HERVÉ RYSSEN

THE JEWISH MAFIA
INTERNATIONAL PREDATORS

Hervé Ryssen

Hervé Ryssen (France) is a historian and an exhaustive researcher of the Jewish intellectual world. He is the author of twelve books and several video documentaries on the Jewish question. In 2005, he published *Planetary Hopes*, a book in which he demonstrates the religious origins of the globalist project. *Psychoanalysis of Judaism*, published in 2006, shows how intellectual Judaism displays all the symptoms of hysterical pathology. There is no "divine choice", but the manifestation of a disorder that has its origins in the practice of incest. Freud had patiently studied this question on the basis of what he observed in his own community.

France is home to one of the largest Jewish communities in the Diaspora, with a very intense cultural and intellectual life. Hervé Ryssen has been able to develop his extensive work on the basis of numerous historical and contemporary sources, both international and French.

THE JEWISH MAFIA
International predators

La Mafia juive: Les Grands Prédateurs internationaux,
Levallois-Perret, *Baskerville, 2006.*

Translated and Published by
Omnia Veritas Limited

www.omnia-veritas.com

© Omnia Veritas Limited - Hervé Ryssen - 2023

All rights reserved. No part of this publication may be reproduced by any means without the prior permission of the publisher. The intellectual property code prohibits copies or reproductions for collective use. Any representation or reproduction in whole or in part by any means whatsoever, without the consent of the publisher, the author or their successors, is unlawful and constitutes an infringement punishable by articles of the Code of Intellectual Property.

PART ONE 13

FROM YIDDISHLAND TO BROOKLYN 13

1. American gangsters 13
- Yiddish Connection 15
- Torah Nostra - The Crime Syndicate 22
- Murder incorporated 28
- The song of the canary 35
- Bugsy Siegel in Hollywood 38
- Fight fascism, support Israel 44
- The Wanderings of Meyer Lansky 46
- The invisible mafia 51

2. Russia under the yoke of the oligarchs 59
- Pillage of Russia 59
- Mafia democracy 72
- There's nothing like a good war 78
- The fall of the oligarchs 83
- The Invisible Mafia II 90

3. The "Russian Mafia" takes over the world 94
- On the Azur coast 94
- From Berlin to Marbella 97
- The Organizatsiya in the USA 100
- M&S International - Antwerp, Vilnius, Bangkok, Bogotá 105
- International predators and a world without borders 110
- The quest for respectability 121
- The Mafia in Israel 132

PART TWO 140

BUSINESS WITHOUT BORDERS 140

1. Guns, drugs and diamonds 140
- The diamond industry 140
- Paramilitary militias in Colombia 148
- Hashish, cocaine, heroin 153
- Ecstasy trafficking: 100% Kasher 161
- Diamantists and the laundering of dirty money 167
- A long tradition 172
- Detoxification and decriminalisation 177

2. The porn mafia 182
- Sexual liberation 182
- The promoters of porn cinema 186
- Porn in every home 191
- The pioneers of pornography 195
- Sex shops and prostitution: the Sefarade Connection 197

3. The White slave trade 206
- Sex slaves in Israel 206
- Cyprus and migrant smuggling 218
- The Golden Age of the White Slave Trade 220
- The Lemberg Trial 232

Eros centre in defeated Germany 235
A long tradition 240
The dialectic of Jewish intellectuals 243
4. *The Black slave trade*.. *248*
The Atlantic Trade I: The Portuguese 248
The Atlantic slave trade II: in the United States 255
In Martinique and Guadeloupe.. 257
The Debate... 259
5. *Christian slaves*... *264*
Towards America... 264
Slavery in the Mediterranean... 265
In the Middle Ages and in Antiquity... 268
6. *Organ trafficking* *273*
The bodies of the Palestinians 274
Fresh meat from Moldova.. 279
From Brazil to South Africa 281
Chinese suppliers 284
From Ukraine to Azerbaijan 285
Traffic continues in Israel 285
The yellow house in Kosovo 286
The accusatory inversion.. 292
Cosmetic surgery.. 296
Organ trafficking and Jewish morality 301

PART THREE **303**

SWINDLERS AND TRAFFICKERS.. 303
1. *The big scams* *303*
Claude Lipsky, "the swindler of the century". 303
Jacques Crozemarie and the ARC scandal 308
The case of the Sentier... 312
Racehorses and mechanics 319
VAT fraud... 321
Defrauding the community 321
Samuel Flatto-Sharon... 324
In England and the United States 327
Under the Third French Republic (1870-1940)... 330
2. *The Traffickers* *340*
Monsieur Michel and Monsieur Joseph... 340
Shenanigans and company... 343
The gold rush 346
The plunder of the defeated countries 351
3. *Anti-Semitism* *356*
Anti-Semitism through the ages... 356
Jewish uniqueness 366

EPILOGUE **372**

OTHER TITLES... **379**

When we think of the mafia, we think first of Sicily and the world around it. Indeed, everyone has heard of the Sicilian mafia: it is the most mediatised, the one we see most portrayed on the big screen and in television series. In the early 1990s, after the collapse of the Soviet Union, we regularly heard about the "Russian mafia", then the "Chechen mafia" and the "Albanian mafia". The "Jewish mafia" does not exist; the Western media never talk about it. It is, however, and without a doubt, the most powerful mafia in the world. The fact is that the phenomenon is generally unknown, for the simple reason that within so-called "democratic" societies, the media is largely in the hands of people who have no interest in it being widely publicised.

Jacques Attali, who was an advisor to President François Mitterrand before serving the very liberal Nicolas Sarkozy, is an intellectual eminence thus recognised by the French media who wrote in one of his books: "Among the 3 million American Jews after the Great War, a few hundred isolated criminals emerge…". According to *The Jewish Almanach*, "it is no exaggeration to say that their influence on organised crime in the United States in the 1920s and 1930s equalled, and even surpassed, that of the Italians."

But the phenomenon, as we shall see, is not limited to the interwar period. In the 1990s, it was still the Ashkenazi Jews from the former Yiddishland of Russia and Poland who were in the limelight. Attali added: "But, among them, as always, things are not done by halves: since they are criminals, it is better to be the first[1]."

---

[1] Jacques Attali, *Les Juifs, le monde et l'argent*, Fayard, 2002.

PART ONE

FROM YIDDISHLAND TO BROOKLYN

Before World War II, the vast majority of Jews lived in central Europe and western Russia. Two million of them had emigrated to America by the end of the 19th century. A second major wave of emigration arrived in the 1970s. Soviet Jews, supported by Western governments, then left the Soviet Union, which they had helped to build fifty years earlier. After the fall of communism in 1991, we witnessed a new massive outflow of Russian Jews. Each time these waves of immigration occurred, crime was on the rise in the Western world.

1. American gangsters

Jews are invariably portrayed in the media as the victims of history. The idea of the Jew always persecuted for no reason is as old as Judaism itself. Thus, it is almost axiomatic that Jews are incapable of evil. Therefore, a Jew who was both a gangster and a murderer may at first sight seem surprising.

Joseph Roth, a famous Austrian Jewish writer between the two world wars, wrote, for example, about the criminality of Eastern Jews: "There is hardly a single mugger. And no murderer or robber who murders[2]." But the reality is quite different, however, when you look into it a little more.

The famous writer Elie Wiesel, a "survivor of the death camps", had the opportunity to do some research on the gangsters who spread terror in American cities. This is what he wrote in his memoirs: "I am preparing an investigation of the American underworld, the Mafia, and

---

[2] Joseph Roth, *The Wandering Jews*.

most particularly the Murder Incorporated hit men. Rummaging through the archives of various newspapers and municipal libraries, I have discovered, to my astonishment, Jewish names. That's right, in the 1920s and 1930s, Jewish professional killers offered their services to this criminal society. They agreed to murder men and women who had done nothing to them and whom they did not even know. It is said that some of them boasted of being a practising Jew, wore the kippah during their "work" and scrupulously observed the Sabbath rest."

Elie Wiesel continued: "I confess that my research left me shocked, shocked, disgusted. How can it be conceivable that a Jew could become a hitman or simply a murderer? Perhaps I have a too idealised view of the Jew, but the fact is that in Eastern Europe my people could be reproached for everything except being involved in murder. In my homeland, we used to say: there are some things that a Jew—whoever he is and wherever he comes from—will never do. He will let himself be killed, but he will not kill. That, even our enemies had to recognise. Of course, I am not talking here about the "ritual murders" of which fanatical Christians have often accused us over the centuries. I am talking about real crimes. The Jews could be reproached with lies, deceit, fraud, smuggling, theft, perjury—but not with being murderers… So we must admit the unthinkable: as in all things, we are becoming a people like other people, neither better nor worse, with its Righteous and its wicked, a people capable of violence, hatred and vileness as much as of goodness, sacrifice and greatness[3]."

However, one did not have to wait for the American gangster phenomenon of the 1930s to become aware of certain secular dispositions of the Jewish people. In Russia, for example, the Bolshevik revolution of 1917 had ushered in a "liberation" during which, as we have already seen in our previous books, very many Jews had played an absolutely appalling role, both as doctrinaires and as officials and executioners[4].

In a book published in 1998, entitled *Yiddish Connection*, the American Rich Cohen also noted the difference between the media image of the persecuted Jew and a more prosaic reality: "Hardly anyone has heard of Jewish gangsters," he wrote. Their existence is even questioned. The very notion of the Jewish gangster runs counter to the basic stereotypes applied to Jews… Physically, Jews are creatures of office, incapable of inspiring fear." Thus, "how can one believe in the

---

[3] Elie Wiesel, *Mémoires, tome I*, Le Seuil, 1994, p. 364, 365.
[4] On the role of the Jews in communism, see the chapters on the subject in *Planetary Hopes* and *Jewish Fanaticism*.

existence of Jewish gangsters, capable of violence? "

It seems that after the Second World War, Jews had voluntarily erased this episode from their memory. Rich Cohen explained: "Today, after less than two generations, even Jews find the idea inconceivable. They keep that image of the Holocaust before them: never forget. Never forget the time when we were victims. They have put away the image of the gangster—forgotten. Forgotten the time when we were beasts. When I talk about my book to older Jews, they change the subject. They turn pale. Sometimes they get angry. When I told one of my friends about the book, he got upset. He warned me that it would be a text inspired by self-hatred, a book that would give a bad impression of Jews." And Rich Cohen confessed in turn: "I wouldn't mind if Jews made a bad impression from time to time. I wish our freedom had some of that brutality[5]."

Yiddish Connection

During the last two decades of the 19th century, almost two million Jews had left Central Europe and the Russian Empire to settle in the United States. After their arrival in the United States, some of them manifestly continued what they had been accustomed to practising in Chisinau and Odessa. At the end of the 19th century, wrote Rich Cohen, "it was not uncommon to discover, in a dark alley, an old man, an immigrant, his skull crushed, his pockets emptied and turned inside out, as a kind of message to the body snatchers: save your time, there is nothing left to take from this one." Criminals fought with guns against rival gangs, but sometimes also in real pitched battles against regiments of police." That was the era of the Wild West in New York, when the biggest gangsters were really nothing more than petty street thugs."

Gangs of pickpockets wreaked havoc throughout the city, organised by *"fagins"*—from the name of the hideous character in Charles Dickens' novel *Oliver Twist*: in London, the Fagin of the story is a receiver who recruits a gang of young boys whom he teaches the art and manner of stealing the wallets and watches of passers-by. He piles his gold and valuables in a chest hidden under the floor of his hovel, and his eyes sparkle as he gazes at his ill-gotten gains[6]. Historian Albert Fried cited some of these New York-based *"fagins"*: Harry

---

[5] Rich Cohen, *Yiddish Connection*, 1998, Denoël, 2000, Folio, p. 222
[6] *Oliver Twist*, 1837. In 1948, director David Lean gave a characteristic physiognomy to the Jew Fagin. Fifty years later, in Roman Polanski's film, none of the character's Jewishness remained.

Joblinsky, for example, who supervised the work of some fifteen young pickpockets, or Abe Greenthal, who commanded the Sheeny Gang. There was also the burly Fredrika Mandelbaum. At the turn of the century, wrote Albert Fried, Jewish criminals "regularly made the front page of the newspapers."

Zelig Lefkowitz, who had originally been a thief and pickpocket in his youth, became a *"fagin" after a while*, i.e. the leader of a gang of thieves. Lefkowitz was self-employed. His services had a fee: ten dollars to slash a cheek, twenty-five dollars for a bullet in the leg, fifty dollars to plant a bomb, and up to a hundred dollars for a murder. He was killed in 1912 by a member of a rival gang[7].

But organised gangs engaged in other, probably more lucrative, activities. In the early 1890s, a series of fires broke out in New York. These fires were actually criminal in origin. After a while, the police managed to arrest the arsonists responsible and eighteen of them ended up in prison, some for life. Their boss was called Isaac Zucker. He ordered the fires that allowed the owners to collect the insurance premium[8].

The gangsters made their profits from gambling, prostitution, robberies and burglaries, and even from murder under command. In April 1911, 400 Jewish clothes horse traders had reported numerous robberies and decided to testify in court against the presence of gangs in their neighbourhood.

The first to achieve a certain notoriety was a certain Monk Eastman. Zelig Lefkowitz had joined him in the late 1890s and had become one of his lieutenants. Monk Eastman was originally named Edward Osterman. Rich Cohen drew an interesting portrait of the character: "Monk was monstrous, of a monstrosity not often seen any more—typical of the 19th century… His pockmarked face showed the marks of smallpox … his ears were like cabbage leaves, his flat nose reduced to its minimum expression, his mouth grim, notch-shaped… To anyone who saw him suddenly appear on an underworld street, he must have embodied death in person[9]."

Criminals also had their dealings with the men of the New York Democratic Party in power in the city since the 1850s, and for whom they stuffed ballot boxes during elections or lent a hand in influencing

---

[7] Albert Fried, *The Rise and fall of jewish Gangster in America*, 1980, Columbia University Press, 1993, p. 31.
[8] Albert Fried, *The Rise and fall of jewish Gangster in America*, 1980, Columbia University Press, 1993, p. 25, 26.
[9] Rich Cohen, *Yiddish Connection*, 1998, Denoël, 2000, Folio, p. 61, 66, 67

a decision. In return, politicians used their contacts in the judiciary to reduce the effects of arrests.

These delinquents also sometimes served as shock troops for the bosses. In 1897, when the textile workers went on strike for the first time, "the factory owners—German Jews from the wealthy neighbourhoods, Rich Cohen pointed out—expressed their concerns to the bosses of the Jewish gangs, and one of the bosses hired Monk Eastman to force the strikers back to work. In short, some Jews had gone to seek the help of their co-religionists[10]."

At the turn of the century, Monk Eastman's gang numbered around 75 members and was battling for territory on the *Lower East Side* in lower Manhattan with another mostly Italian group called the *Five Points Gang*, led by Paolo Antonio Vaccarelli, a former Sicilian boxer. The fight between Monk Eastman and the *Five Points Gang* culminated in 1903 in a full-blown street battle that the police were barely able to contain. One hundred gunshots had left three dead and seven wounded[11].

The reign of these gangs declined throughout the 1910s after several arrests, including that of Monk Eastman himself. Monk Eastman was sentenced to ten years in prison for the death of a detective in 1904. After serving most of his sentence, he was drafted as a soldier and sent to fight on the European front in 1917. On his return, he returned to the *Lower East Side*, but was shot five times in front of a café in 1920. A matter of course.

Monk Eastman had sponsored the career of Arnold Rothstein, who became the first great godfather of gangsterism, the first crime boss in New York. Unlike most gangsters, Arnold Rothstein did not come from the underworld. He was the son of a millionaire. His father Abraham was a Jewish immigrant from Bessarabia who owned a textile emporium and a spinning mill." Abraham had one of those grim, haunted faces that some Jews have," wrote Rich Cohen. Arnold one day introduced his father to his future wife. But she was not Jewish. This is usually a serious problem for pious Jews, as exogamous marriage is considered a real catastrophe for the community. Even today, when a member of an orthodox family marries a Gentile, the family performs the rite of *Shiva*, normally reserved for deaths. Doing *Shiva* means declaring that the person is considered dead in all respects. Rich Cohen wrote: "The older man shook his head and declared: "Well, I hope you

---

[10] Rich Cohen, *Yiddish Connection*, 1998, Denoël, 2000, Folio, p. 135.
[11] Albert Fried, *The Rise and fall of jewish Gangster in America*, 1980, Columbia University Press, 1993, p. 27.

will be happy". After the wedding, when he had declared his son dead, when he covered the mirrors and read the *Kaddish*[12], that moment was a big step forward for crime in America. For Rothstein, that was the decisive breakthrough."

Arnold Rothstein had begun his career as a teenager as a professional gambler and gambler at craps, cards and billiards, under the aegis of Monk Eastman. By his early twenties, he had become a bookmaker on horse races, baseball games, boxing matches and political elections. In 1909, he had acquired his own bookmaker in the spa town of Saratoga, New York State, a town known for receiving large investments from the mob. Soon after, the town would become his domain; all the local authorities had been corrupted. In the gambling world, his reputation had spread across the United States. He rigged boxing matches and baseball games. Legend had it that he rigged the 1919 baseball championship final, but he was eventually cleared by the courts.

He did not personally run any gangs, but he had become the grey eminence of the underworld, its organiser. He settled disputes, financed it with money, manpower and protection, and when the going got rough, he covered the costs of bail bonds and lawyers. In New York, which by 1920 was already the largest Jewish city in the world, Arnold Rothstein had built a gambling empire. He opened a luxurious casino in the centre of the city where many of New York's great fortunes and personalities such as Joseph Seagram, the "Canadian" whisky baron (his company would later merge with that of Samuel Bronfman, whose son would head the World Jewish Congress), and Harry "Sinclair", the oil tycoon, regularly gathered.

Rothstein was also involved in drug trafficking (opium and cocaine) and horse breeding. With alcohol prohibition beginning in January 1919, he concentrated his efforts on taking over this underground trade. Waxey Gordon managed Rothstein's entire East Coast liquor trade. He imported large quantities of whisky across the Canadian border and bought up numerous taverns, distilleries and speakeasies. Gordon was born into a family of Polish Jewish immigrants on New York's *Lower East Side*. His real name was Irving Wexler. He had been a pickpocket before marrying a rabbi's daughter, then joining Arnold Rothstein's gang during the early years of Prohibition in the 1920s. Waxey Gordon lived extravagantly, in the most luxurious suites of Manhattan's grand hotels. His position began to decline after the death of his boss in 1928.

---

[12] *Kaddish*: the main Jewish prayer that is also recited at duels.

To protect his convoys against attacks by rival gangsters, Rothstein had managed to bring into his service fearsome gang bosses who would later become the leading figures of gangsterism in the 1930s: Bugsy Siegel, Meyer Lansky, Lucky Luciano, Frank Costello, Louis "Lepke" Buchalter, Arthur Flegenheimer (Dutch Schultz), Gurrah Shapiro, Legs Diamond.

Arnold Rothstein's recruits came mainly from the *Lower East Side*. They were "Jews and Italians—but mostly Jews", wrote Rich Cohen. They were to become the most notorious criminals of the 20th century. Rothstein was thus the "Moses of the Mafia: he led the new generation to the promised land, but he could not get there[13]." On 4 November 1928, he was found in a New York hotel on a bloody carpet, writhing in pain with a .38-calibre bullet in his stomach. According to Broadway chronicler Damon Runyon, he had been "shot in the crotch". He agonised for two days in hospital. The case was never solved, but everyone knew that he had failed to repay a gambling debt from a poker game that he believed had been rigged[14].

Of the Jewish gangsters who left their mark on the American crime world of the time, we find Charles "King" Salomon. Originally from Russia, he ran the Boston underworld. Along with Longy Zwillman, Meyer Lansky, Dutch Schultz, Benjamin "Bugsy" Siegel and Lepke Buchalter, he was one of the East Coast's *Jewish Big Six*. In the early 1920s, King Solomon controlled all the gambling and drug business in Boston and New England. He then moved into bootlegging. He also owned the city's major nightclubs. In 1922, he was indicted for drug trafficking, but was acquitted thanks to his political supporters. Later, he spent a year in prison for having coerced a witness in a trial for drug trafficking. He was finally liquidated in 1933 in one of his nightclubs, the famous *Cotton Club* in Boston. Meyer Lansky had just got rid of his last rival.

Abner "Longy" Zwillmann was also an important alcohol dealer in Prohibition times and the head of the mafia in New Jersey, a state west of New York. At school he was already nicknamed "Longy" because he was the tallest. He had corrupted every cop and judge in New Jersey. The police escorted his convoys and guarded his warehouses. When the FBI was finally going to arrest him in 1959, he was found hanged in his Newark home, although he was probably

---

[13] Rich Cohen, *Yiddish Connection*, 1998, Denoël, 2000, Folio, p. 73, 71, 80–89
[14] Arnold Rothstein inspired the American author Francis Scott Fitzgerald for the character of Meyer Wolfsheim in his novel *The Great Gatsby* (1925). The latter introduces Gatsby to bootlegging and the New York underworld.

previously strangled. Zwillmann had put part of his fortune into the service of his community. He donated large sums of money to Jewish associations.

The Purple Gang was the core of the Jewish mafia in Detroit, on the Canadian border. The gang ran the liquor trade and gambling halls, ran the drug trade, swindled insurance companies, and carried out kidnappings and contract killings. The twelve members of the Purple Gang were all Jewish, as noted by Jewish historian Robert Rockaway, who noted that they were also involved in the murders of uncooperative prostitutes[15]. The Purple Gang's bootleg alcohol came from the distilleries belonging to the Canadian-based brothers Sam and Harry Bronfman. The Bronfman family was to have a bright future, as Samuel's descendants would become the world leaders in the sale of alcohol in the world and would become presidents of the World Jewish Congress and directors of Universal film studios. Robert Rockaway claimed that half of the top bootleggers were Jewish and that they controlled racketeering activities in some of the country's largest cities[16].

There were also the "Cleveland Four": Moe Dalitz, Sam Tucker, Morris Kleinmann and Louis Rothkopf, who ran the city's liquor trade. The Cleveland police had established a blacklist of the most dangerous criminals in 1930. Of the 74 American-born "white" criminals, 27 were Jewish. Germans numbered fifteen, Italians thirteen and Irish nine. Among the foreign-born, there were thirty Italians and twelve Jews[17].

There, as elsewhere, gangsters ran the nightclubs. In New York, Dutch Schultz owned the *Embassy Club*; in Boston, Charles King Solomon owned the *Coconut Grove*; in Newark, Longy Zwillman owned the *Blue Mirror* and the *Casablanca*. Detroit's Purple Gang ran *Luigi's Café* and the *Picadilly,* among others.

Arthur Flegenheimer, known as "Dutch Schultz", was the undisputed king of beer in the Bronx. He was born in 1902 to German Jewish parents. Dutch Schultz was also known to have a very bad temper. He was cynical and paranoid and suffered great mood swings. The young Flegenheimer had been abandoned by his father at the age of fourteen. He began his career playing craps and robbing houses.

---

[15] Robert Rockaway, *But he was good to his mother: The lives and the crimes of jewish gangsters*, Gefen publishing, 1993, p. 113.

[16] Robert Rockaway, ... *The lives and the crimes of jewish gangsters*, in Jean-François Gayraud, *Le Monde des mafias*, Odile Jacob, 2005, p. 115.

[17] Albert Fried, *The Rise and fall of jewish Gangster in America*, 1980, Columbia University Press, 1993, p. 111.

During one of his expeditions he was arrested in the Bronx and sent to work on a farm, from which he escaped before being recaptured. Upon his release from prison, he was nicknamed "Dutch Schultz", the name of a recently deceased notorious gangster. This ruse spread the rumour that a once fearsome rooster was still alive and kicking.

Dutch Schultz worked first for Arnold Rothstein, then for Jack "Legs" Diamond. In 1928, he went into business for himself as a *bootlegger*, specialising in beer. He did not hesitate to torture those who were a little reluctant to buy his drinks. With his right-hand man Bo Weinber, he set up shop in Manhattan, vying for territory with his former boss, Legs Diamond.

Legs Diamond had been in jail for deserting the army in 1918. He would later become a celebrity of the New York nightlife scene. He also had a reputation for cruelty: in 1930, he had kidnapped and tortured a truck driver to extract information about a shipment of alcohol. He had ordered the murder of a henchman of Dutch Schultz, but one day, on his way home, he ran into Bo Weinberg, who put three bullets in his head. Jack "Legs" Diamond was 34 years old.

At the end of Prohibition, in 1933, Schultz went into the rigged lottery business in Harlem. The procedure had been worked out by his accountant, Otto Abbadabba Berman. At the same time, Dutch Schultz's "Bronx Legion" was battling Bumpy Johnson, a black gangster, for control of Harlem. This confrontation forms the plot of the film *Hoodlum* (1997).

Already in September 1908, New York police chief Bigenheim had revealed that half of all American gangsters were Jews. The big Jewish organisations were shocked by these words, but their complaints did not change the reality[18]. At the end of the 1920s, in Minneapolis, the denunciation of gangsterism took an anti-Semitic turn. Thus, in November 1927, the *Saturday Press* unusually accused Jewish gangsters of having corrupted the judges, the police chief and his men, and of having rigged elections. Jewish gangsters were accused of beating up businessmen, of defying "our" laws, of corrupting "our" officials: 90% of the city's crimes were committed by Jewish gangsters[19]. The newspaper was denounced in court and convicted in the first instance.

Indeed, it always takes some time before the truth can finally be told. Thus, the Jewish historian Robert Rockaway could afford to write

---

[18] Jacques Derogy, *Israël Connection*, Plon, 1980, p. 193.
[19] Albert Fried, *The Rise and fall of jewish Gangster in America*, 1980, Columbia University Press, 1993, p. 112, 113.

a long article in the *Jerusalem Post Magazine on* 20 April 1990. In the introduction, he explicitly wrote: "As in many other areas, Jews knew how to create a dominant position for themselves in the world of crime."

Torah Nostra— *The Crime Syndicate*

Of all these gangsters, Bugsy Siegel was one of the most influential, and also one of the most dangerous. Born into a family of Jewish immigrants from Russia, Benjamin Siegelbaum was born in 1905 in Williamsburg, a neighbourhood in Brooklyn, New York. Bugsy dropped out of school early and quickly realised on the street that violence would allow him to achieve what he prized most: power, money and influence. From an early age, he and his friends began extorting money from street vendors. Those who thought they could do without the protection of a gang of minors had their carts doused with paraffin and reduced to ashes[20].

One of the first members of Bugsy's Williamsburg gang was Meyer Lansky. They had grown up together in the same neighbourhood and were great partners, setting up shop on the streets of Manhattan's *Lower East Side*. Their gang was known as the "Bugs and Meyer mob". They extorted money from shopkeepers, immigrants and loan sharks, although their main speciality, thanks to Lansky's skills as a mechanic, was car theft. Later, their activities diversified even further, ranging from contract killing to alcohol smuggling and armed robbery. Bugsy and Meyer Lansky thus formed a duo destined to become famous.

Lansky was born Mair Suchowljansky in 1902 in Grodno, in present-day Belarus. His family had emigrated to New York in 1911. In his childhood, Lansky profited from watching craps players on the street, while continuing his religious studies. In 1921, Arnold Rothstein proposed that he join his network of bootleggers with a Sicilian gangster who would also become famous: Lucky Luciano, whom Siegel and Lansky had met at school, and a Calabrian named Frank Costello. Together, they would organise their first drug deals, their first swindles and robberies. This close cooperation symbolised the new links between Jewish and Italian criminal groups. With Prohibition and the clandestine alcohol trade, thousands of dollars were to turn into millions. Lansky convinced his associates to create a common fund to corrupt the authorities and thus continue their lucrative activities. A gifted number cruncher and accountant, Lansky was soon doing all the

---

[20] Don Wolfe, *Le Dossier Dahlia noir*, 2005, Albin Michel, 2006, p. 204.

accounting for his business.

Meyer Lansky had a cold, calculating spirit and was capable of devising all kinds of perfidious and treacherous manoeuvres. He was later described by the press as the *"mastermind of the mob"*. For many years, he was the treasurer of the crime syndicate. His first wife, on the other hand, ended up in a psychiatric hospital[21].

In 1933, when Prohibition ended, Lansky invested massively in the gambling industry throughout the country, generously bribing the governors of the various states. He built up a gambling empire, controlling hotel-casinos from Las Vegas to Miami, via New Orleans, Arkansas and Kentucky. As Jacques Attali wrote, Lansky, together with Schultz, "became the great bosses of American Jewish gangsterism[22]."

Bugsy Siegel was very different from his partner and congener. He was a crazy head, and was known for his fits of rage and brutal violence. At the age of twenty-one, he was already excelling in all sorts of criminal activities—kidnapping, human trafficking, robbery, rape, extortion, drug trafficking, alcohol trafficking, murder. His fits of violence have often been likened to seizures and explosions of a pathological nature that transformed him into a murderous monster. These crises of murderous violence soon earned him the nickname "Bugs" or "Bugsy[23] ", but it was better not to mention this nickname in front of him, as he was known to beat those who committed this recklessness almost to death with the butt of his revolver." He took great pleasure and enjoyment in knocking off or stabbing his victims," wrote Don Wolfe. He had a split personality: "There was Bugsy, the heroin-addicted murderous monster, and Benny, the handsome young man with movie-star airs who could be charming, affable and generous. But it was Bugsy who used Benny as a front[24]."

Bugsy Siegel had taken over from the Sicilian tradition the art of making his victims disappear. In 1934, he decided to kill his old friend Bo Weinberg, who, stalked and harassed by prosecutor Thomas Dewey, could testify against his boss Dutch Schultz. He phoned him to have dinner together. The two men drove around in a car before stopping on a dark, deserted street. There, Bugsy went on a rampage, pistol-whipping Bo and slashing his face and neck with a knife. The bodies of

---

[21] Mental and genetic illnesses are common in the Ashkenazi Jewish community (see *Psychoanalysis of Judaism*).
[22] Jacques Attali, *Les Juifs, le monde et l'argent*.
[23] From "bugs" or "buggy", which means "crazy", "crazy" or "buggy" in Anglo-American.
[24] Don Wolfe, *Le Dossier Dahlia noir*, 2005, Albin Michel, 2006, p. 204, 205.

Bugsy's victims were rarely found. Indeed, it is said that he himself removed their viscera so that intestinal gas would not float the bodies from the bottom of the East River, their watery graves. In the police files kept on Bugsy, the FBI estimated that before settling in California, Benjamin Siegel had savagely killed at least thirty people[25]. One of his favourite tortures was to douse his victims with gasoline and ignite their shoulders with his lighter. He would then extinguish the fire and relight it on another part of the body. Terrified to the core, the tortured would eventually reveal everything Bugsy wanted to know. But the victim ended up with two shots in the head anyway.

In the spring of 1928, at the age of twenty-three, Benny had married Esta Krakower, his childhood sweetheart, with Meyer Lansky witnessing the wedding. At first, she did not suspect that Benny was a gangster. To her, her husband ran a truck rental company with Meyer Lansky on *Cannon Street* on the *Lower East Side*. In reality, the rental company only served as a front for alcohol smuggling and kidnapping activities. The gang received its liquor deliveries by boat from the New Jersey shore. But such was New York's thirst in the Roaring Twenties that Siegel often stole shipments from other dealers to fill his stocks. These operations sowed discord and provoked a war between gangs[26].

The Jewish gangsters had to contend with the dreaded Sicilian mafia. After a trip to Sicily in 1925, Mussolini had launched a major campaign to root out the mafia. He sent an "iron prefect", Cesare Mori, who carried out mass arrests, sometimes even surrounding and besieging entire villages. For the first time, the Mafia was backing down. In his speech in the Chamber of 26 May 1927, Mussolini had clearly announced that the fight against the Sicilian Mafia would be one of the most important objectives of his government and that he would act relentlessly against it: "You ask me, when will the fight against the Mafia end? It will end when there are no more mafiosi. Just as it will end when the memory of the mafia has definitively disappeared from the memory of the Sicilians[27]."

Some Mafia bosses then left the country. Salvatore Maranzano thus arrived on American soil in 1927. A gangster who met him gave this testimony: "When we arrived, everything was very dark. We were led before Maranzano: he looked absolutely majestic, with two pistols in his belt and surrounded by about ninety men armed to the teeth. I

---

[25] Don Wolfe, *Le Dossier Dahlia noir*, 2005, Albin Michel, 2006, p. 204, 205.
[26] Don Wolfe, *Le Dossier Dahlia noir*, 2005, Albin Michel, 2006, p. 206.
[27] William Reymond, *Mafia S.A.*, Flammarion, 2001, p. 51.

would have thought I was in the presence of Pancho Vila[28]."

Maranzano immediately fell out with Giuseppe Masseria, an established Sicilian who called himself *"Joe the boss"*. The rivalry between the two factions was exacerbated in the late 1920s by the frequent robberies of alcohol convoys, and war was finally openly declared in 1930 when Joe Masseria had a ringleader executed who was going over to Maranzano's side. Gunshots were heard at night and in the morning the policemen came to count the dead. After several dozen deaths, the conflict, known since then as the Castellammarese war, seemed insoluble. Lucky Luciano and Vito Genovese then commanded the assassination of their own boss, Joe Masseria.

Charles Luciano had landed from Sicily in 1906. In 1923, he was introduced to Joe Masseria, but the relationship between the two men quickly deteriorated. Masseria distrusted his new protégé, in whom he saw a potential rival. For his part, Luciano reproached Masseria for his virulent anti-Semitism—common in the Mafia—which closed off to the Cosa Nostra the juicy traffics controlled by the Jewish gangs of New York. At the time, Luciano already frequented Meyer Lansky, and together they had taken control of the loan sharks, bookmakers and insurance brokers in the Jewish neighbourhoods and Little Italy.

As a warning, Luciano was beaten up in an open field. From then on he would be called Lucky, as he had been very lucky to get out alive. When war was declared against Maranzano, Luciano took the opportunity to make a deal with him. On 15 April 1931, he invited *"Joe the Boss"* Masseria to lunch to talk business at the Nuova Villa Tammaro restaurant in Coney Island, opposite Brooklyn. Rich Cohen wrote: "Maybe Masseria talked about the Jews, repeating once again to Charlie that a man can only trust his own kind." After lunch, they played poker. At about three o'clock, Luciano excused himself to go to the toilet. A moment later, the front door of the restaurant was blown open and gangsters of the worst kind emerged: Bugsy Siegel, Albert Anastasia, Joe Adonis and Red Levine. They went to the back of the room and fired a score of shots. When the cops asked Luciano where he was during the shooting, he simply replied, "In the bathroom, taking a piss." After thinking about it, he added: "I always take a long time to pee."

Maranzano was thus victorious in the war against Masseria. It was a milestone in the history of organised crime. Maranzano had become the sole boss of the Sicilian Mafia. A few weeks later he organised a meeting. The Italian Cosa Nostra would henceforth be divided into five

---

[28] Rich Cohen, *Yiddish Connection*, 1998, Denoël, 2000, Folio, p. 95.

families, of which he named the bosses: Genovese, Gambino, Bonanno, Colombo and Luchese. He was now the *capo di tutti capi*, the boss of all bosses. But Maranzano's reign was short-lived, for that agreement lasted no more than five months. Like Masseria, Salvatore Maranzano remained attached to the Mafia's ethnic identity and refused to join forces with the Jewish gangsters. His taste for tradition and his anti-Semitism did not sit well with the young Mafiosi led by Luciano who felt more American than Sicilian.

Maranzano had already planned the execution of Luciano, Vito Genovese, Al Capone and Frank Costello, but did not have time to take action. In September 1931, Luciano, who had heard about the affair, went ahead and, with the agreement of his associates, once again sent a team of Jewish gangsters to take out Maranzano. His friend Meyer Lansky had assembled a group of assassins that included Abe [Abraham] Levine of Toledo, Ohio. He was "an orthodox Jew who refused to murder on the Sabbath." With him came Bo Weinberg, Dutch Schultz's right-hand man. All were men Lansky had chosen for their cold-bloodedness. Together with Bugsy Siegel, Martin Goldstein and Abe Reles, they posed as federal agents in charge of suppressing alcohol trafficking and penetrated Maranzano's headquarters: "Federal agents, Treasury control, nobody move! "they shouted. They disarmed the bodyguards and took Maranzano into a locked room with double padded doors. They stabbed him one after the other and Bugsy gave him the coup de grâce by slitting his throat. Maranzano's murder marked the beginning of the purge. The killing began on 10 September and ended on the morning of 11 September. That night went down in the annals of crime as "the night of the Sicilian Vespers", a reference to the massacre of the Angevins in 1282 in Palermo[29]. Forty bosses of the old mafia were liquidated.

From then on there was no longer a *capo di tutti capi* but a federal system. Under Charlie Luciano's leadership, five Sicilian families would continue to exist with the notable difference that they could now work closely with the Jewish gangsters.

The creation of a "Syndicate" had been decided two years earlier, in May 1929, after the death of Arnold Rothstein. Why spend fortunes

---

[29] Sicilian Vespers is the name given to the historical event of the massacre of the French in Sicily in 1282, which led to the end of the reign of Charles of Anjou on the island, who was replaced by the kings of Aragon. Some authors see it as the historical origin of the Mafia: according to them, the war cry of the insurgents would have been *"Morte Alla Francia! Italy Aviva!"* or *"Morte a i Francesi! Italia Anella*! These two phrases would be acronyms for the word mafia.

to get rid of judges and police if they ended up killing each other? A central power was urgently needed to stop the vendettas. So a meeting was organised by Lansky and Luciano at the seaside resort of Atlantic City. It was the first "Yalta" of crime. The six-day meeting had brought together all the crime bosses of the American East: Al Capone of Chicago, with his financial adviser Jacob Guzik; Joe Bernstein of Detroit; Moe Dalitz, Lou Rothkopf and Chuck Polizzi of Cleveland; Boo Boo Hoff and Nig Rozen of Philadelphia; Weissman and John Lazia of Kansas City; Longy Zwillmann of Newark. From New York were Joe Adonis, Waxey Gordon, Lucky Luciano, Frank Costello, Albert Anastasia, Meyer Lansky, Louis "Lepke "Buchalter, among others. The aim of the meeting was to divide up crime sectors outside the old Sicilian Mafia order and to divide up the respective territories and profits.

After Maranzano's death, a new meeting took place in 1931 at the Blackstone Hotel in Chicago. It was agreed that no one Mafia boss should dominate all organised crime and that there would be collegial leadership. Collaboration would be sought rather than confrontation in cases of litigation. The system would operate like a business, with a board of directors voting on policy before implementing it. The United States and Canada would be divided into twenty-four territories under the responsibility of the members of the Commission. In addition, a system of pooled funds was established to pay bribes to the authorities and to finance special investments. It was the birth certificate of organised crime.

At the end of Prohibition, the management was composed of seven permanent members (the "Big Seven"): Lucky Luciano, who controlled prostitution; Frank Costello (who had married a Jewess) controlled gambling; Meyer Lansky was the financial expert; Bugsy Siegel managed the nightclub rackets and alcohol distribution; Albert Anastasia controlled the ports and the longshoremen's union with his partner Joe Adonis of Broadway; Louis "Lepke" Buchalter was in charge of extorting the textile industry, the teamsters' union, the bakeries and the cinemas.

At the same time, the Commission created a special branch charged with the execution, after deliberation, of members guilty of non-compliance or deemed unreliable. Known as Murder Incorporated, this team of assassins operating throughout the territory was led by Louis "Lepke" Buchalter, Anastasia and Bugsy Siegel. Henceforth, before killing anyone anywhere, the Syndicate had to give its approval and the council appointed the executioners.

The cops did not suspect the existence of the Syndicate for a long time. When they did manage to arrest a gangster willing to talk, they got little information because of the law of silence that the Mafia had imported from Sicily. In fact, before the creation of the Federal Bureau of Narcotics in 1930, few people in law enforcement and the judiciary understood organised crime. John Edgar Hoover, who headed the FBI at the time, was not interested in the Mafia. He didn't even believe it existed and thought it was a hoax invented by the mayors of big cities to justify their difficulties. When investigators produced evidence of the existence of a vast criminal conspiracy, he continued to dismiss the idea as absurd, telling reporters, "There is no Mafia in America[30]."

Hoover ignored the problem throughout the 1930s and 1940s until 1957, when police officers in a rural region of New York State raided a large isolated property in the countryside and discovered more than sixty gangsters gathering and conspiring in the dark[31].

Upon arriving at the meeting place, wrote Rich Cohen, the cops "had a vision that must have led them to believe they had found a car dealership[32]." This raid definitely changed the way Americans viewed organised crime.

Murder incorporated

Louis Buchalter was born in 1897 in Brooklyn to German Jewish parents. His mother called him 'Lepkelech', which meant 'Little Louis' in Yiddish, which his friends shortened to 'Lepke'. In his youth, Lepke was a member of a gang, the Amboy Dukes (of Brooklyn's Amboy Street), with which he engaged in all sorts of robberies. By 1919, he had

---

[30]In his biography *Official and Confidential: The Secret Life of J. Edgar Hoover* (1993), journalist Anthony Summers alleged that the Mafia had blackmail material on Hoover, which made Hoover reluctant to aggressively pursue organised crime. According to Summers, organised crime figures Meyer Lansky and Frank Costello obtained photos of Hoover's alleged homosexual activity with Tolson (Hoover's second in command at the FBI) and used them to ensure that the FBI did not pursue his illegal activities. However, most biographers consider the Mafia blackmail story unlikely in light of the FBI's ongoing investigations of the Mafia. Biographer Kenneth Ackerman says Summers' accusations have been "widely discredited by historians". (NdT).
[31]*Apalachin meeting*: The Apalachin meeting was a historic American mob summit held at the home of mobster Joseph "Joe the Barber" Barbara at 625 McFall Road in Apalachin, New York on November 14, 1957. The meeting was allegedly held to discuss various topics, including loan sharking, narcotics trafficking and gambling, along with the division of the illegal operations controlled by the recently assassinated Albert Anastasia. It is believed that about 100 gangsters attended the meeting.
[32] Rich Cohen, *Yiddish Connection*, 1998, Denoël, 2000, Folio, p. 229–233.

already served two prison terms. Lepke formed a duo with Jacob "Gurrah" Shapiro whose fiefdom was in Brooklyn, in the Brownsville neighbourhood. At that time, in Brownsville, power was in the hands of the Shapiro brothers. The eldest, Meyer Shapiro, was born in the neighbourhood. He was a lanky kid who would become obese in adulthood." Everything about him was fat: fat eyes, a fat nose, fat ears, a fat mouth," wrote Rich Cohen. The Shapiro brothers ran some fifteen brothels in the underworld. Like the Jews of Odessa, the city from which they originated, they terrorised the shopkeepers and shopkeepers of the neighbourhood. In 1930s Brooklyn, any shop or restaurant owner who wanted to rent or buy a slot machine had to go through the Shapiros, who, in addition to taking a percentage of the profits, charged a flat five dollars for each machine." What if the Shapiros weren't paid, what if you got your own jukebox, your own cigarette machine or your own flip-flopper somewhere else? Then, something unfortunate could happen—your shop could burn down or be broken into and robbed[33]."

Lepke and Shapiro occasionally escorted Arnold Rothstein's alcohol deliveries. But they had other profitable activities. They extorted money from small shopkeepers and had taken over the *Prêt-à-porter* market on the *Lower East Side*. Lepke explained: "How fragile the rags are! What damage can be done with a bottle of ink. The shopkeepers are quick to understand." Buchalter then managed the pension funds of the textile workers. They used the same methods with striking workers. They organised criminal gangs to break strikes (*the schlammers*), preventing strikers from disrupting work and receiving for these services large sums of money from factory managers. This is what Rich Cohen wrote about it: "It is worth remembering that it was the company bosses who first resorted to gangsters… In general, when they broke strikes, the gangsters beat the workers with iron bars wrapped in newspaper. They called that *schlamming* (beating)."

They also extorted money from large bakeries in New York by offering them "protection". These extortions then spread to other sectors, such as movie theatres and trucking. Buchalter carried out this activity with an iron fist, and continued to do so after he became a leading member of the American Mafia Commission. The extortion of labour unions was practised by other New York gangsters, but Buchalter's ruthlessness towards non-payers surpassed that of his colleagues. Where others would simply break the legs of the recalcitrant, Buchalter would simply kill without warning. He also ordered looting and arson to bolster his reputation.

---

[33] Rich Cohen, *Yiddish Connection*, 1998, Denoël, 2000, Folio, p. 31, 32

Then the union leaders also turned to the gangsters, as they had no other way to protect themselves. Arnold Rothstein was the first to agree to help them[34]. At the beginning of the 1930s, Lepke already controlled a thousand workers through the truck drivers', cinema operators' and construction painters' unions.[35]

Buchalter's extortion successes propelled him to the top of the criminal world. During the formation of the Crime Syndicate, Lepke was in charge of Murder Incorporated, the organisation in charge of assassinating unreliable or guilty members of the Mafia. They had agreed to prohibit the murder without prior authorisation of policemen, judges or any important public figures. The gangsters were also forbidden to kill people who were not members of the mafia in order to avoid thorough investigations or national mobilisation against organised crime. Instead, they were allowed to take the law into their own hands among members of organised crime, provided that the sentence was endorsed by the "Commission". It was in order to centrally decide this "dirty work" that the "Murder Incorporated" (so called by the press) was created, a kind of mutuality of murder whereby a local boss could benefit from the services of a murderer from another locality and thus avoid prosecution. Murder Incorporated was a gang of hired killers, as Don Wolfe wrote, "composed of Jewish criminals who did the dirty work of the Crime Syndicate. [36]"It is estimated that, between 1933 and 1940, the organisation was responsible for more than 700 murders, although some say as many as 2,000. By the end of his career, Lepke was personally suspected of dozens of murders. Executions with firearms were easily identifiable, so drowning, a bladed weapon, baseball bat, piano wire, and, above all, the ice pick were preferred.

Murder Incorporated was co-directed by Bugsy Siegel and Albert Anastasia. They were the ones who collected the requests and chose the modes of execution. Sometimes they hired *freelance* killers, but most often they used a group of young Jewish and Italian gangsters based in Brownsville who were paid an annual salary. The most famous were Louis Capone, Harry "Happy" Maïone, Frank Abbandando, Vito Gurino, Mendy Weiss, Harry Strauss (called "Pittsburgh Phill") and

---

[34] Rich Cohen, *Yiddish Connection*, 1998, Denoël, 2000, Folio, p. 135. Rich Cohen further informed us that Sydney Hillman, the adviser to President Franklin Roosevelt and former leader of the textile workers' union, "had worked in the past with Lepke." (p. 400)
[35] Rich Cohen, *Yiddish Connection*, 1998, Denoël, 2000, Folio, p. 145.
[36] Don Wolfe, *Le Dossier Dahlia noir*, 2005, Albin Michel, 2006, p. 209, 214.

Martin "Bugsy" Goldstein.

Abraham Reles, called Abe Reles, or "Kid Twist", was the leader of the group. He was born in 1907, his parents came from Galitzia, a region in southern Poland. His nickname, "Kid Twist", came from his youthful face and his ability to wring the necks of his victims. Rich Cohen described him as follows: "Over time, Reles became a leader. Although he was barely over six feet tall, something about him commanded respect... He spoke slowly, in a throaty voice, with a lisp. He had a curious gait: in the street, he looked like a man trying to pull his shoes forward by shaking his feet."

In the early days, "the first person the Kid recruited was Martin Goldstein... He had the same small-mouthed, duck-walking, tough-guy attitude as the movie stars. Marty was shy, but the Kid knew how to spot a peculiarity in him. If his shyness was put to the test, he could be driven out of his wits, put into a psychotic crisis. That's why he was called Bugsy (the Bugsy)—because he was a bit crazy, and that was a quality you always saw in some gangsters[37]."

Abraham Reles' weapon of choice was the ice pick, which he inserted through his victims' ears into their brains, simulating death by cerebral haemorrhage. He was known to be a particularly vicious psychopathic killer. He once killed a gas station attendant because the attendant had failed to clean a stain from the side of his car. During prohibition in the 1920s, Reles and his friend Martin Goldstein, still in their teens, had worked for the Shapiro brothers who ran the Brooklyn racket.

It was Reles who finally dethroned the Shapiro brothers in the Brownsville neighbourhood of Brooklyn. Reles had invested in one of Shapiro's strongholds: gambling and loan sharking. Things got ugly fast: one night, Reles received a call from a "friend" informing him that the Shapiro brothers had left their East New York lair. Reles, Goldstein and their henchmen rushed to the Shapiro headquarters, but the information was a hoax and they were ambushed. Reles and Goldstein were wounded in the firefight. Meyer Shapiro wanted to teach Reles a lesson by kidnapping his girlfriend and taking her to an open field where she was beaten and raped several times.

After several attempts on both sides, Reles managed to get his hands on Irving Shapiro. He dragged him down the hallway of his house to the street where he brutally beat him before killing him with eighteen

---

[37] Rich Cohen, *Yiddish Connection*, 1998, Denoël, 2000, Folio, p. 35, 37, 41. On physical and mental defects read *Psychoanalysis of Judaism*, (2022).

shots, two to the face. Two months later, on a deserted street, Reles found Meyer Shapiro and shot him in the head. It was three years before the last Shapiro brother, William, was finally kidnapped off the street and taken to a gang hideout. He was savagely bludgeoned to death. Harry Strauss then tied him up and loaded him into the car to take him for burial. A few years later, when his body was found, exhumed and autopsied, the coroner found traces of mud on his rib cage: he was still alive when he was buried.

The Brownsville gang's reputation reached all the way to Manhattan, to the *nightclubs* and hotel suites where Charlie Luciano, Meyer Lansky and Bugsy Siegel projected and planned the future of organised crime. Soon, Abe Reles and his accomplices would be working for the "Syndicate".

Harry Strauss was the famous assassin of the Abraham Reles gang. He was a pious Jew. Rich described him as follows: "He lived in a world deeply shaped by morality. His views—on punishment, on responsibility, on any formal commitment—were, in many ways, Hebraic views. For Strauss, God was present in every act, every gesture, every gesture... Strauss was the image of the God of the Old Testament; he saw, he judged, he punished[38]."

Strauss killed more than thirty men in more than a dozen cities, but he could probably be credited with a hundred murders." He travelled with a small leather suitcase containing a pair of trousers, silk underwear, a white shirt, a pistol and a rope. He followed in the tradition of the Jewish peddler, the ambitious immigrant who moved westward on muddy roads... The Syndicate had invented the "contract"; a foreigner comes, kills and leaves. The local cops have nothing to do— no motive, no suspects, nothing[39]—". Most of the time, if the situation became complicated, the contract killers could hide in isolated regions of the United States where local politicians were bought off and turned

---

[38] Rich Cohen, *Yiddish Connection*, 1998, Denoël, 2000, Folio, p. 120–122. Let us recall here what the Talmud says: A pious Jew is always considered intrinsically good, despite the sins he may commit. Only his shell is tainted, never his inner self. Talmud (*Chagigah, 15b*). [The Gemara asks: (...) one source states that one may only learn from a scholar who is blameless in his ways, while another indicates that it is permitted even to learn from someone whose character is not blameless (...) Rava taught: What is the meaning of what is written: "I went down to the walnut grove to see the greenness of the valley" (*Song of Songs 6:11*)? Why are Torah scholars compared to walnuts? Just as this nut, even though it is stained with mud and excrement, its contents do not become repulsive, for only its shell is stained; so too a Torah scholar, even though he has sinned, his Torah does not become repulsive." (www.seforia.org). On the Talmud, read *Psychoanalysis of Judaism*].

[39] Rich Cohen, *Yiddish Connection*, 1998, Denoël, 2000, Folio, p. 162.

a blind eye.

In Williamsburg, the Ambergs were the only Brooklyn gangsters with the will and guts to challenge Kid Twist (Abe Reles), showing up on their own turf to extort money from merchants. They had imposed themselves in the early years of the century and had been quite successful in robbery, extortion of funds and murder. The gang was led by Joey Amberg, a Russian Jewish immigrant. In 1935, members of his gang had a run-in with Harry Kazner, a small-time crook working for Murder Inc. He was taken one day to a basement where he was tied up, beaten to death and his body chopped up. The killers had dumped the pieces in a bag in the sewer that led to Jamaica Bay. The tide carried Kazner's remains out to sea[40]. The response was swift, and Lepke got the go-ahead from the other Syndicate bosses to kill the members of Joey Amberg's gang, who were all liquidated one after the other.

By the mid-1930s, the Brownsville Boys had mixed with Lepke's henchmen and it was difficult to distinguish the two gangs, as Reles, Goldstein, Strauss, Happy Maione and Abbandando could be seen everywhere in the company of Lepke's best marksmen, such as Albert Tennenbaum, Charlie Workman, Mendy Weiss and Pretty Levine.

Albert Tannenbaum worked for hire, renting his services to anyone with the necessary cash." He had a dark, narrow face with a comically long nose, sad eyes and bushy eyebrows," wrote Rich Cohen.

Charlie Workman "always kept a cool head, despite the sirens wailing in the distance, to take the time to search the pockets of the corpse[41]. By the end of his career, his number of murdered victims must have been in the mid-twenties. When the cops caught him, he claimed to be Jack Harris or Jack Cohen or whatever name would cross his mind. He told people he was a Brooklyn businessman or that he sold cars." In fact, almost every member of Murder Inc. was in a declared profession, thus having the necessary financial means and an alibi to tell the cops. Tannenbaum worked in textile manufacturing. Pretty Levine drove a rubbish truck, which he sometimes used to dispose of dead bodies. But his real source of income evidently came from extorting money from the shopkeepers he mistreated or from smuggling alcohol.

Loan sharking was also part of the gangsters' arsenal for preying on their victims. Abe Reles had a gambling table at the intersection of Court and State Street in Brooklyn. This is what Rich Cohen wrote about the scam: "When a gambler lost his money, Reles would lend him

---

[40] Rich Cohen, *Yiddish Connection*, 1998, Denoël, 2000, Folio, p. 197
[41] Dispossessing corpses is a long and ancient tradition of the Jews; See Hervé Ryssen, *Planetary Hopes*, (2005–2022).

more, often at an interest rate of twenty-five percent. To repay Reles, the player would often borrow from Strauss, Pretty Levine or Dukey Maffeatore. Before he realised what he had got himself into, the gambler owed everything he had to the little troop[42]." So we see how the American gangsters used the same methods that had earned the Jews a reputation, perhaps deservedly so, since ancient times.

The massive arrival of Russian and Polish Jews in the United States seemed to have enriched America with a 'different' population. In general, though, it seems that Jews were more inclined to criminal activities than the other newcomer populations.

This was the testimony of one Frank Moss, quoted by Rich Cohen. After a visit to the Jewish neighbourhoods of New York, he noted "the ignorance, the prejudice, the persistent refusal to conform to the ideals, religious customs and demands of America, the clan spirit and the distrust of Christians." And he added: "There is no place in the world where so many human parasites can be found, in a properly incalculable quantity… The criminal instincts which are often observed to be the natural state in Russian and Polish Jews come to the surface, in such a manner as to accredit the opinion that these people are the worst elements of the whole New York population[43]."

One day, a Union accountant named Walter Sage suffered the consequences of his recurring mistakes: Gangy Cohen stabbed him in the chest with an ice pick and stabbed him thirty-six times to teach him to count correctly. The accountant ended up at the bottom of the bay tied to a slot machine. But after killing Walter Sage, Gangy Cohen had a kind of revelation: "If they made me kill Walter, then sooner or later they would find someone to kill me. Gangy Cohen took the train to the far west, to Hollywood. There he made his film debut, first as an extra, then as an actor under the name Jake Cohen. A few years later, a police officer, who had been tracking Gangy Cohen for a long time and thought he was missing, saw him on the big screen in a film playing the role of a policeman. Cohen was arrested, handcuffed and extradited

---

[42] Rich Cohen, *Yiddish Connection*, 1998, Denoël, 2000, Folio, p. 208. This is the classic method of usury which has fostered the anti-Semitism of all the peasants of Europe throughout history.

[43] Rich Cohen, *Yiddish Connection*, 1998, Denoël, 2000, Folio, p. 62. The former Chilean socialist president, Dr Salvador Allende made the same analysis: "The Hebrews are characterised by a certain category of crimes: fraud, mendacity, slander, defamation and above all usury. These facts allow us to suppose that race plays a role in criminality." (Excerpt from Salvador Allende's 1933 medical thesis, quoted by Victor Farias in his book entitled *Allende, Antisemitism and Euthanasia*, in *Faits et documents* of 1 June 2005).

from California. His trial took place shortly afterwards, but he was acquitted for lack of evidence. Rich Cohen concluded: "If things got really tough, there was always the solution of going to Hollywood and becoming a movie star[44]."

The song of the canary

In 1933, when prohibition was abolished, gangsters still made a lot of money from gambling, narcotics, prostitution and the telephone betting system. Then there were the rigged horse races. Don Wolfe wrote: "The Syndicate only rigged one race out of a hundred so that it would not be suspected, but that was still more than enough. They agreed with the riders, who received their bribes. Those who refused to cooperate risked serious trouble. Bets were placed at the racetrack, rarely at the Syndicate's bookmakers. As soon as Bugsy found out that a race had been rigged, he would call his Turf Club colleagues and they would bet at the last minute and win the jackpot[45]."

However, the gangsters were increasingly under siege. Al Capone had been arrested in 1932 for tax fraud. Prosecutor Thomas Dewey had locked Waxey Gordon behind bars in 1933. It must be said that Waxey Gordon was at odds with Lansky over alcohol trafficking and gambling. Their rivalry had turned into an open war that would result in several deaths on both sides. Lansky had finally provided the police with the information that led to Waxey Gordon being charged with tax evasion and sentenced to ten years in prison. After his release, he left for California where he trafficked heroin on a large scale. In 1951, aged 62, he was re-arrested and sentenced to 25 years in Alcatraz. He died the following year.

In 1935, Dutch Schultz (Arthur Flegenheimer) was also on the verge of going under. Thomas Dewey had ordered the seizure of a hundred slot machines in several of Shultz's gambling halls. Shultz then decided to ship over a thousand machines to New Orleans, where the state's governor, Huey Long, was at the time on the gangsters' payroll[46].

---

[44] Rich Cohen, *Yiddish Connection*, 1998, Denoël, 2000, Folio, p. 213. Read the chapter on plasticity in *Psychoanalysis of Judaism*. In Sergio Leone's *Once Upon a Time in America* (1984), one of the Jewish gangsters (James Wood) also changes his identity to enter politics. He becomes a senator.

[45] Don Wolfe, *Le Dossier Dahlia noir*, 2005, Albin Michel, 2006, p. 204. On rigged horse races, see Laurent Heynemann's beautiful film, *Le Mors aux dents* (France, 1979), with Michel Piccoli, Jean Benguigui, Michel Galabru, Jacques Dutronc and Roland Blanche ("the Greek"), although they do not appear as such.

[46] William Reymond, *Mafia S.A., Flammarion, 2001, p. 33.*, Flammarion, 2001, p. 33

Shultz was indicted, but his lawyers obtained a change of venue, and the trial took place in a small town in New York State, in Malone. A small town with only one church. One small street. A single traffic light... He set up shop in a small hotel, introduced himself to locals he didn't know, made donations during local charity sales, wore very simple suits." He was seen at small meetings organised by the church, at neighbourhood festivals and at bingo games. A week before the trial, he showed up at a local church and converted to Catholicism," wrote Rich Cohen." By the time the jury had to deliberate, Schultz had cheated and corrupted the entire town. There is a photo of him, taken just after the verdict acquitting him, grinning like a little boy who had just rigged his election as class deputy." In this tough-guy world, there's no room for donkeys," he told reporters[47]."

Schultz had called for Dewey's elimination before the Syndicate Commission. But the other members did not share his opinion: Dewey was too important a target, and his assassination could have put the whole organisation in jeopardy. Since Schultz was obstinate in this project and attended meetings only irregularly, it was decided to eliminate him. On 23 October 1935, he was gunned down with his bodyguards and his accountant in a Newark restaurant by a team of three Murder Incorporated assassins. His body was found in the bathroom, where Charlie Workman had had time to empty his pockets[48].

In June 1936, Charles Luciano himself was convicted of solicitation of prostitution by the Manhattan Supreme Court, sentenced to thirty years in prison for pimping, and locked up in the New York penitentiary. Meyer Lansky hastily retired to the coast of Miami.

Bugsy Siegel settled permanently in Los Angeles, where the DA and city administration were still willing to sell out to the highest bidder. In November 1939, Bugsy had to eliminate "Big Greenie" Greenberg. The wanted man was demanding cash from his former boss Louis "Lepke" Buchalter, threatening to blackmail him. Bugsy, accompanied by Abe Reles, went to Hollywood where Greenberg was hiding." Abe Reles tells how Bugsy quickly got out of the car, approached Big

---

[47] Rich Cohen, *Yiddish Connection*, 1998, Denoël, 2000, Folio, p. 283
[48] In the film *The Cotton Club* (USA, 1984), Francis Ford Coppola paints a psychopathic Dutch Schultz. Schultz and his henchmen, Bo Weinberg, Lulu Rosenkrantz, as well as his financial advisor Abbadaba Berman appear in E. L. Doctorow's novel *Billy Bathgate* and in Robert Benton's film of the same name, starring Dustion Hoffman. In fact, he bears a striking resemblance to Dutch Schultz. Doubles are quite common in the Jewish community, which has favoured inbreeding for centuries. For example, Elie Wiesel's father and Bela Kun, the Bolshevik tyrant who ruled Hungary in 1919, looked like two peas in a pod.

Greenie and hit him with the butt of his gun, before firing four shots into his fractured skull. Big Greenie's lifeless body slumped over the steering wheel as Bugsy returned to the stolen Mercury[49]."

Shortly afterwards, Abe Reles was also arrested in New York. In January 1940, Abe Reles and Bugsy Goldstein were summoned to appear at the police station, not suspecting that an unexpected statement from a witness in an old murder case threatened to cost them their heads. Kid Twist had already been arrested forty-two times in fifteen years, so this new appearance was of little concern to him. But two months later, he realised that his life was at stake and that he could end up in the electric chair. So he began to "sing". He finally reached an agreement with the Kings County Prosecutor, William O'Dwyer, proposing to reveal the existence and workings of Murder Incorporated, hitherto unknown, and to denounce his accomplices, including his boss, Lepke Buchalter. Buchalter was already in prison, charged with drug trafficking by prosecutor Thomas Dewey, who was still unaware that Buchalter had had dozens of potential witnesses executed to avoid a conviction. Reles testified to police "enough to fill twenty-five notebooks with hair-raising stories of murder and violence," wrote Don Wolfe. Reles exposed his twenty-four murders in Brooklyn alone, and thus earned the top spot in the *"hit-parade* of the Jewish parallel world[50]".

Among the killers Abraham Reles mentioned in his confessions was the name Bugsy Siegel. He further reported that he was one of the founders of Murder Inc and that he was the mob boss involved in the recent elimination of Big Greenie Greenberg. His confessions provoked a chain reaction from the other gangsters, so much so that the police set up special housing for informers of justice.

The talk of the traitor (the "canary's song" in Mafia slang) led to the prosecution of Murder Incorporated's top killers. Harry Strauss, Pittsburg Phil, Happy Maïone, Frank Abbandando, Louis Capone, Mendy Weiss and his childhood friend Bugsy Goldstein were all executed in the electric chair. After the trial, Goldstein shouted to reporters: "Tell that rat Reles that I'll wait for him. Maybe it will be in hell. I don't know, but I'll wait for him. I bet I'll have a pitchfork in my hand!"

Murder Inc.' s Albert Anastasia, a top Cosa Nostra leader, was scheduled for trial on 12 November. Anastasia had previously organised a bloody purge to prevent the appearance of new witnesses who could

---

[49] Don Wolfe, *Le Dossier Dahlia noir*, 2005, Albin Michel, 2006, p. 216.
[50] Rich Cohen, *Yiddish Connection*, 1998, Denoël, 2000, Folio, p. 377

compromise the Syndicate bosses. Her indictment was based on the sole testimony of Reles. Fortunately for him, on the morning of the 12th, Reles' body was found under the window of the Coney Island hotel where he was staying, guarded by the police. Unfortunately, despite the extensive security measures taken to protect him, Reles had fallen from the fifth floor. The cause of his death was never clearly established and it was never known whether he had thrown himself out of the window or had been pushed, or whether he had attempted to flee. Frank Costello was said to have paid off the policemen guarding Reles so that he could not testify. The future repentant Joe Valachi later revealed that it was indeed a murder committed with the help of one of the policemen guarding Reles. Abraham Reles earned a new nickname after his death: the canary who sang but couldn't fly.

Lepke Buchalter eventually turned himself in to the FBI in April 1939 to avoid a harsher sentence, beginning a 14-year sentence for drug trafficking at the federal penitentiary in Leavenworth, Kansas. However, the sentence was later extended to thirty years because of his misconduct within the Union. The testimonies of Reles and Albert Tannenbaum were fatal for him. Lepke had committed the reckless act of participating in person in a settling of scores—only one of hundreds committed by the organisation. The evidence communicated to the prosecutor about the murder of knick-knack shop owner Joseph Rosen led to a new sentence in December 1941: the death penalty. Buchalter was executed in the electric chair in January 1942 at Sing Sing Prison in New York State. He was the only crime boss of that rank to have been executed. It was the end of Murder Incorporated[51].

Bugsy Siegel in Hollywood

Bugsy Siegel had gone to sea, settling in Los Angeles in 1936. Since 1934, Siegel had travelled several times to serve the interests of the Syndicate in the region. His ambition was to infiltrate the movie business by setting up gambling dens, prostitution rings, gambling rings and drug rings. In Hollywood and the west side of the city, their nightclubs served as fronts for the Syndicate." According to the

---

[51] Murder Incorporated was the subject of a single Hollywood film, by Stuart Rosenberg in 1960. Kid Twist (Abe Reles) is played by Peter Falk. In 1975, Menahem Golan made a film about Lepke, starring Tony Curtis (born Bernard Schwartz), in which the Jewishness of the gangsters is perfectly reflected. The film presents a Lepke betrayed by the Syndicate and cornered. At the end of the film, it is emphasised that Lepke was the first boss of the Mafia Syndicate to be executed.

California Crime Commission, the Syndicate operated more than thirty bars, at least seventy-five gambling dens, nineteen brothels, seventeen casinos, and fourteen *nightclubs* in the Hollywood region[52]."

In 1938, Bugsy Siegel moved in with his wife and children in a lavish thirty-five-room mansion. He also had a suite in a large hotel where he met Virginia Hill, the Syndicate's fund-raiser, and a whole swarm of Hollywood beauties chosen from among the studios' young stars. Bugsy was also in touch with Hollywood stars and the great eminences of the production companies, such as Jack Warner, Harry Cohn and Louis Mayer, with whom he did business[53]. He was a friend of some stars, such as Clark Gable and Cary Grant, and the lover of Lana Turner—a co-religionist—and Rita Hayworth. A sportsman and showman, few people in Hollywood knew that he was also a ruthless killer and one of the founders of Murde Incorporated. He took control of several unions of extras and technicians (set designers, sound technicians, editors, editors, etc.) that could bring any film shoot to a standstill in a short time. Thanks to his control over the workforce, he extorted money from the studios in exchange for their protection against wildcat strikes.

When Siegel arrived on the West Coast, the Sicilian mobsters were already present: Jack Dragna (born Anthony Rizzotti), was the Los Angeles mob boss. His lieutenant was Johnny Rosselli, a man with the soft, cloying manners that Dragna lacked. They had come to power during Prohibition, when gangs were raiding the black market for alcohol. Born in Sicily, Dragna had emigrated to the United States in 1914 and frequented Al Capone's Chicago gang before becoming a mob boss in Southern California.

The arrival of Bugsy Siegel in the region quickly raised tensions and Lucky Luciano had to impose his will to get them to cooperate and Dragna to renounce the war. Luciano, who retained all his authority from his prison cell, demanded that they cooperate because according to the Mafia code, refusing to obey the godfather meant signing his death warrant. The city was then divided into territories controlled by Siegel and Dragna. Siegel got the western part, with Hollywood and Beverly Hills, while Dragna was given downtown, the outskirts of the valley, Long Beach and the port of Los Angeles[54].

Bugsy had been summoned to testify before the police in

---

[52] Don Wolfe, *Le Dossier Dahlia noir*, 2005, Albin Michel, 2006, p. 211.
[53] Universal, Fox, Paramount, Columbia, Warner Bros, MGM, RCA and CBS are all creations of Eastern European Jewish immigrants. See *under Planetary Hopes*.
[54] Don Wolfe, *Le Dossier Dahlia noir*, 2005, Albin Michel, 2006, p. 211.

September 1940. Charged with Greenberg's murder, he was incarcerated in the Old City Prison in downtown Los Angeles. His brother-in-law, Whitey Krakower, who had also been implicated by Reles in Greenie's murder, appeared before the police shortly afterwards, but was shot dead in the street in Manhattan. Bugsy had killed an inconvenient witness. Siegel's marriage would not get over the drama. Bugsy's wife filed for divorce and returned to New York with their children.

Bugsy Siegel's conditions of incarceration were not very harsh, as he received favourable treatment. He lived in a flat inside the prison and had his dinner brought in from the best restaurants in town. He even continued to frequent Hollywood nightclubs where he was taken at night. When the scandal broke in the press, it turned out that prison doctor Benjamin Blank had received more than $32,000 from Siegel to let him move into his private flats. The public learned in passing that, during his first month of detention, Siegel had made eighteen nocturnal outings and had been allowed to receive visits from young women in his prison "flat". Even his prisoner's jean suits were custom-made. The murder charges were eventually dropped thanks to a $30,000 donation that helped fund the Los Angeles prosecutor's campaign.

Bugsy had been ostracised by Hollywood society, but he continued to run his criminal business. He recruited Mickey Cohen, a former boxer, and began to expand into Jack Dragna's territory by annexing a luxury telephone prostitution ring. Next, Siegel visited Las Vegas, then just a small town. Nevada was a small oasis in the heart of the American judicial system where everything was legal: telephone gambling, gambling, prostitution. Siegel dreamed of establishing his empire there so that he could make astronomical sums of money legally. So Siegel started the construction of the Flamingo Hotel, which was to be the largest and most luxurious hotel-casino in the world. That project was the origin of the fortune of Las Vegas, the city of gambling. In 1943, following Lansky's advice, Luciano loaned Siegel $5 million to finance the Flamingo. Naturally, Siegel kept in touch with the Syndicate. Joseph Epstein, alias Joey Ep, the treasurer and confidant of the Chicago mob, worked with him.

While he was busy in Vegas, Bugsy had left Mickey Cohen to manage the business in Los Angeles. But the latter was not as slick as he was, and the rivalry with Jack Dragna soon turned into open warfare. When Cohen began to interfere aggressively in the Sicilian's gambling network, the Sicilian had enough of gritting his teeth. War broke out in 1946 after a Syndicate bookie working for Mickey Cohen was murdered and two other Siegel and Cohen associates were gunned down. These murders were all over the front pages of the press for several days, but the investigation stalled even though everyone knew Dragna was in charge.

In Las Vegas, the construction of the pharaonic hotel-casino was dragging on. The bill was mounting and the Syndicate bosses began to have doubts about the marble palace in the middle of the desert. Bugsy then asked his henchman Albert Greenberg to organise a series of jewellery store robberies. Al Greenberg, who also ran a drug ring, had years earlier been involved in the alcohol trade with Bugsy and Meyer's gang.

On 26 December 1946, the casino finally opened its doors. The many Hollywood stars who were supposed to be there, such as Clark Gable, Lana Turner and Cary Grant, had been stranded at Los Angeles airport because of the storm that had made it impossible for planes to take off. The Flamingo, located in the middle of the desert, initially had some difficulty in finding a clientele. Al Greenberg's gang continued to rob and rob jewellers' shops to finance the project. The jeweller Maurice Reingold suffered continuous robberies of his insured merchandise. Al Greenberg finally had to make a hasty escape from the city to New York.

Young Elizabeth Short frequented this world of delinquents and criminals. She was in contact with Al Green. This beautiful 23-year-old woman, who had ambitions of becoming a film star, always dressed in black and wore a dahlia in her hair, which is why she was nicknamed the "Black Dahlia". On 15 January 1947, her body was found at dawn in an open field, atrociously mutilated. Elizabeth Short had sadly been awarded the most horrible crime ever committed. The coroner was stunned: her mouth had been "prolonged" with a knife, cut open in two. Her skull and face had been savagely bashed in with the butt of a gun. The breasts had been severed, but most spectacularly, the body had been cut in two from the waist, where the spine is easiest to cut, between the second and third lumbar spine, and the letter "D" had been carved into her pubis[55].

---

[55]"Jack the Ripper", who savagely murdered at least five young women in London in 1888, was never caught by the police. The victims' throats were slit, then the Ripper removed their intestines, kidneys and uterus. The precision with which the killer worked at night indicated that he had a background in medicine or butchery. After the first murder, police arrested a Jewish butcher named John Pizer who the mob wanted to lynch. The second murder, that of Elizabeth Stride, took place in the courtyard of a building occupied by German Jews. Catherine Eddowes, the third victim, was horribly disfigured. Her nose and left ear had been cut off and her face slashed and marked with

The gruesome murder was on the front pages of the Los Angeles press for thirty-one days, but it took decades for the original photos of the victim's body to be published. 400 police officers became entangled in that investigation. According to Don Wolfe, who published a book on the case in 2005, the man responsible for the act was none other than "Bugsy Siegel, the number two in the Jewish mafia", as could also be read in an article in the weekly *Le Point* on 2 November 2006 following the release of Brian de Palma's film: "Siegel was the right-hand man of Meyer Lanski, the head of the Jewish mafia." He had taken over a number of garets, brothels and Brenda Allen's network of prostitutes, which had offended Jack Dragna. According to Don Wolfe, Betty Short was one of these girls in Brenda's network. Betty Short's body had been found two hundred yards from Jack Dragna's house, as if Siegel had wanted to pin the murder on his enemy.

In front of the grand jury, Sergeant Charles Stoker had revealed under oath the existence in Los Angeles of a network of Syndicate abortionists. These were protected by Lieutenant Willie Burns and members of the anti-mafia squad by means of bribes. According to Stoker, the head of this network was Dr. Leslie Audrain, who officially committed suicide at his home in May 1949 when he was about to be interrogated. Don Wolfe hypothesised that Elizabeth Short had been impregnated by Norman Chandler, the most powerful man in Los Angeles. Her body had been mutilated in order to ablate her uterus and foetus.

Siegel had become more violent and a danger to everyone. In fact, his mistress Virginia Hill had opened two secret accounts in Switzerland from which she was taking some of the money that could have been used to repay Luciano. Four years later, Lucky had not seen another dollar, and he was convinced that Siegel was trying to swindle him. At the Havana conference on 22–24 December 1946, Siegel had even become enraged and declared that he would repay when he decided to do so. From then on, his fate was sealed, and Lansky tried unsuccessfully to prevent his execution. On 20 June 1947, Benjamin

---

a V. She had been almost decapitated, cut open, her head cut off. She had been almost decapitated, cut open "like a pig in a shop window", her stomach and intestines placed over her right shoulder, her liver cut out, her kidneys and genitals removed. At around 3 a.m., police inspector Alfred Long discovered graffiti near the crime scene: *"The Juwes are the men That Will not be blamed for nothing"*, which meant without misspelling: "The Jews will not be blamed for nothing". In order not to provoke a wave of anti-Semitism, the inscription was immediately transcribed and erased. Another murderer had been in the news in the early 1990s: David Berkowitz, known as "Son of Sam". He had killed 17 women, mostly prostitutes on Long Island, New York.

Siegelbaum was executed at his lover's villa in Beverly Hills with a long-distance rifle. He was shot twice in the head56. Dragna took it upon himself to liquidate him and the case was declared "unsolved", as was the murder of Elizabeth Short. Jack Dragna carried out his personal vendetta against Mickey Cohen. He got away with several assassination attempts, but six of his men were killed in 1948. The management of the Flamingo was handed over to three faithful collaborators of Meyer Lansky: Moe Sedway, Morris Rosen and Gus Greenbaum. So it was all in the family.

The link between Bugsy, the Syndicate and the Black Dahlia murder was never publicly established by the police and the press." The irony of the story," wrote Don Wolfe, "is that the only person publicly punished after the 1949 grand jury was Sergeant Charles Stoker—the honest cop. Demoted in rank and assigned to traffic, Stoker was the victim of a frame-up by the LAPD, which charged him with robbery and found him guilty of "insubordination and conduct unbecoming a police officer". Stoker, a fervent Catholic, spent twenty-five years of his life working as a trainmaster at the Southern Pacific Railway depot in Los Angeles, where he died, forgotten by all, on March 10, 1975[57]."

Of course, Brian de Palma's *The Black Dahlia* (2006) showed no Jewish gangsters guilty of atrocities, and placed the full weight of infamy on the WASP (White Anglo-Saxon Protestant) bourgeoisie. Similarly, Barry Levinson's film *Bugsy* (USA, 1992) recounted the life of Bugsy Siegel with almost no evidence of the psychopath's Jewishness and emphasised Warren Beatty's idealistic, Anglo-Saxon traits. This is what the American nationalist David Duke wrote in his book *Jewish Supremacism* (2003): "The film depicts the most bloodthirsty of American gangsters as an elegant and romantic man with a big heart, with the traits of an Anglo-Saxon." David Duke quite rightly added: "Invariably, Jewish films and television producers give gangsters the features of a blond-haired man with blue eyes."

---

[56] In the first part of the cult film *The Godfather* (1972), Bugsy Siegel is portrayed by the character Moe Green. The Corleone family tries to buy his hotel in Las Vegas from him and he ends up murdered. In the second part, Hym Roth (portrayed by Meyer Lansky) mentions him as a friend, business partner, and creator of Las Vegas.

[57] Don Wolfe, *Le Dossier Dahlia noir*, 2005, Albin Michel, 2006, p. 287. In a footnote, Don Wolfe wrote the following: "Sergeant Jack Clemmons, the first policeman to arrive at the scene of Marilyn Monroe's death, met the same fate. Clemmons claimed on several occasions that Marilyn Monroe had been murdered and that all the officers of the LAPD's information division (the former anti-mafia squad), including Archie Case and James Ahern, had covered up the crime…"

Fight fascism, support Israel

From the depths of his prison cell, Lucky Luciano continued to run his business and still seemed to control New York harbour. Apparently, the massive presence of the US armed forces was not enough to guarantee the security of the port. On 9 February 1942, the French ocean liner *Normandie*, renamed *La Fayette*, was severely damaged by fire and sank. So in March 1942, when his second application for parole had just been rejected, Luciano was visited by Navy emissaries. The deal was simple: Lucky guaranteed the safety of the port in exchange for his freedom. In addition, he offered his cooperation to the US army officers who were planning a landing on the Sicilian coast and the overthrow of Mussolini. Luciano enthusiastically put the American officers in touch with his friends in Sicily. The latter drew up detailed maps for the state-major and guided the American soldiers through the territory. In return, Luciano demanded that the Sicilian mafias resume their dominant position after the fighting. The Americans promised that they would not exert any pressure and control over the conduct of the elections. Without saying so explicitly, they had handed Sicily over to the Mafia, which would soon regain the power it had lost under Mussolini.

Meanwhile, Luciano ordered that New York harbour be cleared of all Fascist or Nazi sympathisers. Before the invasion, he had contacted senior navy officials: he wanted to accompany the troops ashore to serve as a liaison officer. Perhaps he imagined himself returning home at the head of an army. His request was turned down, but the US government was grateful for his contribution. In 1946, Tom Dewey signed his application for parole. Luciano was released on the condition that he leave the United States permanently. On 10 February 1946, he embarked for Naples. On the dock, Frank Costello and Meyer Lansky accompanied him. They would continue to take care of business on American soil.

The Jewish and Sicilian gangsters were naturally "anti-fascist". It is known that Bugsy Siegel had planned to assassinate Goebbels and Göring, guests like himself at the Italian villa of his then mistress, Countess Di Frasso. Charlie Birger (born Sacha Itzik Berger), the Missouri mob boss, had been hanged in 1928 for the murder of the mayor of West City. But he was suspected of murdering at least a dozen people, including a head of the Klu Klux Klan. In Minneapolis, David Berman, who ran the local criminal underworld, attacked the conferences of American pacifists who refused to launch the country into a new war in Europe. Mickey Cohen, Bugsy Siegel's lieutenant, recounted, for example, in his biography *In My Own Words*, that one day, a judge had called on him before an extreme right-wing rally: "I said OK, don't worry about it. So we went over there and tore them to pieces." Rich Cohen had this sentence: "For many gangsters, fighting the Nazis was an expression of their patriotism[58]."

Jewish gangsters, in fact, did not at all disavow their membership of Judaism: "Even the most violent gangsters considered themselves good Jews, people of the Book, wrote Rich Cohen. They went to synagogue during the religious holidays, turned their thoughts to God when things went wrong, had their children circumcised and accompanied them on their Bar-mitzvahs[59]... How did they match their criminal lives with the Bible? Like most people, they introduced a distinction: this is the life of the soul, and that is the life of the body. Next year in Jerusalem. But while I am in the Diaspora, this is how I live[60]."

If the Sicilian Mafiosi were always able, in case of need, to take refuge across the ocean in the villages of their ancestors, the Jews would soon have the new state of Israel, created in 1948. Rich Cohen wrote here: "For the Jews, there was Miami, the other holy land. And soon there would be Israel ... a victory for the fugitive Jews[61]."

After the war, Mickey Cohen raised money for the Jewish fighters of the Irgun who were fighting against the British to create a Jewish state in Palestine. But the Jewish racketeers sometimes thought less of the cause than of their own interests, and the money raised did not always go to its intended recipients. In 1950, Cohen organised a charity gala." That night, wrote Don Wolfe, more than two hundred thousand dollars were raised for the cause—but mysteriously, the money never reached Palestine. According to Mickey Cohen, the ship carrying the money had been torpedoed and sunk. But for Ben Williamson and Ben Hecht there was little doubt that the money had ended up in one of those big betting pots for poker games at Hecht Castle on Angelo Drive[62]."

Elie Wiesel transcribed in his memoirs this curious episode: "The writer Ben Hecht recounts in his memoirs that, "kidnapped" by strangers, he was taken to a garage where, in front of the underworld

---

[58] Rich Cohen, *Yiddish Connection*, 1998, Denoël, 2000, Folio, p. 337, 339
[59] The Bar-mitzvah is the rite of passage to adulthood. A person who is Bar-mitzvah has the same responsibilities as an adult under Jewish law.
[60] Rich Cohen, *Yiddish Connection*, 1998, Denoël, 2000, Folio, p. 266
[61] Rich Cohen, *Yiddish Connection*, 1998, Denoël, 2000, Folio, p. 255.
[62] Don Wolfe, *Le Dossier Dahlia noir*, 2005, Albin Michel, 2006, p. 248.

gathered there, a suitcase full of dollars was handed over to him on behalf of the Irgun[63]."

Meyer Lansky was also involved in these operations in support of the Jewish fighters in Palestine and had not hesitated to have an arms exporter assassinated who had had the bad idea of supplying the Arab countries as well. Lansky, like the other Jewish gangsters, was an ardent supporter of the Jewish state. In *Jewish Supremacism* (2003), David Duke quoted this *Newsweek* article of 17 November 1971: "Each year, Lansky and his associates donate large sums of money to the Israeli Treasury and philanthropies." When he took refuge in Israel, Lansky continued a tradition dear to his heart, contributing to social organisations, as he had done to the *United Jewish Appeal* and Brandeis University. Shortly after arriving in Tel-Aviv in 1970, he received at the Sheraton Hotel, in the company of his friend Jo Stacher, the president of the Ilan organisation for handicapped children to which he donated the modest sum of 300,000 Israeli pounds. Lansky also contributed to the construction of a synagogue in Jerusalem, which was to be named after him. In *Israel Connection*, Jacques Derogy recounted this anecdote: "One Saturday, anxious to go to 'his' temple, he took the precaution of parking his car a respectable distance from the building. But once inside, the faithful gave him uncomfortable looks: he had forgotten to put out his cigarette[64]! "But above all, Lansky became one of the biggest donors to the Tel Hashomer hospital, whose fundraising association was sponsored by a certain Mordechai Tsarfati, also called Mentesh. Mentesh was an honourable member of the public committee supporting David Ben Gourion, the former head of the government. He was also the leading figure in organised crime in Israel at the time.

The wanderings of Meyer Lansky

After prohibition in 1933, Lansky had invested massively in the gambling industry. He had started with casinos in the resort town of Saratoga, where he had already set up shop in the Rothstein era in partnership with Frank Costello and Joe Adonis. Then he had generously bribed the governor of Louisiana, Huey Long, so that the New York gangsters could exploit the hotel-casinos of New Orleans, and repeated the same operation in Arkansas, Kentucky and Florida,

---

[63] Elie Wiesel, *Mémoires, Tome I*, Le Seuil, 1994, p. 364, 365. The Irgun was a Zionist paramilitary formation. Ben Hecht was a famous and successful Hollywood writer and screenwriter, nicknamed "the Shakespeare of Hollywood".
[64] Jacques Derogy, *Israël Connection*, Plon, 1980, p. 75.

around Miami.

After World War II, Lansky was at the head of an empire that he ran from his *Fontainebleau* hotel in Miami. His casinos, which he also owned in New York, New Jersey and Louisiana, were open 24 hours a day. But in the early 1950s, Senator Kefauver, who headed the mob investigation commission, had vowed to bring Lansky down one way or another. After a tax investigation, his American casinos were shut down. But Lansky was not discouraged and began negotiations with Cuban dictator Fulgencio Batista to set up shop in Havana[65]. He took control of the Hotel Nacional and created one of the most important casinos in the Caribbean. Havana seemed to become a mafioso's paradise[66].

But with the fall of Batista and the victory of Fidel Castro in 1959, Lansky's business was seriously damaged and he had to leave the island. He settled in the Bahamas, about 100 kilometres from Miami. The government was autonomous and everything could be bought. Even the head of government himself, Ronald Simons, was on the payroll for services rendered. In 1961, Lansky set up a company there that guaranteed a monopoly on the construction and operation of casinos. Air travel for clients to the casinos was organised from the continent, while the millions of dollars in profits were transported to Switzerland, to Geneva, and more precisely to a unique bank of its kind: International Credit, "run by a very special Jew, Tibor Rosenbaum". Jacques Derogy described him as follows: "Chubby of waist and face, a kippah concealing his baldness, Tibor Rosenbaum managed to successfully reconcile his rabbinical piety with the role of European treasurer of the American mafia." He received "suitcases full of dollars, deposited them in special coffers under the pseudonym of Lansky, "Bear", and, through trust companies, reinvested them in the United States and elsewhere in perfectly legal businesses, especially in real estate[67]."

---

[65] Jacques de Saint Victor, *Mafias, l'industrie de la peur*, Editions du Rocher, 2008, p. 224. For Jacques de Saint Victor, the Jewish mafia does not exist. There are only Italians.

[66] In the second part of *The Godfather*, Francis Ford Coppola portrays Meyer Lansky through the character of Himan Roth, the Jewish mafia man who tries to bring down the Corleone family. We see him trying to convince Michael Corleone to invest in a Havana casino. Richard Dreyfus also played the character in the 1999 TV series *Lansky*. British actor Ben Kingsley played the role of Meyer Lansky in Barry Levinson's 1991 film *Bugsy*. Patrick Dempsey also played the role of Meyer Lansky in the 1991 film *Mobsters*. Meyer Lansky is played again by Dustin Hoffman in the film *The Lost City (2005)* directed by Andy Garcia.

[67] Jacques Derogy, *Israël Connection*, Plon, 1980, p. 69–71.

Tibor Rosenbaum was also the only banker to pay interest on gold deposits. His clients included the notorious swindler of the 1970s, Samuel Flatto-Sharon[68]. There was also the Israel Corporation, in which Edmomd de Rothschild was a shareholder. In 1967, the scandal exploded in the columns of *Life* magazine. The public then learned that Rosenbaum's representative in Israel was Amos Manor, the very head of Israeli counter-espionage, the notorious Shin Beth.

In the United States, Lansky's long-time friend Jo Stacher had been sentenced to five years in prison for various tax offences. Jacques derogy wrote on this point: "Fortunately, he was able to escape detention by agreeing to leave the United States. To Israel, of course[69]."

It was in Havana, before the Castro revolution, that Luciano organised a conference in December 1946 during which he presented his international drug trafficking project. In fact, Lucky Luciano was the first to break with the traditions of the Sicilian Union and to partner with Lansky in heroin trafficking.

At that time, most of the smuggled opium came from Turkey, and to a lesser extent from Indochina. From Turkey, the real poppy seeds were smuggled to Lebanon, where the airport director and most of the customs officers were bought by the gangsters. In Lebanon, the royal poppy was transformed into morphine base. This morphine was then transported to the Marseille region to be refined.

Meyer Lansky was the main organiser of what the Americans would call the *"French Connection"*. At the end of 1948, Lansky had been in Europe, in the south of France, visiting the palaces of Nice and the clandestine laboratories of the Marseilles region. He had met several times with Joseph Renucci and the Guerini brothers, before leaving for Naples to talk to Luciano about the advantages of the Corsican network.

The transformation of morphine base into heroin is a complex operation. Dominique Albertini, a retired pharmaceutical laboratory worker, had the secret to making heroin of high purity compared to others who could not achieve more than 60 or 70%. With him, the Corsican network had become indispensable. From then on, heroin destined for the American market would pass through the Marseilles region. The drug was prepared and packaged in 500 gram bags and sent

---

[68] On Flatto-Sharon read the chapter on "scams".
[69] Jacques Derogy, *Israël Connection*, Plon, 1980, p. 72." It must be said that in the United States, where Senator Robert Kennedy had taken over the fight against the Mafia after Kefauver, Meyer Lansky was still the target of investigations, interrogations and other annoyances. In fact, his long-time friend, Jo "Doc" Stacher, had been sentenced to five years in prison and fined $10,000 for various tax offences."

to the United States via Montreal, where François Spirito had taken refuge since 1944, or via Florida, which benefited from the proximity of Cuba[70].

The Castro regime was very conciliatory towards cocaine traffickers. The Cubans turned a blind eye to cargo ships crossing their territorial waters, and had proposed the use of their ports for repairs and refuelling. In exchange for their cooperation, the Cubans demanded that the freighters make the return trip with their holds full of weapons to deliver to their Marxist brothers in Latin America." Cuba would buy the cocaine from communist militias in Colombia, who would use the money to buy weapons. Once the cocaine arrived in Cuba, the regime would negotiate with a few families on the East Coast or with one or two Mexican gangs" that flooded California, thus weakening the US enemy. Without the drug money, Castro would not have lasted all those years, claimed William Reymond[71].

In the United States, the number of regular heroin users had exploded. Whereas in 1946 there were twenty thousand, by 1952 there were more than sixty thousand Americans "addicted" to the drug. By the early 1970s, with the help of the hippie wave and "liberationist" ideas, the United States now counted half a million drug addicts, a figure probably much lower than the reality. But the fate of the victims mattered little: it was the profits that mattered. In 1974, a kilo of morphine base was bought for $220 on the Turkish markets and traded, once processed, for $240,000, which was 1000 times the initial price.

But the *French Connection* quickly perished after Nixon became president of the United States in 1968. Nixon had declared war to the death on drug traffickers and asked the French government to cooperate. Numerous traffickers were arrested on US soil. On 28 February 1972, the fishing boat *Le Caprice des Temps*, which had just left the port of Villefranche for Florida, was searched by French customs. The police found 425 kilos of pure heroin on board. It was the largest quantity ever seized. The *French Connection*, already faltering, was severely weakened. The laboratories were then dismantled. But at that time, most of the heroin was already coming from Asia. The Corsican network had expired[72].

---

[70] William Reymond, *Mafia S.A., Flammarion, 2001, p. 84.*, Flammarion, 2001, p. 84
[71] William Reymond, *Mafia S.A., Flammarion, 2001, 59–70*. Flammarion, 2001, 59–70. His book is completely incoherent. For him, there is no Jewish mafia either: there are the Italians (Cosa Nostra), the "Russians", the Yakusa (in Japan), the Triads (in Hong Kong, Taiwan and China), and also the terrible Nigerian mafia, "a fearsome group" (page 343).
[72] In the film *French Connection* (USA, 1971), apart from a brief mention of a drug

In 1970, Lansky was still living in Miami, in a relatively modest house, spending little and paying all his taxes, at least apparently. But he was still the target of US tax investigations. Senator Robert Kennedy had continued Kefauver's anti-mafia fight, helping to bring Lansky down. When Lansky learned that he was about to be indicted for tax fraud, he tried to flee to Israel, invoking the law of return by which the Hebrew state guaranteed Israeli citizenship to any Jew.

In Tel-Aviv, his friend Sam Rothberg besieged every ministry to help Lansky get his residence permit. Rothberg had been a figurehead of the American mafia during Prohibition, becoming king of the underground distilleries and producing whiskey instead of importing it from Scotland and Canada. He had achieved a semblance of irreproachable dignity by getting himself elected president of the *United Jewish Appeal* of the *United* States and investing massively in Israeli businesses, especially in real estate. Louis Boyar was another friend of Meyer Lansky. He was a former San Francisco gold dealer. He had also enhanced his image by generously funding various institutions, such as the Hebrew University of Jerusalem. His arguments were simple: Lansky, an older man retired from business, thought only of ending his days in Israel and investing his considerable fortune in Israel's needy national economy[73]. Nor could the Israeli state forget that, in 1948, Lansky had delivered weapons to the Haganah, the Israeli army.

However, Golda Meir, the prime minister, was adamant, and after a two-year legal battle, Israel finally refused asylum to the Mafia boss. It must be said that the US government had insisted strongly on his extradition and threatened to deprive Israel of the Phantom aircraft necessary for his defence. Moreover, prosecutor Bach had convinced Golda Meir that, far from living a quiet life in Israel, Lansky had been meeting in Tel Aviv with all the members of the American mafia. Thus, all of Lansky's appeals to the Supreme Court were in vain.

A week before his visa was due to expire in November 1972, Meyer Lansky left on a Swissair overnight flight with several laissez-passers issued to him by the diplomatic missions of Latin American countries, confident that at least one of them would accept his presence and his promises of investment. But he was unaware that FBI agents

---

dealer at the beginning of the film, the role of Jewish criminals does not appear. The film is by William Friedkin.

[73] The Hebrew state encouraged and promoted investment. In August 1967, Levi Eshkol, Israel's prime minister, had appealed to Jewish billionaires in the diaspora to come to Israel's aid. Sixty billionaires from fourteen countries had gathered in Jerusalem. Jean-Jacques Servan-Schreiber's French weekly *L'Express* had reported the event in a few succinct and discreet lines (Archives d'Emmanuel Ratier).

were following him closely. In Zurich, Switzerland, he was met by a friend who arranged his passage to Rio de Janeiro with a stopover in Buenos Aires. From there to Paraguay, where he planned to bribe officials, change his name and disappear. But the FBI had sent a telex to every airport in the world. When the plane landed in Paraguay, Lansky was surprised to be met by police officials who informed him that he could not get off the plane. Lansky had the same reception at successive stopovers in Bolivia, Peru and Panama." Somehow," wrote Rich Cohen, "during those hours, the seventy-five-year-old gangster was once again reliving the history of the Jews: the arrivals and departures, the exile and the wandering."

After a ruse by the FBI, Lansky finally ended up on a US plane that flew him to Miami. When the plane landed on 7 November 1972, he was greeted by a crowd of journalists.

—Welcome back! the cops told him[74]." He was on his way back to Miami, where so many old Jews carry their dreams to their deaths[75]," wrote Rich Cohen.

Over the next few years, Lansky faced two charges of tax fraud, but was miraculously acquitted due to a procedural error. He finally passed away in 1983, never having set foot in a prison. Before his death, he had taken care to bequeath his ill-gotten fortune to the *United Jewish Appeal* charity. In one of his books, the American novelist Philip Roth presented the testimony of a certain Sheftel, who was one of Lansky's lawyers. He apparently told everywhere that "this American gangster was the most brilliant man he had ever met in his life." If Lansky had been at Treblinka, the Ukrainians and the Nazis would not have lasted three months[76]."

The invisible mafia

Jewish intellectuals are clearly reluctant to talk too much about the criminality emanating from their community. This is a tendency we also see when, for example, they try to account for the terrifying role played by numerous Jews during the Bolshevik revolution in Russia from 1917 to 1947. The aim was to create a "world without borders". Despite the most compelling and irrefutable evidence, Jewish intellectuals continue to vigorously deny the participation of very many

---

[74] Jacques Derogy, *Israël Connection*, Plon, 1980, p. 76, 77
[75] Rich Cohen, *Yiddish Connection*, 1998, Denoël, 2000, Folio, p. 457, 458
[76] Philip Roth, *Operation Shylock*, Debolsillo Penguin Random House, Barcelona, 2005, p. 394–395.

of their fellow Jews in what remains by far the most criminal experience in human history, second only to the Maoist revolution. The fact is that Jewish doctrinaires, Jewish officials and Jewish executioners have borne a crushing responsibility for the nearly thirty million deaths caused by the communist revolution in Russia[77].

In analysing the mafia phenomenon, these communitarian intellectuals always use the same Talmudic contortions to avoid tarnishing the image of a Jewish community that has always been persecuted for no reason. The best thing to do, of course, is not to talk about it and to divert the public's attention to other mafias: Sicilian, Turkish, Albanian, Russian, Nigerian, Chechen, Galician, etc...

In the United States, a mafia figure became very famous: Jacob Leon Rubinstein. His parents, of Polish origin, had emigrated in 1903, and he settled in Dallas in 1947, changing his name to "Ruby". He then took control of several discotheques and nightclubs. In 1959, Ruby had travelled to Cuba to visit some mafia friends and deal arms. Jack Ruby was no softie. The Warren Commission report stated that he had repeatedly attacked meetings of American nationalist militants with his bouncers. He often used violence against his employees. Once, he hit one of his musicians with a *brass knuckles*; another time, he was seen beating an employee's head in with a club, and he was also frequently seen beating up those who did not perform fast enough for him.

Ruby was often armed with a revolver, as he carried large amounts of cash from his nightclubs. On Sunday morning, 24 November 1963, he was guilty of the first assassination in history to be broadcast live on television. He had shot Lee Harvey Oswald, the suspected assassin of President Kennedy who had been arrested two days earlier and was being transferred to another prison. Ruby later claimed that he had killed Oswald in a stroke of madness, and, indeed, his lawyer tried to pass him off as a madman. Most analysts thought Ruby would get off with a conviction for manslaughter, a light sentence of five years. But on 14 March 1964, Ruby was sentenced to death for murder. Questioned in his cell by members of the Warren Commission, Ruby had begged to be transferred to Washington, fearing for his life. Some argued that if Ruby felt threatened, it was because there had been a plot and that Ruby had killed on the orders of the mob. Ruby died on 3 January 1967 of a pulmonary embolism as a result of cancer. The Mafia was "very probably one of the main commanders of the assassination" of President Kennedy in Dallas in 1963 (*Les Echos* newspaper, 16 August 2007). Kennedy was allegedly "guilty of not having paid his debts—the

---

[77] See *Planetary Hopes* and *Jewish Fanaticism*.

purchase of ballots in several states—and of having allowed his brother Bobby to attack the mafia." The journalist from *Les Echos* immediately added: "Such is the power of the Cosa Nostra." The Sicilians are really fearsome: they are everywhere, they have everything under control, and we don't notice anything[78]!

The *Courier international* of 19 July 2007 provided a good example of intellectual "poaching". An article presented the Chicago mafia of the 1970s and '80s in the wake of a historic trial that opened on 20 June 2007 in Chicago federal court, in which old gangsters in their sixties and seventies were to be tried for their former crimes. Joey Lombardo, 78, and Frank Calabrese, among others, were finally appearing before the judges. The hearings were watched by millions of Mafia crime-loving television viewers eager to learn a little more about the customs of those horrible Catholics: "This trial," wrote the journalist, "should normally shed some light on the Mafia's initiation ceremonies, during which the aspirants swear, with their hands outstretched on the image of the Holy Virgin, to protect the Cosa Nostra. The tribunal will also bring to light eighteen cases of murders never elucidated and attempt to expose the Mafia's lasting influence over Chicago's underworld."

The Italian-American mafia had been "hit hard in the 1980s by aggressive prosecutors like Rudy Giuliani, at a time when its decline seemed inevitable." The journalist explained: "Italian immigration to the United States had been replaced by Colombians and other Latinos. Drugs had become the main source of income and the big Mafia families were no match for the ruthless Colombian drug traffickers. In Chicago, the gangsters are now but a shadow of their former selves. If what prosecutor Donald Campbell says is true, they cling to petty extortion in strip joints and occasional burglaries." He told the *Los Angeles Times*: "They have lost a lot of ground to other organised groups, whether it's the Russian mob, Latinos or street gangs on the

---

[78] Swiss researcher René-Louis Berclaz noted that on 4 June 1963, Kennedy signed Executive Order 111,110, which gave the state exclusive authority to issue bank notes, a decision "contrary to the interests of the international usury lobby, since it abrogated the privilege of monetary issuance held by the *Federal Reserve Bank*, which serves as the central bank in the United States." (*Le système bancaire est-il la cause des crises économiques?* Avril 2008). Kennedy had become the number one enemy of the entire US economic and political-military establishment (bankers, politicians, military, oil and arms oligarchs, CIA, mafia, etc.). [The assassination of President Kennedy has given rise to many theories, such as the famous one-bullet theory invented by Arlen Specter. On the Kennedy assassination, read William Reymond, *JFK, autopsie d'un crime d'État*, Flammarion, 1998].

East and West coasts." The Jewish mafia? It doesn't exist. It should be noted that *Courier international* was directed by Alexandre Adler, who obviously preferred to avoid talking about certain uncomfortable subjects.

In the cinema, the image of the Jewish mafioso is so furtive that the untrained viewer sees nothing of this reality. However, the Sicilian mobster is always much more visible than the Jewish gangster. In the three episodes of Francis Ford Coppola's *The Godfather* (1972, 1974, 1991), or in Martin Scorsese's *Goodfellas* (1990), some Jewish characters appear (men or wives), but it is the Sicilians who call the shots.

In Scorsese's *Casino* (1995), Robert de Niro, the casino manager, plays the Jewish Sam Rothstein, but he is subordinate to the Sicilian mobsters, his bosses whom he makes a lot of money, and to the goodwill of the governor of the State of Nevada. The role of the villain is played by Joe Pesci, the hyper-violent little bad guy of Sicilian origin. The murder of Joe Pesci at the end of the film, bludgeoned and buried alive in a cornfield, is inspired by the murder of Anthony Spilotro in June 1986.

Mel Horowitz, the Las Vegas underworld lawyer, was a friend of Alvin Malnik, the heir to the Meyer Lansky business, who was considered by the US federal authorities to be a pre-eminent figure in organised crime, which Alvin Malnik naturally strongly rejected. Since the late 1960s, Malnik had been the partner of Sam Cohen, the majority owner of the Flamingo Hotel. Lawyer, real estate developer, restaurateur of renown in Miami Beach, Malnik was also the owner of the national chain of lending agencies for private individuals: "Loans with such a high interest rate that one attorney general spoke of "legalising usury"[79]." During his long career he was never convicted.

Casinos play an important role in laundering dirty money. Let us recall that the "Pope" of Las Vegas at the beginning of the 21st century was one Poju (Haïm) Zabludowicz, an Israeli living in London who owned several hotels and six casinos in the city, i.e. 40% of the gambling city centre. Poju was also a great collector of contemporary art. After leaving Finland to settle in Israel, his father Shlomo had set up Soltam, an arms factory that was to become the jewel in the crown of Israeli industry. Arthur Goldberg was the owner of the largest casino chain in the United States. In Las Vegas, he owned the huge *Paris* Casino and the famous *Caesars Palace*.

In 1999, the election of Oscar Goodman to the mayoralty of Las

---

[79] Jean-François Gayraud, *Le Monde des mafias*, Odile Jacob, 2005, p. 117.

Vegas testified to the fact that the mafia's hold on the city was still real. Indeed, Oscar Goodman had long been the Jewish mafia's lawyer. He had defended Meyer Lansky and Frank Rosenthal.

There was also the brilliant Sol Kerzner, a Russian-born Jew who owned *Sun City*, a gigantic hotel-casino created in 1979 in South Africa. Kerzner had casinos all over the world: in Las Vegas, in Atlantic City, in Mauritius, in Dubai and in the Bahamas, where he built the *Atlantis Paradise* hotel and holiday club. His son, Butch Kerzner, was tragically killed in a helicopter crash in October 2006. The aircraft crashed into a property in the Dominican Republic while he was prospecting the region with an investor.

Hollywood cinema never shows us this reality. In *The Departed* (2007), Scorsese portrayed the Boston Irish mob. Its boss, played by Jack Nicholson, was cruel and Machiavellian in a way that no Jew could ever appear in an "American" film. The film *Road to Perdition* (USA, 2002), depicted the Irish mob in Chicago in the 1930s. Despite always having the word "God" or "Lord" in their mouths, these strong-believing Catholics were terrifying murderers. The film was directed by Sam Mendes, who is clearly neither Irish nor Catholic.

However, the Jewishness of the protagonists appears in some films. Apparently, there can also be a certain pride in seeing some mafia leaders from their own community. Thus, we saw how the beautiful film, Once Upon *a Time in America* (1984), very complacently depicted a gang of Jewish gangsters in Prohibition times (starring Robert de Niro and James Wood). Anything goes: prostitution, alcohol, nightclubs, murder, armed robbery, diamond theft, drugs, union control and finally ... political consecration. But there again, an untrained viewer will not see all the little details that show the Jewishness of the gangsters. In any case, they are so sympathetic that it is difficult to condemn their actions.

In *L.A. Confidential* (USA, 1997), a film by Curtis Hanson adapted from James Ellroy's novel, Jewishness appeared more discreetly. The opening of the film introduced the godfather of the local mafia in 1950s Los Angeles, Meyer Cohen as "Mickey C., to his fan club". He was the "king of organised crime in the region: the king of drugs, extortion and prostitution. He "takes out a dozen people a year" and is on the front pages of the press.

Meyer Lansky, on the other hand, appeared on screen as an innocent victim of anti-Semitism. In the 1999 American TV series (Lansky), the two opening scenes set the trend. The first showed old Lansky in Jerusalem, trying to buy a plot in the cemetery near his grandparents' grave. In a second scene, in a *flashback*, we see him at the age of seven, petrified, watching a poor Jew being massacred by Polish peasants during a pogrom in Grodno, his hometown, just like that, for no apparent reason. In other shots, he is also forced to defend himself against Irish drunks. In the series *The Sopranos* (1999), the only Jew is a kindly horse-breeding yayo whose only crime seems to have been swindling the copyrights of black singers.

The fact of erasing the trace of Jewishness of major criminals in American films is even acknowledged by specialists. This is what we read in the daily *Libération* on 10 February 2000, under the pen of Philippe Garnier: "Historically, the importance of Jewish gangsters has been hidden by American writers, but especially by Hollywood. Hemingway, who knew how to mind his own business, let us hint that *"The Killers"* in his novel of the same name were Jews… In Robert Siodmak's film produced by Mark Hellinger [in 1946], any allusion has disappeared, and one of the killers is played by Charles McGraw, a goy brute if ever there was one."

In the 1930s, the great actors of the Yiddish theatre such as Paul Muni and E.G. Robinson were offered the roles of Italians such as Scarface or Rico. *CinémAction* magazine confirmed: "During the great period of film noir, no leading gangster character had been Jewish; the change only came about from the 1950s onwards when the biographies of "Legs" Diamond, Arnold Rothstein and "Lepke" Buchalter were shot—and even then, the ethnic and religious background was almost overlooked[80]."

In 1931, producer Howard Hughes bought the rights to a novel entitled *Queer people*. The story told the tale of a journalist new to Hollywood who discovered that all the film studios were run by Jewish businessmen. No actors agreed to be in the film, except William Haines, and eventually Hughes, who had received death threats over the phone, had to give up his film[81].

After the war, this absolute dominance was somewhat officialised. Several American Jewish organisations founded the *Motion Picture Project* in 1947, a body that was to monitor Hollywood's portrayal of Jewish themes and the image of Jews. A certain John Stone was hired

---

[80] CinémAction, *Cinéma et judéité*, Annie Goldmann, Cerf, 1986, p. 104.
[81] All Hollywood studios have been created by Ashkenazi Jews. Read in *The Planetary Hopes*." Jack Warner demanded that all his employees pay a percentage of their salaries to the Jewish Unified Social Fund…" It was enough for him to say: If you don't donate anything to the *United Jewish Appeal*, you'll never work here again," his son, Jack junior, acknowledged." (Neal Gabler, *Le Royaume de leur rêve*, 1988, Calmamnn-Lévy, 2005, p. 336).

to enforce its objectives on the studios: "To eliminate anything that might generate anti-Semitism, especially in films about the life of Jesus Christ; to avoid unsympathetic Jewish characters; to orient public opinion towards an awareness of the persecutions of which Jews were victims[82]". So, for example, Stone pressured the screenwriter of *Murder Inc*, the story of the Jewish gangster Louis Lepke, to include a combative Jewish prosecutor in the script.

The 19 July 2007 issue of Alexandre Adler's newspaper, *Courier international*, quoted Tim Adler's book, *Hollywood and the mob*, devoted to "the murky links between the film industry and the crime syndicate... However, Hollywood's dubious links with the mafia have not disappeared. Today, the Russian mafia is at the forefront of the scene. Their control of the film industry has already resulted in the bankruptcy of an Australian insurance company, and it looks like the mafia story is far from over." Admittedly, these "Russian" gangsters are pretty scary, as we will see in the following chapters.

The highly influential Jacques Attali, a former adviser to socialist president François Mitterrand before becoming an adviser to liberal president Nicolas Sarkozy in 2007[83], was somewhat more honest. In the weekly *L'Express* of 10 January 2002, he presented his latest book, *The Jews, the World and Money*. The journalist asked him: "You bluntly evoke another taboo: the power of Jewish gangsterism in the United States." Jacques Attali replied: "It would have seemed dishonest not to talk about this marginal and fascinating episode." And we ourselves would be dishonest if we did not transcribe here these details provided by Attali, which relativise the phenomenon of Jewish criminality: "One of the bosses of the American mafia is a certain Meyer Lansky. He is part of that small minority of Jewish criminals—perhaps 2000 out of 2 million Russian Jews who immigrated to the United States at the end of the 19th century and the beginning of the 20th century."

But Attali added: "This totally "disintegrated" fraction of the community is a great historical novelty. Until then, Jews had had a phobia of delinquency and criminality for theological reasons, but also for reasons of survival, since the behaviour of a single individual could endanger the security of the entire community[84]."

---

[82] Jean-Luc Doin, *Dictionnaire de la censure au cinéma*, Presses Universitaires de France, 1998, p. 316.
[83] And Emmanuel Macron's mentor in 2017. (NdT)
[84] "One Jew is like the whole of Judaism", wrote the founder of the World Jewish Congress, Nahum Goldmann, quoting the famous verse from the Talmud (*Le Paradoxe juif*, Paris, Stock, 1976, p. 43).

In reality, this Jewish criminality was by no means a "historical novelty[85]", as we will see below. Nor had it disappeared, as Jean-François "Gayraud" tried to make us believe in his book *The World of Mafias*, published in 2005. In fact, he tried to make us understand that Jewish gangsterism had died out and that it was an exceptional and ephemeral phenomenon: "Unlike the Italians, the Jewish community after the Second World War had definitively distanced itself from illegality[86]."

And again, with great concern for the truth, Jacques Attali stated: "Meyer Lansky has no connection with the community… When he was later arrested—for tax reasons, like Al Capone—and asked Israel for the right to benefit from the Law of Return, Golda Meir did not grant it to him." He explained in his book: "A few years later, Lansky will try to take refuge in Israel, which will deny him the benefit of the Law of Return: for his crimes, he will have lost the right to be recognised as a Jew[87]." And Attali continued to the end with his intellectual honesty: "Meyer Lansky, the Jewish gangster was a novelty; in fact, he was no longer a Jew at all[88]."

You have understood, Jewish gangsters do not exist, for the simple reason that one cannot be a gangster and a Jew at the same time. In fact, this reasoning is exactly the same as that used by Jewish intellectuals who claim that in reality the Bolshevik criminals were no longer "Jews at all", since they were communists and atheists. The point is quite clear: you have simply had a hallucination.

---

[85] "The Jewish element in the world of gangsterism was a very serious and grave matter for American Jewry; something that could not be ignored—a problem of great magnitude. Such communication between Jews and non-Jews in the basements of society found expression in the fact that the jargon of the German underworld was essentially Yiddish, or Jewish. The whole underworld made it their own, simply as a secret language, and precisely the Hebrew elements of Yiddish spoken by the Jews were accepted with special gusto as code words by the non-Jewish underworld, as those languages with which prisoners communicate with each other." *Everything is Kabbalah. Dialogue with Jorg Drews, followed by Ten ahistorical theses on Kabbalah.* Gershom Scholem, Editorial Trotta, Madrid, 2001, p. 22.
[86] Jean-François Gayraud, *Le Monde des mafias*, Odile Jacob, 2005, p. 116.
[87] Jacques Attali, *Les Juifs, le monde et l'argent*.
[88] Jacques Attali, *Les Juifs, le monde et l'argent*, Fayard, 2002, p. 485.

2. Russia under the yoke of the oligarchs

However, the best way to build large fortunes quickly is still to operate legally and act in the open. But this requires certain favourable circumstances. Wars, revolutions and major changes are very opportune for the most reactive individuals, the most familiar with money management and the most unscrupulous.

One example in a thousand: we know that the Rothschild fortune was made following the defeat of Napoleon's armies at the Battle of Waterloo in 1815. Informed of the outcome of the battle before everyone else, Rothschild turned up at the London Stock Exchange with an air of gloom that suggested Napoleon had won. This allowed him to take all the securities that had been hastily sold at a very low price. This famous episode had inspired some verses by Victor Hugo, who thus watched the financier pass before him in his *Contemplations*:

"Old man, I take off my hat! This one who passes/Made his fortune, in the hour when you were shedding your blood/He was betting low, and rising as he went/That our fall was deeper and surer/There had to be a vulture for our dead, he was it."

The chaos that followed the collapse of communism in Russia represented a formidable hunting ground for predators. Russia then became the prey of a few cosmopolitan businessmen who bought up all the former collectivised enterprises and factories for ridiculously low prices. Some individuals amassed colossal fortunes during the privatisations of the 1990s, while the vast majority of the population fell into abject poverty and destitution.

Russia's plunder

Of the books written about the 'Russian' mafia that came out after the collapse of communism in 1991, Paul Klebnikov's *Boris Berezovsky and the Pillage of Russia*[89] was the most successful. Paul Klebnikov,

---

[89] Paul Klebnikov, *Godfather of the Kremlin: Boris Berezovsky and the looting of Russia* (2000). Paul Klebnikov was shot dead on a Moscow street in 2004. He was the victim

who was the Russian specialist for the famous American magazine *Forbes*, had interviewed a large number of personalities and carried out extensive research. The information presented in this chapter is taken from this book.

In August 1991, Boris Yeltsin, who had just been elected President of the Russian Republic, had thwarted the communist coup attempt in front of the parliament[90]. In order to unseat Soviet President Gorbachev, Yeltsin had agreed with the presidents of the Ukrainian and Belarusian republics that the Soviet Union would officially cease to exist. On 8 December 1991, the USSR gave way to fifteen new independent states. Russia lost 50 million inhabitants and returned to its 1613 borders.

The transition to a market economy was a forced march. At the beginning of 1992, prices were liberalised and inflation soared. By the end of the year, price increases were 1900% for eggs, 3100% for soap, 3600% for tobacco, 4300% for bread and 4800% for milk. In the same time interval, savings accounts and deposits reported less than 10% annual interest and wages increased slightly. All the savings of the population were thus rapidly devoured by inflation. Prime Minister Gaïdar's "shock therapy" consisted—as the Russians used to say—of "many shocks and little therapy". More than a hundred million people fell into misery.

President Yeltsin, a heavy drinker, was in reality largely manipulated by a group of scoundrels whose aim was to seize Russia's natural resources. The people closest to him were businessmen led by Boris Berezovsky.

Boris Berezovsky was born in 1946 'into a Jewish family of the Moscow intelligentsia', and had studied computer science at one of the USSR's leading secret scientific institutes. In 1989, he founded a car distribution company called LogoVaz, which marketed the vehicles of AvtoVaz, whose main factory was on the Volga, and quickly established itself as the largest reseller of Lada cars. His fortune made him a coveted target for the criminal gangs that were thriving with impunity at the time. Gang shoot-outs were not uncommon in Moscow, and to survive,

---

of a contract killing.

[90] "The new Jewish elite did not fully identify with Russia, but pursued a separate policy. This had a decisive effect in 1991, when more than 50 per cent of Jews supported President Yeltsin's pro-Western coup, while only 13 per cent of Russians supported it. In 1995, 81% of Jews voted for the pro-Western parties and only 3% for the Communists (while 46% of Russians voted for the Communists), as published by Jewish sociologist Dr Ryvkina in her 1996 book, *Jews in Post-Soviet Russia.*" In Israel Adam Shamir, *The Other Face of Israel*, Ediciones Ojeda, Barcelona, 2004, p. 125, 126.

leading businessmen had to be heavily protected. As the Russian government descended into chaos, the most effective security services turned out to be those of the mafia. Boris Berezovsky worked in coordination with organised criminal groups from the small southern republic of Chechnya. These were the "terrifying Chechen gangsters" who protected him.

After the collapse of the USSR at the end of 1991, Russian troops had withdrawn from Chechen territory, leaving behind large arms depots. At the same time, one of the first measures of the new Chechen government was to open the prison doors and release about 4,000 professional criminals. Paul Klebnikov wrote here, "Many of the underworld bosses became members of the small republic's government while maintaining their contacts with Chechen groups in Moscow and other major Russian cities."

In the early 1990s, the seven main Chechen mafia gangs in Moscow had a potential of five hundred fighters. They had set up a network to extort money from shops, restaurants and hotels throughout the city. They quickly took control of the Beriozka state chain and Soviet-era luxury supermarkets reserved for members of the Nomenklatura and foreigners. When casinos started to appear in 1992–1993, the Chechens took control of the most important ones. With the huge revenues generated by their criminal activities, they penetrated the financial markets and took control of dozens of banks. They also controlled the gigantic Rossïa hotel opposite the Kremlin. A large part of the proceeds from extortion were repatriated to Chechnya.

Grozny airport then became the centre of smuggling activities in the Chechen Republic and one of the international hubs for heroin trafficking[91].

Klebnikov informed us that most of the other mafia bosses belonged to one of the numerous ethnic minorities. Thus, in 1993, of the sixty gang bosses operating in Moscow, more than half came from Georgia and a dozen were from other regions of the Caucasus." There were numerous luxury cars parading through the streets of the capital without registration plates. No police would risk stopping them[92]." After two years of democratic experience, most Russians had realised that their country had fallen into the hands of a criminal caste.

29,200 murders had been committed in 1993, which represented a

---

[91] Paul Klebnikov, *Parrain du Kremlin, Boris Berezovski et le pillage de la Russie*, Robert Laffont, 2001, p. 22-26.
[92] Paul Klebnikov, *Parrain du Kremlin, Boris Berezovski et le pillage de la Russie*, Robert Laffont, 2001, p. 37.

murder rate twice that of the United States, which was also experiencing its highest crime wave. In Moscow, the number of murders had increased eightfold between 1987 and 1993, but these murder figures represented only a fraction of the real number of murders in Russia, as many victims were recorded in the statistics in other categories: suicides, accidents, disappearances. In addition to the thirty thousand victims a year, there were some forty thousand missing persons. The police, unable to channel this violence, suffered 185 fatalities among its officers in 1994." When I questioned Berezovsky about the causes of the crime epidemic in Russia," wrote Paul Klebnikov, "he also told me about the collusion between gangsters and high-ranking government officials[93]."

Against the Chechen gangsters, Slavic gangs such as the Solntsevo Fraternity, created in a grey Moscow neighbourhood called Solntsevo, rose up. A gang war began in 1993, in which Boris Berezovsky became involved because he was the Chechens' ally. In the spring of 1994, he suffered several attacks in which several of his close associates were killed and he himself was wounded. After months of massacres, the Slav and Chechen gangs had exterminated each other. The Chechen leaders withdrew from the limelight and their Slav counterparts emigrated abroad. At the end of 1994, two years of madness came to an end. The real winners were the new businessmen who had worked with the underworld and would henceforth stop resorting to contract killings. On 11 December 1994, the Russian army invaded Chechnya.

The Soviets already had a tendency to deal with shady middlemen in their foreign dealings. Commodities trader Marc Rich, for example, was an oil trader who had had his heyday in the 1970s. He had fled the US in 1983 after being charged with extortion, racketeering, tax fraud and trading with Iran, a hostile power. Now a multi-millionaire, Marc Rich, in his fifties, lived in Zug, Switzerland, where he combined his life as an international businessman with that of a wanted outlaw. He was high on Interpol's "red notices", which meant his capture was a priority, but Switzerland refused to extradite him to the US.

Rich traded all kinds of goods with the Soviets. He sold them grain, sugar, zinc concentrate, alumina (an extract of bauxite, the main compound in aluminium), and got paid in oil, aluminium, as well as nickel, copper and other metals. Raw materials gave Rich considerable weight in some of the world's most important markets. Thanks in large part to his Soviet contracts, Rich dealt, for example, in two million tons

---

[93] Paul Klebnikov, *Parrain du Kremlin, Boris Berezovski et le pillage de la Russie*, Robert Laffont, 2001, p. 45, 50

of aluminium per year, which meant that he controlled a third of the world market for that metal." In fact, wrote Klebnikov, Rich swindled the Russians by buying the raw materials with inside information on prices." He resold abroad, pocketing his profits in his tax shelter in Zug, Switzerland.

Other Russian businessmen engaged in similar operations in the 1990s, although Rich's specificity was that he did it before everyone else and on a large scale, corrupting factory managers." Many of his actions were illegal under Soviet law, but he had ingenious collaborators inside the country. His contracts usually contained secret agreements with the directors of oil and aluminium companies and provided for complex payment mechanisms all over the planet[94]."

One of Rich's most important partners was a forty-year-old businessman named Artem Tarasov, a man who would be considered one of the pioneers of Russian predatory capitalism. Half Georgian, Tarasov had grown up on the Black Sea coast. He had done his higher education at the Institute of Mining Extraction and the Higher School of Economics of Gosplan (the State Planning Committee). When the creation of private companies was legalised in 1987, Tarasov founded a cooperative called Tekhnika, which sold Russian raw materials and imported individual computers and from which he made a small fortune. The company he founded after that, Istok, became an economic empire dedicated to the export of equipped trains, warehouses, port facilities, ships and warehouses, all leased from the state. The Russian government under Boris Yeltsin also granted it a licence to export Soviet fuel oil and authorised it to keep its profits abroad—"an unprecedented privilege for a private entrepreneur", wrote Klebnikov— on condition that it used part of its revenues to cash the promissory notes that the government had issued short of money to pay the Kolkhoz farmers[95]. The peasants could then exchange these promissory notes against imported consumer goods." Tarasov sold the fuel oil abroad, but the Soviet farmers never received their consumer goods. It was a notorious scandal," wrote Klebnikov. Tarasov was indeed our master," Oleg Davydov, a high-ranking official in the Ministry of Trade, later acknowledged with an air of regret. He bought fuel oil within the country for $36 a tonne and resold it abroad for $80… Evidently, the ministry did exactly the same thing; only the difference in domestic and world prices did not go into Tarasov's pockets, but into the

---

[94] Paul Klebnikov, *Parrain du Kremlin, Boris Berezovski et le pillage de la Russie*, Robert Laffont, 2001, p. 77-79.
[95] Kolkhozes were collective farms in the Soviet Union.

government's budget[96]."

Berezovsky then adopted many of Marc Rich's capital flight strategies. Paul Klebnikov had the opportunity to discuss the issue of capital flight in the final years of the USSR with Egor Gaidar, the first Russian head of government in the post-Soviet era: "There was a lot of mystery about Soviet foreign trade contracts, he told me. We were buying all kinds of equipment at abnormally high prices which we paid in cash, while a significant part of our production was sold at very low prices." And Klebnikov added: "One thing is clear: the gold and currency reserves of the Soviet Union disappeared around 1990". The coffers were emptying." In the early 1980s, the Soviet gold reserve amounted to 1,300 tons (approximately 30 billion dollars at the time). In two years, between 1989 and 1991, most of the gold (about a thousand tonnes) was sold. In the same time, foreign exchange reserves fell from $15 billion at the beginning of Gorbachev's reign to only $1 billion." Alexander Yakovlev, Gorbachev's closest adviser and the main architect of Perestroika, was accused by the anti-Semitic Pamiat movement of being a "Zionist spy".

Supported and encouraged by the chieftains of the International Monetary Fund and other Western advisors, the young Yeltsinianreformers decided that the state should no longer intervene in foreign trade. They removed barriers that could prevent traders from buying raw materials at domestic prices for resale abroad. Within a few months, 30 per cent of Russia's oil exports and 70 per cent of metal exports were done outside state trading agencies, and by 1994 the bulk of Russia's foreign trade was in the hands of private import-export companies. Berezovsky quickly emerged as one of the leading traders. His LogoVaz company sold hundreds of thousands of tons of aluminium and crude oil in Switzerland and the US, and tens of thousands of wood-burning stereos abroad.

To avoid paying taxes, most of these traders resorted to an old KGB trick: false import-export invoices. Good quality construction wood, for example, was registered as heating wood and exported at a low price, with the foreign buyer paying the difference into foreign bank accounts. The same procedures were applied to aluminium, steel, nickel, strategic metals, furs and fish. Imports of foodstuffs, clothing, consumer electronics and industrial equipment were imported in the same way, with commissions paid into Russian buyers' offshore accounts. The largest Russian companies thus became entangled in

---

[96] Paul Klebnikov, *Parrain du Kremlin, Boris Berezovsky et le pillage de la Russie*, Robert Laffont, 2001, p. 80-81.

shady business deals. These new import-export companies tended to hide almost all of their profits abroad." It is estimated that Russian capital flight at that time amounted to some 15 to 20 billion dollars per year, siphoned off into the bank accounts of mafia ringleaders, corrupt high-ranking officials and complicit factory managers."

In this shameless plundering of the country's natural resources, oil exports generated the most significant profits. The oil industry was therefore "one of the main battlegrounds of organised crime in Russia." Criminal groups liquidated those who refused to work with them, and many refinery managers were murdered[97].

On 14 December 1992, Boris Yeltsin appointed a new prime minister: Viktor Chernomyrdine. After Gaidar's measures, Russia's GDP had collapsed by more than 50%, making Russia poorer than Peru on a per capita GDP basis. Decades of technological successes were lost; renowned scientific institutions were left in ruins and Russian culture seemed to have disappeared." All those who had travelled to Russia in the early years of the Yeltsin era were stunned by the spectacle of Russian citizens trying to survive," wrote Paul Klebnikov. Former fighters sold their medals in order to buy food, and the highest Soviet decorations ended up on flea market stalls exposed for sale as common trinkets.

Rumours of food shortages drove millions of city dwellers to the suburban gardens to grow potatoes and cabbage. If famine was averted, it was thanks to the soil of mother Russia. The recession in Russia was worse than the Great Depression of the 1930s in the United States. Between 1990 and 1994, the male mortality rate rose by 53% and the female mortality rate by 27%. Male life expectancy plummeted and every month, thousands of Russians died prematurely. Many of these deaths involved elderly people who had lost all their savings.

According to official estimates, the number of drug addicts in the country was between 2 and 5 million, mainly young people. Alcohol also took its toll. A 1993 survey found that 80% of Russian men drank and that their average consumption was more than half a litre a day. In 1996, more than 35,000 people died of poisoning from adulterated alcohol compared to only a few hundred in the US during the same period. Drinking and crime contributed to the dramatic explosion in violent and accidental deaths. From 1992 to 1997, 229,000 people committed suicide, 159,000 died of intoxication after drinking

---

[97] Paul Klebnikov, *Parrain du Kremlin, Boris Berezovsky et le pillage de la Russie*, Robert Laffont, 2001, p. 116-121.

adulterated vodka and 169,000 were murdered[98]. Many young Russian women gave up motherhood, not by choice but out of necessity. Several million of them were forced into prostitution, of whom hundreds of thousands were taken abroad to be sex slaves[99]. The declining birth rate combined with even faster rising mortality rates resulted in a demographic deficit of 6 million Russians in 1999. In parallel, hundreds of thousands of children were abandoned.[100]

The Russian state itself was led by an alcoholic president who provoked embarrassing diplomatic incidents. On 31 August 1994 in Berlin, Boris Yeltsin presided over the ceremonies marking the departure of the last Russian occupation troops with his German counterpart, Chancellor Helmut Kohl. The Russian president had started drinking very early in the morning. Korjakov, his security chief, later explained that Kohl had understood the situation perfectly and that he discreetly carried Boris Nikolaievitch to the ceremony by the waist. After lunch and a few drinks, Yeltsin reviewed the troops in front of the audience. Arriving near the Berlin police orchestra, the president suddenly leapt onto the podium, grabbed the conductor's baton and began to wave it ridiculously against the music. A little later, he began to sing a drunken version of "Kalinka". The Berliners had never seen anything like it.

Berezovsky was introduced into Boris Yeltsin's inner circle during the winter of 1993–1994. The Russian parliament, hostile to Yeltsin, Gaidar's reforms and Chubai's privatisation plans, blocked his reforms and threatened to impeach the president. On 21 September 1993, the president announced the dissolution of parliament, but Aleksandr Rutskoi's supporters, gathered inside, refused to leave and the

---

[98] Aleksandr Solzhenitsyn has evoked the anti-Semitism linked to the problems generated by some Jews with the production and distribution of alcohol in Russia in Tsarist times (read in *Jewish Fanaticism*). In *Testament d'un antisémite*, Édouard Drumont already wrote about alcohol production and trafficking: "Nothing can give an idea of what the Jews of Poland and Russia are. They annihilate the populations of entire villages with poisoned spirits. I have heard it directly from a great Polish gentleman: An eight-year-old boy passes by on the road. The Jewish innkeeper calls out to him from the door of his tavern: "Hey boy! Stop there for a moment, I'll give you a glass of schnapps." And he gives the boy a glass full of adulterated schnapps… The gentleman approaches the tavern keeper and says: "Why corrupt this boy? You have no interest in it since he doesn't pay you. —No doubt," replies the other with that sinister smile of the people of his race, "he doesn't pay me … but, you see, you have to get them used to it from a young age." (Édouard Drumont, *Testament d'un antisémite*, 1891, p. 150).
[99] See chapter on the White Slave Trade.
[100] Paul Klebnikov, *Parrain du Kremlin, Boris Berezovski et le pillage de la Russie*, Robert Laffont, 2001, p. 124-129.

confrontation turned into a bloodbath during the days of 3 and 4 October. This time the battleships were on Yeltsin's side and killed hundreds of people. A draft new constitution, giving more powers to the president, was finally approved days later in a referendum, and privatisations of the Russian economy continued under the supervision of Anatoly Chubais.

The plan envisaged the transfer of more than half of Russia's industrial enterprises to the private sector within two years. The implementation of the plan was to sell 29% of the shares of a state-owned company at public auctions and distribute 51% to managers and employees. The rest would be retained by the state to be sold later. A privatisation bond had been sent to every Russian citizen. 151 million bonds were distributed. Everyone could thus become a shareholder and the best companies would not be bought by the rich. But poverty meant that many Russians immediately sold their bonds on the streets for cash. Their prices were ridiculously low, around 10,000 roubles, which corresponded to 7 dollars. It was barely enough to buy two bottles of cheap vodka. At $7 a bond, Russia's immense industrial wealth was worth only $5 billion.

Instead of starting with shops and small businesses, the whole economy was privatised all at once: the big oil companies, the mines, the biggest forestry companies, the car manufacturers, the big engineering companies, the main commercial ports, etc., everything was privatised. Chubais immediately privatised Russia's most important and profitable export companies. While few Russians got shares, some investors amassed immense fortunes.

Berezovsky's first target was the state television channel ORT, the only one broadcast throughout the country and reaching 180 million viewers. Many Russians only watched ORT for information. Berezovsky managed to convince Yeltsin, and in November 1994, 49% of the channel was privatised.

Berezovsky's main rival at the time was Vladimir Gusinsky. Gusinsky was a Muscovite born into a Jewish family and known to be the protégé of Mayor Yuri Luzkhov. Moscow was 'plagued by casinos, corruption and rival gang wars', wrote Klebnikov. Luzkhov's strategy was not to fight organised crime directly (he did not have the means to do so), but to tax it. In this way he managed to persuade even the shadiest businesses to contribute to the realisation of his municipal projects: a luxurious underground shopping centre, the extension of the peripheral motorway, the identical reconstruction of the gigantic Cathedral of Christ the Saviour (destroyed on Stalin's orders and under

Kaganóvich's supervision) and the rebuilding of Moscow's historic centre. The city experienced a veritable building frenzy. So that, "in a country where everything was falling apart, Moscow was an oasis of prosperity and success[101]."

Gusinsky's Most group was one of the largest business conglomerates in the country. It included the financial sector, media, an insurance company, a security company, an import-export company, real estate agencies and building materials companies. His security service had no less than a thousand armed men. Gusinsky owned newspapers (daily and weekly), a radio and a television station since 1993 (NTV) which "broadcast a lot of pornography, horror and violence (even by American standards)[102]."

Berezovsky argued that Gusinsky posed a threat to the president and attempted to assassinate him. In December 1994, a massive operation had been organised and executed when Gusinsky, as usual, was driving down a major artery of the capital at 140 km per hour, running at all traffic lights. His armoured car was flanked by two other vehicles occupied by bodyguards armed to the teeth. The chase was unsuccessful, but after that intense gun battle, Gusinsky decided to bring his wife and children to safety in England. The car dealer had succeeded in driving his rival out of the country.

Berezovski accused Gusinskyin particular of having been the commander of the car bombing he had been the victim of in June 1994. A car had exploded in front of his car and Berezovski had seen his chauffeur's head blown off in front of his eyes. The attack had obviously disturbed him. General Alexander Korzhakov, the head of presidential security, left this testimony: "Berezovsky used a special terminology. Instead of saying 'kill', he preferred to say 'finish'. It was a term from the vocabulary of gangsters... Berezovsky seemed to believe that the SBP had been created to 'eliminate' people he did not like. From then on, I had the conviction that Berezovsky was psychologically deranged and I started to keep an eye on him[103]."

Berezovski was also the prime suspect in the murder of Vlad Listiev, Russia's most popular TV presenter. In February 1996, he had announced that he would revoke Lissovsky and Berezovsky's

---

[101] Paul Klebnikov, *Parrain du Kremlin, Boris Berezovski et le pillage de la Russie*, Robert Laffont, 2001, p. 175.

[102] Paul Klebnikov, *Parrain du Kremlin, Boris Berezovski et le pillage de la Russie*, Robert Laffont, 2001, p. 173-177.

[103] Paul Klebnikov, *Parrain du Kremlin, Boris Berezovsky et le pillage de la Russie*, Robert Laffont, 2001, p. 179.

advertising monopoly on the ORT channel. He was assassinated on 1 March, shot twice in the head. A few days earlier, wrote Paul Klebnikov, Berezovsky had met with an underworld "justice of the peace" to hand over $100,000 in cash. Popular outrage was immense and tens of thousands of people attended Listiev's funeral.

Berozovsky also took control of the sixth television channel, a magazine (*Ogoniok*) and a daily newspaper. The car dealer was now at the head of the country's largest television network. ORT's news service became a sounding board for his interests, singing Yeltsin's praises during the 1996 elections or denouncing General Lebed after a dispute between the two, or attacking a major businessman competitor, while presenting Berezovsky as a statesman[104].

It was not necessary to buy a private company in order to control it, Klebnikov explained. It could very well remain in the hands of the state. It was enough to take over its management and then channel its profits, which amounted to "privatising its profits". In 1989, Berezovsky had begun to privatise the profits of the car manufacturer AvtoVaz, buying cars at a price that guaranteed him a large profit but resulted in a net loss for the factory. In 1992, it went into commodities trading, exporting oil, timber and aluminium, paying domestic Russian prices for the goods and then reselling them abroad at world market prices at a huge margin. In 1993, with the start of bond privatisation, Berezovsky moved to the second stage of his plan: ownership privatisation, acquiring a majority stake in AvtoVaz. In 1994, he undertook the privatisation of ORT's profits through the channel's advertising management body, before moving to full privatisation the following year. He did the same in 1996 with the country's first airline, Aeroflot." When Aeroflot delegations abroad asked why the airline did not receive the money it billed and why it ended up in private accounts, they were told that the money was going to Yeltsin's presidential campaign, said General Korzhakov. In reality, Berezovsky kept the money for himself[105]."

The figures for capital flight (an estimated $15 billion a year) showed that a huge part of the profits of Russian companies escaped both the tax authorities and the shareholders." Such looting, Klebnikov wrote, ruined great jewels of Russian industry, depriving them of

---

[104] Paul Klebnikov, *Parrain du Kremlin, Boris Berezovski et le pillage de la Russie*, Robert Laffont, 2001, p. 187, 195.
[105] Paul Klebnikov, *Parrain du Kremlin, Boris Berezovski et le pillage de la Russie*, Robert Laffont, 2001, p. 197-204.

necessary investments, while capital flight undermined and ruined the country's monetary stabilisation efforts."

Two months after taking over Aeroflot in 1995, the tycoon pulled off his masterstroke: the privatisation of one of Russia's largest oil companies. That was his greatest success. He had a 29-year-old partner, Roman Abramovitch, and together they created Sibneft in the summer of 1995. When Ivan Litskevitch, the director of the Omsk refinery, heard about Abramovitch and Berezovsky's takeover of his refinery and its integration into Sibneft, he protested. On 15 August 1995, his body was found in the Irtich river, but the militia found no evidence of a mafia crime[106].

It was from then on that the oligarchs fine-tuned the system to take over the country's big exporting companies: the principle was simply "loans for shares". Vladimir Potanine, the thirty-six-year-old "golden boy" of the *establishment*, was responsible for proposing the measure to the Council of Ministers in March 1995. Potanine was accompanied by a certain Mikhail Khodorkovsky of Menatep bank and Aleksandr Smolensky. The government accepted the plan, and immediately the major "Russian" banks launched a battle for the right to lend money to the government in exchange for shares in major companies.

One of the first winners of the loans for shares was Mikhail Khodorkovsky, a former associate of Berezovsky's who was then 31 years old. He ran one of Russia's largest business empires at the time, and was also one of Russia's biggest fortunes. His list of assets included the Menatep bank, as well as twelve other banks, substantial real estate in Moscow, a steel mill, the country's main titanium and magnesium producers, numerous food factories, fertiliser factories, and textile and chemical companies. Mikhail Khodorkovsky's office was in a Victorian castle in the centre of Moscow. The building was surrounded by a large cast-iron gate. Security men, some in suits, others in black uniforms, patrolled the entire property.

In 1987, when he was in charge of the Moscow Communist Youth, he had set up a trade cooperative with communist party funds. The following year, he founded a bank. So we see that anti-Semitism in the Soviet Union was not as virulent as some claim. Between 1990 and 1993, he went into state service, first as economic advisor to the Prime Minister, then as Deputy Minister of Petroleum and Energy. His trading companies made substantial profits in oil, wheat, sugar and metals. The Menatep bank was enriched by various accounts with the city of

---

[106] Paul Klebnikov, *Parrain du Kremlin, Boris Berezovski et le pillage de la Russie*, Robert Laffont, 2001, p. 225.

Moscow and some federal ministries. Menatep also took care of its foreign relations. The first vice-president of Menatep was Constantine Kagalovsky, whose wife, Natacha Gurfinkiel-Kagalovsky, was the head of Russian operations at the Bank of New York. Paul Klebnikov provided the following information: "Natacha Gurfinkiel would be forced to resign in 1999 during the US government's investigation into money laundering at the Bank of New York."

In addition, Khodorkovsky attempted to penetrate the West by advertising Menatep's name in the United States. In 1994, he bought several advertising pages in the *Wall Street Journal* and the *New York Times for a* million dollars. Paul Klebnikov confirmed here the existence of community ties: "However, some of his foreign trade deals were not of a nature to endear him to the United States. In particular because he had worked with Marc Rich, the American commodities trader who had been on the run from the US justice system for several years. Moreover, between 1994 and 1996, he had sold Cuba the equivalent of hundreds of millions of dollars worth of oil in exchange for sugar. As if that were not enough, Khodorkovsky also contributed to the creation of an establishment called the *European Union Bank* on the Caribbean island of Antigua, a notorious money laundering tax haven."

Of the "loans for shares" auctions, Khodorkovsky was particularly interested in the 45% of Yukos, Russia's second largest oil company. However, the body responsible for registering the auctions for Yukos was none other than his bank, Menatep. Competitors were therefore pushed aside and a Menatep front company won the bidding by paying only $9 million more than the starting price of $150 million. Another consortium had bid up to 350 million but had been disqualified on the pretext of lack of guarantees.

The same script was repeated in Vladimir Potanine's purchase of Norilsk Nickel. This company was one of the first Russian exporters, whose mines were located in the Arctic Circle. The Norilsk mine, which mined the world's most abundant lode, was bought for about $100,000 above the $170 million starting price at auction.

Similarly, the same process was repeated for the transfer of shares in other Russian industrial giants, such as the oil giant Sidanco: "Rossinski Kredit executives explained that their representatives had not been allowed to enter the Onexim bank building on the day of the auction."

The sale of 51% of the shares of Sibneft, one of the world's largest private oil companies, was the last in the series. The auction took place on 28 December 1995. The starting price was ridiculously low: 100 million dollars." It had already been decided months ago that Sibneft would be awarded to Berezovski[107]," Klebnikov wrote. Berezovsky generously offered 100.3 million and rival Inkombank's bid of 175 million was rejected. On the day of the sale, Inkombank's representative announced his withdrawal in the most succinct manner, without further explanation. Two years later, Sibneft's shares had a market capitalisation of USD 5 billion on the Russian stock exchange.

In the two years that followed, the market capitalisation of these companies increased by a factor of between 18 and 26. The chief architect of the "loan-for-share" sales, Anatoli Chubais, denied that the auction sales had been manipulated and that the state had received ridiculously low sums. But in reality, for the Russian state, it was undoubtedly an unmitigated disaster.

Mafia democracy

In the December 1995 parliamentary elections, the Communists and Vladimir Khirinovsky's nationalists had overtaken the ruling party and held a majority in the Duma, Russia's parliamentary assembly. Following the pro-Yeltsin party debacle, Yeltsin was forced to get rid of the liberals in his government, and Chubais was sidelined. Six months before the 1996 presidential elections, his main challenger, the communist Guennadi Ziuganov, was far ahead of him in the polls. According to opinion polls, the president's share of confidence varied between 5 and 8 percent.

As for the "oligarchs", they no longer had a choice: the rigged auctions forced them to support Yeltsin's re-election. Berezovsky and Gussinsky had put aside their quarrels." Between the oligarchs and the Yeltsin government there was now a partnership of evildoers," wrote Paul Klebnikov. Thus, the main members of Yeltsin's campaign team were Boris Berezovsky, Anatoly Chubais, Vladimir Gussinsky, Boris Nemtsov, Yevguiny Kiselyov and his own daughter Tatiana Diatchenko.

The law stipulated that campaign expenses could not exceed three million dollars for each party, but it was estimated after the fact that Yeltsin's total expenses had been more than a billion dollars. In Washington, one think tank had even estimated the total at two billion dollars." The money was used to smear local political bosses and

---

[107]Paul Klebnikov, *Parrain du Kremlin, Boris Berezovsky et le pillage de la Russie*, Robert Laffont, 2001, p. 231-235.

corrupt people," said the head of the anti-corruption service. Large amounts of money were also spent on producing pro-Yeltsin documentaries, rock concerts and billboards. The whole campaign was supervised from Berezovsky's LogoVaz house, the tycoon's palace in the centre of Moscow. He was the orchestra leader. Businessmen had donated hundreds of millions to the phantom HQ's black box." In return, they received the amount of their contribution multiplied in the form of state subsidies[108]." The oligarchs were promised new packages of shares in privatisations after the elections. Thousands of companies thus participated in the financing.

The president was on the news almost every night, while his communist opponent Ziuganov hardly ever appeared. Yeltsin's team had paid journalists and editors." Payments ranged from a hundred dollars to a provincial correspondent to write a positive article, to millions paid to the owners of major Russian newspapers" and to the owners of television stations. Most Russian media also depended on state subsidies, mainly the press. The Berezovsky-controlled public television station received more than 200 million in public funds per year.

Yeltsin's campaign manager was officially Anatoli Chubais, but Boris Yeltsin's team also called on the best American communication specialists, in this case the famous political strategist George Gorton. He and his staff were based near the election campaign headquarters at the President Hotel. They were asked to be very discreet and to leave the hotel as little as possible. Yeltsin's daughter, Tatiana Diatchenko, liaised with the presidential team. Boris Yeltsin's photo sessions and appearances were thus staged to appear spontaneous and the election strategy fluctuated according to the ongoing polls.

Every day, Yeltsin was seen on television visiting pensioners in the Far North, promising to release large budget allocations for isolated communities, joking with workers on a collective farm, shaking hands with the mayor of some distant industrial town. He was also seen with the soldiers or with the Kolkhozians. Another time, he appeared wearing a miner's helmet to go down a coal shaft. In Moscow, during a rock concert, Yeltsin went on stage to dance to the music in front of the audience. Millions of letters bearing his signature were sent to former World War II combatants. Yeltsin thanked them for their services to the homeland. Since this was the first time a political mail campaign had been conducted in Russia, many recipients believed that the letters had

---

[108] Paul Klebnikov, *Parrain du Kremlin, Boris Berezovski et le pillage de la Russie*, Robert Laffont, 2001, p. 241-253.

actually been signed by the president himself. The advertisements featured troubled townspeople who ended up declaring: "I believe. I love. I have hope. Boris Nikolayevitch Yeltsin[109]." Television stations also repeatedly broadcast documentaries on the atrocities of the communist regime. In the face of this unrelenting roller coaster, the hundreds of thousands of communist militants and patriots had no money and no television coverage at all.

Meanwhile, teachers, doctors, soldiers and workers waited for months for their pay and millions of elderly people did not receive their pensions. But in the spring, the IMF granted Russia a large loan: 10.2 billion dollars to be repaid over three years. The money was used to quickly pay the salaries and pensions of civil servants, and thus to indirectly finance Yeltsin's campaign. It was also around this time that the Chechen leader Dzhojar Dudayev died. A ceasefire with the rebels came into effect two months later and the Russians were relieved.

On 16 June 1996, Yeltsin won the first round of the election with 35.1% of the vote to Ziuganov's 32%. Lebed was a surprise third place with 14.7%. On 3 July, after the second round, Boris Yeltsin was re-elected for a second term with 53.7% of the vote. Western observers had naturally concluded that the elections had been free and democratic.

All suppliers involved in Yeltsin's campaign had inflated their expenses and transferred the difference to foreign accounts. According to an investigation carried out by the SBP, between 200 and 300 million dollars had been embezzled from the election fund, "mainly by businessmen close to the campaign headquarters in Moscow[110]."

But at the end of June, Boris Yeltsin suffered another heart attack and had to rest for several months. Kremlin spokesmen had not revealed the seriousness of the president's heart problems until then. Anatoly Chubais took over the reins of government and the banker Vladimir Potanine was appointed deputy prime minister from the economy portfolio. The time had come to repay the businessmen who had contributed to Eltsine's re-election. So Vladimir Gussinsky was authorised to buy the fourth television channel and Alekansdr Smolensky and Berezovsky's Stolitchny bank doubled in size by absorbing the state-owned Agroprom bank.

Yeltsin had appointed General Lebed to head the Security Council. But he began to attack corruption and was dismissed only four months

---

[109]Paul Klebnikov, *Parrain du Kremlin, Boris Berezovski et le pillage de la Russie*, Robert Laffont, 2001, p. 257-259.
[110]Paul Klebnikov, *Parrain du Kremlin, Boris Berezovsky et le pillage de la Russie*, Robert Laffont, 2001, p. 271.

after his appointment and replaced by Boris Berezovsky, who coordinated security and defence policy. Berezovski now held an official position within the state apparatus." From now on, the fox would guard the henhouse," wrote Klebnikov.

A few days later, the *Izvestia* revealed that Berezovsky held an Israeli passport. This revelation could seriously jeopardise his appointment to the government executive, as foreign citizens were forbidden by law to hold official functions. He initially denied this and threatened to take the newspaper to court. But the Israeli government, harassed by the press, confirmed the information. Berezovsky was then forced to admit that he did indeed have an Israeli passport and announced that he was going to give it up." According to Israeli law, anyone with Jewish blood, whether half or only a quarter, is a citizen of Israel, he said. Every Russian Jew has de facto dual citizenship." The tycoon complained of being a victim of the rising tide of anti-Semitism, but nevertheless remained in his post. He had in fact confessed one day in the *Financial Times* "that he and six other financiers controlled 50% of the Russian economy and had enabled Yeltsin's re-election in 1996[111]."

Within the Security Council, Berezovsky was in charge of relations with Chechnya. He appeared to have "excellent relations with the Chechen leadership" and his former relations with Chechen gangs in Moscow were undoubtedly useful. At the time, Klebnikov wrote, "almost the entire country was controlled by autonomous militias and criminal gangs whose leaders were former commanders of the Chechen forces... Each of them ruled their own little feudal kingdom, largely built on old clan loyalties and financed by smuggled oil, drugs, arms trafficking and other criminal operations[112]." They also practised kidnapping. Within two years, more than 1300 people had been kidnapped in Russia, many of them Western generals and journalists. In December 1996, twenty-two Russian policemen were captured on the Chechen border. Berezovsky travelled there and managed to free them. This was the first in a series of hostage-takings that the tycoon managed to resolve. General Lebed saw them primarily as a political manoeuvre. In January 1997, he also went to Chechnya to try to free two journalists, but without success. A few days later, Berezovsky managed to convince the Chechen military commander to release them. Contrary to

---

[111] Paul Klebnikov, *Parrain du Kremlin, Boris Berezovsky et le pillage de la Russie*, Robert Laffont, 2001, p. 16.
[112] Paul Klebnikov, *Parrain du Kremlin, Boris Berezovski et le pillage de la Russie*, Robert Laffont, 2001, p. 289-292.

government claims, officials came from Moscow with briefcases full of money with orders from Berezovsky to pay the ransom to the kidnappers. Moreover, the tycoon made no secret of the fact that he had helped finance various Chechen groups in return for his benevolence. For more than two and a half years, Berezovsky thus maintained close relations with the warlords and criminal gangs that carried out the kidnappings. The leader of the Chechen Republic of Ichkeria himself, Aslan Maskhadov, told Russian and British newspapers one day that Berezovsky "endorsed the Chechen criminal gangs, often organising the payment of ransoms." Berezovsky's interlocutors were not moderates like President Maskhadov, who abhorred such arrangements that discredited the Chechen people, but rather terrorist leaders like Shamil Basayev and Islamic fundamentalists like Movladi Udugov[113].

The auction sales of large companies continued in the same way. The oil company Yukos was bought by Menatep, Khodorkovsky's bank, for a price of $350 million, when in fact it should have been more or less $6.2 billion. Alfred Koch, the man responsible for overseeing the sales, explained: "We could not get a better price because the bankers who had taken control of these companies had previously sought to put these companies into debt with their banks. If we had sold these companies to another buyer, they would have bankrupted them the next day." Klebnikov added: "On this point, Koch was right. By siphoning off the funds of Russia's leading companies, the financiers who had won the first stage of the auctions had managed to ensure that none of these companies was viable on its own…" We are a group of bankrupt companies," Mikhail Khodorkovsky of Menatep cheerfully admitted in front of me. The whole country was a bunch of bankrupt companies[114]."

On 12 May 1997, the remainder of the Sibneftoil company was auctioned. Alfa bank was removed because it had failed to submit the required documents, while Onexim was removed because of an alleged violation of a banking rule regarding the transfer of a deposit. From now on, the company would belong entirely to Berezovsky and Abramovitch.

In March, the *Izvestia* published detailed reports of Berezovski's negotiations to buy Promstroi Bank, a company linked to a notorious swindler, Grigori Lerner, who was imprisoned in Israel. Berezovski

---

[113] Paul Klebnikov, *Parrain du Kremlin, Boris Berezovsky et le pillage de la Russie*, Robert Laffont, 2001, p. 293-298. Paul Klebnikov transcribed here a telephone conversation between the two men recorded by the Russian security services.
[114] Paul Klebnikov, *Parrain du Kremlin, Boris Berezovski et le pillage de la Russie*, Robert Laffont, 2001, p. 300.

immediately denied the newspaper's allegations.

On 25 July 1997, the auction of Sviazinvest, the Russian telecommunications monopoly, took place. This time, Berezovsky and Gussinsky lost out to Vladimir Potanine's group, backed by "American" billionaire George Soros[115]. Paul Klebnikov wrote of that episode: "The jewels of the industry were handed over to a handful of unscrupulous financiers who stripped them of their assets, avoided paying taxes and siphoned off their wealth to tax havens[116]."

Yeltsin, fresh from convalescence, seemed determined "to put an end to the crony capitalism that had tainted his regime." Berezovsky, who had accused the government of favouring Potanine in the sale of Sviazinvest, was removed from his post on the Security Council. The banker and oligarch Vladimir Potanine was also removed from his post as deputy prime minister and replaced by Anatoli Chubais. A young Jewish reformer, Boris Nemtsov, was appointed deputy prime minister.

In January 1998, a French weekly magazine described Boris Nemtsovas "the man of the year", and that he had been "acclaimed by the Russian people". The journalist Thomas Hofnug praised him with superlative adjectives, exemplifying the famous community solidarity: 'A rock star physique, a Marlboro at the corner of his mouth, Nemtsov seduces above all with his insolence and intelligence. During a televised debate, he ridiculed the ultra-nationalist Jirinovski, who spitefully threw a glass of water in his face... At 31, he became the country's youngest governor after the failed coup of 1991. In five years, through unbridled reforms, Nemtsov has made the Nizhny Novgorod region the showcase of the new Russia." So, if Thomas Hofnung is to be believed, Russia had finally found the providential man who would lift it out of depression and misery.

Nemtsov was also in charge of social reforms. Thanks to him, for example, the phasing out of housing subsidies was announced, leaving the most vulnerable populations, impoverished or ruined by the reforms of the "oligarchs", on the street. On a television set, he had indeed been taught a lesson by being given a glass of water in the face, which must have cheered up a few million humiliated Russians.

As in all democratic societies, the state had become heavily indebted to the banks it had in fact copiously subsidised with public funds a few years earlier. The Russian state's debts were mainly in the form of Treasury bonds called GKOs. Between 1995 and 1998, the

---

[115] On George Soros, read *Planetary Hopes* and *Jewish Fanaticism*.
[116] Paul Klebnikov, *Parrain du Kremlin, Boris Berezovsky et le pillage de la Russie*, Robert Laffont, 2001, p. 313.

annual return on these securities rose from 60 to 200 per cent (even taking inflation into account), ensuring the banks huge profits. GKO issuance continued unabated after Yeltsin's re-election and reached 70 billion two years later. When Sergei Kirienko took over as head of government in March 1998, all the financial revenues generated by the GKOs were to repay the interest on previous issues. The government was forced to issue bonds at ever higher interest rates simply to maintain its debt. The international usurious lobby was triumphing.

There's nothing like a good war

Paul Klebnikov returned to Moscow in the winter of 1998–1999 to continue his investigation into Berezovsky. The former foreign trade minister, Oleg Davydov, warned him that there had been recent assassinations and that 'it was not the time to go back to the Berezovsky case. With a guy like him, you have to be very careful. He has, so to speak, contacts with the world of organised crime[117]."

In reality, Russia was gradually becoming safer. In September 1998, the government of Yevgeny Primakov took the first real measures against organised crime since the end of communism and numerous investigations were opened into various personalities, such as Berezovsky.

At dawn on 2 February 1999, an absolutely forceful search took place at Sibneft's headquarters. Men in balaclavas, military fatigues and armed with assault rifles entered the oil company's premises. Money laundering, violation of the law on currency transfer, tax fraud and embezzlement were the main charges brought. Searches were also carried out at Aeroflot's headquarters, the offices of NFQ (the advertising agency) and FOK, Berezovsky's financial company. The ORT television station was deprived of government subsidies and put into bankruptcy proceedings. Other legal proceedings were initiated against companies linked to Berezovsky for fraud and money laundering, such as the car manufacturer AvtoVaz.

In the United States, FBI agents launched an investigation into the laundering of at least seven billion dollars from Russia through the Bank of New York. In Switzerland, the focus was on Berezovsky's and Aeroflt's scams. Andava's bank accounts were blocked, as were Berezovski's personal accounts.

---

[117] Paul Klebnikov, *Parrain du Kremlin, Boris Berezovski et le pillage de la Russie*, Robert Laffont, 2001, p. 320.

It was during this period that NATO forces launched air strikes against Serbia in March 1999 in order to force the withdrawal of its soldiers from Kosovo. Primakov, who was willing to take an anti-Western hard line, was dismissed by Yeltsin in May." Primakov's dismissal was a personal victory", Berezovsky explained a few months later[118].

Berezovsky was thus at that time the grey eminence of the Kremlin. The new Prime Minister was one Sergei Stepachine who had been Minister of Justice and Interior. Although loyal to Yeltsin, he refused to interfere in the investigations against Berezovsky and was replaced in August by Vladimir Putin, a former agent of the KGB, now FSB, which he himself had headed since July 1998.

Putin was obedient and everything suggested that with him the investigations would be discontinued. The members of the "family" therefore decided that Putin would be the man to guarantee their impunity, and Yeltsin officially appointed him as his ward for the 2000 presidential election. In the December 1999 legislative elections, Berezovsky and his Kremlin allies in the Unity coalition mobilised all their resources. The polls gave them no more than 2–5%, and Berezovsky knew he could not repeat the 1996 feat. This time he no longer had a quasi-monopoly on television, as Gussinsky's NTV supported the Primakov-Luzkhov coalition. The situation called for a dramatic event. A war was needed.

The invasion of Dagestan by Chechen soldiers in August 1999 and the proclamation of an Islamic republic served as a pretext. On 9 September, a huge explosion ripped through a building in a poor Moscow suburb, killing hundreds of people. The attacks were not claimed but the Kremlin immediately attributed them to Chechen fundamentalists. In fact, a majority of Russians were now in favour of a war against Chechnya. Klebnikov wrote: "These attacks were reminiscent of the mysterious explosion in the Moscow metro a week before the first round of the 1996 presidential election, which had been blamed on 'communist extremists' and whose immediate result was to reinforce the Yeltsin regime's claim to be the only one capable of guaranteeing peace and stability in Russia."

The daily *Le Figaro* of 29 September 1999 published an interview with General Aleksandr Lebed, the governor of the Krasnoyarsk Territory. He declared himself "almost convinced" that the Russian government had organised the terrorist attacks against his own citizens. Lebed's statement caused a sensation. For the first time, a high-ranking

---

[118]On those responsible for the war in Serbia read *Planetary Hopes*, (2022).

politician was publicly voicing a suspicion that the national press had hitherto only alluded to in passing. A few days later, Berezovsky took off for Krasnoyarsk where his aluminium business required his presence, taking the opportunity to meet the general in passing. It is not known what they talked about, but the general was never heard from again after his visit." So far, Klebnikov wrote, he has remained ostensibly aloof from the political scene[119]." General Aleksandr Lebed later had these words: "Berezovsky is the apotheosis of state-level bureaucracy: this representative of the small caste in power is not content with stealing. He wants everyone to see how he steals with impunity[120]." Aleksandr Lebed died on 28 April 2002 in Siberia in a helicopter crash. The helicopter had collided with some electrical wires due to fog… That was the official cause.

It is difficult, however, to see Prime Minister Putin's hand behind these attacks," Klebnikov added. Nothing in the man's past allows us to believe that he was capable of committing such a monstrous crime in order to seize power." In fact, he did not yet control all the powers in September 1999. Nor was there any evidence against Berezovsky." The most likely explanation is that the attacks were actually perpetrated by Chechen militants[121]." Be that as it may, more than 100,000 Russian troops poured into the small breakaway republic, triggering the second Chechen war. The Berezovsky-controlled ORT television network supported the war and praised Putin's actions.

The elections were a success for the Kremlin. The Unity bloc garnered 23.3 percent of the vote, just behind the Communist party with 24.3 percent, while the Luzkhov-Primakov duo was left with 13.9 percent. Berezovsky, who was running for a deputy's mandate to benefit from criminal immunity, ran in an obscure constituency: the autonomous republic of Karachayevo-Cherkessia, a poor region of the North Caucasus with a population of three hundred thousand. He easily won his seat and thus secured a guarantee that he would not be prosecuted unless the Duma voted to lift his immunity. Roman Abramovitch, his associate, was also elected. He had chosen a constituency in the Chukotka Autonomous Okrug, an icy land across from Alaska that was the poorest and most primitive region of Russia.

---

[119] Paul Klebnikov, *Parrain du Kremlin, Boris Berezovsky et le pillage de la Russie*, Robert Laffont, 2001, p. 338, 339.

[120] Paul Klebnikov, *Parrain du Kremlin, Boris Berezovsky et le pillage de la Russie*, Robert Laffont, 2001, p. 20.

[121] Paul Klebnikov, *Parrain du Kremlin, Boris Berezovsky et le pillage de la Russie*, Robert Laffont, 2001, p. 341.

Other gangsters had already been elected in previous elections. As it was, it was not surprising to see the Duma hit by mob violence: at least three deputies were killed, as well as a dozen parliamentary assistants and staff.

Putin's victory encouraged Yeltsin to resign. On 31 December, during his traditional New Year's address, he announced that he was resigning to complete his term in office and handing over his powers to Prime Minister Vladimir Putin, thus bringing forward the presidential election to 26 March 2000.

By February 2000, Berezovsky and Abramovitch had acquired three huge aluminium plants. Russia was the world's second largest producer after the United States and aluminium was one of the country's main sources of foreign exchange earnings. Having acquired a dominant position in the automobile, television, airline and oil industries, aluminium was now Berezovsky's fifth largest sector of activity[122].

Aluminium was one of the sectors of activity most affected by the mafia. The three factories bought by the two businessmen had previously been run by the Trans World Metals Ltd group, headed by Lev Chernoi, a businessman from Tashkent in Uzbekistan. This was what one could read in the daily *Le Monde* of 27 November 2002: The Chernoi brothers had conquered "almost the entire aluminium industry of the CIS[123] with Trans World Group, a company listed on the London Metal Exchange. But the dozens of corpses that marked this conquest had forced the brothers to fake the transfer of their assets in the CIS to some of their trusted men." It should be added that Lev Chernoi was also Jewish, that he had Israeli citizenship and that the profits he made from Russian aluminium were partly invested in Saviom, the Israeli "Beverly Hills." The battle for Krasnoyarsk aluminium was particularly bloody, even by Russian standards, Klebnikov wrote. At least five managers had been killed in the purest style of gang warfare."

Alan Clingman, a thirty-four year old "South African" had become one of the most successful traders in the aluminium market, but also in copper, nickel, zinc, steel, ferrous alloys, coal and precious metals. My return on investment is close to 100%," Klebnikiov boasted

---

[122] Boris Berezovsky declared a net worth of $39,000 in 1997, while *Forbes* magazine of the same year put his fortune at around $3 billion (William Reymond, *Mafia S.A.*, Flammarion, 2001, p. 318).

[123] The Commonwealth of Independent States (CIS) is a supranational organisation, composed of ten of the fifteen former Soviet republics, created in December 1991. (NdT)

in front of me in 1994,[124]," he wrote. Clingman had established fruitful relations with Krasnoyarsk Aluminium and benefited from a barter contract on exports. At the end of 1995, the body of his representative, Felix Lvov, was found on the edge of a forest.

How can the Russian mafia thrive in the shadow of the Kremlin, headlined *Le Monde* on 28 December 2002: Djalol Khaidarov, an Uzbek businessman who had started working with Mikhail Chernoy in the early 1990s, testified against his former boss. Khaidarov was in charge, he said, of the "legal side" of a group that distributed "between 35 and 40 million dollars in bribes" each year. He was also in charge of the evasion of their capital to Western tax havens. In 1999, as director of a copper complex in the Urals, Khaidarov had refused a redistribution of shares and the exclusion of a foreign partner, for which he had received death threats and had to expatriate. In July 2001, he testified in the Southern District Court of New York. Djalol Khaidarov told the US court how his copper complex had been confiscated: blackmail of the managers, private militias, bought-off court decisions and finally the occupation of the site by the special forces of the governor of the Ural region, Edouard Rossel. Khaidarov accused the latter of having been bought by Chernoy's group. In the summer of 2002, his driver was found murdered and decapitated in Siberia.

Khaidarov further explained how his foreign partner, the Israeli-American businessman Josef Traum, had had to give up his shares. In the bathroom of his offices, police officers had conveniently found a kilo of heroin. The Israeli authorities had turned to the Russian ministry to request that Traum be allowed to leave the country. Khaidarov's account coincided with the testimony of another aluminium businessman, Mikhail Khivilo, who had taken refuge in France at the end of 2000 and filed a complaint for "corruption, murder and links to organised crime".

Mikhail Chernoy had moved to Israel in 1994, as he was beset by investigations that suspected him of being the instigator of some of the dozens of assassinations that had peppered the aluminium war. He continued to run his businesses from Israel: real estate in the US and Canada, finance in Switzerland and tax havens, banking and telecommunications in Bulgaria. But 80 per cent of his business was still based in Russia.

In the spring of 2000, Mikhail Chernoy and his partner Oleg Deripaska had teamed up with Roman Abramovitch and Berezovsky to

---

[124] Paul Klebnikov, *Parrain du Kremlin, Boris Berezovski et le pillage de la Russie*, Robert Laffont, 2001, p. 350.

create Roussal, an industrial behemoth that would produce 80% of Russian aluminium. Oleg Deripaska was born on 2 January 1968 into a Jewish family in Djerzinsk. In 1994 he had acquired two thirds of the shares of the Russian pulp giant (49,000 employees). After that he invested in aluminium. Deripaska had been declared persona non grata by the World Economic Forum in Davos because of suspicions about him. Mikhail Chernoy told the Russian daily *Vedomosti* that he had known Deripaska since 1994: "I liked him immediately," he admitted. "I am a shareholder, that's all," he replied to his accusers and to the police services whose reports included a long list of murders, crimes and financial crimes of which he was suspected. However, Mikhail Chernoy constantly denied having any links to the world of crime: "If that were the case, I would already be behind bars!"

The fall of the oligarchs

Berezovsky thought of Vladimir Putin as a friend whose career he had promoted. He had been instrumental in Putin's rise to the head of the security services in 1998 and in his appointment to the post of prime minister the following year. He was also instrumental in the media campaign to boost his popularity. Having financed and orchestrated the election of a pro-Putin parliament, Berezovsky was pleased to see his protégé elected president in the March 2000 election. The tycoon's future seemed assured. But within a few months, he realised that he had misjudged the new Russian president. Far from being a docile instrument in the hands of the oligarchs, Vladimir Putin quickly showed that he was determined to assert his authority and independence. He was "healthy, sober and hard-working", wrote Klebnikov.

The new president, eager to restore the state's prestige, turned sharply against the oligarchs. His first victim was media tycoon Vladimir Gussinski, who was accused of fraudulently transferring assets of the NTV television network abroad. He was arrested in June 2000 and remanded in custody for three days and forced to relinquish his control of NTV for non-payment of debts. After his release, Gussinski immediately travelled to Spain where he was arrested in 2001 on an Interpol warrant. The oligarch managed to avoid extradition to Russia and settled comfortably in Israel, although he had lost his media empire[125]. Heavily indebted, NTV remained dependent on its creditors

---

[125] Paul Klebnikov, *Parrain du Kremlin, Boris Berezovsky et le pillage de la Russie*, Robert Laffont, 2001, p. 356.

and state subsidies. Gazprom, which held the Russian natural gas monopoly, took control of the channel.

In September, in New York, before the prestigious Council on Foreign Relations[126], Gussinski presented himself as the champion of democracy, freedom of expression and the book market in Russia and "dressed himself in the dignity of a great fighter for human rights", wrote Paul Klebnikov: "According to the tycoon, President Putin was betraying the ideals of the Yeltsin era and was taking Russia back to the authoritarianism of the past." In November, in a letter to the international press, Berezovsky also accused the president of "violating the constitution with his administrative reforms and handing the country over to the security services and bureaucrats"[127].

Berezovsky felt that his situation was rapidly becoming uncomfortable. In February 2000, he left the majority of his shares in Russian Aluminium to Abramovitch. In August, two months after Gussinsky's fall, the government, which owned 51% of the shares in ORT—Russia's leading television network—used its majority power to force Berezovsky, a minority shareholder, to leave the channel and thus lose his influence. Three months later, one of his main partners in Aeroflot, Nikolai Gluchkov, was charged with fraud, embezzlement and money laundering and imprisoned. The following July, Berezovsky resigned his seat and moved to England where he was granted political refugee status, claiming the title of Putin's number one opponent.

Berezovsky and Gussinsky now presented themselves as the victims of Russian authoritarianism and declared themselves standard-bearers for the defence of "human rights". In the following years, they financed all democratic causes, following the example of other American Jewish billionaires, such as George Soros, who boasted of having financed the Georgian revolution, as well as the famous Ukrainian "orange revolution"[128]

Putin's government increased taxes on the barter contracts that were the key to the profits of the company of Mikhail Chernoy, the

---

[126] CFR: The *Council on Foreign Relations*. Founded in 1921, it is a US non-profit organisation specialising in US foreign policy and international affairs. It is based in New York City. Its membership includes senior politicians, more than a dozen US secretaries of state, CIA directors, bankers, lawyers, professors and media figures. The CFR promotes globalisation, free trade, reduced financial regulations on transnational corporations and economic consolidation in regional blocs such as NAFTA or the European Union and develops government policies that reflect these goals. (NdT).

[127] Paul Klebnikov, *Parrain du Kremlin, Boris Berezovski et le pillage de la Russie*, Robert Laffont, 2001, p. 18, 19.

[128] On Soros: *Planetary Hopes* and *Jewish Fanaticism* (2022).

'aluminium king'. Chernoy had moved to Israel, but his Russian business continued to thrive. He, too, was in the crosshairs of justice. Mikhail Chernoy was arrested twice by the police—once in Switzerland, and once in Israel—and questioned about his alleged links to organised crime. However, the authorities were unable to prove any violation of the law. Chernoy was again indicted for tax fraud in Israel and sentenced to house arrest. He lived comfortably in Tel-Aviv where he had founded an association for victims of suicide bombings.

Obviously, the fact that nine of the country's ten largest fortunes were in the hands of former Soviet citizens of Israeli confession who had been able to accompany the institutional changes so well, provoked an anti-Semitic fever in Russia: "Nine Russians out of ten think that the current fortunes have been badly acquired and more than fifty percent approve of the legal proceedings", wrote Helena Despic-Popovic in the daily *Libération* on 19 July 2003. The journalist added: "The campaign is willingly accepted by a society still contaminated by traces of anti-Semitism, as a good part of the oligarchs are Jewish."

In 2003, the "campaign against the oligarchs" continued and Mikhail Khodorkovsky was arrested. According to *Forbes magazine*, Khodorkovsky, at 41, had become Russia's richest man. The billionaire, who headed the oil company Yukos, was accused of tax evasion: his company had a colossal tax debt of nearly $27 billion. Yukos owned two large oil fields and six refineries in Russia, as well as a thousand gas stations. The company had set up in Houston, Texas, backed by the London-based Menatep bank, registered in Gibraltar. The new main shareholder of Menatep was now Leonid Nevzline, to whom Mikhail Khodorskovsky had transferred part of his assets. Leonid Nevzline, number 2 of the Yukos oil company, had also replaced Vladimir Gussinski as head of the Russian Jewish Congress in exchange for the cancellation of a 100 million dollar debt that the latter was unable to repay[129]. Menatep bank recruited influential personalities: former European Commissioner Frits Bolkestein, in charge of the internal market, was appointed to the international committee of the bank's board (*Le Monde*, 2 June 2005).

The Russian prosecutor's office also announced the opening of five investigations against Khodorkovsky for murder and attempted murder involving the Yukos company. But before his arrest, the billionaire had sought to hand over the management of his bank to his British co-religionist Jacob Rothschild. Market prices continued to

---

[129]La lettre d'Emmanuel Ratier, *Faits-et-documents* du 15 avril 2001 (https://faitsetdocuments.com/index.html).

plunge, while the *New York Times* described the Russian government's takeover of Yukos as "the biggest spoliation of Jewish interests since the 1930s." In addition, it can be noted that the billionaire Khodorkovsky was also a friend of Richard Perle, one of the neo-conservative Zionist "hawks" in the White House and an ardent supporter of the 2003 invasion of Iraq[130].

Vladimir Putin supported the prosecutor's enquiries against the plutocrat, but reassured the other oligarchs that they were content to conduct their business within the framework of the law. In Russia, the president hammered, no one can impose himself above the law with billions; all must be equal before the courts to fight crime and corruption.

Le Figaro of 17 May 2005 reported on the financier's trial. For journalist Laura "Mandeville", the Yukos case obviously "tarnished" Moscow's image and Mikhail was a poor victim of fascism. Even so, we learned that his fortune was in the region of 15 billion dollars. An army of twenty lawyers was going to work to defend him, while several of his associates had fled: "Three of them live in Israel, a country from which they will not cease to accuse the Russian justice system of being in the pay of power." As usual, Khodorkovsky declared his innocence: "The case was fabricated out of thin air". And he named the culprits: "A criminal bureaucracy." In the newspaper's editorial, we could read a few lines full of common sense about the oligarchs: "The fact that these men, who started from scratch, have been able to appropriate whole chunks of Russia's natural resources for a plate of lentils has not made them particularly popular in their own country." Khodorkovsky was sentenced to eight years in prison. In reality, Vladimir Putin's policy filled the Russian people with joy.

In August 2003, after the arrest of Mikhail Khodorkovsky, Leonid Nevzline also fled to Israel. The Russian prosecutor's office wanted to try him for a series of murders and tax evasion. On 29 April, the daily *Le Monde* published a particularly illuminating article entitled "Leonid Nevzline tries to organise the Russian opposition in exile". This is what the article read: 'Sitting in the living room of his villa north of Tel-Aviv, surrounded by a collection of Japanese samurai statues, Leonid Nevzline is leading his fight against Vladimir Putin. This 45-year-old Russian oligarch has been living in Israel since August 2003, where he has taken refuge to escape Russian justice… Leonid Nevzline has become the leader of the Russian oligarchs in exile who have vowed to defeat Vladimir Putin. Although his fortune, evaluated in 2003 at

---

[130] On neoconservatives read *Planetary Hopes* and *Jewish Fanaticism*.

2 billion dollars by *Forbes magazine*, has suffered the repercussions of the judicial investigations and the confiscation of his assets in Yukos, it still remains significant. Leonid Nevzline now alone controls 67% of the Gibraltar-based Menatep holding company, which owns more than 60% of Yukos. In the tranquillity of the affluent seaside resort of Herzliya Pituah, bathed in pine, lilac and palm trees, Leonid Nevzline spends most of his days on the phone talking to Moscow and other Russian businessmen in exile in Israel or London. He regularly receives emissaries from Moscow in this Californian-style house. The windows open onto the garden with swimming pool and the garage houses a luxurious convertible."

Leonid Nevzline had invested in the Israeli petrochemical sector and founded an institute named after him, the Leonid Nevzline Research Centre, for Russian and Eastern European Jews wishing to emigrate to Israel. But his political action was even more feverish. He multiplied his forums in the Russian press and tried to unite political forces against Vladimir Putin's power by coordinating his action with the other exiles: Vladimir Gussinski, Boris Berezovsky, refugees in London, as well as a close associate of the latter, the businessman Badri Patarkatsichvili.

Jewish-born Georgian billionaire Badri Patarkatsichvili was Berezovsky's partner in the large-scale vehicle diversion company Avtovaz (Lada), as well as in the ORT television network. He had boasted of having "brought Putin to power". In 2002, after the rift between Berezovsky and Putin, he had also left Russia where he was wanted for "grand theft" (the Lada vehicles). Known to be an opponent of the Georgian regime, he had tried to federate the opposition, which had earned him an arrest warrant for "attempted coup d'état". Since then he had been living between London and Tel Aviv and claimed to be under threat. In February 2008, his lifeless body was found at his property in Leatherland, south of the English capital.

"All these millionaires claimed by the Russian justice system are of Jewish origin", we read in *Le Monde*. This would make Leonid Nezline, who claimed to be a "Zionist and Russophile", say that the Kremlin's policy was "animated by strong anti-Semitic prejudices"." Putin has no friends in Israel", he insisted.

On 2 July 2007, the Russian news agency RIA Novosti reported that the Russian Prosecutor General's Office had indicted Boris Berezovsky for his calls for the overthrow of power by force. Indeed, in an interview given to the British newspaper *The Guardian* and published on 13 April 2007, Boris Berezovsky had declared that he was financing his supporters who were preparing a coup d'état in Russia. A year earlier, in 2006, he had already declared that he was financing "an underground movement in Russia" to fight against Putin's "criminal regime".

On 29 November 2007, RIA Novosti reported that the Savelovsky district court in Moscow had sentenced Boris Berezovsky in absentia to six years in prison for the theft of Aeroflot airline funds. But Berezovsky was still in exile in Britain, which refused to extradite him." Some would have you believe that I am only seeking revenge against Putin. But that is not true. What bothers me is the criminal and dictatorial regime he has set up."

After the loss of their political hegemony in Russia, some oligarchs continued to prosper with their businesses both in Russia and abroad. Among Russia's great fortunes listed in *Forbes magazine*, Roman Abramovitch appeared just behind Khodorkovsky. He had rapidly prospered and amassed an immense fortune from oil exports alongside Berezovsky and came to own 80 per cent of Sibneft, the Russian oil company, 50 per cent of Rusal, the aluminium monopoly, and 25 per cent of Aeroflot. In 2005, while Khodorkovsky was convicted, Abramovitch sold Sibneft for 13 billion euros to Gazprom, i.e. to the state, a company he had bought for only 100 million dollars at the time of privatisation. While his former friends were in jail or in exile abroad, Abramovitch had escaped the wave that had swept away the oligarchs. Unlike the others, he had demonstrated his loyalty to President Putin by returning the ORT network to the Russian state, a gesture much appreciated by the Kremlin[131].

The weekly *Le Point* of 8 February 2007 published an article about him: At the age of 40, he stood out with a fortune of 18 billion dollars, making him the 11th largest fortune in the world. If the magazine was to be believed, Abramovitch was a good and generous man. He had suffered much during his childhood: "His mother died before his first birthday. His father was killed in a construction accident when he was two and a half years old. Raised by his uncle in Ukhta, 1200 kilometres northeast of Moscow, little Roman had it hard. On top of that, he was Jewish, which in the Soviet Union closed off many careers for him."

In 2005, he had been re-elected governor of the Chukotka region in eastern Siberia, a territory about one and a half times the size of

---

[131] Roman Abramovitch and Oleg Deripaska were the main oligarchs to escape judicial repression. In 2007, Oleg Deripaska dethroned Roman Abramovitch and became Russia's richest man with a fortune of $21.2 billion, according to the *Forbes* magazine list.

France but with a population of barely 50,000. Some said he was seeking parliamentary immunity. Others revealed that a tax cut he had voted into the Duma in 2000 had allowed a Sibneft buying and selling subsidiary, domiciled in Anadyr, to save hundreds of millions of dollars. But that tax gimmick had been banned after two years." Since then, Abramovitch has carried the full weight of Chukotka."

Étienne "Gernelle's" article was moving. Here is the good Abramovitch arriving by helicopter in his province: "In the village school, Abramovitch refuses to make a speech and asks to be asked questions. A fisherman takes the floor: "Roman Abramovitch, give us hooks to go fishing". A month later, i.e. with the next plane, the fisherman received a box of hooks. The others ask for flour, sugar, etc. Later, a school, buses and more money would arrive. Hated in Russia because of his ill-gotten wealth, Abramovitch is celebrated here as a demigod. Posters with his effigy are displayed in many homes." Abramovitch's generosity knew no bounds: "Every citizen is entitled to a three-minute free call to a London call centre to complain about the local administration. No oligarch has ever been so committed to Russia."

In 2005, at the end of his term, Abramovitch did not wish to repeat his mandate, but governors were now appointed by the president and Vladimir Putin decided to confirm him for an additional term: bad luck!

In his immense generosity, the billionaire also financed the construction of dozens of football pitches in Russia. He even took over the payroll of the Russian national team coach. In England, he was the owner of the London football club Chelsea, which won him the adoration of thousands of fans. Football was his passion. He organised major tournaments in Israel. The discreet Abramovitch had finally emerged from his anonymity, displaying his fortune more and more ostentatiously. He owned palaces all over the world, a submarine, three helicopters, two Boeings, all equipped with electronic devices worthy of Spectre, the criminal organisation of the "James Bond" films. His Boeing 767 was a real flying palace with 250 seats. He also owned four yachts: the *Pelorus*, 115 metres, the *Grand Bleu*, 112 metres, the *Ecstase*, 86 metres, and the small *Sussurro*, just 49 metres. The last of his yachts would be the *Eclipse*, a 167-metre boat costing 300 million euros that he was building in Germany. The yacht, equipped with bulletproof windows, was longer than any Royal Navy vessel except aircraft carriers, and—like his personal Boing—was fitted with an anti-missile system. Abramovitch now lived between Moscow and London where he had settled his family and was discreetly evacuating his money, as if preparing a sudden escape.

The Invisible Mafia II

Westerners were never informed of the real nature of this mafia, which all the media called "Russian", as if they had received a slogan. Pavel Lunguin's film *Tycoon: A New Russian* (2002, Russia) did not divulge any of this reality. This was the plot in a nutshell: in the late 1980s, Plato Makovski and his friends, young and brilliant university students, abandon their scientific studies to go into business. Plato, originally from one of the southern regions, has established links with the (Uzbek) mafia. But we must understand that he did this to defend himself against other hostile gangs. In any case, he and his friends are so nice that they can be forgiven for anything. He becomes the richest man in the country, controlling television, but always acting in a good cause. Unfortunately, Plato is killed in an assassination attempt. The bad guys in the film, responsible for this vile murder, are the Russian Marxist-Leninist patriots, big, strong and clear-eyed, but who deceive the people and will not back down from anything until they have eliminated Plato, the nice billionaire. Once again, the white man plays the role of the bastard. Of course, it is not necessary to study the family tree of Pavel Lunguin to understand which mafia he belongs to.

The weekly *L'Express* of 16 July 1998 had to surrender to the evidence of the mafia's control over the country: 'The criminal oligarchs completely control some branches of Russia's economy and territories', we read in its pages. In October 1997, in the daily *Izvestia*, Anatoly Kulikov, former Russian Interior Minister, wrote: 'The representatives of organised crime have established themselves in the organs and structures of the state. In some regions, the forces of law and order do not control anything, if they are not directly involved... Let us remember that at the end of the 1980s, around twenty freight trains disappeared every day in Soviet territory." Since then, the situation has worsened. Thus, Hélène Blanc wrote in *The Black Dossier of the Russian Mafias*[132]: "The various mafias inherited from the Soviet era control nearly 85% of Russia's economy and natural resources." But in this article, nothing in the article made it possible to identify the true nature of this mafia.

L'Express recalled that this "Russian" mafia already existed in Soviet times. Under Stalin, however, the Nomenklatura was too afraid

---

[132]Hélène Blanc, *Le dossier noir des mafias russes*, Balzac éditeur, 1998.

of purges to give free rein to its appetites. The phenomenon appeared in the Khrushchev era, when corruption began to gangrene the state apparatus, and the evil worsened especially under Brezhnev. Constantine Tsvigun, a KGB general in the Moscow region, son-in-law of Brezhnev, committed suicide after the search of his flat where gold and dollar notes, etc., were discovered.

In his book entitled *Jewish supremacism*, David Duke, an American nationalist, cited two books that explained the workings of organised crime in the defunct USSR: *Hustling on Gorky Street* by Yuri Brokhin (1975, Dial Press), a former Jewish pimp, and *USSR: The Corrupt Society* by Konstantin Simis (1982, Simon and Schuster), the latter a leading advocate of the Jewish mafia in the Soviet Union. Both books, wrote David Duke, clearly showed that Jewish mobsters controlled organised crime in the Soviet Union. Brokhin further explained that only Jews could run this mafia, as the Slavs were only capable of street crime.

In 1992, a book, published and distributed by the major commercial distributors to the general public, delved into this little-known subject. Arkadi Vaksberg's book, simply titled *The Russian Mafia* (Albin Michel), told us about another aspect of the influence of mafia groups: the trade in pirated VHS tapes and the emergence of the pornographic industry in Russia: "A new distraction that is all the rage and brings the mafia fabulous profits," wrote Vaksberg." The profits generated by this industry make a whole network of local mafias live[133]." Vaksberg also briefly mentioned in his book the havoc caused by the hard drugs sold by gangsters. In 1990, there were 130,000 drug addicts in Russia. By the end of 1990, there were 1.5 million.

But Arkadi Vaksberg presented a very unique analysis of the mafia phenomenon, at any rate very characteristic of the Jewish intellectual who seeks at all costs to beat around the bush and avoid uncomfortable subjects. Vaksberg first of all denounced the Soviet system and the communist mafia under Andropov and Brezhnev in the 1970s and 1980s: "The political regime, he wrote, established for more than 73 years, and despite all its modifications, was a real mafia; a totalitarian despotism cannot be anything else. The structures and phenomena which we call today a mafia, and which we identify as illegal, criminal and anti-state, are in reality nothing more than the natural development of the totalitarian state[134]."

---

[133]Arkadi Vaksberg, *La mafia russe*, Albin Michel, 1992, p. 167.
[134]Arkadi Vaksberg, *La mafia russe*, Albin Michel, 1992, p. 21.

We must therefore believe that the mafia in Russia was communist. Vaksberg went further and taught us to see what was really going on behind the scenes: "Marxist-Leninist dogmas and red flags are nothing more than camouflage, he said, and can, if necessary, be replaced by the Suras of the Koran, for example, and the green colour of Islam. Changes in colour and vocabulary do not change anything in substance: the mafia is not giving any ground. The author was indignant: "While I am writing these lines, all the leaders of the Uzbek mafia are at liberty"[135]." Vaksberg did indeed denounce the Uzbek mafia: "The revelations about the Uzbek mafia had an immense impact on the country[136]." (page 128). But there was also the Kazakh mafia: "The Kazakh mafia was not entirely spared." (page 151).

Other mafias had emerged after the collapse of the communist system. This is what Vaksberg wrote: "One evening we were having a discussion at a friends' house on the subject: 'Which is the most powerful mafia in the Soviet Union: the vodka mafia, the fruit mafia, the transport mafia?'... In reality, they are all equally powerful and, above all, they all support each other[137]."

Arkadi Vaksberg again managed to reverse the roles in the conclusion of his book, once again demonstrating that intellectual tendency so symptomatic of the cosmopolitan spirit. According to him, the mafiosi were those who opposed the market economy: "The political mafia and the economic mafia", he wrote, wage a "fierce battle" against the market economy. This fight "is in reality the fight of the mafia defending its positions. The paradox is that it is done in the name of the anti-mafia struggle; "No to the parallel economy!", shout the mafiosi who are skilled in taking advantage of popular sentiment, while they want the parallel economy to prosper[138]. Arkadi Vaksberg introduced here a grain of truth in his Talmudic demonstration: "If the market economy is eventually established, he said, the mafia will cease

---

[135] Arkadi Vaksberg, *La mafia russe*, Albin Michel, 1992, p. 275, 285.

[136] The weekly *Le Point* of 28 April 2005 revealed that in 1999, the well-known "French" writer Marek Halter had interceded with the Minister of the Interior to ask him to lift the residence ban on an Uzbek. However, this individual was "an important member of organised crime." The French services were even more perplexed by the fact that another Uzbek mafioso, turned back at the French border, had said: "I am a friend of Marek Halter! Journalist Christophe Deloire mischievously added at the end of his article, "When Marek Halter is asked awkward questions, he responds gently, placing his hand on the forearm of his interlocutor."

[137] Arkadi Vaksberg, *La mafia russe*, Albin Michel, 1992, p. 245.

[138] Arkadi Vaksberg, *La mafia russe*, Albin Michel, 1992, p. 257. On the accusatory inversion, see the chapter in *Psychoanalysis of Judaism* (2006). The word "paradox" appears very frequently under the pen of Jewish intellectuals, which is logical.

to be a market economy and will become a normal economic actor" (page 265)." (page 265). We are finally entering the Western democratic system, a fully democratic and egalitarian society where everyone has the nationality of the country, allowing the foxes to manage the henhouse as they see fit.

The truth is that Arkadi Vaksberg's book was more like a buffoonery than anything else, and had evidently been commissioned to fill the media field and serve as a substitute for a public asking questions about the phenomenon. In the last pages of the book, we learn that Arkadi Vaksberg had nevertheless suffered some heartache: "Since I got an answering machine, the number of calls from people who want to express their feelings to me has been increasing all the time. Threats and insults are becoming more and more frequent. Normally, I delete the messages immediately, but I saved the last one I received four days before writing these lines. It read: *"You scoundrel, you whore, you dirty Jew, try to keep your mouth shut or you will regret it. Stop pouring your filth into your shitty Zionist newspaper and shut up if you want to stay alive. I have heard you in the Library of Foreign Literature swell the heads of honest Russians with your mafia stories. The mafia, it's you dirty Jews. Leave the Party alone, don't touch our homeland*[139]*."*

---

[139] Arkadi Vaksberg, *La mafia russe*, Albin Michel, 1992, p. 282.

3. The "Russian mafia" takes over the world

The new "Russian" ruling class had bought flats, villas, castles and chalets everywhere in Europe and the United States. The mafiosi invested their capital in the West and bought blocks of buildings in the big capitals of Central Europe. The magazine *L'Express* of 16 July 1998 explained: "There are many other promised lands for Slavic mafiosi." These "New Russians", as they were called at the time, were the talk of the town because of their eccentricity and arrogance.

On the Azur coast

In France, the oligarchs had bought the most beautiful mansions on the Côte d'Azur, the best yachts, and organised grandiose parties at Cap Antibes. According to a disturbing French intelligence report of May 1998, which analysed the activities of businessmen from the former Soviet Union, investments in France directly linked to the mafia amounted to some 200 billion francs, mainly concentrated in luxury real estate, especially on the Côte d'Azur. But many French companies would have worked—often unknowingly—with businessmen linked to or members of the Moscow mafia. In fact, it was very difficult for the French authorities to obtain reliable information about ex-USSR nationals who came to invest their capital.

Among these "*nababs* from the cold", as *L'Express* headlined on 2 May 2002, were Boris Berezovski, Arcadi Gaydamak (now a refugee in Israel), Boris Birstein, Serguei Rubinstein, Alexandros Kazarian, Alexander Sadadsh, and Georgy Khatsenkov. Naturally, the journalist deliberately avoided mentioning their true nationalities.

The magazine referred to a confidential report by the Alpes-Maritimes tax investigation and control brigade, which listed the properties, villas and flats—only high-end goods—bought by the '*nababs*'. Some of them had already made the news, like Berezovski, when he bought the Château de la Garoupe in December 1996 and, in July 1997, the Campanat de la Garoupe, two of the most prestigious properties in Cap d'Antibes, for a total of 145 million francs (22.1 million euros), a vastly underestimated price. Berezovsky regularly hosted Tatiana Datchenko, the daughter of former President

Yeltsin.

The second "star" of the billionaire peninsula was Arcadi Gaydamak, recently implicated in an arms sales case in Angola. He had acquired the Isleta, in Cap d'Antibes, for some 59.3 million francs (8.13 million euros). It was the famous villa Pellerin, named after the defence developer who had it built with its 2000 square metres of illegal construction. The man ended up taking refuge in Israel.

Less well known, his neighbour's name was Boris Birstein. He was born in 1947 in Vilnius (Lithuania) and was a Canadian national, like his wife. The couple had bought the villa La Cloute under her name in April 1995 for 1.3 million euros. The tax investigators stated: "Boris Birstein conducts most of his business activities from Switzerland, where his company Seabaco AG is based...".

Telman Ismailov, born in 1956 in Baku (Azerbaijan), was the owner since 1999 of the beautiful villa Istana, purchased for 36,667,000 francs, about 5.59 million euros. The walls of the compound, the facades, the railings and balustrades and the floors were all made of marble, inside and out. The man loved to be noticed at the wheel of his white Bentley convertible. On 11 September 1999, for his birthday, the council banned him from setting off fireworks on his property. He therefore moved to a large terrace of a room in the Meridien hotel in Juan-les-Pins to satisfy his whim. A witness told the next day that a bodyguard came to pay the bill for the evening: 450,000 francs (68,600 euros) in cash, notes stuffed anyway in a plastic grocery bag.

A little further on, at Marina Baie des Anges, was an undulating architectural complex, built "with its feet in the water". A dozen "Russians" had their homes there, which had cost them between 1.25 and 7 million francs each. The services investigating them spoke of the "Villeneuve-Loubet group": "These individuals are linked to each other by businesses they run from various places in Europe", we read in a Treasury report. There was also Arcadi Gaydamak and Sergei Rubinstein, born in 1971 in Odessa, who was one of the fifteen Russians expelled from Monaco between 1994 and 1997, which, by virtue of the Franco-Monegasque convention, also obliged him to leave the Alpes-Maritimes department. Domiciled in Berlin, he was the owner of an import-export company that was largely supplied by Russian companies. In August 1995, Rubinstein had rented the *Club Med* sailing boat, anchored in the port of Cannes, to host the 400 guests at his wedding. The cost of the festivities was 10 million francs, of which 100,000 francs paid for the floral decorations alone.

Less prestigious, but also remarkable, the Atoll Beach

programme, close to the port of Saint-Laurent-du-Var, was home to some striking personalities such as Alexandros Kazarian. Born in 1951 in Tbilisi (Georgia), he had bought a 200 square metre flat in January 1996 for 3 million francs near another individual called Alexandros Pavlidis. In reality, Kazarian and Pavlidis were the same person.

Another example: in July 2005, the "British" billionaire Philip Green opened the season with his son's *bar-mitzvah*. The *nabob* had booked the 44 rooms and 9 suites of the famous Grand Hotel de Cap-Ferrat. A fleet of racing cars from Monaco had been made available for the 200 guests. "Real estate prices have soared to such an extent that most French people have retreated to the less sought-after hills of the hinterland" (*Courrier international*, July 2005).

These "Russians" were not just rich, partying, spending tourists. In the second part of their reports, the tax investigators showed that a good number of them also invested in shady businesses. Generally speaking, these investments actually ended up in service or import-export companies. Some of them had even recycled Colombian drug money through international trading companies.

The "Russians" came to the Côte d'Azur simply to do business in a pleasant atmosphere. In 1997, thirty or so merry businessmen accompanied by about forty "women of the night" were seen disembarking at Nice airport. The group did not go unnoticed by the intelligence police. On their arrival in Cannes, the women settled in the palaces on the Croisette and the men isolated themselves on a 30-metre yacht, the *Inéké IV*, which could sail outside territorial waters. It was on this boat that in August what could be called the "Yalta of privatisation" took place, i.e. the distribution of the large Russian national companies bought from the state at a vile price. The meeting was held with large quantities of vodka and champagne on board, first among the men, then in the rooms where the young women awaited the return of the new capitalists.

But the most disturbing aspect of this major investigation, concluded the *L'Express* journalist, was that public representatives, a former policeman, a lawyer, a notary, a private detective and French businessmen appeared here and there, i.e. citizens who, in principle, were above suspicion and perfectly in tune with more or less notorious mafiosi[140].

---

[140] Nessim Gaon, an 80-year-old businessman and director of the Noga company, was a Sephardic Jew from Sudan who had come to Geneva in the late 1950s. In December 2004, the Nice correctional court sentenced him to three years in prison for having bribed Michel Mouillot, the former mayor of Cannes (read in *Planetary Hopes*, [2022],

Some more discreet but no less disturbing characters appeared on the Azur coast. On 14 December 1994, the Grassepublic prosecutor's office had opened proceedings for drug trafficking against a certain Tariel Oniani, born in Kutaisi, Georgia, who lived in Vésinet, in the Yvelines, and in Cannes. The French justice system had become interested in him thanks to information leaked by Interpol Brussels. A few months earlier, an Israeli citizen, Raphael Michaeli, born in Georgia and registered as a drug trafficker, had been arrested in Belgium. The day before his arrest, Raphael had sent two stolen and forged passports and two residence permits to Tariel Oniani. The French police later found out, thanks to Interpol in Israel, that Tariel Oniani was suspected of being the head of the Kutaiskaya gang—the name of his home town in Georgia—and that he was supposed to meet in France with the head of another mafia gang—the Solntsevskaya—a certain Sergei Mikhailov. Oniani's wiretaps revealed a kidnapping plan. But the gang was also suspected of other criminal activities: diversion of Iran's oil embargo, extortion and robbery to take over Georgian or Russian banks and factories, kidnappings and murders in the context of settling scores, etc. In October 1999, the Grasse correctional court opened the trial of the "Georgians" (*L'Express* of 16 July 1998), accused of "illicit association with a view to preparing a crime". The defendants were released after having spent a year in prison and paid a bail of 1 million francs each, but had to answer for a kidnapping and an "offence of extortion of funds under threat".

In France, as in Israel, the most visible part of the mafia activities exported from the countries of the former Soviet Union was obviously prostitution. In Nice, prostitutes from these countries plied their trade at the end of the *Promenade des Anglais*, in the direction of the airport. They arrived via Rome or Hamburg. They did not speak a word of French, so they wrote their rates on the palm of their right hand. But the presence of these girls on the coast may have seemed anecdotal compared to the 25,000 of their female colleagues, also from Eastern Europe, who worked on German soil.

From Berlin to Marbella

Soon after the fall of the Berlin Wall, Germany was on the front line of an influx of 200 to 300 rival gangs from the former Soviet bloc

---

also claimed 600 million dollars from Russia for failing to honour its commitment to a huge barter contract, oil for goods, signed in 1991.)

countries, and Berlin became the home of Russian organised crime. According to Jurgen Roth, author of two books on the Russian mafia, some fifteen Mafia godfathers wreaked havoc in the country.

The first sector to develop was the trade in stolen cars. Within a year, the German authorities had experienced an unprecedented wave of disappearances of luxury Berlins. A 1993 *Spiegel* investigation revealed that the Russian mafia already controlled a considerable part of Berlin's restaurants, discotheques and shopping arcades and that many of the city's merchants paid up to 20,000 marks a month for their "protection".

The expansion of this "Russian mafia", according to William Reymond, the author of *Mafia S.A., was* also manifested by the massive arrival of "Natachas" on the pavements of Berlin and in the shop windows of Hamburg. In 1993, a quarter of the prostitutes in Germany came from Eastern Europe, but seven years later it was already three quarters. Strip clubs and brothels multiplied. The black market exploded. Imported goods, intended to supply soldiers, were diverted duty-free and sold on the black market[141]. By the end of the decade, with the opening up of the East, Berlin had become Ali Baba's den of electronic goods. Televisions, calculators and hi-fi equipment could be sold duty free. Trucks arrived and left immediately for Eastern Europe and the USSR.

Reports by the Bundeskriminalant (BKA), the Federal Criminal Agency in Wiesbaden, identified economic crime as the most important source of crime, along with drugs. The Berlin police had searched 350 companies run by the "Slav mafia" in the German capital or at least suspected of being so (*L'Express* of 16 July 1998). The nightmare of the German police was the laundering of dirty money from Eastern European mafias. According to an Interpol estimate, 1.3 billion dollars were laundered every year in Germany. According to some intelligence services, between 20 and 30 per cent of the federal state's annual credit came from organised crime.

Austria was not spared from dirty money either. A large Russian company from Moscow, headquartered in Vienna and employing 8,000 people, was suspected of being a mafia enterprise. Its activities encompassed banking, oil, energy and telecommunications, and it had two subsidiaries in Düsseldorf and Berlin.

Belgium was also an important centre, wrote William Reymond: "In Brussels and Antwerp, the Russians were involved in prostitution, the diamond market, port activities and various traffics. Cyprus and

---

[141]William Reymond, *Mafia S.A.*, Flammarion, 2001, p. 325–327.

Israel are also targets of Russian organised crime[142]."

The Iberian peninsula was another favourite haunt of the Mafiosi. For them, it was a kind of European Florida. Marbella played a role similar to that of Yalta, a seaside resort for the "rich Slavic criminals" (*L'Express*, 16 July 1998). The sumptuous yachts of Puerto Banus in Marbella belonged to these "Russians" who relaxed in the most beautiful mansions on the Costa del Sol. But the *nababs* were not just there for a siesta. They laundered drug money by the bucketload.

In Marbella, "narco-rubles" converted into dollars had taken over from British and Arab capital. Passengers on Aeroflot's direct flights— five flights a week in high season between Málaga and Moscow—did not arrive empty-handed. Sometimes they disembarked with ordinary plastic bags full of dollars and presented Spanish customs officials with a certificate from the Russian administration authorising them to take capital out of the country. Others, more discreet, preferred to legally set up a limited company in the tax haven of Gibraltar, so that they could then buy real estate on the mainland in the name of this shell company.

The local economy benefited from this financial manna, but episodic events reminded the public of the true nature of these businessmen. On 15 February 1998, for example, one Roman Frumson was found murdered in his bed in his sumptuous pink villa in Los Verdiales, a residential neighbourhood of Marbella: shot twice in the head while he slept. The man, a multi-millionaire, had long been identified as a godfather of the mafia. This "naturalised German Russian" (*L'Express*) had made headlines in the Marbella tabloids for his lavish three-day wedding celebration at the Don Carlos palace. He was closely linked to other "Russians" who were on the Spanish police's books for kidnapping company bosses, trafficking in arms and works of art and forging documents. He had built his colossal fortune in the 1980s as a supplier to the Red Army in the GDR. He also owned the *Planet Hollywood* bar in Zurich, which went bankrupt in May. According to the Spanish daily *El Mundo*, Roman Frumson also had interests in the luxury prostitution business on the Costa del Sol. In the end, he had been the victim of a settling of scores.

A significant number of bars and restaurants on the Spanish coast had been bought by "Russians", wrote William Reymond. The same phenomenon was observed on the Adriatic coast and generally throughout the European Mediterranean[143].

---

[142] William Reymond, *Mafia S.A.*, Flammarion, 2001, p. 325–327.
[143] William Reymond, *Mafia S.A.*, Flammarion, 2001, p. 302.

The Organizatsiya in the USA

The collapse of the Soviet empire had unleashed some energies hitherto repressed by communist institutions. Since then, the notorious "Russian Mafia" had become the talk of the world, but first and foremost in the United States. In his book *Red Mafiya: How the Russian Mob has invaded America*, the American journalist Robert Friedman was categorical: In the early 1990s there were already about 5,000 Jewish gangsters from the Soviet Union operating in New York City. That was more than all the members of Italian families in the entire country.

Because this Russian underworld is *mostly jewish*, stamping it out is eminently political, especially in the New York region," wrote Friedman, who noted that "respectable" Jewish associations such as the Anti-Defamation League of B'nai B'rith, the most important American anti-racist league, put pressure on the police pursuing these gangs not to mention publicly "any origin which might lead the Christian public to protest against the steady stream of Jewish criminals, the most important American anti-racist league, were pressuring the police pursuing these gangs not to publicly mention "any origin that might lead the Christian public to protest against the steady stream of Jewish criminals presenting themselves as refugees." Senior police officers had confessed to the journalist: "The Russians are ruthless and crazy. It's a lousy combination. They shoot for any reason[144]."

Friedman had also met the former attorney general of the Soviet Union, Boris Urov: "It's wonderful that the Iron Curtain is gone," he said, "but it was a protection for the West. Now that we have opened the gates, the whole world is in danger."

The American nationalist William Pierce wrote in August 2000, in volume VI of *Free Speech* devoted to the *"Jewish Mob in* America", that the Anti-Defamation League had facilitated their entry into the United States." The groundswell had begun thirty years earlier, when Congressional politicians, in collusion with Jewish organisations, lobbied to facilitate the departure of Jews from the Soviet Union under the pretext that they were being persecuted. They had become, by media magic, the main victims of communism[145]."

In the 1970s, Leonid Brezhnev had authorised the emigration of Jews from the USSR in return for sometimes very large sums of money. Hundreds of gangsters of Jewish origin were encouraged to seek their

---

[144]Robert Friedman, *Red Mafiya*, Ed. Little, Brown and Co., 2000, p. 85, 84, 74
[145]natvan.com7free-speech; jewwatch.com

fortune abroad and emigrate to Israel or to Jewish communities in Europe or America. In 1998, in an article entitled *"Paying the Organizatsiya"*, William Pierce explained that in 1989, a Jewish legislator from New Jersey, Senator Frank Lautenberg, had succeeded in having Jews from the Soviet Union officially declared a "persecuted minority" and therefore eligible for unrestricted admission to American soil, when it was almost impossible for a simple Russian or Ukrainian goy to be admitted to the United States. Fifty thousand Jews from the Soviet Union arrived each year, presenting themselves as "refugees" who had suffered "persecution". On arrival, they received state aid and various and sundry subsidies on top of that.

In New York, this wave of *Russian "refuznik"* immigration was concentrated in the Brighton Beach neighbourhood at the southern tip of Brooklyn. They numbered 7,000 in 1975 and 75,000 five years later, and their numbers only increased after the fall of the Soviet regime. This neighbourhood, called Little Odessa, was home to most of the Russian-speaking community and it was sometimes difficult to make oneself understood when speaking English. At the beginning of the 21st century, 70% of the 400,000 Russians in New York State still lived in this neighbourhood.

Among these new immigrants was a character named Evsei Agron. When he arrived on US soil in October 1975, he declared that his profession was jeweller and that he was a native of Leningrad. In reality, the man had been sentenced in Russia to seven years in the camp for murder. He had been living for four years in West Germany, where he had organised "one of the most efficient prostitution networks in Western Europe" (*L'Express*, 16 July 1998).

Fake jeweller Evsei Agron settled in New York in the Brighton Beach neighbourhood, where he quickly became known for his ruthlessness. The electric cattle prod with which he enforced his law became famous. He used it to correct and torture the victims he extorted[146]." Who in Brooklyn does not remember his reprisals? "wrote Belgian journalist Alain Lallemand in his book on the Russian mafia: "One man found his wife beaten to death, her eyes gouged out of their sockets and stolen. Stolen? Indeed, the fashionable belief among these criminals was that the image of the killer was etched in the back of the retina. Without eyes, there was no more evidence."

With such methods Evsei Argon had established himself as the godfather of the "Russian" mafia in Brooklyn." His build, 64 kilos for 1.71 metres, should not deceive us, for even if the lawyer's analogy did

---

[146]https://www.lexpress.fr/informations/salades-russes-a-brooklyn_601064.html

not refer to him, it fits him like a glove: "Go buy a ten-kilo sack of shit and try to put it all in a five-kilo sack. You'll get a good picture of what[147] stands for."

The gangster extorted money from local businesses, which ensured him an income of USD 50,000 per week. But he had also diversified his activities with prostitution and illegal gambling. After five years, Agron was surrounded by a veritable court of advisors and bodyguards.

Thus, Agron and his henchmen embarked on a gigantic oil tax fraud scheme that consisted in multiplying the number of shell companies that resold petrol to each other and then declared bankruptcy before they were able to pay the taxes and duties. Oil was thus resold at discounted prices, reporting the tax liabilities to bankrupt companies. The State of New Jersey thus lost 40 million per year. Thus, these oil shenanigans allowed it to control one third of the petrol pumps in the New York metropolitan area, a market it shared with the Italian mafiosi.

It was also he who laid the foundations for collaboration between the various Russian bands in New York and other cities. He had managed to sign a principled agreement, valid in the United States and Canada, for the exchange of enforcers. Extortionists and hitmen could be passed from one clan to another for one-off operations so that police investigators could not link a murderer or a criminal act to a particular family.

But Evsei Agron did not get to enjoy the fortune he had amassed for long. In May 1985, while waiting for a lift in a building, a man emerged from the stairs and coldly shot him twice in the head.

Another, more educated Jewish godfather was to succeed him: Marat Balagula. In Odessa, where he was born, Marat Balagula, a graduate in economics, was already the king of the black market. He had arrived in New York in 1977 where he established himself as the owner of a restaurant where all the elite of the Brighton Beach underworld would eventually gather. He would become Evsei Agron's personal advisor. His responsibility for the murder of his own boss was never proven. Agron's assassination may well have been commandeered by a rival organisation led by Boris Goldberg, who was charged in 1991 with drug trafficking, armed robbery, extortion, arms trafficking and attempted murder.

After a deal with the Genovese clan that controlled the port, Balagula became the most important oil smuggler on the East Coast and

---

[147]Alain Lallemand, *L'Organizatsiya, La mafia russe à l'assaut du monde*, Calmann-Lévy, 1996, p. 34.

lived like an emir. However, in November 1986, he was forced to flee the United States in a hurry due to an indictment for credit card fraud. In fact, his mistress had used one of his credit cards without limit. The police tracked him down in thirty countries, from Hong Kong, Germany, Paraguay, South Africa to Sierra Leone. In Sierra Leone, Marat Balagula had collaborated with a certain Shabtaï Kalmanovitch in the trafficking of gold, diamonds and oil.

Kalmanovitch was at the time the Sierra Leonean president's security officer, but he had once been a ministerial adviser in Golda Meir's Israeli Labour government and was still an important Mossad informer. He was also seen accompanying Sol Kerzner in South Africa, the owner of the huge *Sun City* hotel-casino. In 1987, Kalmanovitch was indicted in North Carolina for forged cheques worth more than two million dollars. But his downfall came later that year in Israel, where he was charged with espionage on behalf of the USSR. He was sentenced to nine years in prison, but was pardoned in March 1993 by President Haïm Herzog. According to the FBI, he settled in Budapest, where he has since managed the financial interests of Marat Balagula.

During this time, Balagula was in prison. He had been identified by a customs officer at Frankfurt airport in February 1989 and locked up in a high-security prison before being extradited at the end of the year to New York, where he would eventually serve his eight-year prison sentence. In 1992, his sentence was extended by ten years because of his fuel fraud. The following year, the ongoing investigation led to a new conviction for fuel fraud. It was now estimated that he had siphoned off 3.6 billion litres of fuel through a network of eighteen oil companies, thus evading all taxes and duties. This time, Balagula pleaded guilty, bringing down almost all of his accomplices.

In his 1996 book, *The Russian Mafia is storming the world*, Belgian journalist Alain Lallemand wrote that in the mid-1980s, according to the US feds, twelve different Russian crime groups were then divided up in New York. Ten to twelve "Russian" mafia bosses had been identified in Los Angeles, a hundred or so criminals in Philadelphia. There were also gangs in Cleveland, Chicago, Dallas, Portland, Portland, Boston, Miami, San Francisco, organised in flexible and mobile structures but very active in activities such as extortion, counterfeiting, drug trafficking, ransom racketeering, murder, prostitution, tax fraud and money laundering. All linked to Brooklyn." If we trust the analysts of the German BKA, the Russian MVD and the FBI, dozens, even hundreds of murders bear their mark—from Moscow to Berlin, from Los Angeles to Paris[148]."

In 1991, score-settling in Brooklyn was almost continuous. A fratricidal war pitted Boris Nayfeld, Evsei Agron's former chauffeur, confidant and alleged executioner, against Monya Elson, a former Agron bodyguard released from prison in 1990. Their rivalry was to reverberate across the European continent, from Rome to Berlin, Amsterdam to Antwerp.

Monya Elson was born in Chisinau, Moldova. He began his criminal career in Moscow, before arriving in New York in 1978 where he was immediately detected in credit card fraud, gasoline smuggling and narcotics trafficking. But Elson was also an extortionist who specialised in intimidation and murder—he had a hundred murders to his credit—as he confessed to Robert Friedman when he interrogated him in prison: "Don't show pity or remorse when you kill someone. Don't even think about it[149]." He was a spendthrift. He had a passion for Rolexes, flashy suits and Bentley cars. He controlled most of the export of diamonds and jewellery to Russia and was a regular at *Raspoutin*, the Brooklyn nightclub owned by the Zilber brothers[150]. It was there that he settled disputes between small-time Mafia groups, taking a percentage of their illicit activities in return[151].

Boris Nayfeld was his competitor in the heroin trade. He was born in Belarus in 1947 and arrived in the US shortly after Elson. He had followed Balagula during his African journey and was also capable of setting up international operations.

Within a few months, the war between the two gangs resulted in a dozen dead bodies in the streets. Elson had tried to get rid of his rival with a car bomb, but the explosive used could not take full effect because of the very low temperatures in those days. Nayfeld was to repay him in kind on 6 November 1992, when a hired assassin managed to get close to Monya Elson and shoot him almost point-blank. Elson

---

[148] Alain Lallemand, *L'Organizatsiya, La mafia russe à l'assaut du monde*, Calmann-Lévy, 1996, p. 33, 12. On 14 September 1998, ABC News spoke of 25 "Russian" criminal groups operating on US territory. The FBI had opened 250 investigations in 27 states.

[149] Robert Friedman, *Red Mafiya*, Ed. Little, Brown and Co., 2000, p. 12.

[150] The "Zilberstein brothers" were "brought down" in May 1993, after four years of investigation, for a $60 million oil fraud.

[151] James Gray's film *Little Odessa* (USA, 1995) dealt with Jewish criminality in 1990s New York. Joshua Shapira is a hitman who returns to his Brooklyn neighbourhood to execute a contract. In the Russian Jewish community of Little Odessa, word of mouth spreads fast, and the scores are settled in a morbid and sinister atmosphere. This beautiful film also shows the sufferings of a Jewish family, and the terrible hatred that separates a father and son.

survived, but with a shattered hand, although it was later fully recovered. Nayfeld sought his revenge to the end, and on 26 July 1993, two gangsters machine-gunned Elson's vehicle while he was accompanied by his wife and a bodyguard. Elson was again wounded, this time in the back, as was his wife. After the murder of his bodyguard two months later, Elson realised that he had better leave Brooklyn for good and decided to settle in Europe. In March 1995, Monya Elson was arrested in Italy where he was organising a Thai heroin trafficking operation. He was extradited to the United States in August 1996.

M&S International—Antwerp, Vilnius, Bangkok, Bogotá

Boris Nayfeld had become the most influential man in Brookilyn's "Russian" circles, but he was also a target for the assassins of his rivals, so he preferred to settle in Antwerp, Belgium, and continue to manage his US financial interests from the other side of the Atlantic. From Antwerp, Nayfeld was to represent the interests of the Antwerp-based M&S International, founded by his friend Rachmiel Brandwain, in the former Soviet Union. They had met in 1987, when Nayfeld had followed his boss Marat Balagula in his flight from American justice.

Rachmiel Brandwain was born in 1949 in a Jewish community in the Ukraine, where he spent the first nine years of his life. His family later moved to Israel, but in the mid-1980s, "Mike" preferred to settle in Antwerp, in the heart of the famous Jewish diamond dealers' quarter. He had opened an electronics shop, but also sold gold and precious stones clandestinely.

At the end of the decade, after the opening up of the Eastern countries, "Mike" Brandwain immediately understood where the new market was and was a forerunner in doing business with the former Soviet bloc countries. While Moscow was poor, there was also an affluent class discovering the abundance of the West and desiring a steady supply of luxury goods, alcohol, chocolate, cigarettes, electronic gadgets, computers and the latest fashionable clothes.

Although he had opened another electronics shop in Berlin, Brandwain managed his business with Eastern Europe from the port of Antwerp. Certainly, at the time, the legislation in force in Belgium did not allow wiretapping.

In 1990, Rachmiel Brandwain and a certain Riccardo Fanchini set up an import-export company called M&S International." M' for Mike Brandwain, and 'S' for Sacha Krivoruchko, the brother-in-law, 'who was only good for playing tennis and walking the dog', as Brandwain put it. Computers, electronic equipment, jewellery, luxury clothes, cosmetics, alcohol, cigarettes, etc., were sent to Russia. Business with the East was very lucrative. Boris Nayfeld, for his part, officially managed the company's interests in Russia, which was an unassailable facade. The fact is that his reputation had a certain influence on the Russians for the repayment of loans.

M&S was also the first company to do business with the Russian army stationed in Germany since 1945. Some shipments arriving at the entrance to the barracks were duly registered, but then left the warehouses for the black market or directly to Poland and Russia. The traffic was then covered up by high-ranking officers. Millions of cigarettes, truckloads of wine or vodka bottles were sold to the mafia. The scandal was reported in June 1994 in the weekly *Moscow News* by journalist Alexander Zhilin.

Riccardo Fanchini, who was of Polish origin, was, contrary to what his surname might suggest, linked to a German-born Jew named Efim Laskin who shook the entire "Russian" Berlin community. On 27 September 1991, Laskin's body was found with dozens of stab wounds in the boot of a car in a Munich car park. Laskin had the misfortune to meet Monya Elson in Italy, while Elson was still seeking revenge against Nayfeld.

In September 1992, Fanchini set up his own company, Trading Unlimited. He was a partner with Leonid Barnchuck and Yakov Tilipman, both from New Jersey, near New York. They imported alcohol into Russia, tax-free thanks to a special exemption granted to a Russian company, the Russian National Sports Fund. It was headed by a well-known "Georgian" mafioso, Otarik Kvantrichvili, who was assassinated in April 1994 in Moscow by a sniper. Yeltsin had granted him three years of exemption from import taxes, as well as from export quotas on cement, iron, titanium, and aluminium. Riccardo Fanchini, for his part, settled in Monaco, where he produced vodka and sponsored a Formula 1 racing team.

In the early 1990s, M&S had branches in New York, Moscow, Berlin, Tel Aviv and Warsaw and served as a front for the activities of the 'Russian' clan. The trade in electronic equipment was in itself an excellent cover for drug trafficking. In Antwerp on 24 March 1992, 18 tonnes of Japanese televisions and refrigerators were seized. The shipment, coming from Cristobal in Panama, was transiting via Belgium with final destination Tel-Aviv. The equipment concealed 650 kilos of Colombian cocaine.

On 16 February 1993, Russian policemen in Viborg, on the

Russian-Finnish border near St. Petersburg, made the biggest catch in their history: more than a tonne of Colombian cocaine concealed in tins of cured meat. An Israeli resident in Bogota, Elias Cohen, married to a Colombian woman, in collusion with one of the clans linked to the Cali cartel, organised the supplying of the network together with a certain Yuval Shemesh. The final destination of the cocaine was a group of Israeli traffickers based in the Netherlands[152]. A cargo ship usually transported the cocaine from Colombia to Gothenburg in Sweden. A smaller vessel transported the goods across the Gulf of Finland to Kotka, where a Russian truck took it over, and a Belgian truck finally transported it to the Netherlands.

In September 1993, Elias Cohen was arrested in Colombia at the same time as Yuval Shemesh, who also resided in Colombia, although he was arrested in Tel Aviv on his way back from Holland. In exchange for clemency from Israeli justice, Shemesh agreed to talk: the head of the network was a man known to Rachmiel Brandwain and Boris Nayfeld: a certain Jacob Korakin. Korakin was a kippah-wearing religious Jew, highly respected in the Antwerp diamond district. We also find in this case the names of Boustain Cohen and Aharon Wiener, both of whom ran two Antwerp companies. Jacob Korakin, betrayed by Shemesh, was arrested in mid-October. He was caught in a Jerusalem flat by Tel Aviv drug investigators." Once again," wrote Alain Lallemand, "no one knows whether to speak of a Russian or an Israeli trail[153]."

Brandwain and Nayfeld were also involved in heroin trafficking. The heroin, which came from Thailand, was concealed inside the cathode ray tubes of imported television sets. Nayfeld and his associates ordered Malaysian televisions for Singapore. There, they would collect the Thai heroin brought to them to refill some of the TVs. The shipments were then shipped by sea to Gdansk, before being unloaded at a warehouse in Warsaw belonging to an Amberian accomplice of Nayfeld. The heroin could then be shipped to the United States by 'mules'. Each trafficker wore a "bar" strapped to his belly and behind his legs. The candidates were Russians or Ukrainians from New York, all in good standing with the administration, who claimed to be on a family visit to Poland, a country that at the time did not arouse the suspicions and strict control of US customs. Nayfeld was hanging

---

[152] Alain Lallemand, *L'Organizatsiya, La mafia russe à l'assaut du monde*, Calmann-Lévy, 1996, p. 217.
[153] Alain Lallemand, *L'Organizatsiya, La mafia russe à l'assaut du monde*, Calmann-Lévy, 1996, p. 218.

around the port of Antwerp while a certain David Podlog was picking up the white powder in New York. Denmark could also serve as a transit point. In fact, it was a Danish customs officer who discovered a heavier than normal television set: it was loaded with 3.5 kilos of heroin. The US Drug Enforcement Administration (DEA) later caught Podlog and 15 of his accomplices in April 1993. He was sentenced to 27 years in prison.

The "Russian" mafia was also present in Lithuania where it spread terror in the early 1990s. Members of the Vilnius Brigade were known to be involved in criminal activities such as robbery, illegal trade in gold and narcotics, smuggling of video equipment and sound equipment, etc. Alcohol smuggling was also one of their specialities. Alcohol was illegally imported, or even distilled in Lithuania and then labelled with false import documents. The "Russians" were also involved in tobacco smuggling. In 1993, the documents covering the illicit transactions came from Antwerp, which was the first European point of traffic in American cigarettes. In the first nine months of 1994, via Antwerp, little Belgium imported up to 4.5 times more Philip Morris cigarettes than the whole of Germany.

At that time, most of the companies in the Lithuanian capital were victims of extortion. Lithuanians knew above all the acronym and logo of the M&S company, the black panther—the "Jewish panther", wrote the *Respublika* newspaper. M&S Vilnius was founded by David Kaplan, who was involved in the import and export of all kinds of goods, including luxury clothing with the panther on it.

Mafiosi did not hesitate to resort to murder and bombings. Thirty-two-year-old Vita Lingys, deputy editor of the daily *Respublika*, was one of their many victims. He had had the courage to denounce their activities by publishing a series of articles on organised crime in Lithuania. On 12 October 1993, he was found dead, shot three times in the head. The murder of Vitas Lingys provoked great emotion in Lithuania, and the police immediately made arrests. Suspicion first fell on David Kaplan, a young Israeli who had been living in Lithuania for a few months and who had signed a contract with the Lithuanian state to sell Kalachnikov assault rifles.

David Kaplan was in contact with two Israeli brothers of Lithuanian origin, David and Michael Smushkevitch, based in Los Angeles, who had been indicted in 1990 for a gigantic insurance scam. The two Smushkevitch brothers, together with their wives, eight accomplices and a doctor named Boris Jovovich, had devised a telephone canvassing system whereby they lured Californian clients to their mobile clinics "free of charge". Once there, the client would sign a form transferring, in exchange for a specific medical operation, his insurance benefit to the "clinic". The bills for the medical acts 'prescribed by a doctor' were then submitted to the insurance company for reimbursement. The amounts taken individually were not very large—never more than $8000—but the number of clients was such that it had reached $1 billion, so that the scam had generated an increase in the private insurance rates of all Californian subscribers[154].

Michael Smushkevitch, the mastermind of the operation, held three passports at the time of his arrest: in addition to the 1981 Soviet passport, he held a Mexican passport issued in 1988 and an Israeli passport issued in 1990. He was convicted after his trial in September 1994, but was not arrested until 2006 in Los Angeles. The journalist of the weekly *L'Express* added without a hint of irony: "The apparent specialisation of white-collar crime confirms the level of training of the new Slavic criminals."

David Kaplan had met him in Vilnius: he had come to explore the country's real estate possibilities in order to buy whole blocks of buildings as cosmopolitan financiers did all over the world. After his interrogation and the press campaign against him, Kaplan sold his M&S shares and went into exile in Israel. He declared himself the "victim of a plot" hatched by the Lithuanian anti-mafia boss and journalist Lingys against "good and honest traders."

The murderer of Vitas Lingys turned out to be one Igor Achremov, a 28-year-old Russian who confessed to the crime and gave the name of the instigator: Boris Dekanidzé. He was a Georgian whose father was the owner of the splendid Vilnius hotel in the city centre. Boris Dekanidzé had had to flee the United States because of a case of fraud involving oil products, a "great Russian speciality if ever there was one", wrote Alain "Lallemand"[155].

In November 1993, Dekanidzé was arrested, charged and imprisoned for murder. He was also accused of having formed a criminal gang. The fact is that Boris Dekanidzé had also known Boris Nayfeld long before the M&S penetration of Lithuania: they had met in a Berlin discotheque. On 10 November 1994, the verdict was pronounced: life imprisonment for Achremov and death for Dekanidzé. He was executed in a Vilnius prison with a shot to the head on the

---

[154]Alain Lallemand, *L'Organizatsiya, La mafia russe à l'assaut du monde*, Calmann-Lévy, 1996, p. 188.
[155]Alain Lallemand, *L'Organizatsiya, La mafia russe à l'assaut du monde*, Calmann-Lévy, 1996, p. 170.

morning of 12 July 1995. The Vilnius Brigade, which had terrorised the city for too long, was finally disbanded. A few pages later, Alain Lallemand informed us that Dekanidzé was a "Jew of Georgian origin".

Around the same time, the "fall" of Boris Nayfeldalso took place. On 10 January 1994, after several months of pursuit, the US federal agents of the DEA arrested him on the road to John Kennedy airport at Queen's. He was coming from Miami to catch a flight back to Belgium. He was coming from Miami to catch a flight back to Belgium.

According to the FBI, Mike Brandwain's organisation had been responsible for a hundred murders by the end of the decade[156]. In 1998, Rachmiel "Mike" Brandwain was shot dead in a Flemish town. According to the Israeli daily *Yediot Aharonot* of 2 October 1998, he had probably been liquidated for having provided information to the US police about the Russian mafia.

In addition to the murder of Lithuanian journalist Vitas Lingys, other murders of journalists followed. A year later, on 17 October 1994, Dimitri Kholodov, an investigative journalist with the *Moskovski Komsomolets*, known for his reporting on corruption within the Red Army, was killed when a parcel bomb was opened while he was working on a case and about to publish important revelations. On the 24th of the same month, in Dushanbe, Tajikistan, a thirty-two-year-old journalist, Khamidjon Khakimov, was shot in the head and killed. Also on 1 March 1996, TV presenter Vladislav Listiev was shot dead on the stairs of his residential building in Moscow[157]. Paul Klebnikov, the editor-in-chief of the Russian edition of *Forbes* magazine and author of *The Pillage of Russia* was finally shot dead in the street on 9 July 2004. The culprits were believed to be "Chechens".

International predators and a world without borders

In New York, the war between the gangs of Monya Elson and Boris Nayfeld had lasted until the arrival of Vyacheslav Ivankov. Ivankov, nicknamed Yaponchik or "the Japanese" because of his facial features, was born in Georgia in 1940. This former professional boxer from Moscow was already heading a criminal organisation in the 1970s. He was convicted in the early 1980s for weapons possession, forgery, burglary and drug trafficking. Ivankov became a *"vor v zakone"* (a "thief in law") during the years he served his sentence in the Siberian

---

[156]Dina Siegel, *Global organised crime*, 2003, p. 56.
[157]Alain Lallemand, *L'Organizatsiya, La mafia russe à l'assaut du monde*, Calmann-Lévy, 1996, p. 166.

gulag, i.e. an organised crime boss. The *vory v zakone* included indigenous Russians, Georgians, Armenians and Azeris. They numbered about 400 in Russia, just over 300 in the other republics of the former USSR, and could be identified by tattoos on their bodies and finger phalanges. Ivankov was surprisingly released in 1991 for "exemplary behaviour". In Moscow, he was linked to another influential godfather of the Solntsevo gang, one Otarik Kvantrichvili. He later became an Israeli citizen.

Ivankov's arrival on US soil in 1992 augured the worst for the New York police, for he quickly established himself as the undisputed leader of the Jewish mafia from Russia[158]. He had become the boss of drug trafficking, prostitution and extortion. But Ivankov also took over the market segments left free by the competition, such as forgery of official documents and trafficking in automatic weapons. The manufacture of fake driving licences and taxi licences had enabled him to take control of the New York paid transport market.

He lived in a luxury Manhattan flat in one of the Trump Towers, although he often travelled to London, Tel Aviv and Moscow. During the summer of 1994, Ivankov chaired two conferences in Tel-Aviv in the halls of the luxurious Dan Hotel to plan international drug trafficking. A few weeks earlier, he had been in Miami where he had met with representatives of the Cali cartel. In exchange for privileged access to Colombian cocaine, the "Russian" offered his services to launder the Orejuela brothers' money. That same year, another conference, this time in New Jersey, brought together Ivankov and other gangsters to discuss investments in Thailand, Brazil and Sierra Leone, where Yaponchik planned to take control in a few months of the diamond trade[159]. At the same time, he was developing his activities in Los Angeles, Houston and Denver, where he placed trusted men in charge of monitoring part of the drug market and establishing a quick method of laundering *"street money"*. The FBI's voluminous 1995 report on his organisation also detailed the state of his establishment in Central Europe.

US police had identified 47 companies around the world linked to his mafia network. He had a fortune estimated at hundreds of millions of dollars. But his attempt to extort money from a Russian investment company in Brighton Beach led to his downfall. On 5 June 1995, police

---

[158] "Ivankov quickly seized control of the Russian Jewish mob." Robert Friedman, *Red Mafiya*, Ed. Little Brown and Co., 2000, introduction, p. 15, 277.
[159] Robert Friedman (*Red Mafiya*) in William Reymond, *Mafia S.A.*, Flammarion, 2001, p. 307, 309.

broke down his door. He had on him four mobile phones and a Tsarist-era gold ten-ruble coin with his profile engraved on it instead of Nicolas II's. He was sentenced in 1996 to nine years in prison. He was sentenced in 1996 to nine years in prison and incarcerated in Lewisburg Federal Prison, from where he continued to run his empire. Then, in 1999, he was taken to the high-security Allenwood Penitentiary after traces of heroin were discovered in his urine[160]. Upon his release from prison, he was deported to Russia and immediately arrested on a murder charge. But the closed trial, held in July 2005, resulted in his release: witnesses had refused to testify.

In 1994, the "Russian" mafia was significantly represented in twenty-four countries. By 2000, according to Louis Freech, then director of the FBI, it had directly entered more than fifty countries[161]. During a congressional session, Louis Freech, himself of Jewish origin, declared that 27 groups linked to the Russian mafia were operating in the United States and that there were more than a hundred around the world. Jimmy Moody, another FBI official, had warned Congress: "The Russians are becoming the number one mafia group in the United States. They are more numerous and richer. Even more than the Colombians of Medellin." In 1996, it was estimated that some 100 million US dollars in cash was being repatriated daily from the US to Russia." They import heroin into the United States from Southeast Asia and the poppy fields bordering Chernobyl," wrote American journalist Robert Friedman in *Vanity Fair*. Because they control the gas stations in New York and the country, Russian gangsters siphon off $5 billion a year, a fraction of which goes to the Italian mafia" (*Le Nouvel Observateur*, 27 April 2000).

Among the best-known godfathers was also Ludwig Fainberg, nicknamed "Tarzan", a muscular comrade of the ill-fated Yaponchik. He was born in 1958 in Odessa, Ukraine, and was thirteen years old when his parents emigrated to Israel. In 1980, he settled in Berlin where he thrived on extortion and credit card fraud. Four years later, he travelled to New York and settled in the Little Odessa neighbourhood of Brooklyn. As he recounted: "It was like the Wild West out there, I carried my gun everywhere I went[162]." As several of his associates had been liquidated, Fainberg decided to emigrate to more clement latitudes. In 1990, he settled in Miami HQ at *Porky's Club*, where he thrived on extortion, gambling and prostitution. Behind the extortion,

---

[160]William Reymond, *Mafia S.A.*, Flammarion, 2001, p. 307-310.
[161]William Reymond, *Mafia S.A.*, Flammarion, 2001, p. 310.
[162]Robert Friedman, *Red Mafiya*, Ed. Little, Brown and Co., 2000, p. 146.

his favourite sport was beating up women. In one scene recorded by FBI agents from the roof of a building, he was seen throwing a dancer out of his *Porky's Club* and brutally beating her with fists and kicks. On another day, he had brutally knocked another dancer to the ground in the club's car park, forcing her to eat gravel. On another occasion, he repeatedly slammed his lover's head against the steering wheel of his Mercedes until he spilled blood on the floor[163].

Ludwig Fainberg had imported tons of marijuana from Jamaica and exported hundreds of kilos of cocaine from Ecuador to St. Petersburg. Later, a search of his nightclub revealed his collaboration with several investment banks in Caribbean tax havens. Russian bank branches in Antigua and Aruba provided generous financing for a chain of nightclubs in Florida and ensured the connection to the Colombian cartels.

Tarzan's gang exported weapons to Colombian drug traffickers, as reported in the magazine *L'Express* of 16 July 1998. Several shipments of automatic weapons had been supplied, as well as Russian surface-to-air missiles to shoot down Colombian army helicopters used to locate cocaine laboratories in the jungle. Ludwig Fainberg had also provided Pablo Escobar, the head of the Medellín cartel, with six former Red Army combat helicopters, sold for a million dollars a unit by former KGB officers bribed by the mafia. The jewel in the arsenal was a 1992 Baltic Sea diesel submarine, with its crew of seventeen sailors from Kronstadt hired for two years. The submarine was to be used to transport cocaine along the Pacific coast to California, thus avoiding the Mexican cartels' toll[164].

In 1997, before the transaction came to fruition, the US Drug Enforcement Administration (DEA) had managed to arrest him on his way back from Russia. He had the plans for the submarine with him, as well as photographs of him posing with the crew in front of the ship. Fainberg was sentenced to 33 months in prison. The sentence had been reduced thanks to his cooperation with the US authorities. He had provided information about the relations of high-ranking officers of the former Red Army with the Russian mafia, as well as about their Colombian associates.

---

[163] Robert Friedman, *Red Mafiya*, Ed. Little, Brown and Co., 2000, p. 155.

[164] During the collapse of the USSR, corrupt Russian generals resold their huge stocks of weapons to gangsters. See the film *Lord of War* (USA, 2005), by Andrew Niccol and starring Nicolas Cage: the smuggling arms dealer is from the Jewish community of Brooklyn. At the beginning of the film, he is introduced to his first contact in front of the Little Odessa synagogue. This contact allows him to make his first machine gun transaction.

Fainberg explained to Robert Friedman, who came to interview him in his Miami prison cell for the *New Yorker*, that life in the USSR in the 1960s and 1970s was not so hard, at least for Jews. For him, "being a Jew in Ukraine simply meant having some privileges. Jews were the richest people in town, he said. They had cars, money, lived in beautiful flats and paid to have the most beautiful women. My mother had beautiful dresses and jewellery. We used to go on holiday to Odessa[165]." While the Russians struggled to get some potatoes, the Jews ate in the best restaurants in town, frequented the brothels where they enjoyed the favours of the most beautiful Russian women. But Tarzan preferred America: "I love this country," he said, "It's so easy to steal here! "He added: "In America, you can make people believe anything. It's Disneyland. I'm surprised Mickey Mouse isn't the president[166]!"

After serving his sentence, Fainberg settled in Quebec, where he opened a strip club that concealed a network of prostitutes. There he brought young women from Russia, Ukraine, the Czech Republic and Romania. And this is when we realise that Fainberg had a generous soul when he told an American journalist: "The girls come here and send money to their families... I give them a chance to earn money. For me, it's not just a business. I also help them to move on." In short, one had to understand that Fainberg was a benefactor of humanity. But he also crudely acknowledged that a girl "bought" for $10,000, if she was young and pretty, could be profitable within a week. Two days after this interview, Ludwig Fainberg was arrested at his home in Ottawa and deported. Address: Israel. However, he had stopped over in Cuba, where, according to various sources, he had set up a start-up company specialising in the sale of pornographic services on the internet[167].

In a *History Channel* report available on the internet (Youtube, "Russian mafia"), Fainberg explained his helicopter and submarine transactions with the Red Army during the fall of communism: "Everything was for sale, it was chaos..."." At the end of the report, he finally explained his vision of the world of the future, very much in tune, by the way, with that of the planetary financiers: "If you can make money in China, go to China, if you can make money in Africa, go to Africa, if you can get rich in Alaska, go to Alaska. We have no borders."

This is now the case with Semion Mogilevitch. The New York *Village Voice* of 26 May 1998 published an article by Robert Friedman about the enigmatic Organizatsiya mafia boss. He was "the world's

---

[165]Robert Friedman, *Red Mafiya*, Ed. Little, Brown and Co., 2000, p. 144.
[166]*Le Nouvel Observateur*, April 27, 2000
[167]William Reymond, *Mafia S.A.*, Flammarion, 2001, p. 362, 363

most dangerous gangster", Friedman wrote, claiming that Mogilevitch had amassed an immense fortune from his various trades: arms trafficking, trafficking in nuclear materials, money laundering, drug trafficking, prostitution, smuggling of art objects and precious stones. In his book *Red Mafiya*, Robert Friedman wrote: "Mogilevitch is the representative of a new type of Russian gangster, the prototypical godfather of the new millennium. He has created a global communications network using encrypted satellite phones, undetectable mobile phones, encrypted faxes, an e-mail system and supercomputers, all run by highly skilled and highly qualified engineers whom he employs... Mogilevitch is protected by a network of personal relationships made up of the heads and top brass of security services around the world, the elite financiers and politicians... He has built around himself a highly structured organisation, based on the "classic" American mafia model where blood ties bind key figures together."

Semion Mogilevitch was "a Ukrainian of Jewish confession", Friedman wrote. He was born in Kiev in 1946 to a mother who was a doctor and a father who ran a major state printing house. He had earned a degree in economics at Lvovo University, but his career began in the 1970s as a henchman in the Moscow Lyubeetsky clan. Thanks to access to the presses and the talents of some of the employees of his father's printing house, he had started printing counterfeit currency in the early 1970s, which led to a four-year prison sentence[168].

In the 1980s, he made his fortune by proposing to Jews who wanted to leave the Soviet Union to sell their property and transfer the money to them in Israel. Naturally, the money was not sent, but invested in illegal trafficking. He then managed to attract powerful mafia groups such as the Solntsevo clan. He was also the co-founder of the first commercial undertakers' company in Moscow.

In 1990, he fled from the settling of scores between rival gangs in Moscow and became an Israeli citizen. According to the CIA, from 1991 onwards, he opened a large number of bank accounts in Israel and took part in several meetings with other known criminals. In 1992, after his marriage to a Hungarian Jew, he settled in Budapest in a fortified villa on the heights of the capital. His new Hungarian nationality was added to his Russian, Ukrainian and Israeli passports. He now ran his empire from Hungary, specifically from his headquarters: the *Black and White Club* in Budapest. He also used to reside in Tel Aviv and Moscow.

His organisation was responsible for numerous thefts from Orthodox churches in Russia and Central Europe. Among the works of

---

[168]Robert Friedman, *Red Mafiya*, Ed. Little, Brown and Co., 2000, p. 295–297.

art he trafficked, some came from the Hermitage in St. Petersburg. In addition to the looting of art treasures and religious relics, there was also forgery. Robert Friedman, citing a CIA report, reported that Mogilevitch had taken over a major Budapest jewellery shop, one of the few in the world specialising in the restoration of Fabergé Eggs. The original pieces delivered by the owners were stolen and replaced by imitations made in the jeweller's workshops[169].

A 1994 British intelligence report claimed that the godfather controlled the black market 'from Moscow to the Czech Republic'. Mogilevitch was also suspected of setting up a large-scale scam selling tax-deductible heating oil, causing huge tax losses for the Czech Republic, Slovakia and Hungary.

The man was linked to the Neapolitan Camorra and the Genovese mafia family. He also had contacts with the Colombian Medellin and Cali cartels. An FBI report from May 1995 stated: 'Telephone listings indicate that during his visit to Warsaw in February 1994, Semion Mogilevitch made two calls to Vienna to numbers belonging to registered drug traffickers working with the Colombian Cali and Medellin cartels[170]." Mogilevitch had also bought an airline from a former Soviet republic in Central Asia—for cash—to transport heroin from the Golden Triangle.

The FBI report mentioned the name Shabtai Kalmanovitch. The man provided Israeli passports at very short notice to members of Mogilevitch's organisation." Such ease in obtaining identity documents suggests that Kalmanovitch has connections to some Israeli government officials," wrote William Reymond.

Semion Mogilevitch still ran a major prostitution network. In Prague, Budapest, Riga and Kiev, he exploited Russian girls in his *"Black and White Clubs"*, giving them false cover jobs. In 1995, a police operation in his restaurant in Prague led to the arrest of two hundred people and dozens of prostitutes[171].

In 1996, Semion Mogilevitch suddenly acquired, one after the other, three Hungarian arms manufacturing companies: Army Co-Op, a company specialising in the manufacture of mortars, machine guns and surface-to-air missiles; Digep General Machine Works, which built

---

[169] Robert Friedman, quoted by William Reymond, p. 299. Read the case of a Treblinka survivor, Martin Gray, who recounts in *Au Nom de tous les miens* how he made his fortune in ruined Germany by making fake 18th century porcelain and selling it to the United States.

[170] William Reymond, *Mafia S.A.*, Flammarion, 2001, p. 298, 299

[171] The 1995 intervention of the Czech police in the Prague restaurant is available on the internet, as well as several interesting videos about the "Russian mafia".

mortars, but also ammunition for heavy artillery; and Magnex 2000, whose magnets were used in military electronic equipment such as missile guidance." Add to this the fact that Mogilevitch's contacts with the remnants of the Red Army may make him an ideal candidate for uranium trafficking, and one wonders why nothing is being done against him," wrote William Reymond[172]. According to the FBI, it had supplied Iran with surface-to-air missiles and troop transport trucks from Red Army stocks. The business group controlled Inkombank, one of Russia's leading private banks, and owned shares in the Soukoi aviation company.

Semion Mogilevitch had taken in Monya Elson when he had his disagreements in New York with Boris Nayfeld. Elson had finally been arrested in 1995 by the Italian authorities and held in solitary confinement for eighteen months. He had been denounced by one Grecia Rozes, nicknamed the Cannibal, who had himself been arrested in Romania while trafficking heroin on behalf of Boris Nayfeld. The "Cannibal" was, in the words of a Brooklyn sergeant quoted by Robert Friedman, a *"fucking dirty jew"*. He was called the Cannibal because he had ripped off the nose of one of his victims with his teeth. The Cannibal was a good friend of Ludwig Fainberg: "We were like brothers," Fainberg told Robert Friedman." We had grown up together in the same town in Ukraine and lived on the same street in Israel. Our families were very close[173]."

Monya Elson and Semion Mogilevitch were very good friends. At that time, Mogilevitch had not yet made it into the media. The FBI and the Israeli services, however, described him as a threat to the stability of Israel and Eastern Europe. Based in Budapest, his criminal empire also had bases and branches in New York, Philadelphia, Los Angeles, San Diego and even New Zealand. In March 1994, FBI agents photographed one of his lieutenants with a major backer of the Dallas Republican Party.

According to Alain Lallemand, he had an army of 250 henchmen. In 1998, Robert Friedman explained in the *Village Voice* that some police officers refused to investigate to dismantle the mafia because the criminals did not hesitate to attack their families. On the outskirts of Prague, two atrociously mutilated bodies had been discovered. Mogilevitch's presence in Budapest was the obvious cause of the upsurge in crime. Between 1994 and 1999, there were no fewer than 170 bomb attacks in the city.

---

[172] William Reymond, *Mafia S.A.*, Flammarion, 2001, p. 298–300.
[173] Robert Friedman, *Red Mafiya*, Ed. Little, Brown and Co., 2000, p. 160.

Since May 1998, Mogilevitch has been indicted in the United States for several financial frauds related to the Canadian company Magnex International, but also for some 45 federal offences committed between 1993 and 1998 (extortion, wire fraud, mail fraud, securities fraud, money laundering, etc.) which had cost US investors USD 150 million.

On 23 September 2000, *ABC News* announced that Semion Mogilevitch was suspected of having laundered $15 billion through the Bank of New York. Some fifty people were arrested in Europe. The investigation had begun in 1998, when Russian police had asked the FBI for help in tracing the $300,000 ransom paid after the kidnapping of a businessman. The money had been transferred from the victim's bank in San Francisco to an offshore account, and finally to the Sobin bank account in Moscow. Questioned on a television station, Semion Mogilevitch claimed that he was a publisher and consultant for a grain company and that these false allegations had ruined him.

The mafioso now intended to settle in Western Europe. Despite having secretly become an informer for the German federal intelligence service BND and having set up an office in Antwerp, he was still banned from the European Union. He had contacted a "Belgian", Alfred Cahen, former Belgian ambassador to the Congo and France, to negotiate with the French intelligence services for authorisation to enter the EU in exchange for privileged information. Corruption proceedings were opened in Belgium.

Mogilevitch was hiding behind multiple identities: "Between 1 December and 5 December 1997, wrote Robert Friedman, Semion Mogilevitch had travelled to Toronto, to Philadelphia, to Miami and back to Philadelphia... He visited Los Angeles at the end of 1998... In January 2000, according to various European and American services, Mogilevitch was in Boston to attend to his business[174]."

Westerners do not usually hear about this kind of character, or his like, in the media. In his article in the *Village Voice*, Robert Friedman, whose four grandparents were Jewish, as he himself pointed out, had not hesitated to write that Jewish organisations had "corrupted the American justice ministry to minimise the importance of the mafia". Shortly afterwards, according to *Le Nouvel Observateur* of 27 April 2000, the New York cops had warned the journalist that the gangsters had put a price on his head and that he had better not go back to scouring the Brighton Beach neighbourhood. Robert Friedman died in 2002 of a blood disease. But the death threats he had received following the

---

[174] Robert Friedman, quoted by William Reymond, p. 302, 303

publication of his book and his articles in the press supported the hypothesis of death by poisoning, especially as the mafia had put a $100,000 price on his head. Since the fall of communism, thirteen journalists in the Russian Federation had been liquidated by the gangsters, as he had written in the introduction to his book. Friedman had also mentioned the case of Anna Zarkova. This forty-year-old woman had been disfigured with sulphuric acid in May 1998 in Sofia[175].

On 23 January 2008, it was reported that Mogilevitch had finally been arrested. The arrest had taken place in Moscow, where he was living under the name of Sergei Schneider. The French media had kept quiet about it, as usual, but in Belgium, the specialist Alain Lallemand had published an article in the daily *Le Soir. He* wrote: "The Moscow police have arrested one of the most powerful Russian mafiosi of the last quarter of the 20th century, Semion Yudkovich Mogilevitch, 62, alias "Seva". A special feature: during the 1990s, his criminal empire encircled the globe." Since November 1994, German, Italian, American and Russian police had been coordinating their efforts to arrest him. It took them fourteen years to do so.

And Alain Lallemand concluded: "In short, the main activities of the Mogilevitch gang—or rather its international network—were arms trafficking, trafficking in nuclear materials, document forgery, prostitution, drug trafficking, contract killing, trade in precious stones, money laundering, extortion and art trafficking. Lately, a series of complex financial offences had been added to the list[176]."

In France, the only article devoted to Mogilevitch after his arrest in Moscow was published in the weekly *Courrier international,* dated 21 February 2008. His Jewishness was evidently not—or hardly—transcendent. He was "considered the most important godfather of the Russian underworld" and "one of the ten most wanted persons by the FBI on a list headed by Osama Bin Laden." We learned that Mogilevitch enjoyed good relations with some of the men in the new Ukrainian democratic power. His company Arbat International, for example, had acquired the excise stamps (both excise tax and mark of authenticity) of the National Sports Fund (which had a privilege in the matter), and had flooded Russia with imitations of Absolut and Rasputin Vodka

---

[175] It was a method that had already been used in France by Jewish activists against French patriots. See the photos in Emmanuel Ratier's *Les Guerriers d'Israel* (1995).

[176] Everything was for sale in Russia: on 15 August 1994, *Der Spiegel* revealed that the German police had seized 363 grams of 87% pure plutonium 239 from Russia at Munich airport. Two Spaniards and a Colombian had been arrested. From 1992 to 2000, sixteen similar cases had been reported by the FBI and the CIA (Friedman, p. 156).

produced in his factories in Hungary.

But above all, he had become involved with the company Eural Trans-Gas, which bought gas from Turkmenistan and resold it to Ukraine. This new company was based in a village in Hungary, "where it had been set up by three unemployed Romanians and an Israeli citizen called Zev Gordon, who had never concealed the fact that he was Mogilevitch's lawyer." The "Hungarian" Andras Knopp was its managing director. The company had accumulated "billions of profits in Ukraine".

On 8 March, a news report announced the arrest of one of the world's biggest arms and drug traffickers: Victor Anatolyevitch Bout. He had been arrested in his hotel room in Bangkok, Thailand. DEA agents had set up Victor Bout by posing as activists of the FARC (the Colombian Marxist guerrillas) to whom he had been supplying weapons for some time." It was a realistic and credible enough script... For he thought he would actually meet with FARC representatives to shore up the final details of the transaction."

Victor Bout was accused of having sold arms in the four corners of the world. In Afghanistan, he had been the main supplier to the Islamist regime and Al-Qaida, the key man in their air logistics (*Le Monde*, 26 March 2002). According to US and British intelligence services, he had showered Kabul with weapons on the eve of 11 September 2001. He had been wanted since mid-February 2002 by Interpol, at the request of the Belgian justice system.

Victor Bout was born on 13 January 1967 in Dushanbe, Tajikistan. A Russian national and army officer, he was a graduate of the Moscow Institute of Interpreters. A "linguistic chameleon", he was fluent in five languages: in addition to Russian and the Farsi of his Tajik origins, English, French and Portuguese.

He was first seen in 1990 in Angola, where he worked with Soviet helicopter crews. During the great liquidation of the former USSR's military-industrial complex, he had acquired ten Antonovs, an Iliuchine and an Mi-8 helicopter in Chelyabinsk..." For four quid," said Valeri Spurnov, a former civil aviation inspector. A pirate fleet of sixty aircraft was thus formed, flying under a flag of convenience. In Liberia, Air Cess was Victor Bout's first and most important company. From Liberia to Swaziland, via the Central African Republic and Equatorial Guinea, the changes were constant. His planes were stealthy, registered in one country but operating from another, with fictitious flight plans. Faced with the sudden threat of a checkpoint, a few hours were enough to change country prefixes.

After starting out in Africa, Air Cess moved to Ostend in Belgium in 1995, and for two years business went from strength to strength. In one year, the company chartered 38 aircraft to Togo alone, which was then the supply centre of the Unita, the Angolan rebel movement. Its Flemish phase came to an end in 1997, when Human Rights Watch drew the attention of the Belgian authorities and denounced it for supplying arms to Hutu extremists in eastern Zaire who had fled Rwanda after the 1994 genocide. The "Russian" then repatriated some of its aircraft from Africa.

To better sell death to cash-strapped clients, he had specialised in the trafficking of "blood diamonds". Kisangani, a stronghold of the Congolese rebels, had become the centre of their diamond trade. If a Lebanese diamond smuggler is to be believed, the value of Congolese, Angolan and Sierra Leonean gems fraudulently exported from Kisangani would have exceeded $100 million a year.

After leaving Ostend, the "Russian" (according to *Le Monde*) had chosen a new base in the United Arab Emirates. From Sharjah, Dubai and Ras al-Khaimah, he relaunched his operations in Eastern Europe, where he created the Ibis charter company, as well as in Central Asia, especially in Afghanistan, where he used to work with the anti-Islamist mujahideen. But he soon switched sides after the takeover of Kabul by the fundamentalists in late 1998 and ensured the logistical maintenance of the Afghan airline Ariana Airways, which was composed of Soviet aircraft.

Victor Bout had supplied numerous countries under UN embargo, notably Sierra Leone, Rwanda, Congo, Sudan and the entire Great Lakes region. According to a 2005 US Treasury Department report, he was "virtually capable of transporting tanks, helicopters and weapons anywhere in the world." In several investigative reports, the UN had denounced him as a pioneer of mafia globalisation and borderless trafficking that makes a mockery of states and their laws.

The quest for respectability

We have already met Marc Rich, the "American" businessman who had been forced to flee the USA and then prospered in the 1980s by trading with the USSR from Switzerland. Marc Rich was born in Antwerp in 1934. His family had fled Nazism and settled in New York in 1941. It was there that he began his career as an international businessman. At the end of the 1970s, he was prosecuted and charged with fraud. During the course of the investigation, US investigators discovered that the Rich group had not only fraudulently embezzled from the US Department of Energy, depriving the Federal State of $48 million in taxes, but had also violated the oil embargo imposed on Iran by President Carter in 1979. On 19 September 1983, Marc Rich was indicted for fraud, tax evasion, false declarations and trading with the enemy, among other charges. The fraudster did not wait for his conviction to leave the country and flew with his wife to Switzerland, a country that did not have extradition agreements with the United States. He renounced his US citizenship and opted for Spanish and Israeli citizenship, although he remained on the FBI's most wanted list.

On 20 January 2001, Marc Rich was in the news again: US President Bill Clinton had just pardoned the offender a few hours before leaving office. This presidential amnesty triggered a scandal that was further amplified when it was reported that Denise Rich, the businessman's ex-wife, had made a donation of one million dollars to the Democratic Party and the Clinton Foundation. The US president had personally received a cheque for $450,000, while Abraham Foxman, the president of the Anti-Defamation League, the powerful US anti-racist league, had also received a large sum of money from the con man's hands to champion his cause[177].

The FBI was also investigating Rich's involvement in various money laundering operations with Central European, Canadian and US banks. In March 2001, British customs at Gatwick airport had seized $1.9 million from the billionaire under what British law calls the 'prevention of financial transfers suspected of financing drug trafficking." Incidentally, it should be noted that Marc Rich also held a Bolivian passport.

In addition, the FBI was eager to question Marc Rich about his relations with the Mossad—the Israeli intelligence services—as Rich was suspected of having known the identity of a very high-level Mossad informant infiltrating the Clinton administration. Bill Clinton later acknowledged that he had granted the presidential pardon "in part because the Justice Department had not objected, and because he had received a request to that effect from the Israeli government". That request had come in the form of a written note from another old friend of Bill Clinton's: former Israeli Prime Minister Ehud Barak. Rich's clandestine work in relation to Israel consisted of providing Israeli passports to members of the "Russian" mafia.

Among the planet's great predators is Arcadi Gaydamak. This

---

[177] ADL spokesperson Myra Shinbaum stated in March 2001 that the League against anti-Semitism's annual budget was $50 million.

Ukrainian-born businessman had also been able to profit from the chaos generated by the collapse of the Soviet Union. He had built his empire on phosphate mines in Kazakhstan, poultry farms in Russia, real estate and banking investments, and so on. His fortune, which he managed from his mansion in Caesarea (Israel), was worth billions of dollars.

His name became famous after 1996, when it was revealed that he was involved in illegal arms trafficking in Angola. He was also implicated in Russia's $6 billion purchase of Angola's debt and had managed to seize a large part of the country's diamond trade. Gaydamak was also under the scrutiny of the intelligence services who suspected him of having close relations with certain suspicious businessmen in Russia, especially with Mikhail Chernoi's group, with whom he was involved in operations that allowed them to steal tens of millions of dollars from the Central Bank of Russia.

However, Arcadi Gaydamak systematically attacked in court for defamation those reckless enough to link him to the "Russian mafia". Accused by the French justice system of having sold Russian arms to Angola without authorisation, Gaydamak swore that he had acted "in all legality" and had even "put an end to a civil war" in that country.

In December 2000, to the surprise of some police services, he received the National Order of Merit for having intervened in 1995 in the release of two French pilots in Bosnia. However, Gaydamak held the record for the largest tax adjustment ever demanded on French soil: 80 million euros, nearly 500 million francs. Fortunately for him, he held four passports (Angolan, French, Canadian and Israeli). He first took refuge in London, but then chose Israel. In the spring of 2001, an international arrest warrant was issued against him for money laundering, aggravated money laundering, abuse of social assets, tax fraud, breach of trust and illicit arms trading. But repeated requests for his extradition by the French judiciary remained a dead letter. The Israeli judges had not taken the trouble to question the businessman about the acts of which he was accused. In any case, he could not be prosecuted in Israel on the main charge of arms trafficking, as this was not a reprehensible activity in the Hebrew state. As for the offence of money laundering, this also did not exist in Israel at the time of the events. This was indeed what the Israeli Ministry of Justice had replied to the French judges, adding that the arrest warrants contained inaccuracies that they wished to see clarified.

For his part, Arcadi Gaydamak counterattacked by announcing a barrage of accusations against France and openly recounted the ins and outs of the hostage liberation in which he had participated, revealing that the socialist government had paid a ransom of 25 million francs. *Le Parisien* of 28 June 2001 published an interview with the businessman:

—What is your reaction to the dismissal of his prosecution for "arms trafficking"?

Arcadi Gaydamak replied: "I am happy, of course. But I have suffered such an injustice since the beginning of this case that a decision to the contrary would not have surprised me. In this case I am being portrayed as an arms dealer, a mafioso, a criminal... To make up for the evidence they lack, the judges want to give me a negative image. They are even going so far as to cast doubt on my role in the liberation of the French hostages."

In Switzerland, the judiciary was investigating the numerous commissions paid to various Angolan dignitaries in the context of the payment of the Russian-Angolan debt. From Israel, where he lived, Arcadi Gaydamak responded to questions from the newspaper *Le Temps by* defending the legitimacy of the transaction with a strong argument: the largest Swiss bank, UBS, had guaranteed the legality of the operation and had been paid generously for its participation. In *Le Temps* of 1 June 2002, Gaydamak explained his role in the deal concluded between Angola and Russia:

"At the beginning of 1992, he said, Russia inherited the debts owed to the Soviet Union by a number of third world countries, including Angola... An agreement providing for the payment, as of June 2001, of 1.5 billion dollars out of 5 billion owed by Angola was signed in November 1996. It is an agreement negotiated by the two states, not by me or Pierre Falcone. But I acted as a facilitator because at that time Russia lacked administrative structures."

The journalist asked him this question: "How can you explain that Angola has disbursed 775 million dollars, but the Russian Ministry of Finance has only received 161 million dollars?

Gaydamak replied: "That's a good question. The debt was converted into 31 promissory notes with a face value of $48.7 million each and repayable in fixed instalments. The Russian Ministry of Finance was the owner of those notes in November 1996. At that time, it was very important to stabilise the social situation in Russia. They needed money urgently and the Ministry of Finance wanted to sell these bonds to the highest bidder. It was at that time that I created the Abalone company that bought those promissory notes. Six of which were bought for a total value of 161 million dollars; from 1998, at Russia's request, I paid the rest with Russian bonds. The Russian Ministry of Finance was paid in full, it was recently confirmed.

—What benefits did you personally derive from the operation?

—Abalone signed a contract with Angola that allowed me to buy and resell oil paid for with the promissory notes. There was a profit margin depending on the oil prices which were very high at the time, and that margin accrued to me and Pierre Falcone. I don't know what he did with his money afterwards. I suffered damage because the transaction was interrupted by the Swiss justice system which blocked half of the promissory notes. Who is responsible for the damage? Is it the Swiss Confederation or UBS? My lawyers are looking into the matter.

And to the journalist's next question: "Are you prepared to come and explain yourself in court, either in France or in Switzerland", Gaydamak replied: "It would be advantageous for me to come and explain myself. I am ready to go back to France, I want to go back, but the problem is that the French judge who is investigating this case, Philippe Courroye, manipulates opinion through the press and only wants to harm me when in reality his case against me is empty. The Swiss judge, Daniel Devaud, is his accomplice. But if a judge other than Courroye takes over the investigation of the case in France, I am ready to return immediately." It had to be understood that Gaydamak was above all the victim of the judicial system.

In *Le Parisien* of 9 February 2001, we learnt that Gaydamak was suspected of having participated in a dubious real estate operation with the president of the Bernard butcher's shops, Gilbert Salomon, 72, "the king of meat". The latter, under investigation for "money laundering", had been discreetly questioned about his relations with "the French-Russian billionaire". Gilbert's brother Pierre Salomon replied: "My brother has been in hospital since then and has nothing to do with these people. With all that he did in his life, it is sad to be involved in a matter that does not concern him."

Indeed, all this was very sad, especially considering that Gilbert Salomon was one of the hundreds of thousands of "survivors of the death camps". Deported at the age of 14, released at 16, he had built a meat empire with Jean-Baptiste Doumeng, the famous "red billionaire". In 1989, he bought a house in Boulogne-Billancourt, near the forest, for 35 million francs (5.3 million euros). The following year, he bought the villa Montmorency in the 16th arrondissement of Paris for another 35 million francs. He then invested 40 million (6.1 million euros) in 1993 to buy the famous villa Islette (20,000 m²) in Cap Antibes. The following year, Gilbert Salomon met Arcadi Gaydamak, thirty years his junior. Gaydamak was officially in debt in France where he paid no taxes. The "Russian businessman", as the *Le Parisien* journalist wrote, proposed a curious real estate deal to Gilbert Salomon, and in March 1995, the latter bought a 320m flat² a stone's throw from the Trocadero for 9 million francs (1.4 million euros) from Gaydamak. In December of the same year, Gilbert Salomon resold the flat to a Metz real estate company, which was controlled by an English company under Gaydamak's hand. Two years later, in 1997, the meat king also sold his property in Antibes to Gaydamak. Again, in this purchase, the Russian businessman did not appear officially. It was Minotaur, an English company, which bought the sumptuous villa Islette for 59 million francs (9 million euros)." Laundering", said the judges who accused Salomon of having participated in fictitious sales. Gilbert Salomon, who claimed to be "ruined" by the mad cow crisis[178], explained to the magistrates that he had "made a good deal" by selling his property. The new owner, Arcadi Gaydamak, however, was unable to enjoy it. He was on the run in Israel.

In Israel, Gaydamak was reunited with his childhood friend, the scandalous oligarch Mikhail Chernoi, who continued his business under more clement skies. In the daily *Libération* of 30 August 2005, we read that Gaydamak had just invested 11 million euros to acquire and preside over the legendary Jerusalem football club Betar. The club was described thus in the pages of the newspaper: "Populist, epidermic, its fans are openly racist ("Death to the Arabs" is its mildest slogan)."

In the French edition of the *Jerusalem Post* of 29 November 2005, we also learned that the oligarch had been interrogated by the Israeli police and placed in custody. He was suspected of involvement in a very serious case of money laundering with the Hapoalim bank. In March, police had frozen more than $400 million deposited in one of the bank's branches in Tel-Aviv. Gaydamak had been released after posting bail of one million sekels. His passport had been confiscated and he was banned from leaving the country. Naturally, the billionaire accused the police of persecuting him, claiming loud and clear that if he had not been "a very rich businessman and owner of a football team, he would never have been questioned." Even in Israel, Gaydamak was the victim of persecution. In July 2007, he created his political party: Social Justice. For the rest, he continued to run his profitable business in Russia. In Russia, he was also a great benefactor, not hesitating to use

---

[178] The mad cow crisis was a health and socio-economic crisis characterised by the collapse of beef consumption in the 1990s, when consumers became concerned about the transmission of bovine spongiform encephalopathy (BSE) to humans through the ingestion of beef. (NdT)

part of his immense fortune to finance charities and help the neediest Jews.

Edgar Bronfman, who had a fortune estimated at 30 billion euros, was also one of the richest men in the world. His father, Samuel, had made his fortune in Prohibition times, when the four Bronfman brothers, Allan, Samuel, Abe and Harry, worked with Arnold Rothstein in the bootleg liquor trade. In the following period they achieved a certain respectability. As early as 1934, Sam Bronfman had already secured the post of chairman of the *National Jewish People's Relief Committee*. His fortune would help his son become president of the World Jewish Congress. A deeply religious and convinced Zionist, Samuel Bronfman had financed the shipment of arms to the Haganah[179], thus contributing to the creation of the State of Israel.

A few decades later, Seagram, the group led by his son Edgar Bronfman, had become the world's number one spirits and wine retailer. The trust owned Five Crown (the best-selling whisky in the US), Four Roses, Glenlivet, White Horse, Chivas Scotch whisky and London Gin. Seagram had obtained in 1994 the exclusivity of Absolut Swedish vodka sales (60% of the vodka imported in the USA). Paul Masson, Calvert, Seven Crown, Barton et Guestier wines; Mumm and Perrier-Jouët French champagnes. Sandeman port and Martell cognac, acquired in 1988, were also owned by Seagram. The company was also the world leader in fruit juices (40% of the world market) through the Tropicana brand, also acquired in 1988.

Certainly, the alcohol trade seems to have been an Israelite speciality for a long time. In his book on relations between Jews and Russians, the great writer Aleksandr Solzhenitsyn explained that in 18th century Russia, the production of spirits had become their main occupation, so much so that in 1804, under Tsar Alexander I, a decree had forced Jews to leave the villages to prevent them from damaging the health of the peasants[180].

Bronfman was instrumental in getting some of the Soviet Union's Jews out of the country in the 1970s. Together with the World Jewish Congress, they lobbied the US Congress for a bill granting the Soviet Union the Most Favoured Nation clause. This trade right was eventually agreed in exchange for allowing Jews the right to emigrate. Edgar Bronfman and the World Jewish Congress forced the Soviets to accept

---

[179] The Haganah was a Jewish paramilitary self-defence organisation set up in 1920, during the time of the British Mandate of Palestine.
[180] Aleksandr Solzhenitsyn, *Deux siècles ensemble*, Tome I, Fayard, 2002, p. 70. Read in *Jewish Fanaticism*.

their demands.

At that time, part of the Bronfman clan was still linked to gangsterism. In 1972, Edgar's brother Mitchell had been mentioned in Montreal in the report of a criminal commission as an accomplice of Willy Obront, the leader of the local mafia. The report mentioned illegal activities "such as usury, gambling, illegal betting, stock counterfeiting, tax extortion and corruption[181]." Obront and another sharecropper, Sidney Rosen, were both sent to prison.

Since 1981, Edgar Bronfman was the president of the World Jewish Congress. In this capacity, he embarked on a fruitful venture of extortion of funds: the recovery of Jewish property "spoliated" during the war. Indeed, an investigation had established that there were 775 dormant accounts in Switzerland containing 32 million dollars. In 1995, together with Rabbi Israel Singer, the secretary of the World Jewish Congress and a very wealthy real estate agent, they began to put pressure on Swiss bankers and to launch an international media campaign in the Western media. This quickly descended into slander and libel: the Swiss as a whole were denounced as profiteers of "blood money"; they had committed "unprecedented theft"; dishonesty was the "foundation of the Swiss mentality"; their "greed" was unparalleled; they had "profited from genocide"; they had committed the "greatest theft in the history of mankind".

International pressure was such that, in February 1997, Switzerland agreed to set up a "Special Fund for Needy Holocaust Victims" of two hundred million Swiss francs. This sum in no way corresponded to an acknowledged debt, but was to be seen as a gesture of appeasement, a proof of goodwill to stop the defamation campaign. However, the World Jewish Congress did not declare itself satisfied and the pressures increased still further. Jewish financiers now called for an economic blockade of Switzerland." Now the battle is going to be much dirtier," warned Abraham Burg, the president of the Jewish Agency. The states of New York, New Jersey and Illinois adopted resolutions threatening Switzerland with an economic blockade. In May 1997, the city of Los Angeles withdrew hundreds of millions of dollars invested in pension funds in a Swiss bank. New York, California, Massachusetts and Illinois followed suit a few days later." I want three billion or more," Bronfman proclaimed in December. In March 1998, he thundered again against the Swiss: "If the Swiss keep digging in their heels, then I will have to ask all American shareholders to suspend their preliminary negotiations with the Swiss... It's getting to the point where

---

[181]Peter C. Newmans, *The Bronfman Dynasty*, p. 231

it has to be resolved or it will have to be all-out war[182]."

Switzerland was in much the same situation as Germany in 1933. In June, Swiss banks made an offer of $600 million, but the ADL's Abraham Foxman said it was "an insult to the memory of the victims." Other US states—Connecticut, Florida, Michigan and California—threatened Switzerland with further sanctions. In mid-August, the Swiss finally relented and agreed to pay 1250 million dollars. All the Jewish associations then rallied to get their share of the spoils. Lawyers for the World Jewish Congress and the ADL had pocketed $15 million.

Three years later, Adam Sage's report, published in the *Times* on 13 October 2001, stated that the accounts with no heirs could be attributed to a number of 200 deported Jews and that they totalled £6.9 million. In March 2007, Israel Singer, accused of embezzling millions of dollars, was dismissed from the World Jewish Congress. A month later, Edgar Bronfman, who had served as president for 26 years, resigned. Before his death, a journalist asked him what he thought was mankind's greatest invention, Bronfman replied: "Borrowing with interest".

The amounts extorted from Switzerland were small compared to what Germany had been paying Israel for decades. This is what Nahum Goldmann, the founder of the World Jewish Congress, said in 1976 in his biography published in the form of an interview:

"The obtaining of German reparations after the war was, by your own admission, one of your most essential achievements. Expelled from Germany by Adolf Hitler, you returned to talk almost on equal terms with Konrad Adenauer. How did your interviews develop?

Nahum Goldmann responded with these considerations:

—In reality, Germany has paid sixty billion marks to date and will pay a total of eighty billion marks. That is twelve or fourteen times more than we had estimated at the time... One could not reproach the Germans for having been stingy and for not having kept their promises... To put the reparations issue to rest, however, we must remember that today the Germans spend 1.2 billion marks a year on reparations. The public believes that the largest amounts have been paid to the State of Israel, but this is not the case: Israel has officially received the equivalent of three billion marks. The real value is higher, as the prices of the products were set at a time when world prices were at their lowest. But the Jewish victims have received, individually,

---

[182] Norman Finkelstein, *The Holocaust Industry, Reflections on the Exploitation of Jewish Suffering*, www.laeditorialvirtual.com.ar, p. 46. On this case, see the excellent synthesis by the Swiss René-Louis Berclaz, *La Suisse et les fonds juifs en déshérence*.

twenty times as much. Of course, since hundreds of thousands of survivors have settled in Israel, a very large part of the individual payments indirectly revert to the state: there are thousands of Israelis whose livelihood is based on German payments. For the rest, the Russians have never replied to our requests and East Germany has not reacted[183]."

According to the German magazine *Der Spiegel* (no. 18, 1992), the Federal Republic of Germany had already paid 85.4 billion marks to Israel, Zionist organisations and private individuals." Without German reparations," wrote Nahum Goldmann, "Israel would not have half of its infrastructure."

In 1967, Pinhas Sapir, Israel's finance minister, had revealed that from 1949 to 1966, the State of Israel had received seven billion dollars. To realise the significance of these figures, it is enough to recall that Marshall Plan aid, granted between 1948 and 1954 to Western Europe, was thirteen billion dollars. This means that the State of Israel had received for less than two million inhabitants, more than half of what two hundred million Europeans had received, i.e. a hundred times more per inhabitant[184].

In addition, US Jewish organisations send an average of one billion dollars to Israel each year. These contributions, considered charitable, are tax-deductible on the donor's tax return, so in effect they fall on the American taxpayer. However, the lion's share of these contributions came directly from the US state, whose aid amounted to more than three billion dollars per year in the 1990s[185].

By the end of the 1980s, the stagnation of the alcohol market had led Edgar Bronfman Junior, who had taken over the Brongfman empire, to redirect the group's strategy towards the entertainment and audiovisual sector. The sale of Tropicana led to the acquisition of the Polygram record company and control of Deutsch Gramophon, Decca and Philips Music Group. Bronfman also bought half of Interscope Records, a record company specialising in rap music. By 1995, Seagram had taken over Hollywood studios MCA-Universal and owned

---

[183] Nahum Goldmann, *Le Paradoxe juif, Conversations en français avec Léon Abramowicz*, Paris, Stock, 1976, p. 146-164. Goldmann speaks of 600,000 survivors of the "death camps": "In 1945, there were almost six hundred thousand Jews, survivors of the German concentration camps, whom no country wanted to take in." (*Le Paradoxe juif*, p. 237).

[184] Roger Garaudy, *Les Mythes fondateurs de la politique israélienne*, La Vieille Taupe, 1995, p. 211, 212.

[185] See also the joint book by John Mearsheimer and Stephen Walt, *The Israel Lobby and American Foreign Policy*, Harvard University, 2006.

15% of Times Warner. Edgar Bronfman thus became one of the biggest bosses in Hollywood[186]. From that position, he could make Western crowds believe anything.

The Anti-Defamation League (ADL), the powerful American "anti-racist" league, was still linked to some dubious characters. Its president Abraham Foxman, as we saw earlier, had received a very large sum from Marc Rich in 2000 to plead his cause with President Clinton. His predecessor Kenneth Bialkin was also a suspicious character. He had worked in the 1970s as a lawyer at Wilkie Farr & Gallagher in New York. In January 1980, it was discovered that Bialkin had been involved in a scam run by one Robert Vesco, who had to flee to Cuba. Vesco had previously collaborated with 'Colombian' drug supplier Carlos Lehder, thus contributing to the creation of the cocaine and marijuana sales network in the Bahamas. On 17 April 1989, Robert Vesco appeared before a judge in Jacksonville for his involvement in the importation of Colombian drugs.

Kenneth Bialkin had also acted as defence lawyer for banker Edmond Safra, who had been indicted in January 1989 in a dirty money laundering case. Safra's bank in New York was shown to have served as a transit point for drug money from Lebanese, Bulgarian and Colombian gangs.

We also have Paul Lipkin, president of the ADL's regional directorate in Virginia. He had worked for decades as a lawyer for Arthur "Bootsy" Goldstein, one of the pornography kings who was arrested several times.

Long-time Meyer Lanskyacolytes such as Victor Posner, Hollywood lawyer Sidney Korchak and Moe Dalitz had been benefactors of the Anti-Defamation League. Morris "Moe" Dalitz, the godfather of Las Vegas, who was one of the founders of Cleveland's notorious "The Purple Gang", was listed in the 1982 *Forbes magazine list of the* 400 richest people in America. In 1985, he was honoured as a benefactor of the association: the ADL presented him with its highest award, the "Torch of Freedom".

---

[186] In 2001, Michael Solomon's film magazine *Premier* published a list of the 100 "most influential personalities" in Hollywood. Number 1 was Gerald Levin of Times-Warner-AOL, who dethroned Summer Redstone (Murray Rothstein) of Viacom (CBS, Paramount, MTV, etc.). Number 3 was Australia's Rupert Murdoch (Jewish because of his mother, born Emma Greene). Number 4 was Michael Eisner (Disney, ABC, Miramar, etc.) More than half of the list was made up of Israeli personalities. In *Faits-et-Documents* of 15 April 2001.

The mafia in Israel

After the collapse of the Soviet bloc in 1991, hundreds of thousands of Russian Jews arrived in Israel. In 1995, there was talk of nearly 700,000 immigrants in five years, or more than 12% of Israel's total population. Among them were some of the most important representatives of organised crime, taking advantage of the "law of return" which automatically granted Israeli citizenship to all Jews from all over the world who came to settle in Israel. Of course, the Israeli law evoked the possibility of rejecting a candidate for immigration if he or she had a judicial or criminal record, but this provision was very theoretical. The rejection of Meyer Lansky's application to reside in Israel was only an exception[187].

In reality, for the Russian mafia, Israel was a haven of peace, a place of leisure and a place to meet, but also a financial centre offering money laundering opportunities. Indeed, a Jew arriving in Israel did not have to justify the origin of the foreign currency he brought into the country, whatever the amount. In 1996, of the 30 billion dollars that had left the former Soviet Union on behalf of the Russian mafia, four billion dollars had been laundered in Israel[188].

Some of these new immigrants may not have been Jewish. This is an idea that is often asserted to minimise the influence of the Jewish mafia in the world: Russian criminals would have posed as Jews to leave the USSR and then integrated into the diasporas of real Russian Jews, as can be seen for example in the film *Lord of War*, a film that shows the trajectory of a major international arms dealer based in Little Odessa. Alain Lallemand wrote: "This conclusion is fundamental and explains in large part why the Russian mafia's advances are mostly in areas previously marked by a wave of Jewish immigration, much to the chagrin of these religious communities (Brooklyn, Antwerp, Vilnius, Odessa, etc.), and why the development of the Russian mafia is spectacular, using and abusing immigration structures that are foreign to it[189]." This is obviously not serious.

However, at the beginning of his book, on page 13, Alain Lallemand seemed a little uncomfortable when he wrote: "Jews? The

---

[187] In The *Jews, the World and Money* (2005), Jacques Attali had mentioned this exception to mislead his readers.
[188] Alain Lallemand, *L'Organizatsiya, La mafia russe à l'assaut du monde*, Calmann-Lévy, 1996, p. 207.
[189] Alain Lallemand, *L'Organizatsiya, La mafia russe à l'assaut du monde*, Calmann-Lévy, 1996, p. 209.

religious declarations of the persons concerned are their responsibility alone... So, from now on, in this account, only the nationality will be a priori relevant, the declared or presumed religious affiliation will be noted in cases where it plays a determining role." But he finally confessed between the lines: "In this case, it is not a small detail: as we will see, Israeli criminality is complementary to Russian criminality, it is even today its extension, and Tel-Aviv plays a central role in the mafia organisation that interests us[190]."

In 2002, an FBI report stated that most of the members of Mogilevitch's criminal organisation held Israeli passports. Jonathan Winer, an expert in the State Department's criminal bureau, stated: "There is no major organised crime figure that we are pursuing who does not have an Israeli passport." (*Strategic Forecasting*, 8 April 2002). The fact is that the first 75 Russian and Ukrainian criminals wanted worldwide by the US government in the late 1990s were Israeli citizens.

On 18 October 2007, the weekly *Actualité juive* reported 'the impressive number of Israeli passports stolen, lost or sold each year abroad or on national territory': 27,500, while the number of declarations of loss was 6,000 per year. The other documents were sold to "local mafias, in the countries most frequented by Israelis such as India, Thailand, Australia or Japan."

Israel had become a safe base for the mafia: Hundreds of millions of dollars were invested there by mobsters laundering their dirty money. Robert Friedman wrote: "Of all the nations where the Russian mafia has established itself, none is as deeply compromised as the State of Israel."

Some news reports were indeed quite revealing of the atmosphere in Israel. On 24 February 1993 in Tel-Aviv, for example, Yeheskel Aslan, 43, was gunned down by a masked gunman. Yeheskel Aslan was the owner of several restaurants and nightclubs in Israel, as well as casinos in Eastern Europe and Belgium. He had been imprisoned in New York in 1971 and 1979 for drug trafficking, and had been the victim of a first attack in 1982 in which he had been shot seven times. After his assassination on 24 February 1993, about a thousand people followed his coffin in Tel Aviv, giving an idea of his popularity and influence.

On 10 August 1994, Amnon Bahashian was shot three times in the

---

[190] In his book *Le Grand Réveil des mafias (The Great Awakening of the Mafias)*, (JC Lattès, 2003), Xavier Raufer kept silent on the importance of the Jewish mafia. With respect to the Hebrew state, he wrote with clemency: "Often hit by terrorism, this country could well do without another calamity." (page 35).

head at point-blank range by a gunman fleeing in a car with an accomplice. On 14 January 1995, again in Tel-Aviv, a bomb was placed under the car of Moshe Alperon, 42, who lost a leg in the attack. Fortunately, the car's reinforcements had absorbed most of the deflagration. Israeli police turned their investigation towards Gad "Schatz "Plum, who had just arrived in Israel after spending thirteen years in prison in Germany for murder. Everyone feared Gad Plum and his methods of extorting money from brothel keepers and shopkeepers. He also ran casinos and was involved in heroin trafficking. On 31 October 1995, he was shot three times in the torso on a terrace of a Tel-Aviv café. A young gunman had jumped off a motorbike and shot him at point-blank range before fleeing with his accomplice.

Settling of scores was commonplace, but the double murder of 11 May 1995 went down in Israel's annals for the horror it provoked. A 67-year-old grandmother, Sofia Moshayav, and her 20-year-old grandson Siblei, originally from Chechnya, had been found decapitated in their flat in northern Tel Aviv. The heads had probably been sent by mail to the Comorites in the Caucasus, where Siblei's father, Dimitri Moshayav, was doing business with one of his peers. The culprit, Oleg Ya'acobov, was a cousin of Siblei. He had even attended the burial of his victims to appear normal, but a few weeks later he was arrested and prosecuted.

The problems brought by the "Russians", as the Jews from the former Soviet Union were called there, had reached enormous proportions. They had long since formed a state within the state. This community published more than ten newspapers and magazines in Russian, and absorbed the criminality of Russia, the Caucasus and Central Asia. Jews from the former USSR had also caused the extraordinary boom in air traffic to their countries of origin. Destinations to Tbilisi, Baku, Yekaterinburg, Dushanbe, Almati, Kiev, Sevastopol, Moscow and St Petersburg often had several flights a day with Tel Aviv. This constant back and forth between Central Asia, Turkey and Israel worried the Israeli authorities to such an extent that they decided to form a special police unit specialised in the fight against criminality from the former USSR[191].

Within a few years, however, the "Russians" had enabled Israel to double its foreign exchange reserves. It must be said that the Israeli

---

[191] The increase in Israeli flights to Turkey was a result of the strengthening of economic and defence relations with Ankara, but also corresponded to Israeli tourists' enthusiasm for casinos, banned in Israel under pressure from religious parties. London, Las Vegas and Monte Carlo were also popular destinations.

banking system, like that of Cyprus, offers endless recycling possibilities for dirty money. Israeli banks, with branches and *"tax-advantaged"* companies in Europe, the Caribbean, the United States, Canada and Southeast Asia, effectively guaranteed anonymity for all foreign currency deposits and a free flow of money around the world, as well as the possibility of converting it into gold. This was the famous *Pata'h* system (the "foreign account"), praised and advertised by the country's leading banks in their glossy brochures.

L'Express of 16 July 1998 provided further information on the situation in Israel. There, as elsewhere, the criminals thought they were above the law. With their colossal fortunes, they can buy anyone," lamented General Mizrahi. We have dismantled within our interior ministry a network of complicity that allowed them to obtain false documents." He added: "I am not sure that we can prevent them from one day spreading their nets over Israeli politics."

The case of Gregori Lerner, alias Zvi Ben Ari, was emblematic. An Israeli of Russian origin, he had been arrested in 1997 when he tried to take off from Ben-Gurion airport with a billion dollars in bearer shares in his suitcase. He was also accused of having swindled four Russian banks out of some $106 million and of being in Israel to organise a money-laundering ring. Moshe Mizrahi said that the man "might have become a member of the Knesset if he had not been locked behind bars". According to the police, the notorious Lerner, after having miraculously made a fortune in just a few years in the Jewish state, had donated 100,000 dollars to an association linked to the Yissrael B'Aliya (New Immigrants) party, led by Nathan Chtcharanski. Gregori Lerner had been sentenced to six years in prison, but continued to receive several Israeli MPs from the former USSR in his cell.

On 3 April 1998, the BBC interviewed Israeli police commander Meir Gilboa, who told the journalist: 'They come here to Israel because it is not very risky to engage in illegal activities. There are no laws against money laundering or membership of an illegal organisation. It is easy to get Israeli citizenship. They feel safer here than in Russia." Commander Gilboa acknowledged that the gangsters posed a serious threat to Israeli society: "They have the means to corrupt the government and the economic system."

Prostitution provided gangsters with a luxurious lifestyle. Dozens of brothels and "massage parlours" had sprung up in recent years in Tel-Aviv and Haifa. Many were controlled by Russian gangsters who recruited girls from Eastern Europe." They are sold as slaves," said Haifa police officer Tony Haddad. Rita Rasnic, of the Israeli Women's

Aid Centre, claimed that this was a new trafficking in whites.

According to General Mizrahi, traditional local criminals passed for children compared to criminals from the former Soviet Union: "A Russian gangster kills much more coldly. He doesn't hesitate to kill one after the other, the manager and all the girls in a 'massage parlour' before calmly walking away down the street." *L'Express* noted: "Methods that seem to be effective, judging by the near monopoly of prostitution held by Russian gangsters in this biblical land, as evidenced by the countless silhouettes of blonde girls wandering the streets around Tel-Aviv's Diamond Stock Exchange at night."

Israel had become one of the centres of drug money laundering. In 1997, between four and five billion dollars were transiting the country. In September 1995, the *Dépêche Internationale des Drogues* published the following information: heroin and synthetic drugs were openly trafficked in the popular Shaanan Street market near the central bus station in Tel-Aviv. The place was a chaos of people and goods. African and ex-USSR populations mingled, but Jews from ex-Yiddishland, the Caucasus and Central Asia ran the show.

The transit of travellers also supported an almost familiar drug trade: an Uzbek shoemaker from Samarkand who settled in Haifa explained that he had set up his workshop with the money from half a kilo of heroin sold in Israel[192]. However, he later claimed to have had no further contact with the drug. In the major urban centres, especially in Tel-Aviv and Jerusalem, but also in the port of Haifa, heroin doses (one third of a gram) were traded at extremely variable prices, ranging from 30 to 90 dollars. However, the fight against drugs at the borders was not a priority. The control measures and endless interrogations endured by travellers leaving and entering Israel were mainly to ensure security and control weapons and explosives[193].

Police corruption was another indication of the deterioration of the situation. The press had reported that, on Friday 25 August 1995, in Tel-Aviv, three ministers had wanted to "go down" Allenby Street to see for themselves the extent of the traffic. They could see that dealers were distributing their bags of cannabis in front of the local police station. Along the street and in the bars, all drugs were sold. After this media coup, the press reported several cases of police officers who had robbed

---

[192] 300 grams of heroin makes 35,000 doses.
[193] Citizens of Costa Rica, Guatemala, Salvador and the Dominican Republic were not subject to strict controls at Ben-Gurion International Airport, as these countries were the only ones to recognise Jerusalem as the capital of the Hebrew state since 1980. Some travellers took advantage of this to smuggle cocaine into Israel.

dealers or extorted their profits during their arrest. Others were directly accused of involvement in drug trafficking. In January 1997, the Israeli army revealed that a customs officer had been arrested as the main suspect in the diversion of 14 kilos of seized heroin.

According to an August 2001 report by the UN Office for Drug Control and Crime Prevention, 75% of crimes in Israel were drug-related (marijuana, heroin, cocaine, ecstasy, LSD). The country had 300,000 occasional users and 20,000 addicts. But Israel was not only a consumer country: like Colombia, Thailand and Pakistan, the state of Israel had become a centre of international trafficking.

In a 2003 US report, Dina Siegel wrote that organised crime in Israel took the form of hundreds of ethnic groups, of which Caucasian Jews were the most violent." Caucasians and Georgians were part of a single category: the "Russian mafia"." Dina Siegel also told us where the Caucasian mafia came from: during the war in Chechnya, many Chechen Jews had emigrated to Israel.

The Georgian Jewish community was particularly strong and structured. Jacques Derogy wrote in his book: "Stalin himself, the son of Georgia, had not dared to forbid the Jews to worship freely, unlike the rest of the Jews in the USSR." Many of them had left the Soviet Union after the Six-Day War." Of all the Russian immigrants in Israel, the Georgians are the most homogeneous, most energetic and powerful community," Derogy wrote. All the smugglers had surnames ending in *"shvili"*: emigrants from Georgia, they used to be employees of the Lod airport where they stole the goods[194].

But not all Israeli criminality could be blamed on the "Russians". The situation had already deteriorated in the 1970s. In 1980, in his book *Israel Connection*, Jacques Derogy, a pioneer of investigative journalism and a "pro-Israeli and pro- Israel Jew" (page 28), wrote: "From 1949 to 1979, the curve of crime in Israel rose four times faster than that of the population, which in thirty years went from one to three million inhabitants." And he added: "Like its American companion, Israel's mafia makes its fortune in drug trafficking throughout the world, in extortion of funds in all its forms, particularly imposed "protection", in widespread smuggling, especially of stolen diamonds

---

[194] Jacques Derogy, *Israel Connection*, Plon, 1980, p. 101. The English newspaper *The Independent* of 25 January 2001 reported that a member of the Russian Jewish Congress, Mikhail Mirilashvili, had been arrested in St. Petersburg and charged with the kidnapping of two people. Mirilashvili had to flee the country together with Israeli President Moshe Katzav, who was on a state visit at the time. He was the director of the Russian video company, which was bought in 1997 by MediaMost, controlled by Gusinsky.

at Lod's Ben-Gurion airport, in the prohibitive monopoly in the fruit and vegetable and clothing markets, in the large-scale manufacture and dissemination of forged bank cheques, and also in pimping."

Extortion of small traders and commercial companies was already a scourge: "Over the years, it has only developed, institutionalised, expanded, to such an extent that, today, it is very difficult to find a public place—restaurant, discotheque, shop, even grocery store as in the Haifa region—where the owner does not regularly pay large sums of money to individuals who are supposed to "protect" his business[195]."

Heroin trafficking was rampant. See the case of one Hershko Nello, an Israeli underworld figure. He was "a narcotics trafficker who had set up a direct Thailand-Israel network to transport heroin[196]." Hershko Nello and his accomplices regularly travelled to Chiang Mai in northern Thailand to buy heroin.

Derogy also cited one Albert Liani, an Israeli drug trafficker based in Marseilles who reigned over the maritime transport of narcotics between Israel and the United States. There was also Pinhas Goldstein, considered one of the pioneers of cocaine trafficking from Amsterdam to Israel[197].

Samy Shoshana, a sexagenarian, had created a network parallel to that of the Corsicans with the collaboration of a *"pied-noir*[198] " called Jacques Cohen, a former member of Salomon Abou's gang, dismantled in 1970. Jacques Derogy described this individual as follows: "Now back in Paris, in his headquarters in the *Montmartre faubourg,* Jacques Cohen is one of the strong men of the gang created by other North African Jews, the Taieb brothers, who run their business from two Parisian clubs, the *Gibus* and the *Petite Bergère.*" Jacques Cohen went regularly to Israel, until the day, in December 1974, when Samy Shoshana was denounced and arrested with 22 kilos of opium in a flat in the suburbs of Tel-Aviv[199]. So we see that the Sephardic Jews of North Africa were no slouches either, and also knew how to invest in the most lucrative traffics.

The mythical figure of organised crime in Israel was Mordechai Tsarfati, also known as Mentesh. Born in Thessaloniki in 1917, he had been Israel's first "godfather" in the 1950s. He had laid down the law in places of leisure and pleasure and in nightclubs, as well as organising

---

[195] Jacques Derogy, *Israel Connection*, Plon, 1980, p. 29, 34, 92
[196] Jacques Derogy, *Israel Connection*, Plon, 1980, p. 143.
[197] Jacques Derogy, *Israel Connection*, Plon, 1980, p. 110, 111.
[198] French repatriate from Algeria after the war of independence.
[199] Jacques Derogy, *Israel Connection*, Plon, 1980, p. 88.

the drug trade. He also did many favours for the ruling Labour Party leaders, providing thugs for their rallies. He was Ben-Gurion's election agent in the working-class neighbourhoods. It was there that he was to train his deputy, Betsalel Mizrahi. At that time, Tel-Aviv was already infested with organised gangs engaged in all kinds of banditry.

We thus saw that the wishes of the founding fathers of the Jewish state had, after all, been promptly fulfilled. Indeed, they had taken up the words of the theoretician of Zionism, Dov Ber Borokhov, who had declared: "We Jews will have a state like the others when it has its murderers, its criminals and its prostitutes." But truth be told, the criminals had not waited for the creation of the State of Israel in 1948 to commit their misdeeds: "In the 1920s, the Jewish policemen in the service of the British government in Palestine already had to deal seriously with all kinds of bandits[200]."

---

[200] Jacques Derogy, *Israel Connection*, Plon, 1980, p. 35.

PART TWO

BUSINESS WITHOUT BORDERS

1. Guns, drugs and diamonds

With 400 billion in annual profits, international drug trafficking is the world's second largest economic activity, just behind the arms industry[201]. Drug traffickers need weapons. They also need organised networks to launder billions of dollars generated by heroin, cocaine or ecstasy trafficking. This is where diamantaires come in.

The diamond industry

Jews have always played an important role in the diamond industry. Precious stones are easily transported, which presents an enormous advantage in the event of a hasty flight. And the history of the Jews is, as we all know, punctuated by hasty escapes.

The mining and marketing of rough diamonds was entirely in the hands of businessmen from the Jewish community. The De Beers company had long enjoyed a near monopoly in this branch of the industry. The De Beers company's venture had begun in the 19th century in South Africa. In 1869, after the first stones were found, prospectors came from far and wide to dig the earth. Faced with a horde of diamond hotheads, the Beers brothers—Boer farmers—had finally ceded their land in exchange for some £6000 to a syndicate of prospectors, which would prove to be the most abundant diamond deposit in the world. One man stood out for his business sense: the famous Cecil Rhodes. He bought concessions, created partnerships and

---

[201]William Reymond, *Mafia S.A.*, Flammarion, 2001, p. 370.

mergers, so that he managed to take control of the African market and up to 90% of the world's diamond production. To control both production and sales, Rhodes created a marketing syndicate he called the "Diamond Syndicate". However, in 1902, another even more abundant deposit was discovered in the Transvaal province, beyond his control.

The monopoly of production and marketing took place in the 1930s under the leadership of Ernest Oppenheimer. In 1957, his son Harry took over the business and for a decade the "Syndicate" exercised absolute domination over the world's rough diamond industry. The company set prices as it pleased, hoarding rough diamonds in its stocks when prices were low and selling when prices rose. De Beers chose its customers, no more than 160, according to rather opaque criteria." You don't bargain with De Beers; you take what he gives, at the price he asks," was the saying in the diamond world.

The group's activities soon extended to many more branches: gold mines, copper mines, coal mines, steel mills, banks, etc. When Harry Oppenheimer retired in 1984, his son Nicky replaced him at the company's headquarters in London. The Central Selling Organisation (CSO) set commercial policy and regulated the market. The CSO's activities were not limited to De Beers diamonds alone, but also covered almost the entire world production, since the USSR and China also entrusted them with the marketing of their rough diamonds. In the early 1990s, De Beers produced 45% of the world's rough diamonds and marketed about 80% of the world's production. Nicky Oppenheimer, who employed tens of thousands of black workers in his mines, was undoubtedly the richest man in Africa.

During the international embargo against the segregationist Apartheid regime in the 1970s, South Africa maintained very good relations with the state of Israel. Although, on the other hand, Harry Oppenheimer, who had constant relations with the black leaders of the ANC in exile, and another Jewish billionaire, the famous Hungarian speculator George Soros, had been financing the black movements at Captown University since 1981[202].

The fall of the Apartheid regime in the early 1990s was no accident. It had been decided in New York by some Anglo-American multinationals. Journalist Anthony Sampson wrote on 9 May 1994 in *Newsweek*, one of the press organs of the American *establishment:* "In July 1985, Chase Manhattan Bank (David Rockefeller) made a historic gesture: it cut off all financial lending and cancelled the entire credit

---

[202]On the role of George Soros, read *Planetary Hopes*.

channel to South Africa. It was the Chase Bank that caused the international loss of confidence in that country, the collapse of its currency and the international wave in favour of Mandela's release."

Indeed, in South Africa, as elsewhere, financiers and cosmopolitan intellectuals have always encouraged the formation of multiracial societies, since the loss of identity references favours their hegemony[203]. In August 2000, when Harry Oppenheimer passed away, the black leader and newly elected president of the country, Nelson Mandela, paid tribute to the man by calling him "a great South African of our time."

In the 1990s, however, De Beers had to face a formidable competitor in the person of Lev Leviev. Lev Leviev was born and raised in the Jewish environment of Tashkent in Uzbekistan. His father was a textile merchant. In 1971, after seven years of waiting, the family emigrated to Israel after having converted their wealth into diamonds and smuggled them out of the USSR. But on arriving in Israel, his father got only $200,000 instead of the expected $1 million. The 15-year-old Lev Leviev vowed to take revenge. By the end of the 1980s, he had become the biggest gemstone dealer in Israel, and was one of 160 clients selected by De Beers.

In 1994, the Russian government decided to sell part of its decades-old stockpile of rough diamonds on the amber diamond market, thereby breaking the exclusivity contract with the South African company De Beers. Prices then fell by 10–50%. Normally, De Beers would have bought the entire stock, as was the case with Angolan diamonds. But this time the CSO was unable to contain Russian dumping." Since the collapse of the Soviet Union, we have been used to seeing small batches of medium quality diamonds coming in from Russia by the mafia or former members of the KGB. Nowadays, we see official sales of good quality stones that escape the De Beers," said a London dealer, one of the 160 privileged clients in charge of reselling diamonds to professionals[204].

Lev Leviev had bought part of these Russian reserves. A few years later, his Africa-Israel Investments partnership won exclusivity for Angolan diamonds—a contract worth more than a billion dollars a year.

---

[203] On the apology for the multicultural society, read *Planetary Hopes*.

[204] In early 2000, Russian police arrested two "Belgians" at Moscow airport. The two men, in possession of 9259 diamonds, were members of a smuggling organisation that smuggled rough diamonds out of Russia, in violation of the law that the diamonds must be cut in the country. (Dina Siegel, *Global organised crime*, 2003, p. 57). In October 2003, one Abraham Traub was arrested in Hungary at the request of Russian authorities for the illegal sale of rough diamonds from Russia.

At the time, he was in partnership with his friend Arcadi Gaydamak, the arms dealer. Leviev owned diamond mines in Angola, Namibia and the Urals, but also gold mines in Kazakhstan. Other capital had gone into real estate management in Prague and London, and he owned 1,700 Fina gas stations in the south-western United States, as well as the Russian-language Israeli television station. He had also invested $1 billion in real estate in Russia, and an equivalent sum in office complexes and residential buildings in New York and Texas. In Israel, his Africa-Israel company built shopping malls, luxury residences and invested in the fashion industry, tourism and infrastructure. Leviev generously funded Jewish schools. In 2002, he opened a yeshiva[205] for 350 students in Queens, New York. In 1992, he had already fully funded Russia's first Jewish school in St. Petersburg. Leviev, who lived in the ultra-orthodox Jerusalem neighbourhood of Bnei Brak, was completely devoted to the Chabad-Lubavitch movement[206], to which he distributed at least thirty million dollars a year[207].

De Beers had been completely sidelined in Angola, and shortly afterwards it would also be sidelined in Congo. Its market share, which was 80% in the late 1990s, had fallen to 60% by 2003. Leviev had broken its monopoly on diamond trading.

In Israel, this industry had been gradually built up in the 1930s, even before the birth of the Hebrew state. It was mainly located in Tel-Aviv, in the heart of Ramat Gan, the city's business district, and more precisely, at the beginning of the 21st century, in four towers connected to each other by underground passages. This fortress was the most secure place in Israel. 15,000 people worked there every day. The State of Israel had granted this sector very high tax and tariff exemptions. Diamonds, imported in the rough and cut on site, accounted for a quarter of Israel's trade revenue, some $6600 million in 2006. Nearly half of the world's rough diamonds came from there and more than one stone in two bought in the US came from Israel.

The dynamism of the Tel-Aviv square had gradually diminished

---

[205] A yeshiva is a centre of Torah and Talmudic studies generally reserved for men in Orthodox Judaism. They are also often referred to as Talmudic schools.
[206] On Chabad-Lubavitch Chassidic Jews, see *Psychoanalysis of Judaism* and *Jewish Fanaticism*.
[207] *Le Nouvel Économiste*, supplement of 19 December 2003. Benny Steinmetz was one of his competitors. In 2007, this cut diamond magnate was Israel's sixth richest man. Another great jeweller, Hans Stern, also symbolised luxury and the trade in precious stones in all the world's most distinguished neighbourhoods. Hans Stern came from a family of German Jews who had landed in Rio de Janeiro in 1939. In 2001, he employed 3700 people, including 2800 in Brazil.

the importance of Antwerp, the historic capital of diamond cutting. In 1994, 50% of the world's stones (70 tonnes of precious stones) were still cut by diamond cutters in Antwerp's famous Jewish quarter. But the market was weighed down by labour costs, high taxes and cases of dirty money laundering. Of the twenty thousand workers in the 1970s, less than three thousand remained thirty years later.

Antwerp's decline was also due to the relocation of diamond cutting companies to Asia, where the cost of producing a carat was between 5 and 20 dollars, compared to between 100 and 150 dollars in the Flemish port. By the turn of the millennium, India had itself become the world's leading diamond cutting centre. The work of children brought down labour costs considerably. They were paid per stone, up to about 500 rupees per month (14 dollars), and worked 12 hours a day, straining their eyes over tiny stones to polish. In Jaipur, Rajasthan, hundreds of workshops employed thousands of children. Only the fattest diamonds (over two carats, i.e. 0.4 grams) were cut and polished in Antwerp by the best specialists. The Flemish port still had hundreds of workshops and the Antwerp bourse retained its supremacy.

The diamond industry had shocked and outraged the great moral consciences of the West when they learned that raw diamonds were used to finance civil wars in Africa. The African continent (Botswana, South Africa, Angola, Congo and Namibia) produced 60% of the world's diamonds, and part of this production was in the hands of various rebel movements. Those "blood diamonds" aroused the indignation of the virtuous "international community", which expressed itself at the United Nations headquarters in New York. The British government embargoed Sierra Leone's production and De Beers, which was supplied by the Unita rebels in Angola, pledged not to sell any more "blood diamonds"[208].

Israel, which had become the world's leading exporter of cut diamonds, insisted on the need to curb the diamond trade of African guerrillas. In June 2000, the Tel Aviv diamond bourse decided to revoke any trader dealing with rebels in Sierra Leone, Angola and Congo. However, there was nothing humanitarian about the initiative. Indeed, the Leviev Africa-Israel company had just signed an exclusive contract with the Angolan government. A few months later, another Israeli

---

[208] William Reymond quoted a passage from a 1999 report on organised crime: "We have information showing that Russian nationals or Mafia groups are involved in organised criminal activities in several countries in the region, especially in Angola, Botswana, Mozambique, Namibia, Swaziland and South Africa. In Angola, they try to legally obtain diamond mining rights." (*Mafia S.A.*, Flammarion, 2001, p. 333).

company, IDI Diamonds, headed by Dan Gertler, signed another exclusive contract with the Congo.

The diamond business remained a fertile ground for all sorts of scams. In the diamond city of Tel-Aviv, as in New York and Antwerp, the habits were the same. Trading was done without contracts, without certificates, but with a handshake and the established formula "*mazal u baraka*" (luck and blessing). In Israel, moreover, diamantaires were not required to keep a ledger. This was an ideal activity to cover up money transfers. Many smugglers of smuggled diamonds came to launder their money, and naturally the traffic was fraught with bloody settling of accounts. Jacques Derogy already described this in 1980: "The Tel-Aviv diamond exchange has, since its creation, been a very fruitful field of action for the Israeli and international mafia[209]."

In Antwerp, in the vicinity of the central station, Pelikaan Street lined its shops selling shoddy gold and stones of dubious origin. The "Georgians" occupied this large square for the reception and resale of gold. On 13 January 2005, Alexandre Adler's weekly *Courier International* published an article in which one could read that the Israeli mafia, "in the wake of Russian organised crime", had set up shop near the central station, in the diamond dealers' quarter. An Antwerp policeman anonymously declared: 'All criminals use violence, but the Israelis have a reputation for extreme violence. Even the Russian gangsters, who are in many ways their colleagues and allies, find it difficult to keep up with them... There are dozens of Israeli gangsters in Antwerp. Some have come here legally, others are in hiding. What do they do? Everything: money laundering, drug trafficking, money extortion and swindling. At night, they hang out in cafés, discos, strip clubs, brothels and gambling halls. How do you recognise them? They go for champagne, cocaine, ecstasy and especially Viagra. These guys are really into it and are sometimes seen preceded by busloads of prostitutes and *call-girls*."

Diamonds also aroused the greed of thieves. In February 2003, 123 of the 160 safes of the Antwerp Diamond Exchange were emptied without breaking and entering by an 'Italian' diamantaire, Leonardo Notabartolo, who had managed to gain the trust of an employee. In December 1994, three men had carried out an armed robbery at the Antwerp diamond bourse, emptying five chests and taking between 30 and 300 million French francs in diamonds and cash. In December 2003, a jewellery workshop in the 9th arrondissement of Paris was raided. The man, apparently well-informed, had disguised himself as a

---

[209] Jacques Derogy, *Israel Connection*, Plon, 1980, p. 100.

rabbi and pointed a gun at the employees. The losses were estimated at between 500,000 and one million euros. In Martin Scorsese's beautiful film, Once Upon a Time *in America*, we also see how a gang of Jews raided a jewellery workshop and stole the diamonds. In Guy Ritchie's film *Snatch (*USA, 2000), "Francky has just stolen a huge diamond that he must deliver to Avi, a New York mobster."

Asher Doron had been operating from Antwerp since the late 1980s. In 1993 he had been sentenced to 10 years in prison.

Old newspaper clippings show that jewellery store robberies were a national sport: in 1976, a series of robberies of jewellers' shops, post offices and villas took place in Amsterdam. The culprits were "Israelis": Yoram Landsberg and his gang, Isaac Bahadchan and Shlomo Bronstein. A certain Naaman Dieler had been arrested after a blowtorch raid on a jewellery shop in Amsterdam, and was sentenced to three years in prison. Yoram Landsberg had taken refuge in London. See also the case of one Isaac Sperber. In 1955, Sperber, the manager of a diamond buying office, managed to get into the circle of Amber diamantaires, until the day he paid for his diamonds with bad cheques. He travelled abroad with 80 million francs in his pocket.

In his memoirs, Elie Wiesel recounted one of his memories, more or less imaginary as usual, involving one of his co-religionists. This is how he concluded his anecdote: "The guy, who travelled all over the world with false passports, was a criminal wanted by Interpol; he had just stolen diamonds which, thanks to me, were going to be returned to their owner." In passing, Elie Wiesel confessed a little secret in our ear: "Professional ethics, duties and obligations... In Yiddish, this sounds less convincing than in French[210]."

The receiving of stolen diamonds and jewellery was apparently also a long tradition. Thus we see that the Sephardim could compete with the Ashkenazi Jews. In December 1994, Maurice Joffo, brother of Joseph, the author of the famous *best-seller A Sack of Marbles*, which tells the story of the lives of two Jewish children during the Occupation, was arrested in front of his sumptuous restaurant on Place Victor-Hugo in the 16th arrondissement of Paris. He was arrested just as he was getting into his Mercedes with his wife and two gypsies from whom he had just bought 110,000 francs worth of stolen jewellery. Later, the police discovered half a kilo of stolen jewellery in his home, which was only a fraction of the loot from the robberies perpetrated by his gangs of gypsies. They would show up at the homes of elderly people disguised as employees of the gas or electricity company. The Joffo

---

[210] Elie Wiesel, *Mémoires, Tome I*, Le Seuil, 1994, p. 321-325.

treasure, scattered in various bank vaults in Geneva, was estimated at 20 million francs. The arrest of his brother was very bad for Joseph, as it coincided with the publication of his new novel, which dealt with humanity without borders and tolerance. Maurice was sentenced to the maximum penalty: seven years in prison, one year suspended and a million franc fine.

Alexandre Dumas had already evoked the role of Jewish diamantaires and jewellers in some of his novels: "Well then, go to the first goldsmith you meet and sell that diamond for whatever price he gives you; no matter how Jewish he is, you will always find eight hundred pistoles." (*The Three Musketeers, 1844*). And also: "On reaching Leghorn he went in search of a Jew, and sold him four of his smallest diamonds, for five thousand francs each. The (Jewish) merchant should have inquired how a sailor could possess such jewels, but he was very careful not to do so, since he earned a thousand francs on each one." (*The Count of Monte Cristo, 1845*).

South Africa was also the site of some notorious score-settling. In October 1999, the body of Shai Avishar, 36, was found in a grave near Johannesburg. The man had been in contact with an Israeli mafia figure, Yossi Harari, and police suspected a settling of scores in the illegal world of diamond, arms and drug trafficking. The network operated in Johannesburg, Cape Town and Durban, according to the *Jewish Bulletin of Northern California*.

Some time later, one Lior Saad, a member of the Israeli mafia, was charged with the murder of Shai Avishar. In November 2003, Lior Saad was the victim of an attempted murder when the van transporting him to court was machine-gunned by the rear passenger of a motorbike, leaving 18 bullet holes and another prisoner dead in his place.

Avishar's wife Hazel Crane was also gunned down in her Mercedes on her way to court to testify against the diamond dealers accused of her husband's murder. Two other witnesses had been liquidated shortly before by Israeli gangsters. Now, it turned out that Avishar and Hazel Crane were two close friends of Winnie Mandela, the former wife of the South African president. It turned out that Hazel Crane worked for Sol [Solomon] Kerzner, the flamboyant billionaire who owned the gigantic Sun City hotel-casino and entertainment complex set up in 1979 in South Africa and where many prostitutes also worked. Nelson Mandela, the new president of South Africa, after years in prison and the icon of democrats around the world, was also on very good terms with Sol Kerzner. In 1992, Kerzner had built Lost City, a pharaonic and extravagant complex with its tropical forest, artificial waterfalls and thousands of slot machines.

In September 2005, also in Johannesburg, one of the most notorious Jewish gangsters, Brett Kebble, was murdered in his luxury Mercedes. He was a member of Nelson Mandela's ANC (African National Congress) and financed the organisation to the tune of millions of rands. After his assassination, black children's unions had called for prayers for him.

Paramilitary militias in Colombia

In the United States in the 1970s, the situation had only worsened since the Jewish gangsters had been joined by their Israeli counterparts. Several hundred of them had settled in California at that time. They were, as Jacques Derogy wrote, "fed up with dealing heroin in grams in Israel, when in the USA they were offered the possibility of dealing in kilos[211]." Yossef Zakharia was the biggest trafficker at the time. He organised the trafficking of Colombian cocaine throughout the territory.

With the arrival of the "New Russians" in the 1990s, things did not improve. In September 1994, a report submitted to the US government denounced the "Cocaine Triangle", whose three sides were the Colombian drug lords, the Jews and Israelis, who were in charge of laundering, and the "Russian" mafia, which was in charge of security. A 1997 report by the *Center for Strategic International Studies* (CSIS) also established the links between "Russian" organised crime and the Colombian drug cartels in Miami[212].

The fact is that there was indeed a strong Israeli presence in Colombia. It seems that Israelis working in the country were involved with the government in both the fight against the extreme left-wing guerrillas and the drug cartels. Israel was the main supplier of weapons used against the Marxist guerrillas of the FARC (Revolutionary Armed Forces of Colombia) and the ELN (National Liberation Army). The Israelis also supplied light weapons, drones, surveillance and communication systems, as well as special bombs to destroy coca plantations. Officially, they were also in charge of training the Colombian government's anti-terrorist formations. Colombia also had excellent trade relations with Israel. In April 1988, Israel had bought two million tons of Colombian coal in exchange for Colombia's purchase of 14 Israeli Kfirfighter planes.

---

[211] Jacques Derogy, *Israel Connection*, Plon, 1980, p. 193.
[212] Israeli daily newspaper *Maariv*, 2 September 1994

In reality, it was not until the 1970s that ties between the countries of the region and the State of Israel were forged. General Zeevi, a friend of the Israeli mafia, had offered his services as an advisor in the fight against terrorism to all the South American states. He was accompanied by the man who was supposed to finance these operations: Betsalel Mizrahi, the Israeli mafia's chief financier. General Zeevi himself was a drug trafficker, as Jacques Derogy noted: 'The Israeli police intelligence chief, Samy Nahmias, had already noticed that Betsalel Mizrahi made dozens of trips abroad intermittently, and that on his return he was always met by General Zeevi at Ben-Gurion airport, as well as by the director of the El Al company's VIP service, Mike Pinhasi. This meant that luggage was not checked[213]."

In 1987, banana producers seeking to combat the Marxist guerrillas who were extorting them and attacking their plantations had recruited former Israeli reserve colonel Yair Klein and mercenaries from his security company Hod He'hanitin (Spearhead Ltd.). Colombian President Virgilio Barco Vargas had given financial support to the operation at the instigation of the Minister of Justice, José Manuel Carrizosa. It should be noted that he was also the president of the Association of Banana Producers and was directly linked to the large fruit groups in the United States.

Carrizosa first contacted Lieutenant-Colonel Yitzhak "Mariot" Shoshani, who was the head of ISREX, a company that had been supplying military technology to Colombia for years. He advised the recruitment of Yair Klein, a former paratrooper who had left the Israeli army in 1985 to set up a mercenary company. Klein and his men formed the militias for the large landowners who were to form the basis of the paramilitary groups AUC (Autodefensas Unidas de Colombia). The wars between these groups and the Marxist guerrillas caused the deaths of tens of thousands of civilians over the years.

Yair Klein soon began to work for the drug traffickers who fought relentlessly for control of certain production areas. The AUC's growing involvement in the drug trade was to exasperate Washington, especially as the militias were not above attacking the Drug Enforcement Agency (DEA) agents mobilised there. However, while many AUC leaders were wanted by the United States for drug trafficking or serious crimes and abuses, some benefited, like their Salvadoran and Nicaraguan counterparts, from near impunity in Florida or Texas, where they had their secondary residences.

From strategic advisor to the Colombian government, Yair Klein

---

[213] Jacques Derogy, *Israel Connection*, Plon, 1980, p. 140–142.

had become the head of a criminal gang. In 1988, the Colombian justice ministry claimed that Klein was one of four Israelis hired by the drug lord Gonzalo Rodríguez Gacha, nicknamed 'El Mexicano'. El Mexicano had a reputation as one of Medellín's most violent drug barons. One of his favourite techniques was called "the Moshe Dayan method", which he said he had learned from an Israeli commando: it consisted of inserting a small piece of sharp flint under a prisoner's eyelid. The pain is apparently so extreme and unbearable that the prisoner goes mad before his eye is lacerated.

Yair Klein later admitted in an Israeli court to having trained Rodriguez Gacha's troops in Puerto Bocaya in 1988. When the army searched Rodríguez Gacha's house, they found a stock of 200 Israeli machine guns. However, these weapons were part of an official shipment from the Israeli government that Klein had diverted. Numerous documents found there also attested to Klein's role as a trainer of "sicarios" of all ages. In 1989, El Mexicano was killed during a shootout with the Colombian army and Klein then went into the service of another famous drug lord of the Medellín cartel, Pablo Emilio Escobar Gaviria, who had also surrounded himself with several Israeli advisors, such as Lieutenant-Colonel Yitzhak Shashono, and 3,000 hitmen. In Medellín in 1992, no fewer than 6662 people died in armed clashes, to which must be added 1292 unidentified corpses and 967 missing inhabitants. The Cali cartel and the Medellín cartel were at that time the two largest Colombian drug cartels. The death of Pablo Escobar, killed by police in December 1993, had weakened the Medellín cartel, so that the Cali cartel now distributed 80 per cent of the world's cocaine and a third of the world's heroin, generating $25 billion a year in the US alone[214].

Klein was arrested in Israel in 1990, and finally appeared in court, accused of illegally exporting arms and military technological equipment to Colombian terrorist groups, but was only sentenced to a ridiculous penalty: one year in prison and a fine of $13,400. The new Colombian government then issued an international arrest warrant for him for having formed the illegal paramilitary groups.

After his release from prison, Yair Klein used his good contacts with former Rhodesian and South African officers to work in Sierra Leone. In 1999, he was interrogated by the army while supplying arms to Johnny Koroma's rebels and Charles Taylor's Liberian rebels, two warlords known for their sadistic violence and abuses against the

---

[214] Abraham Majuat was a capo of the Medellín cartel. He owned a ranch near Medellín where 4.5 tons of cocaine were found in 1989.

population²¹⁵. Released after 16 months in prison, Klein took refuge in Israel, which refused to extradite him to Colombia. He stated on Israeli television that he had worked for the Colombian government, had done nothing wrong and was willing to return to Colombia to help train the country's security forces in their fight against the FARC. Klein had also travelled several times to London and the United States without ever being bothered by the British and US police, despite being wanted by Interpol.

In the spring of 2007, *Agence France Press* reported that Colombia had issued another international arrest warrant for several Israelis: Yair Klein, Melnik Ferry and Tzedaka Abraham were accused of atrocities against civilian populations. The information, however, was not reported again in the French media.

On 27 August 2007, Klein was finally arrested in Russia, where his society was very active, as he was preparing to embark on a false passport to Tel Aviv. He was to be extradited to Colombia. Colombian Vice-President Francisco Santos said: "We want Klein to be handed over to us so that he can rot in jail as punishment for all the evil he did to our country."

But Israeli involvement in Colombia did not end with Klein's escape. In an article published on 10 August 2007 by the newspaper *Semana*, Colombian Defence Minister Juan Manuel Santos acknowledged that Bogotá had discreetly recruited former Israeli army officers to train members of the local police force to fight the FARC guerrillas. The team of military advisors—consisting of three former generals, a non-commissioned officer, an Israeli-Argentine officer and three interpreters—had been recruited under a $10 million contract. The Israeli mercenaries were specialists in prisoner interrogation and came to bring their expertise in "special interrogation techniques". For Laude Fernández, a Colombian national security expert, "it would have been better to rely on the British, who have a good intelligence system and better human rights standards" (Diario *Semana*, 4 August 2007). However, for Sergio Jaramillo, deputy defence minister, Israeli help was valuable: "They are a kind of psychoanalyst. They ask us the questions [that we would not have thought of] and they help us to see all the problems we have that we don't see" (*Ynet News*, 10 August 2007)²¹⁶.

---

²¹⁵ In the film *Lord of War* (2005), we see the arms dealer in Colombia, where he gets paid in cocaine, and then in Liberia, where he gets paid in diamonds, in *"blood diamonds"*.
²¹⁶ www.semana.com/nacion/articulo/de-tel-aviv-tolemaida/87449-3/

But even so, the gangsters continued to sell arms to Marxist guerrillas in Colombia and the Andean region. In 1998, "Ukrainian" mafiosi operating from Tel-Aviv and Kiev had participated in the chartering of a shipment of ten thousand AK-47 assault rifles for the Revolutionary Armed Forces of Colombia through a Peruvian spy, a certain Vladimir Montesinos. In May 1999, 3000 Kalachnikovs and 5 million bullets from Nicaragua had been sent by two Israelis to a Colombian armed group considered by the US as a "terrorist" group. In May 2000, the Colombian police arrested two Israelis who were trying to clandestinely sell more than 50,000 weapons of all kinds to the guerrillas[217].

Likewise, this Jewish mafia continued its fruitful collaboration with the Colombian drug cartels. We saw earlier the case of Ludwig Fainberg, who had supplied missiles, helicopters, and almost a Soviet submarine to the drug cartels.

On 15 May 2007, the newspaper *Le Monde* published an article entitled *Mafiapulco*, about the mafia in Mexico, especially in Acapulco. The city was a strategic site for importing cocaine from Colombia. Seven murders were registered every day. At the end of January 2006, municipal police had intercepted a convoy of drug traffickers in a popular neighbourhood of the city. The shootout had lasted twenty minutes and left several dead. A few months later, a video revealed that police officers, paid by a rival cartel, had killed the wounded "narcos" in cold blood. The drug traffickers subsequently took revenge on the four policemen responsible, kidnapping and beheading them. Their heads were found placed in front of an official building with an avenging message.

This low- to medium-intensity warfare is said to have resulted in some 9,000 deaths since 2001, and more than 800 this year. Equipped with state-of-the-art equipment, the drug traffickers could listen to and even threaten the police on the radio frequencies they used. They also had rifles reserved for military forces and ammunition capable of penetrating bulletproof vests, as well as rocket launchers and surface-to-air missiles to shoot down planes and helicopters.

The Mexican government did, however, manage to strike some good blows against the narcos, especially the Gulf cartel. In April, it managed to arrest one of its most dangerous operators, Eleazar Medina, and dismantled a "cell" that transported drugs and illegal immigrants to the United States. That cartel had prevailed over its main rival, the

---

[217]David Marcus Katz was another important arms dealer in Central America in the 1980s.

Sinaloa cartel, led by a certain Chapo Guzman, and "based in the vast northern state of Tamaulipas[218]."

The article in *Le Monde* by Joëlle Stolz did not provide any further details about this Guzmán. Let us simply note that "Guzmán" was also the surname of the leader of the Shining Path, a Maoist-leaning Marxist guerrilla group that had been operating in Peru since 1980, and which was also known for its abuses and atrocities against the civilian population. The Shining Path guerrillas had caused the deaths of more than 30,000 people. Its leader, Abimael Guzman, was sentenced by a military court in 1992 to life imprisonment.

Hashish, cocaine, heroin

Jewish traders have always played a prominent role in international trade. We come across them in the drug trade as well as in the textile, wheat, aluminium and rubber trades. Here are a few cases in which major international traffickers were involved, insofar as the names of the culprits were quoted in the newspapers, which is far from always the case.

In April 2008, the weekly *Rivarol* reported, for example, on an Israeli rabbi named Simha Ashlag. The man was intercepted with his secretary at Roissy airport on his arrival from Turkey. The police had found a "relatively large quantity of drugs" in his luggage. *Actualité juive* of 10 April presented the rabbi as "a guru surrounded by fanatics who had him as a model."

The *Washington Times* of 26 June 2005 published an article on Zvi Heifetz, 48, Israel's ambassador to England and close to Russian oligarch Vladimir Gusinsky. His daughter Lee had been arrested in 2003 in Peru with several kilos of cocaine (*"ten pounds"*) and released after only eighteen months of detention. It should be borne in mind that Peruvian President Alejandro Toledo had married a Belgian citizen of Jewish origin, Eliane Karp, and that his affinities with the ambassador might have favoured an early release.

In April 2002, we learned that Mafia groups in the North Hollywood district of Los Angeles and the Brighton Beach neighbourhood of New York had negotiated an alliance with Mexico's

---

[218] In May 2008, the French press reported the fate of a French woman, Florence Cassez, imprisoned in Mexico since 2005 and sentenced to a heavy prison sentence for kidnapping and arms trafficking. She claimed her innocence, stating that she had never been aware of the activities of her ex-boyfriend, Israel Vallarta, responsible for several kidnappings and head of the "Zodiaco" gang.

Tijuana cartel and Colombian traffickers to distribute tons of cocaine in North America.

In May 2000, Colombian authorities had arrested four Israelis for arms trafficking: Itzik Richter, Ofer Zismanovich, David Birnbaum and Yaron Cohen were doing business with the Cali cartel. They were charged with counterfeiting dollars. A few weeks earlier, another Israeli, Amos Shimoni, had been arrested in Panama on the same charges.

On 17 October 2001, *Los Angeles Time* reported the arrest of a drug dealer: Alen Amor, an Israeli citizen. The police had found several kilos of marijuana, cocaine and heroin at his home.

Two months later, on 26 November 2001, two Israeli women were arrested at Roissy airport. Ortal Biton, 22, and Rozi Benaim, 21, were coming from Bogota. When their backpacks were searched, customs officers discovered no less than nine kilos of cocaine. The two "mules" were facing a prison sentence of ten years, but surprisingly, the examining magistrate decided not to order them to be remanded in custody. The magistrate, Jocelyne Lambert, contacted by telephone by the *France-soir journalist*, did not "wish to comment on her decision". As expected, the two young women did not appear before the examining magistrate on 3 December 2001[219].

Some traffickers also knew how to thrive on 'soft drugs', as the judicial chronicle showed. Cannabis could be a very lucrative business, provided they worked with large quantities. On 9 June 2000, after eleven years on the run, Steven Wolosky, 50, was arrested in California. His partner, Mark Stephen Gayer, 50, was arrested in New Mexico. The two men, among the most wanted in the country, were accused of smuggling more than four hundred tons of hashish and marijuana into the country from Colombia and Thailand with their fishing boats. Their accomplice, Robert Singer, was in charge of road transport across US territory. Eleven members of the network had been arrested. In March 1998, the two men had faked their accidental death in a boating accident off the coast of California.

Here is the case of Howard Marks, better known as Mr. Nice, who was a very important marijuana dealer in the 1980s. He was born in England and educated in London. He had also served seven years in prison in Indiana, USA. On his release from prison, in July 2000, he published an autobiographical book in which he championed the legalisation of cannabis. He was at the origin of the legalisation movement in England. The US Drug Enforcement Agency in Miami had dubbed him the "Marco Polo of drug trafficking". His daughter

---

[219]*France-soir*, 6 December 2001. Archives of Emmanuel Ratier.

lived in Israel (*The Guardian*, London, 26 April 1995).

In the Israeli daily *Haaretz, dated* 10 May 2002, we read the news that an Indian court had just acquitted two Israeli women. Ravi Shriki and Berta Cohen had been arrested a year earlier with two and a half kilos of cannabis. The two women had pleaded their innocence, claiming that the backpacks did not belong to them, but were nonetheless sentenced to a heavy penalty before finally being released. Their lawyer stated that the Indian authorities had probably heeded the thunderous media hype orchestrated in the US and Israel to demand the release of the two "innocent" women.

India was a popular destination for young Israelis. In January 2003, Daisy Angus, a 22-year-old Englishwoman, had been released from an Indian prison. She had been detained in Mumbai six weeks earlier after agreeing to carry the belongings of her Israeli friend Yoran Kadesh, 37, whose backpack had apparently broken. Indian customs officials found two kilos of hashish in the young woman's suitcase, terrified by the situation. Fortunately for her, her parents, who had volunteered in Calcutta with Mother Teresa, managed to convince the Indian administration of the scheme." A powerful Israeli mafia controls most of this traffic," we read in the *Guardian*.

In 1999, the Thai authorities captured Peres Esat, an Israeli guilty of murdering one of his co-religionists, Shimon Benhamo, in Bangkok. Another Israeli citizen, Shimon Ofer Skriki, had also been arrested. The criminals were at odds with each other over a shipment of cocaine from Brazil. That same year in Bangkok, four other Israelis had been sentenced to life imprisonment for heroin trafficking.

In Canada, Rabbi Eli Gotteman, who had been voted "rabbi of the year" in 1999, was indicted for trafficking cocaine and marijuana from the Montreal prison where he cared for Jewish prisoners.

Rabbi Meyer Krentzman, the former director of the Canadian Jewish National Fund, had already been arrested in Montreal in 1994 for heroin and cocaine trafficking. One of his associates, Andor Galandauer, of the Beth Zion Congregation and also a member of the Jewish Defence League, was arrested at the same time.

On 2 December 1993, Vladimir Beigelman, a Brooklyn-based cocaine dealer, was killed at the wheel of his van: two shots to the head.

In 1995, Norman Max Rosemblum, a cocaine dealer who worked, according to the journalist, "on behalf of traffickers associated with the Italian mafia", was sentenced to 13 years in prison in Canada. He had been arrested when he was about to deliver 558 kilos of cocaine to Hells Angels in England. CCTV footage from cameras on his boat showed a jubilant and triumphant Rosemblum after he had taken possession of the drugs in Colombia. His ex-wife, Wanda Halpert, had been arrested the previous year in British Colombia in a case involving the trafficking of 15 tonnes of hashish. Rosemblum had already been imprisoned several times, in Bordeaux and London, for drug trafficking and also for domestic violence. In 1994, he had fractured his wife's nose with a headbutt.

In 1991, Uri Mizraci, an Israeli hashish and heroin trafficker, was assassinated in Manhattan. That same year, Panama's president, Manuel Noriega, had been overthrown by a US military intervention on the pretext that he favoured drug trafficking to the US. Noriega's right-hand man was a Mossad agent named Mikhail Harari, a former Israeli army general who had become the head of the Panamanian president's security services. According to *Jewish Week*, Panama was then the Switzerland of the Caribbean, and an important financial centre for Israeli businessmen. Steven Kalish (alias Frank Brown), was another Noriega associate. In the 1960s, he had imported tons of Colombian marijuana from San Francisco into the United States, managing all the logistics. He used to drive around in a Ferrari.

In 1994, a bomb exploded on a Panamanian plane killing 21 people, including 12 Jews. The target of the bombing was probably Saul Schwartz, a passenger who was under an international arrest warrant issued by the Italian judiciary. The man was wanted for his links to the Medellín cartel. The media preferred to speak of an anti-Semitic act.

In 1990, Israeli Amiram Nir was killed in a mysterious plane crash in Mexico while visiting a large plantation owned by Avraham Cohen and "Swiss" billionaire Nessim Gaon, whom we have already featured in previous pages. The *Jerusalem Post* reported that Amiram Nir was negotiating a major Israeli arms sale to local drug traffickers, via Vera Cruz.

Again in 1990, Linda Leary, former president of the National Council of Jewish Women, was extradited from Austria to Indianapolis in the United States. Thirty-one other people, including her two sons, Paul and Richard Heilbrun, were accused of having imported tons of marijuana into the United States. Linda Leary pleaded guilty. She had opened bank accounts in the tax haven of the Cayman Islands.

In the 1980s, in the United States, one Israel Abel was the head of a network trafficking cocaine imported from Colombia. Israel Abel had imported no less than three tons to Miami before leaving the business to enjoy a golden retirement in Costa Rica. He had been living there for five years, but federal agents had not dropped the baton and were still after him. In 1992, he was captured and extradited to the US, where he was sentenced to life in prison. (*Pittsburgh Post-Gazette*, 24 November 1998).

Max Mermelstein was at the time the "godfather of cocaine". The man, married to a Colombian woman, had imported at least 56 tons of cocaine into the United States between 1978 and 1985 and was involved in numerous homicide cases on the West Coast. He had for several years imported three-quarters of the cocaine entering the US (*Los Angeles Times*, 6 July 1987). On 5 June 1985, he was finally stopped at the wheel of his Jaguar by FBI agents. On the seat of his car was a handgun, and in his flat the cops found $250,000 in cash and 25 firearms. To save his own head, Mermelstein agreed to cooperate with the authorities. His testimony implicated the heads of the Medellín cartel, the Ochoa family and Pablo Escobar.

In December 1998, a drug trafficking network was dismantled in Paris. Here is what you could read in the pages of *Le Parisien*: "Cocaine, heroin and hashish. You can find it all in the network of dealers in the Sentier in Paris. Their clients are now suffering from abstinence... Eleven people have just been charged and seven convicted in Reims. The trap began to close on them at the beginning of 1987 with the arrest of Jean-Claude Joukoff in Troyes, when he was caught with a stolen Land Rover equipped for drug transport. By tracing the criminal network and thanks to the seizure of 58 kilos of cannabis in another vehicle, the police were able to track down the Hazan brothers. At *Chez Joseph*, in the 11th arrondissement, they discovered 130,000 francs in cash. Marcel had already been convicted in 1986 in Los Angeles for drug trafficking. Among the others arrested were Francis Obadia, David Ben David, Anna Karamanouguian, a former prostitute from Marseille, and Nadi Hafiza. The latter was an Afghan woman who had already been accused in another case of drug trafficking and had just been released four days earlier after paying a bail of 200,000 francs when the police arrested her again... Information from the US drug squad led to her arrest[220]."

Sephardic Jews were often the allies of Israeli traffickers, so they were heavily represented in the high-level drug trade." There are very few Sephardim who are consumers or small street dealers—a breeding

---

[220] *Le Parisien* of 12 December 1998, files by Emmanuel Ratier. There are indeed Jews in Afghanistan, just as there are Jews in Georgia, in Chechnya, in Alaska and all over the world, since their mission is to settle all over the face of the earth and "gather the divine sparks scattered in the four corners of the world" (read *Psychoanalysis of Judaism*).

ground for North Africans and Africans—but there are many large, highly organised dealers who sell very good quality heroin. The 'head offices' of these networks are almost all in the Faubourg Montmartre district', wrote the Jewish monthly *Passages* in June 1989.

The weekly *Actualité juive* of 23 July 1992 confirmed the establishment of Jewish traffickers in the capital: 'A veritable small Israeli mafia has formed in Paris over the last fifteen years. Until recently, all the small-scale drug trafficking, from the Place de la République to the Richelieu-Drouot crossroads, was in the hands of Israeli émigrés or 'tourists'."

In December 1986, small articles appeared in the French press reporting that the Italian judge Giovani Falcone had travelled from Palermo to Israel "to investigate the drug trafficking network nicknamed "French Connection". He was to interrogate in Tel Aviv two men arrested in 1985 in Miami, as well as the commander of a ship carrying eight kilos of heroin. The investigation had implicated about twenty people operating between Sicily, Marseilles and the United States."

In 1985, an Israeli citizen named Shmuel Targan was arrested in New York for trafficking cocaine and heroin. His shoe shop was in fact nothing more than a front. The following year, five other Israelis were also arrested in New York for the same reason. In Los Angeles, Abraham Zarchia and Yitzhak Edvi were sentenced to ten years in prison that same year. Also in 1986, Daniel Whitman and cocaine dealer Robert Cohen were arrested for the murder of Raymond Cohen (no relation to the killer).

The weekly *L'Express* of 29 January 1982 mentioned "a powerful Israeli gang in Los Angeles", following "the double arrest of an Israeli from Los Angeles, carrying one and a half kilos of heroin, on 18 November, and of an American Jew, carrying 2.4 kilos, on 24 November at Lod airport." Jerusalem had also requested the extradition of five captured traffickers, including a 17-year-old girl, following the dismantling of a network by French police.

Traffickers did not seem to have neglected the Asian continent. In 1987, a New Zealander, Lorraine Cohen, was sentenced to death in Malaysia for heroin trafficking. Her son Aaron was sentenced to life imprisonment. Naturally, human rights organisations protested strongly. In 1987, Zvi Gafnis, involved in international cocaine trafficking, was arrested in Hong Kong. He had also smuggled counterfeit dollars into Mexico and the United States.

Evidently, the Jewish mafia does not appear in Hollywood-produced films. Once again, the preference is to project onto the Goyim the crimes for which one probably feels a little guilty. In *Scarface* (USA, 1983), for example, Al Pacino plays a Cuban criminal who rises to the top of the Miami underworld in the early 1980s through cocaine trafficking. A brief dialogue informs us that the mob boss "Tony Montana" works for is Jewish, but the scene is so furtive that few viewers can retain the information. Instead, the cruel Bolivian "boss" is played by a man with Nordic features, and some of the influential men around him are also portrayed as blond with blue eyes. The beautiful blonde women, they, invariably end up in the arms of the mobsters[221]. The film is by Brian de Palma, who dedicated it to Ben Hecht.

In *Carlito's Way (*USA, 1993), also by Brian de Palma, Al Pacino plays this time a Puerto Rican criminal whose lawyer manages to get him out of prison. He is a Jew named Kleinfeld who has gradually adopted the methods of gangsters: he uses his gun, sells cocaine, hangs out in nightclubs, knocks off other gangsters and ends up betraying his friends.

The film *Lethal Weapon* (USA, 1987) shows the methods of these horrible drug dealers very well. Two policemen—one white and one black—have to take on the job of stopping these scum. The two cops are atrociously tortured in the basement of the discotheque run by the drug dealers. But make no mistake: the bastards are Vietnam War veterans, white men with blue eyes. The poor Jews have nothing to do with it. The film is by Richard Donner.

The second part of *Lethal Weapon* (1989) is even more caricatured. The two cops, symbolising the triumphant multicultural society, are this time fighting a fearsome gang of South African drug dealers. The bastards are all white, Nordic types, frankly blond and above all horribly racist. It should be noted that Richard Donner was born with the surname Schwartzenberg. This is a piece of information that may be useful to understand the messages that his films spread.

In 1973, there were 2,000 drug addicts in Frankfurt willing to do anything to get the 500 marks needed to pay for their daily double ration. Frankfurt was the hub of heroin trafficking from Thailand and the headquarters of Yossef Amiel. Amiel was not only involved in the local market, but also sent goods to Israel. Jacques Derogy wrote: "Flight attendants, stewardesses, flight captains, sailors, security agents, models, models, students, a whole motley population, thanks to Yossef Amiel, was able to earn a lot of money without risk, often in

---

[221] On this racism, read our chapters on cinema in *Planetary Hopes* and *Psychoanalysis of Judaism*.

order to provide their own rations." How can I resist temptation?" asked an Israeli student employed as a security agent on El Al flights." Every time I carry a kilo of heroin, I earn 8,000 Marks, which is the equivalent of a whole year's salary!

Drugs were concealed in luggage, the heels of shoes, women's dusters, the crutches of wounded or disabled soldiers and, of course, in the private parts of individuals. When large quantities were involved, some customs officers were bribed to turn a blind eye and let the trafficker pass. Yossef Amiel had thus won a veritable army to his cause, with his soldiers and his staff. At his side was an individual named Avner Kedem, whose duties as security officer in the Israeli foreign ministry led him to travel regularly to Asia and Europe. He took advantage of the sacrosanct diplomatic bag to transport cocaine and heroin safely from the producer to the distributor. In 1975, Avner Kedem was arrested after a routine check of his luggage. The customs officers found 300 grams of heroin.

On 17 March 1975, six policemen broke into the building occupied by Yossef Amiel and his gang. One of the policemen was hit in the shoulder with an axe, but the traffickers were caught. Germany's largest heroin smuggling and distribution network had been dismantled. Imprisoned Yossef Amiel had managed to escape and get out of Germany, but seven of his accomplices were tried in 1976 by the Frankfurt criminal court. More than 40 kilos of heroin had been distributed." A gigantic quantity, wrote Jacques Derogy, enough to kill thousands of people and make a fortune out of thousands more." The victims were Germans and American soldiers stationed in Frankfurt, as well as women transformed into prostitutes. Nine heroin addicts had died during the week of the trial.

The court listened to recordings of the defendants' telephone conversations made by the police a few days before the arrests in which one could hear: "Those cretinous German cops will never catch us", or again: "Hey, you can make the delivery quietly. God is with us." Ten years in prison was the most severe prison sentence. After this case, the German police strengthened its vigilance and created an office in charge of "Jewish and Israeli affairs".

In those years in Frankfurt, one prostitute out of three or four wore a Star of David around her neck and spoke Hebrew. After several searches, 300 Israelis were arrested in Moselstrasse, imprisoned or expelled. But for Elie Bolkin, this police operation was only a minor mishap. Elie Bolkin, the perpetrator of two murders, had been released for lack of evidence." Driving around at the wheel of a white Mercedes, surrounded by beautiful German and Israeli women," he declared, feigning virtuous indignation: "Pimp, me? Drug dealer, me? That's all just stories! I'm a restaurant owner! I'm an honest businessman! [222]"

Ecstasy trafficking: 100% Kasher[223]

The ecstasy market was booming in the 1990s, popularised by the wave of electronic techno music. Festivals or *"free parties"* or *"raves"*, which could gather tens of thousands of young people, mostly European, constituted a niche of potential consumers likely to enrich the racketeers.

Big organised crime had "taken control of the drugs of the *free parties*", we read in the newspaper *Libération* of 2 August 2001. According to the National Office for drugs and drug addicts (France), a *"free party"* of 30,000 people generated between 4 and 5 million francs in 48 hours, two thirds of which were from the sale of ecstasy. On 23 July 2001, we read in the same newspaper: "The [Israeli] mafia has taken back the synthetic drugs market." The same observation was made in *Le Figaro* on 11 August 2001: "Ecstasy is the preserve of the Israeli organised crime world."

Israeli organised crime effectively had a monopoly on the distribution of ecstasy in the world. Belgium played an important role, although the Belgians had nothing to do with it. On 11 March 2004, 100,000 ecstasy pills were discovered in Malines, in a car park at the entrance of the motorway. The authorities arrested five people, two of them from Antwerp, the other three from the Netherlands. The other three were from the Netherlands. A few days later, on 18 March 2004, a record seizure of raw materials for the manufacture of 75 to 100 million ecstasy tablets and 400,000 ready-made tablets took place in Maasmechelen.

On 17 April 2004, at Zaventem airport, the Brussels-Asse District Court Service arrested a German woman of Nigerian origin living in Amsterdam who was carrying 10,000 XTC pills in her luggage. On 29 April, one million pills were seized in Knokke-Heist. A fully equipped pill manufacturing laboratory had been discovered during the operation, and eight people were arrested. On 13 July 2004, another record seizure of three million ecstasy pills took place. Four persons from the Antwerp region were arrested. Another member of the gang had been

---

[222] Jacques Derogy, *Israel Connection*, Plon, 1980, p. 173–182.
[223] "Correct" or "proper" to be consumed, i.e. it complies with the precepts of the Jewish religion. The *kosher* seal is a quality seal that carries a tax for the rabbis.

apprehended at the end of June in Australia, where a pill could be sold for up to 40 euros, while in Belgium the price of an XTC pill was around four euros.

On 22 April 2004, the former Israeli Minister of Energy and Infrastructure, Dr Gonen Segev, who had come from the Netherlands, was arrested by customs officers at Ben-Gurion airport in Tel-Aviv: his suitcase contained 25,000 ecstasy pills (about five kilos). He was charged along with his accomplices, Moshe Verner and Ariel Friedman.

The Netherlands was the world's largest producer of ecstasy. The drug was produced in dozens of clandestine laboratories. At the head of this traffic were again Israeli traffickers linked to various 'Russian' mafias who organised the networks that supplied Europe and the United States.

Thirty-year-old Itzhak Abergil was a major international trafficker. His organisation operated from the Belgian port of Antwerp to deploy a whole range of criminal activities: diamond theft, money laundering and ecstasy trafficking." A man like Itzhak Abergil is a man of unbounded brutality, we read in an article in the *Courier international* of 13 January 2005. Any show of competence, mistake or wrong word on the part of his accomplices is punished with blood. Itzahk Abergil is therefore feared by everyone, enemies and friends alike. He knows how to guard his reputation." On 9 September 2004, Itzhak Abergil was finally arrested in the Netherlands. The Amberian judiciary immediately requested his extradition. A few weeks later, he was released by a Dutch judge due to a "procedural error" and flew quietly to Israel. He was in contact with an important member of the Las Vegas underworld, one Gabriel Ben Harosh, 39, a Jew originally from Morocco who thrived on extortion and ecstasy trafficking and had major interests in one of Israel's largest construction companies. Ben Harosh had been apprehended in Canada and was pending extradition to the United States. Las Vegas police were also pursuing his right-hand man, 32-year-old Hai Waknine.

The Israeli daily *Haaretz* of 6 April 2003 confirmed the role of "Israeli" criminals: "Israel is the centre of operations for ecstasy trafficking, according to a document published by the US State Department. According to an official document, in recent years, organised crime in Israel has taken control of drug distribution in Europe in collaboration with criminal organisations in Russia. The document reveals that Israeli criminal groups have the upper hand in the ecstasy trade in North America. Throughout the 2000s, 80 per cent of the ecstasy sold in the United States came from the Netherlands, which was the largest production centre. The State Department is convinced that Israeli organisations are linked to laboratories in the Netherlands and are responsible for worldwide distribution." The article was by Nathan Guttman.

In October 1999, the Australian federal police announced the seizure of 12 kilos of ecstasy, equivalent to 45,000 pills. The operation had taken place in June, but at the request of the Belgian authorities the information had been kept secret. Thanks to this secrecy, two weeks after the Australian raid, 58 kilos were discovered in Germany. Along with the two individuals apprehended in Belgium, 350,000 ecstasy pills were seized. The network, which always used the ruse of shipping with sports equipment, had shipped 45 cartons to the United States. Each carton weighed five kilos, so that 225 kilos of ecstasy (i.e. more than 800,000 tablets) had crossed the US border.

Right after this major operation, Belgian investigators and their Dutch colleagues arrested the mastermind of this international network in the Netherlands. The investigation led to the discovery of those responsible, whom no one had expected: young Hasidic Jews. Sean Erez, a 30-year-old Israeli, was arrested in Amsterdam following an extradition request from the United States. Sean Erez was also a Canadian citizen. Together with his partner, Diana Reicherter, the two were accused by US police of distributing more than one million pills in the US. The five other individuals apprehended by the police were young orthodox Jews who served as "mules" to pass through customs. For a while, the customs officers were not suspicious of these religious Jews in black kaftans, hats and papillotes. Each could carry between 35,000 and 50,000 pills per trip. These "mules", who shuttled back and forth between Europe and the United States, were paid 1500 dollars each way. And for each new recruit they got, they received 200 dollars.

At Paris' Orly airport in April 1999, police arrested a young Hasidic Jewish couple from New Jersey carrying 80,000 ecstasy pills. A few days later, Canadian customs officers arrested a young orthodox woman from New York in Montreal with 45,000 "superman" pills hidden in her suitcase. In fact, the pills often bore various symbols: an elephant, the yin-yang, the eurodollar. The "Superman" was well chosen, as the superhero was a creation of Jewish cartoonists[224].

---

[224] On Superman read *Jewish Fanaticism*. Hasidic Jews could embark on other fruitful ventures. In March 2001, according to the *Haaretz newspaper,* 14 members of the ultra-orthodox community of Kirpas Joel, 60 kilometres northwest of New York, were indicted for fraudulent cheque fraud and insurance fraud through false death declarations. Mordechai Samet, their boss, had transferred millions of dollars into

In October 1999, six Israelis were arrested in New York: Igal Malka, Yariv Azulay, Oshri Ganchrski, Eyal Levy, Robert Levy and Oshri Amar. 300,000 ecstasy pills were seized. Oshri Amar imported the drug from Belgian and Dutch laboratories and flooded the territory from California to Ohio, Florida, Massachusetts, Pennsylvania and New York. Police also dismantled a production laboratory where they found weapons and explosives.

In April 2000, another 25 people were arrested. Their leader was Jacob Orgad, 45, an Israeli living in Los Angeles. His accomplices seemed to be present in all major American cities, noted the *Jerusalem Post* on 15 June 2000. Jacob Orgad, nicknamed "Cookie", had started his career as a supplier of drugs and women to a luxury Hollywood prostitution ring. He then turned to ecstasy trafficking, eventually dominating the Los Angeles market. In April 2000, he was arrested in New York along with his partner, Shimon Levita, a New York yeshiva student. Federal agents had intercepted two packages filled with ecstasy. The recipients, Yaniv Yona and Ereza Abutbul, both Israelis, were also arrested.

Apparently, ecstasy trafficking was not the only speciality of Hasidic Jews: the *Russian Journal* of 15 May 2000 reported that an Orthodox Jew of Russian origin, Mark Simon, had been found shot and riddled with bullets: he was implicated in a case of credit card fraud. In September 2000, the same newspaper reported that Japanese police had arrested another Israeli, David Biton, who was accused of smuggling 25,000 pills into the country.

The *Associated Press* confirmed on 23 May 2001 that the Israeli crime syndicate was indeed the main source of ecstasy trafficking in the United States. The *Jerusalem Post* of 2 August 2001 reported that 17 Israelis had been arrested in May in Spain and the United States. The investigation had led to Oded Tuito, who was indicted in Barcelona. Three other Israelis, Eitan and Erez Elkayam and Yossif Hotvashvili, were arrested in Barcelona after several jewellery store robberies, which led to the arrest of Michel Elkayam and Simon Itach, their lieutenants. Oded Tuito, alias "Fat Man", was reportedly very friendly and spoke several languages. He was also one of those big international

---

offshore accounts. In 1998, Rabbi Joseph Prushinovski was arrested in Israel. He had been wanted for ten years by the FBI, as well as by the Canadian and Dutch police and Scotland Yard for a series of bank and insurance scams that were used to finance his community, the *Hasidic Tasch*. 200 million dollars had gone up in smoke. In 1981, he had already been sentenced to three years in prison for another scam. He then moved to Canada to continue his scams by telephone, fax and telex.

traffickers, as reported in the newspapers. According to the *New York Post* of 25 May 2001, 44-year-old Oded Tuito also used young Hasidic Jews in orthodox dress to cross borders. On 27 June 2001, Tuito was sentenced to 17 years in prison for distributing hundreds of thousands of ecstasy pills. He died of a heart attack in Brooklyn prison on 20 June 2004.

Tuito's arrest did not stop the traffic, as the *Jerusalem Post* of 20 July 2001 reported that two Israeli citizens had been arrested in Manhattan. The police had discovered more than one million ecstasy pills, the largest ever seizure by the NYPD. David Roash, 25, and Israel Ashkenazi, 28, were both based in Tel Aviv.

In November 2001, during their trial in Stanmore, USA, Philipp Lyons and his accomplice Abraham Israel, 31, pleaded guilty to heroin and ecstasy trafficking and money laundering. The money was sent to Spain (*Totally Jewish* of 26 November 2001).

A week earlier, German police dismantled another international network. Two Israelis, Uzi Guttman, 55, and Yosef Raphaelovitz, 41, were arrested in the port of Hamburg while unloading a truck containing 1.5 million ecstasy pills. The pills were hidden in containers of artificial flowers. The Dutch driver had been arrested with them (*Jerusalem Post*, 22 November 2001). At almost the same time, Australian police arrested Elyakim Yacov al-Sheikh, 37, a Dutch resident, and Dror Pachima.

At the end of July 2002, two Israeli drug traffickers were apprehended in New York. In October, six members of a drug trafficking ring had been apprehended by the New York police. The gang dealt mainly in ecstasy, but also cocaine, hashish and marijuana. Zwi Haim Harris, 30, was arrested in his flat where police found ecstasy, two guns and ammunition. The ringleader was a 37-year-old Israeli citizen named Yigal Dobakarov and in possession of 50,000 ecstasy pills worth $1.25 million. Michael Brenman, 29, confessed to being a dealer in the New York underground. Allen Agureyev, 48, and Lior Hajaj, 28, were also charged (*USA Today*, 25 October 2002).

In the same month, some fifteen people were arrested in Miami, New York and Lower Merion. The boss, Lawrence Weinmann, and his lieutenant Neil Smilen were arrested in New York just as they were taking possession of a shipment of pills from Switzerland. The two men were constantly shuttling back and forth between Miami and New York, buying large quantities of drugs which they resold to Alan Chernik, a major distributor in Maine. Stewart and Fred Cohen were also involved in the business, as was Craig Ira Yusem, an individual close to Craig Rabinowitz. Rabinowitz had murdered his wife Stefanie in April 1997.

He would try to pass her death off as an accidental fall in order to collect the insurance premium. This group was known as the "Matzoh Ball Mafia".

The *New York Post* of 10 October 2002 reported the arrest of three members of an ecstasy trafficking ring: 1.4 million pills were seized by federal agents in New York. The pills, worth $42 million on the market, were hidden in the polishing tables of diamond polishers. In August, two men were apprehended in Antwerp, Belgium: Ofer Lebar and Ofer Weizman.

The *New York Times* of 1 April 2003 reported another interesting piece of information: Natan Banda, 31, a Brooklyn-based head of an international network, had been arrested in Florida along with Nathan Weiss and fifteen others, including the Zakay brothers and Ezra Sasson. They were charged with laundering tens of millions of dollars in proceeds from the sale of ecstasy and cocaine. The traffickers were US and Israeli citizens.

The "king of ecstasy" in the following years was called El Al Yoram. This Israeli was one of the most wanted drug dealers in the world. He was accused of smuggling millions of ecstasy pills into the United States and flooding Las Vegas with his merchandise. The trafficker had left the country in 2004 to hide in Uruguay. Arrested in 2005, he managed to escape from prison. He was captured in December 2006 in Brazil, in a flat in Rio de Janeiro.

L'Arche, "the monthly magazine of French Judaism" published this information on page 6 in May 2007: "Zeev Rosenstein, the most famous godfather of the Israeli mafia, has returned to the United States to serve his twelve-year prison sentence for drug trafficking." The man had been convicted of importing 850,000 ecstasy pills into the United States. He served the rest of his sentence in Israel. The weekly *Mariane* of 18 August 2007 reported that Rosenstein's organisation was present on four continents, and used "small Latin American henchmen to distribute his synthetic drug." Rosenstein—"The Fat Man"—had been the target of seven assassination attempts in recent years, including one in the form of a bomb attack that killed three people in Tel Aviv in December 2003. Less than a month later, another drug dealer, Efraim "Freddy" Ran, 60, was fatally shot by a motorist, even though he had recently recycled his activity in the art market. Twenty years earlier, he had been part of the New York Gang, which was involved in the import-export of narcotics, extortion of funds and clandestine gambling.

This synthetic drug called ecstasy, which gives a feeling of strength and well-being for a few hours, is above all a real chemical junk. Its long-term effects are dreadful because they are irreversible: memory loss, behavioural disorders, sleep disorders, concentration disorders, brain damage in the children of drug-addicted mothers. All these complications for the victims were not important for the traffickers. With a production cost of 20 or 25 cents, a pill sold for two dollars to a dealer who in turn sold it for 5 to 10 dollars, even 30 to 40 dollars in some discotheques, the business generated enough profit to support a large family. If, in addition, the dealer owned the discotheque, then he was the "king of the night".

Diamond dealers and the laundering of dirty money

Diamond dealers in Tel-Aviv, Antwerp and New York were at the heart of the Colombian cartels' drug money laundering operations. In Manhattan, 47th Street was the heart of the diamond dealers' activity, as well as the biggest centre for laundering drug money, the Israeli daily *Maariv* reported. US police officers had great difficulty infiltrating this very closed mafia, where transactions were based on trust. Moreover, at least 50 percent of the diamond dealers were Israeli nationals.

Drug money from the Colombian cartels passed through Jewish religious institutions, yeshivas and synagogues. The donations were then returned in exchange for a percentage. The first such operation was discovered in 1984 in Manhattan. The head of the network at the time was David Va'anunu, who worked with the Colombian Cali cartel. The head of the Tifereth Yerushalayim yeshiva, Mendel Goldberger, received cash from Va'anunu every day and deposited the money in a yeshiva bank account. Despite his cries of innocence, he was sentenced to five years in prison and Va'anunu to eight years. Nine other people were implicated in the case, including Rabbi Israel Eidelman, vice-president of the yeshiva. Rabbi Abraham Lau, a leader of the Los Angeles Hasidic community was also arrested.

In the late 1980s, jewellers on 47th Street seemed to be widely implicated. Rabbi Yosef Crozer was arrested in February 1990 on his way to Brooklyn with suitcases and bags full of small notes. Each day he transported sums of up to $300,000. During his trial, he claimed that he did not know he was recycling drug money and thought it was money generated from the diamond trade. However, his cooperation with the police had led to the arrest the following month of some thirty people from the Orthodox Jewish world, notably Avraham Sharir, another pious Jew who owned a gold shop on 47th Street and who turned out to be one of the key figures in the laundering of drug money in New York.

Avraham Sharir, a 45-year-old Israeli citizen, is said to have laundered $200 million for the Cali cartel. His employees, who counted the notes, regularly had to leave the premises to air themselves out because many of the notes had been used to "snort" cocaine. He bought gold at exorbitant prices from other complicit traders, and the money was then donated to religious institutions. Sharir received a 6% commission for this work. He owned a magnificent property on Long Island and drove around in a Jaguar. Avraham Sharir had also agreed to cooperate with the FBI, thus benefiting from witness protection. He denounced Stefaphan Scorkia, who was sentenced to 660 years in prison (a very American sentence), and lived the rest of his life under a false identity to avoid reprisals.

In April 1990, a specialised police unit of 200 officers was formed to seize cash if its origin could not be proven. In the first two years, this unit, called Eldorado, had seized $60 million and arrested 120 traffickers, which probably might seem modest compared to all the trafficking.

The Hasidic community in Williamsbourg went into turmoil after the arrest of several of its members: Naftali, Miklosh, Yotzhak and Ya'akov Shlesinger, as well as Milton Jacoby had all been indicted for money laundering. US Customs had seized millions of dollars concealed in cargo containers and in the hulls of gasoline tankers. In 1990, customs officials found $14 million in cash in a shipment of cables, but it was the 234th such shipment. At Kennedy airport, they found 6.5 million in containers that were supposed to contain frozen semen. On another occasion, they found $210,000 in $100 notes concealed in bowling balls.

In May 1993, five members of these Jewish money laundering networks working for the Cali cartel were arrested by the FBI. At the head of the network was one Zion Ya'akov Evenheim, who had dual Israeli and Colombian nationality. From Cali, he coordinated the activities and supervised the transfer of funds. Raymond Shoshana, 38, Daniella Levi, 30, Binyamin Hazon, Meir Ochayon, 33, and Alex Ajami, 34, had been arrested and ten other suspects had fled to Israel. Investigators had recorded several hours of telephone conversations in Hebrew. For the translation, they turned to Neil Elefant, a New Jersey Jew who had lived in Israel. One day, he was surprised to recognise the voice of a friend among those of the traffickers: Jack Zbeida, an antique dealer from Brooklyn. Elefant then had a moral dilemma and went to his rabbi for advice, who advised him to warn Zbeida. This was a bad decision, for eventually Zbeida was apprehended and offered to cooperate with the police by denouncing Elefant, who in turn was arrested. Elefant defended himself by accusing the FBI agents of anti-Semitism. They were, he claimed, guilty of trying too hard to implicate the State of Israel in a drug trafficking case. Judge Kevin Duffy sentenced him to 18 months in prison.

Adi Tal also worked for the Cali cartel. He had already been arrested in March 1988 with eleven members of a money laundering network in the company of Nir Goldstein. They put the drug money into bank accounts, in deposits of 10,000 dollars, an amount above which a deposit in a US bank was subject to a report. They then converted the money into travellers' cheques which they sent to Panama. They used coded language. Sending a 30.4 carat diamond meant that there were thirty thousand four hundred dollars.

Rabbi Shalom Leviatan, a Chabad-Lubavitch, the main branch of Hasidic Jews[225], was the head of the Seattle network." My intentions were good," he assured the police, arguing that he believed he was helping Iranian Jews get their money out of the country. Leviatan was sentenced to 52 months in prison, but his incarceration would not serve as a punishment, as on his release he would join a gang that was later dismantled. Fortunately for him, this time he had time to flee to Israel.

In 1994, 23 people were arrested for money laundering, including New York rabbis Alexander Schwarts and Menashe Leifer, lawyers Hervey Weinig and Robert Hirsch, policeman Michael Kalanz and a Swiss banker. The cocaine money went into a bank account in Zurich. Rabbi Schwarts had been caught in Puerto Rico with 267,830 dollars in cash.

On 7 July 1995, a certain Moshe Benyamin was arrested in front of a bank in Monte Carlo. In his vehicle, police officers discovered six suitcases full of bank notes worth 5.5 million dollars. Born in Italy but of Israeli nationality, Moshe Benyamin was suspected of being the "chief launderer" of a Colombian cocaine cartel. On 30 August, his brother William was assassinated in Tel Aviv. In 1996, an Orthodox Jew, David Bright, was arrested at New York airport with a suitcase containing $200,000 in cash. He worked for the Cali cartel.

Nachum Goldberg, an Australian Orthodox Jew, had been sent to prison in 1997. He belonged to an international money laundering network that included diamantaires from Israel, Belgium and Australia. Goldberg had laundered 90 million dollars in thirteen years through a bank account of the *United Charity*. In this way he financed the orthodox Jewish community. Most of the money came from the sale of

---

[225]On Chabad-Lubavitch Hasidic Jews read *Psychoanalysis of Judaism*.

diamonds illegally imported into Australia. Tens of thousands of dollars were sent to his brother, who ran the Leumi bank in Jerusalem. In October 2000, Goldberg was sentenced to five years in prison. The judge had criticised the Israeli government for its poor cooperation with investigators.

In 1997, two other New York Hasidic rabbis, Bernald Grunfeld and Mahir Reiss, were indicted along with ten other people for laundering millions of dollars of drug money. Rabbi Weiss was described by the *New York Times* as the ring's mastermind. His brother Abraham, who collected the money from the Manhattan dealers, had also been arrested, as had Israel Knoblach. Jack Pinski was still on the run. Abraham Reiss was also the vice-president of the Conference of Presidents of American Jewish Organisations. The following year, Rabbi Elliot Amsel of Brooklyn, who ran Syrit College, was charged with tax evasion and money laundering. The $700,000 he had amassed was deposited in Israel.

Some Hasidic Jews had gone straight into the drug trade. In 1998, the Antwerp diamond business was found to be a cover for international heroin trafficking. In July, the small diamond community in the Flemish city was hit hard by a series of arrests of Chabad-Lubavitch Jews. The English newspaper *The Independant* of 25 July reported that English police and customs had dismantled a heroin smuggling ring between Israel, Antwerp and London. Fifteen kilos had been seized. An orthodox Jew, Dror Hazenfratz, was at the head of the network. Born in Haifa, Hazenfratz had an Israeli passport and a Belgian identity card. In court, he appeared in traditional dress, black kaftan, hat and papillotes, but this did not spare him from an eleven-year prison sentence.

In 2001, Rabbi Leon Edery was sentenced to one year in prison in Toronto, Canada, for tax evasion. The receipts for donations to charitable and religious institutions were significantly higher than the actual donations.

At the end of 2002, an international drug money laundering network of Colombian cartels was dismantled in New York. According to U.S. Attorney James Comey, it was run by Hasidic Jews who held secret meetings with the Colombians in Miami and Manhattan. Brooklyn-based Avraham Zaltzamn and Aaron Bornstein were jailed. Another man, Akiva Apter, was on the run, but other arrests of traffickers in California and Houston led to the dismantling of the Hasidic network (*New York Daily News*, 2 November 2002). The information was picked up on 10 November in *The Observer*, an English newspaper that was surprised by the involvement of this religious movement with the Colombian cartels. A year earlier, police had broken up another network run by another Hasidic Jew, Sean Erez, who had invested in ecstasy trafficking. The drugs were fraudulently smuggled inside the hats or prayer scrolls of these pious Jews, in the belief that customs officials would not suspect a thing.

Indeed, religious Jews had long been taking advantage of the naivety of customs officials. Jacques Derogy informed us that, as early as the 1970s, there were reports that Abu Hatsira, a relative of the Minister of Religion and Religious Affairs, "had smuggled heroin into Israel, disguised in a scroll of the Law."

In the late 1970s, Isaac Kattan-Kassin, who lived in New York and Miami, was one of the biggest launderers of Colombian cocaine. Other names included Beno Ghitis and Victor Eisenstein, as well as Abel Holtz, the president of the Capital Bank of Miami.

Here is another case highlighted by Derogy: that of Captain Pressman, flight commander of the El Al company, who had been arrested for gold trafficking between Israel and Switzerland." A veteran of the Israeli airline, Pressman had refused for eight years to change Boeing and airlines. And with good reason, for at each stopover in Geneva he took a shipment of gold bars to smuggle them to Israel on behalf of the merchants of Mea Chearim, the ultra-Orthodox district[226]."

In 2002, in his book *The Jews, the World and the Money*, the influential Jacques Attali explained that Jewish criminality was, at most, only a marginal phenomenon: "The relative role of the Jewish 'underworld' in criminality is also diminishing with globalisation, although some of its members are still to be found as brokers in certain types of money laundering in drug trafficking, from Los Angeles to Moscow, from Bogotá to Tel-Aviv." Jacques Attali continued: "A single specifically Jewish network was discovered in February 1990 in New York; it took the following route: part of the Cali cartel's drugs were exchanged in Colombia for diamonds; to transform them into cash, the diamonds were shipped to Milan and mounted on jewellery, which was then sent back to Manhattan to be sold legally—on the count—on 47th Street, where, according to an empathetic comment in the Israeli newspaper *Maariv*, which revealed the case, 'there are more kosher restaurants than in all of Tel-Aviv, and where the largest laundering of drug money in the United States is found'. A portion of the proceeds were then delivered by the jewellers to Jewish institutions in New York, which returned a portion—always in *cash*—to cartel couriers. The ring's leaders led some of their reliefs—Orthodox Jews, such as a

---

[226] Jacques Derogy, *Israel Connection*, Plon, 1980, p. 200.

Brooklyn rabbi whose arrest in February 1990 revealed the whole affair—to believe that they were helping diamond dealers on 47th Street to defraud the tax authorities, or to get their money out of Iranian Jews. The head of this network, an Israeli, confessed to having laundered $200 million on behalf of the Cali cartel, less than 1% of the amount handled annually by the cartel, which distributes four-fifths of the cocaine and one-third of the heroin consumed in the world227." As we ourselves wrote in *Planetary Hopes*: "If Jacques Attali is as discreet about the role of the Jews in criminality as he has been about their role in Bolshevism, this revelation alone represents a great deal."

The film *Blood Diamonds* (USA, 2007) presented a good example of media "stealth" when it comes to Jewish criminality. Indeed, the film barely showed the role of Jews in the diamond industry, only in a brief sequence in which an orthodox Jew appeared on screen ... for half a second! for half a second! Viewers didn't get the point. It has to be said that, in his genre, film director Edward Zwick is a conjurer.

"Information about criminality or the [Jewish] mafia hardly ever appears in the international press," wrote Jacques Derogy as early as 1980. In the mid-19th century, media dictatorship had not yet reached its current levels in Western countries. Thus, in 1864, in its 9 December issue, the Jewish magazine *L'Univers israélite was* outraged that the identity of certain criminals was revealed in the mainstream press: "Four Dutch Israelites, diamond cutters, appear before the jury of the Seine, etc."... It seems that it is finally time for the central council to ask the Ministry of the Interior for a communiqué inviting the newspapers to stop revealing the cult of any person appearing in a court of justice. This simple measure would be enough to put an end to a repulsive abuse that outrages all French Israelis and their religion! [228]"It is indeed important not to "outrage" them: they are susceptible people.

A long tradition

The fictionalised history of Jewish gangsters has always neglected to note their involvement in drug trafficking. Drug dealers are indeed considered intractable." Those Jews don't exist, full stop," wrote Rich Cohen in his book *Yiddish Connection*." Now, Cohen noted, the first

---

[227]Jacques Attali, *Les Juifs, le monde et l'argent*.

[228] *L'Univers Israélite*, September 1864, in Roger Gougenot des Mousseaux, *Los Judíos y la judeización de los pueblos cristianos*, pdf version. Translated into English by Professor Noemí Coronel and the invaluable collaboration of the Catholic Nationalism team. Argentina, 2013, p. 150–151

major American drug dealer was probably Arnold Rothstein himself." It is becoming increasingly clear to us that the drug trade in the United States is conducted from a single source, we read in a federal criminal report from the late 1920s. Moreover, the information at our disposal fuels our conviction that that source is named Arnold Rothstein." "

Rothstein had foreseen the repeal of the alcohol prohibition law and realised before anyone else that drugs could compensate for the loss of the bootleg alcohol trade. His accomplice on this occasion was one Yasha Katzenberg: "Fure one of the great shrouded figures of the Jewish underworld," wrote Rich Cohen. In 1928, when Rothstein died, his narcotics trafficking organisation passed into the hands of Lepke Buchalter, who operated an opium factory on Seymour Avenue[229].

In 1931, a League of Nations treaty had banned almost all world production. From now on, each country could only produce as much narcotic as was necessary for domestic medical use. Lepke's source of supply was exhausted, so he decided to send Katzenberg to the East. Rich Cohen wrote: "Yasha disappeared into the far reaches of China, leaving behind him a trail of letters. He reappeared months later, in the hills around Shanghai, surrounded by an army of bandits. He had taught them how to make heroin and had built a factory in the river valley, and soon the flow of heroin resumed its way to the Lower East Side." In the late 1930s, when the authorities discovered Katzenberg's activities, the League of Nations decreed that he represented a "menace to the international community". Years later, he was indicted along with Lepke and twenty-eight other gangsters for violating narcotics laws. Katzenberg denounced Buchalter, but that did not spare him from being sentenced to eighteen years in prison[230].

The involvement of Jewish traffickers in the drug trade was therefore nothing new. In the United States in the 1940s, there were dozens of heroin dealers in New York, "the remnants of the Rothstein machine", wrote Rich Cohen. Solly Gelb, Solly Gordon, Tudi Schoenfeld, Artie West, Niggy Rutkin, Harry Koch, Sam Haas, Moe Taubman and Harry Hechinger, for example. One Bernard Bergman was an extremely wealthy man and a leading figure in the Orthodox Jewish community. He was "one of the richest Orthodox Jews in the world", wrote Robert Friedman. He had built his fortune in medical care, extending his business throughout the territory. In 1941, the police

---

[229] Rich Cohen, *Yiddish Connection*, 1998, Denoël, 2000, Folio, p. 222–224. Sergio Leone's film, *Once Upon a Time in America*, shows how some gangsters were regular customers of opium dens.
[230] Rich Cohen, *Yiddish Connection*, 1998, Denoël, 2000, Folio, p. 227, 228

seized eight kilos of heroin hidden in his prayer books at his home. Judge Martin Frankel had sentenced him to a ridiculous four months' imprisonment, which generated a purely anti-Semitic rumour. The case was retried and the new presiding judge, Aloysius Melia, added a year's imprisonment to the previous sentence.

In 1942, in France, an author like Léon de Poncins, who had made a list of the criminal activities of certain Jews—major financial swindles, espionage cases and political assassinations, etc.—also mentioned drug trafficking and mentioned two names: Isaac Leifer and Theodore Lyon. Isaac Leifer had been sentenced on 20 June 1939 in Paris to two years' imprisonment and a fine of 5000 francs. The envelopes of heroin sent to the United States were hidden in bibles[231]. Lucien Rebatet, for his part, wrote in the weekly *Je Suis Partout*, dated 17 February 1939: "Recently, following the arrest of a Brooklyn rabbi for international drug trafficking named Isaac Leifer, we witnessed another great defence of the chosen race. This time it was to deny that Leifer was a rabbi. Any more and it would appear that he was not even Jewish. This time, the *Matin* published an article with a headline that read: "The pseudo great rabbi…". The word "great" was accommodated, but it was presented in such a way that the false quality seemed to apply to the word "rabbi" as well. After that, one inquires and ends up discovering that the *Matin's* head of information is called Sam Cohen."

According to Thomas Keyes, in his book *Opium in China*, opium was probably introduced to China by Arab traders during the Tang dynasty (619–907). Opium was then used as a medicine. In 1729, 1780, 1796, and in 1800, imperial edicts addressed to the Portuguese and the British had banned tobacco and opium. But in the 1820s, the British East India Company began exporting opium produced in India to China. It subsequently withdrew from that market, handing over the franchise to the Jardine, Matheson and Co. company, founded in 1832 by two Scotsmen.

During the first decades of the 19th century, Jews from Baghdad had also arrived in India. In Bombay and Calcutta, some of the most powerful families, such as the Kadouri, the Cohens, the Ezra, the Solomons, the Gubbays, the Eliases and, above all, the Sassoons, were to establish themselves among the most powerful. David Sassoon (1792–1864), fleeing the law of the Ottoman governor of Baghdad, arrived in Bombay in 1832 where he set up the David Sassoon and Co and went into the textile business, cotton cultivation and trade, but also

---

[231]Léon de Poncins, *Israël destructeur d'empires*, Mercure de France, 1942, p. 83.

indigo and opium poppy cultivation. David Sassoon and his descendants would later be considered the Rothschilds of the East, as their fortune was considered so fabulous.

David Sassoon found himself in direct competition with Jardine, Matheson and Co in the opium production and trade. Soon, the Daoguang Emperor's commissioner, Lin Hse Tsu, took measures to curb the trade, punish the dealers and detoxify and socially rehabilitate opium addicts. These measures did not impress the enterprising British and Jews, who continued their trade. A First Opium War then broke out (1839–1842) and ended with the Treaty of Nankin, imposed on China by the victorious Great Britain. The terms of the treaty imposed war indemnities to be paid by China, and Hong Kong was ceded to the British. Opium remained illegal, however. A second Opium War broke out in 1858, this time fought by Chinese rebels who wanted to rid the country of opium. This time, the peace treaty no longer specifically prohibited opium.

In the year 1859, no less than 4,800 tons had been produced, and by 1880, the figure reached 6,700 tons[232].

The David Sassoon and Co. company, now in the hands of heirs, already controlled more than 70% of the opium trade and other companies had been set up by other Jewish merchants, so that by the end of the 19th century, the Jardine and other British companies had been driven out of the opium business. By 1900, opium in China was virtually a Jewish monopoly. At that time, the country had at least twenty-five million opium addicts.

Drug trafficking was apparently an old tradition in the Jewish community. In the 15th century, Jewish merchants from the Polish state travelled freely to Moscow. But under the reign of Ivan the Terrible, the situation changed, and entry to Russia was forbidden to Israelite merchants. When in 1550, the Polish King Sigismund-Augustus requested that free access to Russia be allowed again, Tsar Ivan objected in these terms:

"Regarding what you write to us that we should allow your Jews to enter our lands, we have already written to you several times, telling you of the evil deeds of the Jews, who turn our people away from Christ, bring poisoned drugs into our state and cause much harm to our people. You should be ashamed, brother, to write to us about them knowing of their misdeeds. In the other States also they did much evil, and for that they have been expelled or sentenced to death. We cannot allow the

---

[232] This is roughly equivalent to the production of the current Afghanistan "liberated" by US troops in 2002.

Jews to enter our State, for we do not want to see evil in it; we only want God to allow the people of our country to live in peace, without any disturbance. And you, brother, should not, henceforth, write to us any more about the Jews[233]."

Jews themselves were probably heavy users of narcotics. In March 2008, a professor at the Hebrew University of Jerusalem, Benny Shanon, commented on the microphones of an Israeli radio station on one of his articles published in the philosophical journal *Time and Mind*, in which he explained that the Hebrews of ancient times were in the habit of using hallucinatory drugs during religious rites. According to him, the revelation of the Ten Commandments by God on Mount Sinai was probably nothing more than the fruit of Moses' hallucinations, caused by repeated consumption of psychotropic drugs.

This is what we read in the newspaper *Le Figaro* of 4 March 2008. The "voices, the glow, the voice of the horn and the smoking mountain" that the Hebrews saw, according to the Bible, while camping around Mount Sinai (Book of Exodus), had reminded him of his own hallucinatory experiences in the Amazon after taking ayahuasca, a bejuco concoction drunk by shamans in Latin America. Benny Shanon explained that he had consumed it more than a hundred times: "With ayahuasca, I have experienced religious and spiritual visions." The divine transmission of the tablets of the Law to Moses was the result of a hallucination: "During the episode on Mount Sinai, the Book of Exodus mentions that the Israelites perceive sounds. It is a very classic phenomenon in the Amerindian tradition where music is 'seen'," said Shanon, who also pointed out that hypotheses linking the emergence of religions to the use of psychotropic substances have been around for more than 20 years. However, in the deserts of the Negev and Sinai, two hallucinatory plants grow, harmal, still used by the Bedouins, and acacia bark, which produce the same psychedelic effects as ayahuasca.

The acacia is a tree frequently mentioned in the Bible. Its wood had probably been used to build the Ark of the Covenant, the professor insisted. For him, another famous episode in the Torah corresponded to the effects of drug use: the Burning Bush; "Moses believed that the bush had not been reduced to ashes by fire because his perception of time had been altered by the ingestion of psychotropic drugs that persuaded him that he was talking to God." However, for Benny Shanon, the shepherd remained an exceptional character: "Anyone who consumes

---

[233] Léon Poliakov, *Histoire de l'antisémitisme, Tome I*, Point Seuil, 1981, p. 419. These words are also quoted by the great Russian writer Aleksandr Solzhenitsyn, in *Deux Siècles ensemble, Tome I*, Fayard, 2002, p. 26, 27.

hallucinatory plants is not capable of bringing you the Torah, you have to be Moses for that."

Detoxification and decriminalisation

Since the 1970s, and until 1995, help for heroin victims was personified in France and in Europe by a charismatic man who spared no effort to get drug addicts out of their drug addiction. The man, who non-initiates called the "Patriarch", had always looked like a grandfather with his white beard. In the early 1970s, he had set up a community to take in marginalised people and drug addicts who wanted to follow a detox cure and get away from the world of drugs for good.

When you arrived at the Château de la Boère, near Toulouse, you had to strip yourself of everything. Your identity card and money were taken away. The detoxification treatment lasted five days, in secret. The sick person was locked up with a former drug addict who had already been through the same thing. They then took care of him, but he had to work: restoring farms or selling the association's newspaper, *Antitox*. Doctors in the region supported the "Patriarch", and the families of many drug addicts supported him, reassured that their children were no longer self-destructing. For years, the association had operated in this way, with the complacency of the public authorities.

The Patriarch's association then developed considerably, attracting donations for drug addicts all over Europe. In 1995, the structure had 67 centres in France alone, which welcomed 2,500 former drug addicts and 210 centres in 17 countries. The Château de Boère was at the centre of a constellation of eight associations in France, eight commercial companies in Europe and America and four holding companies in Luxembourg. *The Patriarch* had become a true multinational of detoxification.

The funds were largely financed by donations and subsidies. The Ministry of Health contributed 6.6 million francs annually, "without any kind of control or activity report being sent", the court of auditors noted. The sale in Europe of 400,000 copies of *Antitox*, the monthly designed and sold on the streets by drug addicts, represented another important source of cash, especially as the street vendors were not paid. It all fell apart in 1995. Complaints by some pensioners for breach of trust had interrupted the smooth running of the association and it had finally been entered in the register of sects in the parliamentary report. Other legal proceedings had been initiated for rapes and attempted rapes of pensioners. The judicial investigation indicated that 100 million francs had circulated between Switzerland, Luxembourg and Liechtenstein.

For some time now," said Stéphane Hédiard, Lucien Engelmajer's long-time private secretary, "things were no longer going the way they used to. He was out of control. He was only interested in his stories of liquidation, money-raising and real estate investments." (*Libération* of 8 November 2006). The *"Patriarch"*, according to the information we received, was not an easy guy: "Some pensioners who had fled were persecuted and threatened. When criticised, the Patriarch could be extremely violent verbally."

At the age of 86, Lucien Engelmajer was the subject of two international arrest warrants. But this did not prevent him from sleeping soundly. The Patriarch had already been living in Miami for some time, and had subsequently settled in Belize, a country whose citizenship he had acquired (or bought) to escape French justice. In 2006, eight of his collaborators and six of his children were brought before the court for complicity in the abuse of social property, abuse of trust, abuse of weakness, money laundering and receiving stolen goods. Jean-Paul Séguéla, a professor of medicine and former RPR (right-wing liberal) deputy, declared that he "did not understand what he was doing there", in the dock in the middle of the accused, and denied having benefited from free loans from the Patriarch (6 million francs)." Regarding the five sons and daughters of the founder, the lawyer Simon Cohen argued: "Why should they have had to ask where the funds regularly transferred to their accounts came from? Lucien Engelmajer "was a good father, that's all"."

Cosmopolitan intellectuals were also the first to advocate the decriminalisation of drugs. This was the opinion of Daniel Cohn-Bendit, former student leader of the May '68 events and later mayor of Frankfurt, a city where the possession of small quantities of heroin was not criminalised: "The question today is how societies can live with drugs," said Cohn-Bendit. Prohibition is useless. First, in market societies, any prohibition automatically leads to trafficking and a black market that cannot be stopped... The whole strategy of the war on drugs has failed because it does not succeed in eliminating the need for drugs and drug use through repression. We must therefore face the facts... We must decriminalise the use of soft drugs, regulate the situations in which they can be used, control their quality, as for any consumer good." Cohn-Bendit continued: "In Frankfurt, we pursue a risk reduction policy that borders on the limits of the law, distributing methadone and creating places where drug addicts can meet and have access to the heroin they are not allowed to procure. These places are the so-called "drug rooms", set up in cafés, where they can shoot up[234]."

Thus, the left-wing environmentalist Cohn-Bendit said the same thing as the liberal intellectual Guy Sorman, who is also well known to the public. In his book *French Happiness*, published in 1995, he wrote, referring to one of his co-religionists: "Milton Friedman was the first to have analysed the failure of the war on drugs, to have detailed in detail the counter-productive effects and to have proposed the decriminalisation of all drugs. He persuaded me that the damage caused by the war on drugs was greater than the effects of the drug itself, and since this war was universal, it was his duty to propagate his arguments in France in favour of liberalisation." Here is the explanation: "Friedman's calculation was—and still is—essentially based on an economic approach: the billions invested in prohibition enrich the mafias by driving up prices; it also benefits policemen, magistrates, psychiatrists and customs officers whose status and virtue are enhanced. Conversely, drug addicts are driven to commit crimes they would not have committed if the drug were affordable, as they would not have to steal the amounts of money needed for their consumption. Prohibition, Friedman added, floods the market with adulterated products that cause infinitely more victims than the pure drug if it were available at its cost price, which is very low." Guy Sorman added: "An economist, but also a philosopher, Friedman points out that no one should be incriminated for their personal consumption, the state is not legitimate to interfere in an individual free choice that does not cause any external casualties."

In short, planetary intellectuals, whether socialist or liberal, are in agreement in favour of decriminalisation. In France, Michèle Barzach, a right-wing minister, had authorised in 1987 the free sale of syringes whose use was notorious. And it was the famous Bernard Kouchner, a socialist who later turned to the right, who first authorised the distribution of methadone. Simone Veil and her health minister, Philippe Douste-Blazy, would expand and organise its use, not only in hospitals, but also directly in pharmacies[235].

The struggle of cosmopolitan intellectuals and politicians for the decriminalisation of drugs could well be seen as yet another element in

---

[234] Daniel Cohn-Bendit, *Une Envie de politique*, La Découverte, 1998, p. 126-133. Cosmopolitan intellectuals also claim that immigration is "ineluctable", just as they once claimed that the triumph of the proletariat was "ineluctable". Here, drug trafficking is "ineluctable". Be that as it may, we can well understand why they are against the death penalty for drug traffickers. cf.

[235] Guy Sorman, *Le Bonheur français*, Fayard 1995, p. 111, 112.

the war arsenal of the cosmopolitan mafias in their war against the nations[236]. In 1996, for example, a high-ranking Israeli army officer was accused of drug trafficking in Egypt. This was not a common law case, but a covert operation aimed at flooding the Egyptian army with marijuana to undermine its combat capabilities. Following this logic, cannabis and heroin derivatives were destined for the enemy, while amphetamines were part of the Tsahal soldiers' war arsenal.

Some traffickers appeared to be important to the Hebrew state. Thus, in 2004, the Israeli authorities exchanged 400 Lebanese and Arab prisoners in exchange for Elhanan Tannebaum, an Israeli reserve colonel who had been kidnapped three years earlier in Lebanon and was being held captive by Hezbollah. In December 2006, he admitted that he had travelled to Lebanon to traffic narcotics. Indeed, this disproportionate exchange had provoked outrage among many Israelis.

Cosmopolitan intellectuals are also fully committed to the anti-racist struggle. The defence of minorities, of all minorities, in fact makes it possible to weaken little by little the organism of ethnically homogeneous nations impervious to their influence." The hatred of the drug addict coincides with that of the immigrant and the Jew", wrote Guy Sorman.

In Germany, Michel Friedman was a well-known lawyer, very much in the media, and one of the "spokesmen" for the fight against racism and anti-Semitism. Number 2 in the Jewish community on the other side of the Rhine, he was also the president of the European Jewish Congress. A feared talk show host and former member of the leadership of the CDU, the German conservative party, he pontificated on every television set. The French weekly *L'Express* of 26 June 2003 published an article about him entitled *Michel Friedman's lost honour*. The magazine wrote: "Michel Friedman irritated more than a few people in Germany with his dandy airs, his gelled hair and his pink ties. But many people also liked him because he was a brilliant defender of the great principles of morality and human rights, spoke out loud and clear and refused to be pigeonholed into "the role of Jewish victim that many would have liked to see him take on", as the left-wing daily *Tageszeitung* recently noted. In short, Michel Friedman, 47, vice-president of the Central Council of Jews in Germany, was indispensable in the public debate."

On 15 June 2003, however, a search was carried out at his home in Frankfurt, after his name appeared in an investigation into a Ukrainian criminal network operating in drug trafficking, prostitution

---

[236]The war against the nations: cf. *The Planetary Hopes*, and *Jewish Fanaticism*.

and arms trafficking in Germany. Apparently, the worldly consumer also had dubious relations with that world.

The case had begun with bugging of pimps suspected of smuggling Ukrainian and Polish prostitutes into Germany. From the incoming calls, the investigators had recognised the strong familiar voice of the media lawyer behind the pseudonym of a certain Paolo Pinkel. The latter had placed an order for several prostitutes, specifying that they should meet him in his hotel room. Although it did not fit in well with the public discourse of the person concerned, this action in itself was not illegal. But the case took a different turn when two prostitutes claimed, during interrogation, that the lawyer had offered them cocaine.

Psychologically collapsed, his friends said, Friedman had suspended all his television programmes, preferring to go to Italy to rest. The front page of the popular daily *Bild-Zeitung* showed a photo of him sitting at a table on the terrace of a luxury hotel in Venice. *L'Express* journalist "Blandine Milcent" pitied the poor man: he lived "inhabited by a permanent need for social recognition and a constant urge to "poke around where it bothers most". Over the years, Michel Friedman had specialised in denouncing intolerance, racism and hypocrisy in German society. Born in Paris in 1956 (he speaks French without an accent), this son of furriers—Polish Jews saved from the Holocaust by Oskar Schindler—had established himself as the most media-friendly figure in the German Jewish community. Talkative, acerbic, arrogant to a fault, he liked to say that if he made a nuisance of himself in his own country, it was not his problem. These statements were in any case very symptomatic of a certain mentality of some people who constantly boast of being "annoying", "provocative" and "irritating" [237]. And these are the same people who are surprised to be expelled from everywhere.

---

[237] See *Psychoanalysis of Judaism* and *Jewish Fanaticism*.

2. The porn mafia

Sexual liberation

The sex industry has developed considerably since the 1970s and has been growing ever since." In big cities, there is no longer a wall, a bus stop or a newsstand that does not offer sex", wrote Yann Moncouble in 1989 in a book entitled *Politics, Sex and Finance*. In 2008, Westerners could only observe that sex was becoming more and more invasive, on television and on the internet. It was quite clear that this omnipresent pornography did nothing to promote the birth rate, but instead encouraged all sorts of social pathologies. Yann Moncomble quoted an official study that established a link between pornography and the increase in the number of rapes and mild or hyperviolent crime: "In his testimony before the Messe Commission, Ken Lanning, a pornography specialist at the FBI, stressed that in many cases of rape with death, the perpetrator was the owner of a large amount of pornographic material. Statistics also show a marked increase in the number of rapes in states where the sale of pornographic magazines is highest. In fact, rapists have confessed in 40% of the cases that they were inspired by pornographic scenes before or during the perpetration of the crime[238]."

Those profiting from this very lucrative industry were evidently people who did not care too much about "reactionary" Christian morality. Take Jack Kahane, for example. In 1931, he had set up the Obelisk publishing house in Paris and published in English the cursed writers of his country, such as Henry Miller, Anaís Nin and Laurence Durell. His son, Maurice Girodias, innovated by publishing erotic works in English, which were sold after 1944 to American soldiers who took them with them to the USA.

Roger Faligot and Rémi Kauffer, co-authors of a 1987 book entitled *Porno Business,* described Maurice Girodias as follows: "He is always one dream ahead of the others and with the police on his heels... In him, an innate nose for literary genius is mixed with a taste for

---

[238]Yann Moncomble, *La politique, le sexe et la finance,* Faits-et-Documents, 1989, p. 17.

intrigue and provocation. He amused himself by frequenting the conspirators of the Synarchy, the *half-Cagoule* Freemasonry[239], *half-Grand Guignol*[240]. Undoubtedly, this French-English Jew had some contacts that helped him to escape the Nazi raids. During the war, Girodias published art books. But from 1945 onwards, he was seen with Miller, staging spectacular, bloody, gruesome hits—in short, some amazing poker games with the censors[241]."

Maurice Girodias had created a publishing structure, *Olympia Press*. At the time, no publisher in the United States would have dared to publish *Lolita*, the manuscript of a professor at Cornell University in the United States named Vladimir Nabokov. The novel told the story of a man in love with a twelve-year-old girl. Girodias was naturally excited by this kind of literature[242]. He bought the copyright for $1,000 and published it in the autumn of 1955 in two volumes with a print run of 5,000 copies. Thanks to professional smugglers, the book circulated throughout England. The English police intervened through Interpol to get the French censorship brigade to intervene. The novel was banned in France by an order of the Ministry of the Interior, but Girodias appealed to the administrative court. In February 1958, the ban was lifted and the English version of the book was legalised in France.

In the United States, the book that had made it through customs became a *bestseller*. A sign of the times, in 1959, D.H. Lawrence's *Lady Chatterley's Lover* was also authorised and published. The following year, *Tropic of Cancer*, but also Jean Genet, the Marquis de Sade, William Burroughs—the entire *Olympia Press* catalogue was on free sale. However, 65 of the 70 books published by *Olympia Press were* still banned in France. The accursed publisher thus spent his time between Paris and the United States, where he passed as a "liberator of morals". *Lolita was* still a resounding success, and the cosmopolitan filmmaker Stanley Kubrick made a film adaptation of the novel.

In November 1953, the young journalist Hugh Hefner invented the erotic press with *Playboy*. Marylin Monroe inaugurated the magazine by posing on the cover. The magazine went from 70,000 to 900,000 copies sold in four years. *Playboy* undoubtedly played an

---

[239] La Cagoule (The Hood), the popular name for the "Secret Committee of Revolutionary Action". It was an extreme right-wing organisation active in France between 1936 and 1937 and known for its terrorist activities. (NdT).

[240] Famous theatre in Pigalle (Paris) known for its naturalistic horror shows.

[241] Roger Faligot, Rémi Kauffer, *Porno Business*, Fayard, 1987, p. 38, 25

[242] Nabokov had married a daughter of the chosen people. On incest in Jewish families and paedocriminality see the chapters Psychopathology of Judaism in *Psychoanalysis of Judaism* (2006) and *Jewish Fanaticism* (2007).

important role in advancing the values of "tolerance", especially abortion rights, gay rights and soft drug use that gradually permeated Western societies. In fact, the *Playboy* Foundation was committed to the struggle for "gay rights", which it supported financially. Hugh Hefner, following some ancient Jewish customs so well ridiculed by Voltaire, had even defended human beings having sex with animals.

In 1963, *Lui*, the "magazine of modern man", which was then the main competing magazine, came out. It was directed by Jacques Lanzman, an extreme left-wing militant. The central fold-out photo was inspired by the famous *Playboy*. At the beginning of 1964, *Lui*, which had just published its third issue, was already printing 300,000 copies. The founder was Daniel Philipacchi, a friend of Roger Frey, General de Gaulle's interior minister. It was Roger Frey who would smooth things over with the general. Marcel Bleustein-Blanchet, the king of advertising, had also understood the importance of this press, so he too intervened on the magazine's behalf. Frey's son-in-law, Paul Giannoli, was to become the editor years later. There were also strong links between Philipacchi and the Rothschild bank. The bulk of the Philipacchi group's commercial success rested on this specialised press: 360,000 copies of *Lui*, 410,000 of *Newlook* and 145,000 of *Penthouse*.

Philipacchi's career took off during the happy years of triumphant Gaullism. His father, Henri Filipacchi, had landed in Marseilles in 1922, "from Smyrna, with no other luggage than a violin under his arm", wrote Roger Faligot. He became general secretary of the Hachette press distribution company, ensuring the smooth running of business during the Occupation by dealing with the Germans. Henri Philipacchi was also a close friend of Maurice Girodias.

In the years leading up to the May 1986 explosion, Bernard Borderie's *Angélique* series caused a sensation in the cinema. Five films were released between 1964 and 1967. Angelica, the heroine, was sold to the Berbers as a slave and whipped by pirates, but was always saved in extremis, even if she didn't bend to the men's whims. 1967 was also the year of Jacques Rivette's *The Nun*, a film adapted from a novel by Diderot. The film was banned, but André Malraux, General de Gaulle's Minister of Culture, intervened on its behalf[243]. That same year, the National Assembly had voted to form a special commission led by Lucien Neuwirth, a Gaullist deputy for the Loire, to legislate on contraception. The Neuwirth law was voted on 28 December. Abortion was still forbidden, but the text regulated the sale of contraceptives to minors (under 21). The contraceptive pill made its entry into society.

---

[243]Malraux was married to a Jewish woman of German origin.

The events of May 1968 began in the wake of a conference on the sexual revolution, led by a Trotskyist called Boris Fraenkel. Fraenkel was also the translator of the works of Herbert Marcuse, one of his co-religionists who had become the guru of the militants of the radical left[244].

At the time, sales of the magazine *Lui* had exceeded 700,000 copies. Régine Deforges began publishing erotic literature with *Irene*. The book was seized, and Aragon, a Stalinist writer, refused to acknowledge authorship of the manuscript and pretended that it had been stolen. In a small shop in the Rue du Cherche-Midi, Eric and Pierrette Losfeld ran the *Editions du Terrain vague*. Eric Losfeld was the first to publish erotic comics: *Barbarella and Pravda la survireuse.*

In 1969, in a film entitled *Le Désirable et le Sublime*, the director José Bénazéraf showed a couple making love on the living room carpet while the left-wing candidate Alain Krivine appeared on the television screen during an election campaign. A Jew from Casablanca, José Bénazéraf was born into a family of the upper middle class, which was obviously not at all contradictory to his political commitment to the extreme left, as long as it is understood that for these militants the social question is very marginal: for them, the essential issue is the breakdown of traditional European society. In 1961, Bénazéraf had already directed *Le Cri de la chair* (*The Cry of the Flesh*). The director, after twenty-five films, established himself as the undisputed master of this new industry and has since been considered "the father of French pornographic cinema[245]."

The year 1973 saw the publication of the first issue of Playboy in the French version, under the impetus of Daniel Philipacchi and Hugh Hefner. Daniel Philipacchi wanted to extend his empire to the USA and expand his market in France. To do so, he enlisted the services of an erotic specialist, publisher Eric Losfeld. Philipacchi also wanted to publish a version of *Lui* in the United States, and to launch a magazine in France that was a little more *"hardcore"* than that one. For the first time, the magazine's *playmates* showed their sex and fondled themselves[246]. That same year, in October, the International Porn Fair took place in Copenhagen.

---

[244]On Wilhelm Reich and Herbert Marcuse, see *Planetary Hopes*, chapter on *Matriarchal Society*.
[245]Roger Faligot, Rémi Kauffer, *Porno Business*, Fayard, 1987, p. 103.
[246]Roger Faligot, Rémi Kauffer, *Porno Business*, Fayard, 1987, p.100

Porn promoters

The 1970s were the golden age of porn cinema. In his 1982 book on *erotic cinema*, Jacques Zimmer made a short chronicle of the phenomenon. On the cover, we first saw a suggestive photo of the film *Les Onze mille Vierges*, by the great Eric Lipmann. Sweden was then at the forefront of the "liberation" movement. The film *Les Envoûtées* had had 190,000 spectators in 1971.

Erotic films such as *Emmanuelle* (1974) or *Histoire d'O*, produced by Alain Siritzky; *Les Saisons du plaisir* by Jean-Pierre Mocky; *La Bonzesse* by François Jouffa; *Les Onze mille Vierges* by Eric Lipmann; *Emmanuelle II* by Francis Giacobetti, *Godefinger* by Bob Logan, or *La Kermesse érotique* by Jean Le Vitte provoked a great scandal.

In 1975, the new President of the Republic, Valéry Giscard d'Estaing, who wanted to promote a wave of liberalism in France, ordered his Minister of Culture, Michel Guy, to "liberalise cinema" and no longer to decree a total ban. The screening of pornographic films was therefore authorised despite the criteria and opinion of the control commissions. This liberalism led to a tsunami of films, especially foreign films that had previously been banned. In his *Dictionary of censorship in the cinema*, Jean-Luc Doin wrote: "Stupefied, viewers discovered posters showing sexual organs in action and specialised cinemas on the street[247]."

France was concerned about this proliferation of pornographic films, masterpieces such as *Love Variations* (UK); *La Possédée* (Sweden); *Les petites Filles modèles* (France); *Des Filles pour mercenaires* (Italy-Spain); *Edith* (France); *L'Insatiable* (Greece); *La Poupée d'amour* (Sweden-France); *Frustration* (France).

Seventy-seven films were released in 1975. Catholic family associations reacted and the government reversed itself by deciding to tax the most violent or pornographic films. The law of 30 December 1975 authorised the screening of pornographic films in exchange for being categorised as X. This entailed a series of obligations, such as a ban on children under 18 and a fiscal and financial penalty: a VAT of 33% instead of 18.6%, and a 20% tax on profits, with added fees for foreign films. In addition, advertising was banned. The X cinema ghetto had just been created.

In autumn 1975, Jean-Jacques Servan-Schreiber's weekly *L'Express* published excerpts from *Histoire d'O*, while the magazine

---

[247] Jean-Luc Doin, *Dictionnaire de la censure au cinéma*, Presses Universitaires de France, 1998, p. 351.

launched by Michel Caen and José Bénazéraf, *L'Organe*, was banned.

These years were, however, a period of brilliance. In 1975, *Exhibition*, by Jean-François Davy, was the first French *hard-core film*. The leading actress was Claudine Beccarie. With *Exhibition*, Davy earned more than 10 million francs in 19 weeks. *Le Canard enchaîné* of 24 December 1975 noted that the films *La Bête, Suce pas ton pouce* and *C'est plus facile à garder la bouche ouverte*, three licensed pornographic films, had been partly financed by Baron Elie de Rothschild[248]. The great cosmopolitan capital, as we can see, was already compatible with "moral liberation" from the outset.

In January 1976, 161 pornographic films were shown in "specialised cinemas". That year, pornographic films totalled 10 million admissions, compared to 177 million for "normal" films.

Many Jewish directors and producers entered the industry, forming the locomotive. Francis Mischkind, owner of several cinemas, was one of the first, with Max Pécas, to produce and distribute erotic, then pornographic, French and foreign films. Another pioneer of X cinema was the inescapable Boris Gourevitch, owner of the Cinévog Saint-Lazare. At the time, he ran nearly forty Parisian cinemas and generated profits that he immediately reinvested in the production of traditional films[249].

In 1977, a complaint lodged against the broadcasting of *L'Essayeuse*, a film by Serge Korber (under the pseudonym John Thomas), led to a trial that caused quite a stir. The film was not only banned, but the court ordered the physical destruction of the film, which was to be burned.

Here is what Jean-Luc Doin wrote in 1998 in his *Dictionnaire de la censure dans le cinéma*: "In France, the cinema was still exemplarily prudish, even if Paul Éluard had already, in his *Lettres à Gala*, exalted the splendour of "obscene cinema": "A discovery! The incredible life of immense and magnificent sexes on the screen, the semen that comes out. It is admirable. And very well done, of an extraordinary eroticism. The cinema gave me an exacerbated hard-on for an hour[250]"."

José Bénazéraf, very politicised to the extreme left, set the tone with porn-intellectual films full of wise quotations and subversive allusions to current affairs. In addition to José Bénazéraf, "the patriarch", a trio of directors was dominant: Jean-François Davy, who

---

[248]Yann Moncomble, *La Politique, le sexe et la finance*, Faits-et-Documents, 1989, p. 21.
[249]Roger Faligot, Rémi Kauffer, *Porno Business*, Fayard, 1987, p. 113, 120
[250]Paul Éluard's real name was Eugène Grindel.

used to choose his titles with a certain humour *(Bananes mécaniques)*, Gerard Kikoïne and Francis "Leroi". The latter was the director of *Petites Filles* and was the co-director and co-producer of *Sexe qui parle*.

Apart from this "infernal trio", Davy-Kikoïne-Leroi, there were many other directors, not all of them Jewish, of course: Lucien Hustaix had produced a series: *Les Pulpeuses, Les Jouisseuses, Les Lécheuses*. Michel "Lemoine" practised anti-Christian provocation with *Les Petites Saintes se touchent* (*The little saturnines touch each other*). There were also Frédéric Lansac (Claude Mulot), Michel "Barny" (Didier Philippe Gérard), Burt Tambaree (Claude-Bernard Aubert), Pierre B. Reinhart (Reinhart Brulle), John Love (Alain Payet), Gréco de Beauparis (Gérard Grégory), Jean Rollin[251].

According to Jacques Zimmer, from 19 X-films produced in France in 1973, it had risen to 43 in 1974, 78 in 1977 and 167 in 1978, the high point of porn. But only four of these films had achieved more than 100,000 admissions. By 1979, the public had had enough. The attendance of X theatres was falling from more than 10 million to less than eight million. The number of cinemas in France fell from 151 in 1976 to 76 in 1986. Ten years later, these cinemas did not total much more than two million admissions. Competition from VHS videotapes had made its presence felt.

One million video recorders had been sold in France in 1982 and publishers of X films on videotape multiplied in Paris and throughout the country. Jean-Claude Goldstuck then created Scherzo and launched the collection "American X classics". Jean Eckenbaum, who was starting out in X cinema with *Les producteurs du vice,* set up Ski'l Productions. Henri Lenique bought a dozen titles to lay the foundations of Travelling-Productions. Finally, Jean-François Davy added a new activity to his portfolio[252]. In 1986, all these defenders of culture were once again victims of "persecution" when the Supreme Court extended the ban and even the police seizure of material with paedophile, zoophile or sadomasochistic connotations to videotapes. This was a new drama in the history of a people who had already suffered so much.

Elie Oury, *Initial*'s boss, readily confessed that he distributed 35–40% of his video tapes in supermarkets and popular shops. His catalogue included about a hundred titles, a third of which were X-films. Jean-Claude Goldstuck, for his part, focused on another market segment, a more selective clientele. In 1986, 280,000 X-films had been sold in France out of a total of 850,000. But seven tapes out of ten came

---

[251] Roger Faligot, Rémi Kauffer, *Porno Business*, Fayard, 1987, p. 132.
[252] Roger Faligot, Rémi Kauffer, *Porno Business*, Fayard, 1987, p. 252.

from the United States. Richard Fhal and *Editions Concorde later became* one of the largest distributors in France.

Of the twenty or so X-tape publishers identified by Roger Faligot, a dozen had Jewish names. All publishers, wholesalers, distributors, mail-order sellers of sexual products and accessories in France were not Jewish, but in this industry as in others, Jewish businessmen, such as Marc Dorcel (M. Herskovits), for example, were the most influential and took the initiative.

In 1986, Catherine Ringer, the Rita Mitsoukorock star, made headlines. Her lawsuit against George Baruck, president of the videotape distributor VSD-international, was dismissed. She had recorded three porn films in 1982 for money, with no intention of making a career in porn. But Georges Baruck, who had acquired the rights, was going to take advantage of the French singer's newfound notoriety.

Roger Faligot introduced us to the aforementioned individual in his book: "With his thin moustache and his big cigar, Georges Baruck is an *outsider* in the world of videotape X." I like provocation. I'm known for it in the business and I like it that way," he said bluntly." Roger Faligot added: "After winning his lawsuit, he is delighted to have bought the rights to Catherine Ringer's first X movie, *Poker-partouze pour Marcia! He* is even more than happy, because this film benefits incredibly from the notoriety of Rita Mitsouko's singer and sells like hot cakes... His second film, *Le Choc des stars,* will sell just as well. The third, as he himself confesses, Georges Baruck puts it in reserve waiting for Rita Mitsouko to rise in the *hit-parade*[253]."

In the United States, Reuben Sturman was the leading distributor of *hard-core* pornography in the 1970s and 1980s. He distributed shipments of pornographic tapes throughout the United States and Europe. His empire was based in Las Vegas, but Sturman controlled the distribution of pornography in Baltimore, Chicago, Pittsburgh, Denver, Milwaukee, Milwaukee, Buffalo, Toronto, Los Angeles and Detroit. He owned hundreds of specialty shops across the country, according to an FBI report. Some of the films he produced featured scenes of humans eating excrement, or women having sex with horses, pigs and other sadomasochistic acts. In 1976 and 1980, Reuben Sturman had been acquitted by the Supreme Court of obscenity charges. But he complained of being the victim of judicial persecution. In 1989, he was sentenced in Cleveland for tax fraud to 10 years in prison for obstruction of tax inspection. In 1993, the Chicago courts managed to

---

[253]Roger Faligot, Rémi Kauffer, *Porno Business*, Fayard, 1987, p. 264, 265.

get their hands on him and sentenced him to 19 years for extortion. He was also convicted of tax fraud for evading funds to Swiss and Dutch banks. Reuben Sturman died in October 1997 at the age of 73 in federal prison in Kentucky. It was a great loss to humanity, but fortunately, his son David took over the family business. In the 1990s, he would conquer most of the pornography market in Australia.

Roger Faligot's writing about Sturman confirmed the pornography world's links with the Mafia: In the United States, "several pornocrats are of Russian origin, such as Ralph Ginzburg, who spent his youth in Shanghai in the 1930s, where his father was involved in various traffics; or Reuben Sturman, who flew to London to meet Bernie Silver in person... Who is this Sturman really: a pioneer in the distribution of porn films that can be viewed in booths in New York and who wants to establish himself in the London market; but also a direct representative of the interests of the Mafia. With his company Pleasure Books Ltd, Sturman would become one of the main suppliers of the porn business, dominating the world in about forty countries[254]."

Bernie Silver was the king of porn in London, where he controlled two thirds of the nightclubs in Soho, the red light district. In 1974, he had been sentenced to life imprisonment for murder. One hundred and seventy Maltese had accompanied him in prison. But the court decision was appealed, and Silver the "Maltese" godfather was released four years later.

All this money generated by porn obviously aroused great appetites. In a 2003 book entitled *The Great Mafia Awakening*, Xavier Raufer provided some information about this mafia world. The first American porn cult film, *Deep Throat*, shot in 1972 (in seventeen days) in Florida, cost only 26,000 dollars, but earned its producers no less than 600 million dollars. *Deep Throat*'s star, Linda Lovelace, became the first porn star in an atmosphere of erotomania and "women's liberation". But far from consenting, Lovelace was actually the victim of a brutal pimp—her own husband—who, after drugging her, had prostituted her in front of the cameras under threat of a gun. He often beat her and did not pay her a dollar. The whole story was contained in *Ordeal*, the book in which Linda Lovelace recounted her martyrdom in detail. It also revealed that *Deep Throat* had been produced by Gérard Damiano, and that he had to sell his rights under the gun of the Peraino brothers. At the time, a journalist interviewed Gérard Damiano about his exclusion from his own company. His answer was: "I can't say anything... I risk my life." The man was right to be cautious, because

---

[254]Roger Faligot, Rémi Kauffer, *Porno Business*, Fayard, 1987, p. 244.

between 1975 and 1980, the "mafia wars" for the control of porn (magazines, films, sex shops, massage parlours) had caused 25 deaths in New York State alone, not counting the arson attacks and bombings[255].

Where there is a lot of money, there are also necessarily a lot of … criminals. Gérad Leibovici was one of those glittering characters of the 1970s. Editor and producer of porn films, he was also involved in the counterfeiting and smuggling of illegal tapes: sadomasochism, violence, paedophilia and zoophilia. But Gérard Leibovici also had "advanced" ideas in politics, as he was an extreme left-wing militant. He had taken under his wing Sabrina, the daughter of Jacques Mesrine, the number one public enemy killed by the police in 1979. On 5 March 1984, "Lebo" was himself shot four times in the back of the head in a car park on Avenue Foch in Paris. His killers have never been identified (*Marianne*, 28 July 2007).

Porn in every household

Then, everyone should be allowed to watch pornographic films on television screens in their homes and thus finally put an end to all the old prejudices, all the old reactionary morals that hindered the spirit of all those somewhat repressed Christians.

It would be even better if the films were broadcast on television channels. Elie Oury embarked on this adventure with the pay channel Canal+. The director, Pierre Lescure, and his collaborators, including Marc Frydman, introduced X cinema on television. On 17 November 1984, viewers were treated to the small screen premiere of the porn film, *La Bête*, "Walerian Borowczyk's classic", as Roger Faligot described it. On 31 August 1985, Canal+ broadcast *Exhibition*, by Jean-François Davy.

Marc Frydman, who selected the X films shown, then chose *Emmanuelle 4* and *Les Petites filles au bordel* by Francis Leroi. Then *Gorge profonde (Deep Throat)* and *L'Enfer pour Miss Jones* by Italian-American Gérard Damiano, *Histoire d'O numéro 2* by Eric Rochat, *Derrière la porte verte* by Artie James and Adrienne Mitchell and *Hôtesses intimes* by Michel Baudricourt." Canal+ has done an excellent job of demystifying erotic cinema," said Claude Goldstuck[256].

In New York, Abby Ehmann was one of the leading publishers of

---

[255] Xavier Raufer, *Le grand Réveil des Mafias*, JC Lattès, 2003, p. 225, 226.
[256] Roger Faligot, Rémi Kauffer, *Porno Business*, Fayard, 1987, p. 260.

pornographic magazines. Her ambition was to "satisfy the appetites of New Yorkers who were living too tightly confined to the narrowness of their little lives". She had started her career at *Porn Free* magazine, which she left in 1997 to join *Extreme Fetish*. She was also one of the leaders of *Feminist for Free Expression*.

Guy Sitbon, another son of the persecuted community, was also a pioneer of his kind. A former US correspondent for the *Nouvel Observateur*, he had placed an advertisement in the daily *Libération* asking readers to mail him accounts of their sexual experiences. He received hundreds of letters. Thus he founded his newspaper, which was based mainly on these accounts of sexual experiences from his contacts. *Lettres-magazine* quickly reached a circulation of 50,000 copies. By the end of 1985, his newspaper had reached 80,000 copies. Guy Sitbon did not stop there and the following year he created *Femmes libérées* and *Lettres gay*.

In the meantime, the pink telephone and pink messaging via the Minitel (predecessor of the Internet in France) had appeared. A few years later, the porn mafia was to take over the internet. The adventure of "sex.com" was quite emblematic of the interests at stake.

In 1994, in the United States, a certain Gary Kremen had acquired an internet pearl, the domain name sex.com, but without immediately exploiting it. Stephen Michael Cohen, 57, immediately realised the commercial potential of the domain name. He was a repeat offender and had just been released from prison when he sent a fake letter to Network Solutions stating that Gary Kremen's company, the owner of the name, had decided to dump the name and abandon sex.com. NSI withdrew the domain name from Gary Kremen and transferred it to Stephen Cohen without the required checks. Cohen thus illegally acquired the domain name in question and created the most profitable pornographic website on the internet. But with Cohen, it was no longer a matter of eroticism, but of explicit pornography, and sex.com achieved a prodigious turnover.

Gary Kremen then engaged in a lengthy legal and court battle. He sued both Stephen Cohen and Network Solution to recover the ownership of his domain name and the corresponding compensation. In 2000, after five years of proceedings, the judge acknowledged the theft of the sex.com domain name and ordered Stephen Cohen to pay 65 million dollars: 40 million dollars for lost revenue and 25 million dollars in damages.

The sum was never paid, as Cohen had fled. Gary Kremen only received the 20 million paid by NSI in exchange for dropping his complaint. The sex.com thief was however arrested in November 2005 in Tijuana, Mexico. He was extradited to the United States and imprisoned in the San Diego penitentiary. He had spent all that time transferring the illegally obtained money into bank accounts, investing it in multiple shell companies.

This was not Cohen's first scam. In 1991, he had swindled an elderly woman out of $200,000 and was sentenced to 46 months in prison. In the 1980s, he had run a swinger's club in California called *French Connection*. Following complaints from neighbours, he was arrested for having set up his business in a residential area. In 1996, together with three other partners, he bought a hotel in Nevada which he transformed into a gigantic "Polynesian" brothel where dozens of young exotic women were watching over "your comfort and your pleasure".

With the recent opening of the ".eu" domain, the sector's interest had not waned as some 213 applications had been registered for the name sex.eu during the first hours of opening, well ahead of the other domain names (Hotel.eu, travel.eu, job.eu, etc.).

Seth Silverstein, the president of *Cybererotica*, was another eminent personality in the internet pornography industry. He was said to be the "pornography czar".

The weekly *Le Point* of 20 April 2006 published an article on the decline of small businesses and traditional shops in rue Saint-Denis in Paris, where a third of the capital's porn shops are concentrated: "Porn is in crisis, we can't compete with the internet", lamented Simon Zouzoti, manager of *Top Sexy*, who declared he was ready to sell if the city council made him a good offer. This difficult situation was another drama for the community.

But let's take a porn magazine at random. This is what we could read in *Hot Vidéo* from January 2007, on page 55: "Steven Hirsch, the big boss of Vivid is a big man... Indeed, he is among the most influential people in the city of Los Angeles, according to *Los Angeles Magazine*. He is on a list of 122 personalities alongside Steven Spielberg, Hugh Hefner, Magic Johnson and a host of politicians, businessmen, Hollywood celebrities and televangelists. An achievement that was justified, according to the magazine, by his ability, "since 1984, to move the pornographic industry toward the traditional model based on the promotion of Vivid girls, thus recreating the old Hollywood system of contract stars. And still generating a turnover of close to 100 million dollars." That's nothing."

In June 2007, the research magazine *Capital* published a study on the subject: "Eric Larchevêque was predestined to join the orders. However, he preferred to choose a less pure but more remunerative destiny: a pioneer of internet porn, our man was not even 25 years old when he founded the company Carpe Diem with two partners in 1998... Today he is at the head of a pornographic empire that manages more than sixty X portals and hosts more than a thousand free partner sites whose advertising windows serve as hooks to his pay sites." His sites range from *Blondesalope.com* (*Rubiazorra.com*) to *Gaycast.com* (*Elencogay.com*), via *Entrenanas.com* (*entretías.com*)." His small company achieves a turnover of 30 million euros each year, and his profitability (which he refuses to disclose) seems to sweep all[257]."

Another prominent entrepreneur was Patrice Macar, founder of Dreamnex: 18 million visits per month, 2000 transactions per day, 34 million euros turnover in 2006 (eight times more than in 2004), with less than thirty employees on the payroll. At the age of 36, Macar, who owns 30% of the shares, is a very rich man." Some old foxes of porn production have found a second youth. This is the case of Marcel Dorcel (real name Marcel Herkovitz), 73 years old, who created his company a quarter of a century ago. France's leading producer-distributor of pornographic films (12 million euros in turnover in 2006), this grandfather of X—who has just produced an unspeakable *"Presidential Erections"*—is delighted to have been able to jump on the digital bandwagon. It's a real explosion," rejoices his son, Gregory Dorcel, managing director. Every day we sell more than 1000 films via the internet, and the growth rate is 5–8% per month." "

We were also informed that Michel Birnbaum was "the pope of the men's press" in France, owner, among others, of the magazines *Lui, New-Look, Maximal,* as well as *Playboy* France. Birnbaum, with his fifteen million photos in stock, distributes images to some forty mobile phone operators in fifteen countries.

Benjamin Cohen was another leading figure in cyber porn. At the age of 16, he had already launched sojewish.com, a community site that he resold for 600,000 francs two years later. By 2001, at the age of eighteen, he was a millionaire living in London. With his new site, hunt4porn.com, he managed to win 60,000 subscribers. His religious community had not disowned him: "Many of my shareholders are regulars at the synagogue".

As with drugs, pornography could be considered by its main promoters as a weapon of war. In March 2002, for example, the Israeli

---

[257] Larchevêque (The Bishop), Leroi (The King), Sultan (Sultan), Lempereur (The Emperor), etc..... are the surnames used in that business by members of the community.

army, which had taken control of the Ramallah television studios in Palestine, immediately broadcast pornographic films on Palestinian television channels to weaken the enemy.

The pioneers of pornography

The porn industry has long been in the hands of the sons of Israel. Before the First World War, a publisher of Bavarian origin, Moses Offenstadt, had already attracted attention with his licentious publications through his Société Parisienne d'Édition. In France, he had called himself Maurice Villefranche. In 1902, he had created a weekly magazine, *La Vie en culotte rouge*, whose lurid stories and obscene drawings got him into some legal trouble." The French woman was invariably depicted as a slut and in very suggestive positions, most often in the company of a handsome officer in "red shorts", or else on the knees of a colonial marksman with his eyes full of concupiscence[258]." Between 1908 and 1912, the man was convicted several times for offences against public morality and decency, in Lyon, Bordeaux and Orléans.

The advent of cinema immediately enabled some Jews to propagate their obsessive neurosis very effectively. It is known that the founders of the big Hollywood studios were all Ashkenazi Jews[259]. Jean-Luc Doin wrote: "In the United States, cinema was at first restricted to flea markets and flea markets, with their background noise of barrel organs and wooden horses, attracting mainly people from poor neighbourhoods. The first projections were organised by adventurers: future owners of the *majors*, Adolphe Zuckor was an antiques and fur dealer, William Fox, a ragman, Carl Laemmle, a dressmaker. Projected in the dark, the films were suspected of fostering disorders of the soul, of fanning sensual frenzy or a taste for sin, "of disturbing tranquillity and public order[260]"."

From *softcore* to *hardcore*, a new illicit genre had established itself outside the usual underground circuits. Russ Meyer had thus made *The Immoral Mr. Teas, a* film that had been banned after causing a scandal. Russ Meyer had become the champion of legal proceedings, with twenty-three trials in one year.

In his *Dictionary of censorship in cinema*, published in 1998,

---

[258] Yann Moncomble, *La Politique, le sexe et la finance*, Faits-et-Documents, 1989, p. 26.
[259] Read *Planetary Hopes*, (2022).
[260] Jean-Luc Doin, *Films à scandale*, Éditions du Chêne, 2001, p. 12.

Jean-Luc Doin stated that the exhibition of non-simulated sexual acts dates back to 1912 in the United States, where mail-order stag-films circulated." These scenes became a fashionable phenomenon at the end of the 1960s, when they were screened in theatres usually reserved for *peep-shows*."

Pornographic cinema in France also had its era with its Israeli stamp. In 1925, Bernard Nathan, with *Sister Vaseline*, inaugurated this cinema in public, thus attacking the Catholic religion[261].

By the 1930s, the more conscientious goyim were already concerned about the extraordinary aggressiveness of Jewish cinema. In the United States, after some high-profile scandals, the *Legion of Decency* was formed, through which Catholics made their voices heard. The Legion of Decency demanded the establishment of a real "code of decency" to monitor the content of recorded fiction and to verify that "American values" were respected. Part of the Catholic hierarchy was involved in this campaign. In 1933, the Archbishop of Cincinnati (Ohio), Monsignor John McNicholas, declared: "I join all those who protest against these images which represent a grave threat to family life, to the nation and to religion." In the spring of 1934, the Cardinal of Philadelphia, Monsignor Denis Dougherty, called on all Catholics in the United States to boycott Hollywood productions "dominated by Jewish businessmen" and some 11 million of the faithful responded to his call[262]. The results of the boycott were not long in coming: theatres emptied and movie profits plummeted. President William Hays' Hays Code, dictating strict rules of decency, was enforced in 1934. Productions were to be subject to censorship by the Production Code Commission, chaired by Joseph Breen, a Catholic who exercised some power over Hollywood's moral and political standards for twenty years and whose policy was continued by McCarthy's in the 1950s.

But in 1961, the producers decided to violate the Hayscode on homosexuality and after 1968 it was no longer respected[263]. Fifty years later, almost all the dikes have collapsed under the combined pressure of cosmopolitan high finance and libertarian movements, whose activists think they are "revolutionary" but in reality do nothing more than parrot the cosmopolitan slogans of their leaders and doctrinaires.

---

[261] Georges Valensin, *La Vie sexuelle juive*, Éditions philosophiques, 1981, p. 164.

[262] See Thomas Dougherty, *Pré-code Hollywood: Sex, Immorality and Insurrection in American Cinema*, New York, Columbia University Press, 2000. And also: *Courrier international*, 3 February 2000.

[263] Jean-Luc Doin, *Dictionnaire de la censure au cinéma*, Presses Universitaires de France, 1998.

In 2005, the Catholic reaction to the wave of television and film filth was expressed by William Donohue, president of the League of American Catholics. When Mel Gibson's film *The Passion of the Christ*, so criticised by the official media, was released, he did not hesitate to declare in front of the television cameras: "Hollywood is controlled by secular Jews who hate Christianity. It's no secret and I'm not afraid to say it. That's why they hate this film, because it talks about Jesus Christ." He added: "I love family, while Hollywood loves anal sex[264]."

In Germany in 1918, the proliferation of sexually explicit films was already worrying the rulers. Movie theatres multiplied and their revenues doubled when they showed pornographic films. Jean-Luc Doin wrote: "Berlin is the prey of cocaine traffickers, and a haven for decadent nightclubs where numerous films are shown to audiences wearing domino masks to avoid being recognised. This depravity irritated good souls: in 1919, the Catholic Women's Leagues attacked Lubitsch's *Die Puppe*... In Düsseldorf, the audience of *Vow of Chastity* tore the screen apart; in Baden, the public prosecutor seized copies of *Prostitution* and prosecuted the author Oswald. Some anti-Semitic circles suggested that those responsible (the producers) of these sex films were Jews[265]." Indeed, this could prove to be an interesting lead.

In his 2003 book *The Great Awakening of the Mafias*, Xavier Raufer, professor of criminology at the University of Paris II—thus a specialist on the issue—had realised the seriousness of the danger: "In the 1960s, he wrote, the hippie wave of *peace and love*, free love, made the consumption of drugs and pornography explode. The mafia seized the opportunity, making porn the equivalent of Prohibition's bootleg booze: a huge source of cash, associated with a gigantic dirty money laundering machine." Xavier Raufer concluded: "The porn business is, from its origin, plain and simple a creation of the Italian-American mafia, its thing, its "winner" as they say in the underworld[266]." The editor of Xavier Raufer's book was a certain Jean-Claude Lattès, an "Italian-American" as you might have guessed.

Sex shops and prostitution: the Sefarade Connection

The first *sex shops* appeared in France in the 1960s, under the

---

[264]*Faits-et-Documents* du 15 janvier 2005
[265]Jean-Luc Doin, *Dictionnaire de la censure au cinéma*, Presses Universitaires de France, 1998, p. 17.
[266]Xavier Raufer, *Le grand Réveil des Mafias*, JC Lattès, 2003, p. 225, 226.

leadership of "not very Catholic" families. At that time, according to the police, between 60 and 70% of the turnover of the porn show business was in the hands of four "families" from North Africa, and the five Darmon brothers were undoubtedly the most enterprising. It was one of them, Paul, who opened the first *sex shop* in France in 1965[267].

At the forefront of that great moral liberation movement were also the Zemourbrothers, originally from Sétif in Algeria, whose name would become associated with the underworld, not only in France, but also in Germany, Spain and Israel. The eldest, Roland, was the first to arrive in France, but died anonymously in 1947 at the age of 21, probably in a settling of scores. In the 1950s, in Tel-Aviv, the Zemour brothers—William, Edgar, Gilbert and Andrew—frequented the Talmud Tora—the religious school—as well as the Zionism classes given by the kibbutz delegate.

After arriving in Paris, they first tried their hand at pimping, for which they were convicted several times and then released. They then joined Simon Atlan's gang and specialised in extorting money from shopkeepers in the *faubourg* Montmartre and the Sentier. Another clan vied with them for control of this activity: that of the Perret brothers, half-Jews whose mother, Léonie Benaïm, led the gang. On 2 October 1965, the murder of Simon Atlan was the first in a series of thirty-nine murders that decimated the Atlan clan. The Zemour brothers had no choice but to be the modest lieutenants or replace Simon Atlan. At the end of 1967, the Zemours attacked the Perret brothers. The Perret brothers were finally arrested by the police after a long night chase through Paris. The Zemours thus inherited the business.

The Zemourclan had its headquarters in a small bar on rue Pont Louis-Philippe in Paris. From there, the "Z's" revolutionised the landscape of pimping and organised crime by investing in porn in France, but also in several "Eros Centers" in Federal Germany. In their heyday, the Zemour brothers controlled a large part of Parisian prostitution, as well as numerous *sex shops* in the rue Saint-Denis. The Zemours had some two hundred soldiers under their command, so any hint of rebellion on the part of a shopkeeper was severely punished: physical violence or destruction of the establishment. During the Six-Day War, Jewish shopkeepers in the *faubourg* Montmartre turned to them to stop Arab aggression against their shops.

The Zemourbrothers had taken over the underground dens, the basements where small-time mobsters squandered their money by betting heavily on poker tables, baccarat and dice games. Gilbert, above

---

[267]Roger Faligot, Rémi Kauffer, *Porno Business*, Fayard, 1987, p. 176, 54, 55

all, was passionate about gambling.

Due to some problems with the police and the tax authorities, the Zemours left France in 1969 and settled in Israel with Jacques and Elie Aboutboul, their "representatives" in Cannes and owners of the *Vesuvio* restaurant frequented by many Israelis. Together they set up another restaurant in Tel Aviv before splitting up. A little later, the police would find piles of wads of fake dollars there, while a search of Jacques Aboutboul's flat uncovered an Uzi machine gun[268]. But because of their excessive greed they were shunned by the local underworld and returned to France, much to their disgrace. It was at a time when, under American pressure, France had decided to declare war on the French Connection. Although the Zemours had not been involved in this traffic, some of their lieutenants, such as Roger Bacri *"Petit Roger"*, were up to their necks in it. The latter, who had been excluded, declared war on them.

In March 1973, one of the Z's henchmen, Rafael Dadoun, was gunned down in his garage in Neuilly. A few days later, the answer came with the murder of Désiré Dahan in a restaurant in Vincennes. Raymond Elbaz was gunned down on 6 April in a bar in Saint-Germain; Henri Lévite was killed in his car on 27 May in the centre of Paris: twelve dead in seven months. Bacri, feeling cornered, ended up committing suicide.

The hecatomb culminated in the shooting at the Café Le Thélème, which caused rivers of ink to flow in the press for three years. On 28 February 1975, the police were informed by an informer that a meeting between the Zemours and Roger Bacri's "Sicilians" had been organised to put an end to their rivalry. The anti-mafia brigade, which had so far failed to bring a single criminal to justice, decided to intervene and caught them in flagrante delicto for possession of weapons. The meeting was to be held in a hideout in the bar Le Thélème, boulevard Saint-Germain. The inspectors burst into the bar: "Police! Hands up! You are surrounded! "A bodyguard shot and wounded the first inspector to enter the establishment. The shooting erupted. When calm returned, there was blood everywhere. William Zemour, 45, was dead, as was bodyguard Joseph Elbaz. Edgar Zemmour was wounded by four bullets. It would take him three months to recover. According to the police, the anti-mafia brigade had been manipulated by the informer. There was no organised meeting between the Z and the Sicilians. The anti-mafia brigade had been manipulated to exterminate the Zs. William's funeral at the Bagneux cemetery was staged in a grandiose manner.

---

[268] Jacques Derogy, *Israël Connection*, Plon, 1980, p. 62.

Gilbert, who ran a real estate business in Canada, had been expelled from the country and was a refugee in Miami. Edgar joined him in 1976. Andres, for his part, settled in Martinique. In Paris, the dissidents of the clan, the "Sicilians", were liquidating a personal friend of Gilbert. On 17 October 1975, Yzi Spiegel, owner of several discotheques and former friend of the Zemour brothers, was gunned down in the car park of his building. With him, the death toll reached thirty-one, but other murders would follow, all unpunished.

Gilbert, back in France, was sentenced to one year in prison for extortion in January 1978. His lawyer was shouting out loud. In fact, thanks to amnesties and statutes of limitation, Gilbert Zemour was free of any criminal record, even though he had a criminal record with organised crime. At the end of 1979, Gilbert Zemour opened a luxurious discotheque-restaurant club in Brussels. Police discovered that in the evenings the club turned into a poker den, while downstairs the escorts were very docile. Gilbert then bought the casino in Namur, but in November 1980 the casino was burned down.

In 1983, Edgar, who lived in Miami and had been involved in cocaine trafficking, was shot four times. A few months later, in July, Gilbert, who spent most of his time at the bridge club, took two 357 Magnum bullets in the chest at dawn near his home on Ségur Avenue. The third bullet in the head put an end to his career. In all, thirty-nine murders went unpunished forever.

In the small Parisian *sex shop scene*, the end of the Zemour empire caused bewilderment and confusion. The disappearance of Zemour had left the way open for a new generation of young Sephardic Jews. The new Parisian pimps did not run their businesses directly, preferring to leave this task to straw men, sometimes Vietnamese or Cambodian. But experience is not deceiving," wrote Roger Faligot: "When you ask for them on the phone of the *sex shops* with which they have no official relationship, they immediately get on the phone to answer the call. In this complicated architecture of 80 Parisian *sex shops* - 35 of which are on rue Saint-Denis—a few names stand out for their reputation as efficient managers: the brothers Serge and Richard Krief, Philippe Pantel, Mohamed and Ali Ouaghram, Patrick Atlan, Fernand and Jean-Claude Khalifa[269]."

At the beginning of the 1980s, *peep-shows* appeared. These were shows for those who wanted to see without being seen. After New York and Amsterdam, the phenomenon had arrived in Paris. Rue Saint-Denis, the Parisian *peep-shows* bore the number of the street: 25, 88, 109, 129,

---

[269]Roger Faligot, Rémi Kauffer, *Porno Business*, Fayard, 1987, p. 177, 178.

141, 144, 183, 187, 192. Roger Faligot presented some of them: *the Émeraude show* (Richard Krief), *88* (Roger Darmon), the *Christal show* (Joseph Haddad), the *Madison show* (Philippe Pantel), *147* (Eliezer Benhamou), the *Hard shop centre* (Gérard Tourmetz)[270].

Subsequently, the rue Saint-Denis was always "occupied" by Jewish pimps from North Africa. Jacques Perez, for example, owned six shops in rue Saint-Denis. Born in Constantine in 1939, he had been convicted in 1962 for having manufactured counterfeit dollars. Six other convictions followed, until 1989, all for pimping. In March 1991, a police raid on his shops caught three "actresses" performing fellatio. One of them, a big fan of orgies and a great blackmailer, was his trusted wife. Perez was arrested, but a derisory bail allowed him to go free. His luxurious lifestyle had drawn attention to his wealth, such as his beautiful property in Chelles and his numerous bank accounts[271].

Parisian Sephardic criminality was evident in the years 1985–1986 in the rivalry between the Azoulay and Ben Saadoun clans. The Azoulay clan, led by Jean-Claude, had by then taken the lead in extortion, pimping and drug trafficking. Together with the Italians, the gangsters controlled dozens of shopkeepers in the Les Halles district and employed many prostitutes in the rue Saint-Denis. They also had interests in Parisian nightclubs and restaurants. The Ben Saadouns decided to attack, and in September 1985, police from the anti-crime brigade found in the underground car park of the Les Halles forum a Mercedes riddled with 17 9 mm bullets. In the back seat was the lifeless body of a man shot in the chest and head. He was an Italian, a friend of the Azoulays. The Saadouns had the wrong Mercedes.

The counterattack was swift, and several Ben Saadoun shops and restaurants were burned down. Three months later, before Christmas, the Ben Saadoun launched a second offensive. In the Place de Mexico, in the 16th arrondissement of Paris, Jacques Azoulay, 32, and one of his lieutenants, Elie Zerdoun, 37, nicknamed "Willy the Barroso", were gunned down in their BMW, machine-gunned. The Azoulays repaid the Ben Saadoun family in the same way in October 1986, on the eve of Yom Kippur. Two gunmen on motorbikes liquidated Fréderic Ricco, of the Ben Saadoun clan, as well as a former Zemour man as they left a restaurant near Les Folies-Bergères. After that, the Ben Saadouns decided to go abroad. The war had resulted in five dead and several wounded.[272]

---

[270]Roger Faligot, Rémi Kauffer, *Porno Business*, Fayard, 1987, p. 186.
[271]Jacques Solé, *L'Âge d'or de la prostitution, de 1870 à nos jours*, Plon, 1993, p. 275.
[272]June 1989 issue of the Jewish monthly *Passages: La vérité sur les truands juifs*.

The rest of the Sephardic families in that mafia environment limited themselves to managing their interests in well-known restaurants, discotheques, pimping and *sex shops*. Maurice Azoulay and Daniel Morati, for their part, were the specialists of the fixed poker games that were always held in the same flat in Paris XVI. Maurice Azoulay and Daniel Morati were arrested by the Drugs and Pimping Squad after a fake poker game during which they had threatened and swindled 170,000 francs from an honest Swiss citizen. After many years, he had been the only conned player to have the courage to denounce them. But Daniel Morati also had another speciality: marriage fraud. A seducer, he lured wealthy women by promising them an idyllic marriage. Too trusting, they gave him access to their bank accounts. Morati's last two hauls amounted to 380,000 francs and 1.2 million francs.

Baron Sinclair was another emblematic figure of Parisian pimping. He was only "dedicated" to luxury prostitution. In 1982, he had already been convicted for the first time. After that, he had preferred to go to the United States. When he returned to France in 1988, he resumed his usual activities. His clients were industrial magnates, businessmen, princes of the Persian Gulf, some of whom had opened an account for him at the grand George V hotel. Between two appointments, for a dinner or an evening, they paid for the company of beautiful creatures. Between 2000 and 5000 francs for the smallest service; from 20,000 to 60,000 francs for a night or a weekend. A textile industrialist claimed to have paid her 913,000 francs over three years (the cost of a Rolls Royce). A major Italian car manufacturer paid 20 to 30,000 dollars a year.

In court, the baron categorically denied everything. The "clients", he said, were in fact "a constellation of very rich friends for whom he did favours." In fact, he mentioned his friendship with Fahal of Arabia: "I've known him for more than twenty years, we are super friends. I introduced him to a girl with whom he had a son, so of course…"." He claimed to have simply been "a sort of entertainer among my friends and my girlfriends." But by no means a pimp!

In his brand new flat on the Place du Marché Saint-Honoré, police seized eleven high-value paintings. In the United States he had trafficked in works of art: "I bought and sold paintings, he said. I know so many people there, I have so many friends…"." The presiding judge then made this remark: "Paintings are a form of investment for you. In fact, art dealers say you don't understand anything about art[273]."

---

[273] *Libération*, 4 May 1993. Archives of Emmanuel Ratier. In the June 1989 issue of the

The great Italian car tycoon, who was also one of his "friends", was nevertheless in the habit of nicknaming Baron Sinclair "Pinocchio" because of his everlasting lies. The policemen agreed that he was "a talker and a seducer". On top of that, "Jacky" was a lot of fun, for "Baron Sinclair" was mostly known to girls under the name of "Jacky Cohen". He was a repatriate from Algeria. His real name was actually Isaac Sellam. He was a teenager when he landed in Marseille with his mother after the Algerian war. On 3 May 1993, Isaac was sentenced to four years in prison and fined 1.2 million francs. When will the persecutions end?

The June 1989 issue of the Jewish monthly *Passages* reported on other activities favoured by criminals. In 1980, a network of money counterfeiters was dismantled in Lyon. Police officers had arrested Marc-Roger Azan, 38, at his home, where they found hundreds of 17-carat Napoleon coins instead of the standard 22 carats[274]. Marc-Roger Azan had recently bought a flat on the Promenade des Anglais in Nice. In one year, he had changed cars four times.

In the 1980s, the "Marais Gang" raided the flats of elderly women posing as polite and friendly policemen. They were "all of Tunisian Jewish origin". This gang operated mainly in the western part of Paris, in the 16th and 17th arrondissements up to Neuilly. They would spot an elderly woman coming out of a bank, follow her home and note down the flat where she lived and manage to get her name. They would then look up her number in the telephone directory and a "commissaire" would call to warn her of the thefts in the neighbourhood and propose a visit by two inspectors. The criminals sometimes operated in police uniforms that they had stolen from the garment workshops that worked for the Ministry of the Interior.

On 22 February 1983, in Besançon, 23-year-old William Nakache shot six times Abdellali Kahar, a 19-year-old Arab who had disturbed the owners of a discotheque. Nakache had taken refuge in Israel. Shortly afterwards, he was arrested under a false identity with four accomplices, all disguised as policemen, as they were preparing to stop the car of a

---

Jewish monthly *Passages*, devoted to *"The truth about Jewish crooks"*, the lawyer Francis Turquem mentioned the trafficking of works of art: "Israel recovers for its museums the inheritances of property that should remain in France. There are a number of associations and foundations that make a fairly precise inventory of the estates of certain families and put pressure on elderly people to have their property transferred to Israel. This is a crime of illegal export: many paintings are undervalued through some experts, practically in collusion with the Israeli embassy."

[274] Already in the Middle Ages, some Jews were accused of debasing the coinage. When coins were striated, they used acid as a debasement technique.

Greek Catholic bishop and rob him. In prison, William Nakache had a timely bout of religious fervour. He grew a beard, ostentatiously wore a prayer shawl and kippah, and was sponsored by the rabbis. He declared loud and clear that he had brought down a "notorious anti-Semite" and claimed to fear for his life if he was extradited to France. In Israel, Nakache became a hero. Under pressure from the religious community, the Minister of Justice refused to extradite him. In 1986, the Besanzon court sentenced him in absentia to life imprisonment.

André Bellaïche was an illustrious figure in the great banditry. Born in Tunis in 1950, he was the leader of the "Gang of the Postiches". At the time, this gang carried out around thirty armed robberies of Parisian banks. Jean-Claude Myszka, André Bellaïche, Bruno Berliner and Patrick Geay operated in wigs, disguised as English aristocrats, Sherlock Holmes hats or even rabbis. They were arrested in December 1986 and sentenced to 8 to 15 years in prison. In his book entitled *My life without a hairpiece,* André Bellaïche recounted it all: "Those clandestine trips with his wife and son, his Dior suits, his Ferraris, the story of his social climbing, everything except his robberies with the Posticios." (*Libération* of 18 October 2007). The Postizos gang was the subject of a film by Ariel Zeitoun, *Le dernier gang*, released in 2007. The rights to adapt the film had been sold at a high price. After eight years in prison, Bellaïche declared: "To live quietly as a bourgeois retired from business: I had prepared myself for everything but that." The journalist from *"Libé"*, probably enraptured with admiration, had forgotten about the death of a policeman in the shooting in January 1986.

Sephardic Parisian criminality was not over, judging by some discreet articles published in the press. On 4 November 2002, in Place des Fêtes, in the 20th arrondissement of Paris, Felix Lévy, 46, was shot four times, twice in the head, as he sat drinking his coffee and croissant at half past nine in the morning. The man was already known to the justice system for a case involving counterfeit US dollars[275].

Sephardic criminals had more films, such as *The Great Pardon (Le Grand Pardon,* France 1982*)*. The first part is a synthesis of everything: Raymond Bettoun (Roger Hanin, born Lévy) runs casinos and nightclubs, makes girls work on the streets, extorts small businessmen and deals in stolen diamonds. In the second part, we see him in Miami with his henchmen. This time he came to lend a hand to his son who is laundering drug money. But beware, the Jews don't get their hands dirty: they don't deal directly in cocaine and leave the dirty

---

[275]*Le Parisien*, 23 November 2002, archives of Emmanuel Ratier.

work to a goy. He is as rich as he is cruel. We also learn that his father was a Nazi refugee in Chile. He is the real bastard in the film. In the first part, the bastard was already a bleary-eyed white man (Bernard Giraudeau), a criminal who had manipulated the Jews against the Arabs. And the commissioner who pursued poor Raymond Bettoun was also a racist ("I don't like your manners. You smell of oil"). The film is by Alexandre Arcady.

Roger Hanin, who was the brother-in-law of French President François Mitterrand, was the director of the anti-racist film *Train d'enfer* (1985)—the story of three young fascists who defenestrated a Maghrebi from a train. The story was inspired by a real case that took place on 15 November 1983 on the Bordeaux-Vintimilla train. Xavier Blondel, Marc Beani and Anselmo Elviro Vidal, candidates for the Foreign Legion, had beaten up Habib Grimzi in front of several witnesses and thrown him out of the window onto the rails. Elviro Vidal confessed: "He had been drinking, he was an Arab and I don't like Arabs." What Roger Hanin did not tell us in his film is that Vidal was Jewish. Before the trial, Vidal had written a letter to the *Nouvel Observateur* calling for capital punishment. The letter was published on 31 January 1986, and the article was entitled: "I, Anselmo Elviro Vidal, Jew and murderer..."." Following the release of Roger Hanin's film, Rabbi Jacques Grunewald published a review in the weekly *Tribune juive* on 11 January 1985: "Atrocious murder on a train: a young Arab is lynched and defenestrated by three tipsy conscripts. From this case, a racist act by three outcasts, Roger Hanin has constructed a film from which he intends to draw a great moral lesson, this time involving the whole of deepest France. It is no longer about three isolated, drunken kids. It is a real neo-Nazi network involving a whole city, even the whole world." The rabbi added: "Roger Hanin claims that as an Algerian Jew, he has learned since childhood to love Arabs. Apparently, he has not been taught to love the French."

3. The White slave trade

Sex slaves in Israel

Since the fall of the Berlin Wall in 1989, hundreds of thousands of young women from the East had been recruited by prostitution rings and taken to distant destinations. The media remained extremely discreet on this issue. However, in May 2000, an Amnesty International report revealed the magnitude of the phenomenon and identified the State of Israel as the centre of trafficking[276].

The collapse of the USSR in 1991 had led to a considerable impoverishment of the population. Many young Russian, Ukrainian and Moldovan women had responded to attractive job offers published in the press in an attempt to escape poverty and provide for their families. Unfortunately for them, these offers of work abroad often turned out to be traps set by international pimps.

The phenomenon was so important that the very cosmopolitan *New York Times* of 11 January 1998 had been forced to cover the story with an article by Michael Specter on the "naïve Slavic women". The journalist told the moving story of a 21-year-old Ukrainian beauty who had left her village in response to an advertisement in a local newspaper and found herself trapped in Israel, forced into prostitution. The girls were reportedly sent as far as Japan and Thailand by networks of "Russian" gangsters based in Moscow. Remember that, at that time, all the media were talking about the terrible "Russian mafia".

The *Jerusalem Post* of 13 January 1998 picked up on these reports. The newspaper reported that there were more than 10,000 prostitutes in Israel, almost all of them Russian and Ukrainian. The women, bought and sold by pimps, were abducted from bars and brothels, each earning their owner between 50 and 100,000 dollars a year.

The first report on the trafficking of white women was published on 8 April 1997 by CEDAW[277]. That report showed that the trafficking

---

[276] *Amnesty International* 's French-language editions. http://efai.i-france.com. *Human Rights Abuses of Women Trafficked from Countries of the Former Soviet Union into Israel's Sex Industry.*
[277] Committee on the Elimination of Discrimination Against Women.

of abducted white women in Israel was on the rise. In Tel-Aviv, hundreds of bars, brothels and nightclubs were the scene of nightlife. The *Tropicana* was then one of the most prominent brothels. About twenty Russian women worked there, eight during the day and twelve at night. The clients were Israeli soldiers, businessmen, religious men, and immigrant workers—for the latter were not allowed to have sex with Israeli women on pain of immediate expulsion. The owner of the place declared: "Israelis love Russian women. They're blonde, they're hot, and they have a desperate air about them that they like a lot. They are willing to do anything to earn money." The girls were not paid and only pocketed tips. They worked non-stop, seven days out of seven, with no rest during the year except Yom Kippur.

Amnesty International's extensive report presented the testimonies of several young women. They had been lured under pretexts and then handed over to prostitution rings, bought and sold to the highest bidder, most often at auction, like cattle. They were then sequestered by their "owners" in houses or flats from which they could not leave unaccompanied. Their passports and identity documents were confiscated by the pimps to prevent them from leaving the country. They were often beaten if they refused to have sex with certain clients or if they tried to flee. There were numerous reports of torture, rape and other sexual abuse. Traffickers threatened to kill them and their family members if they tried to leave Israel, informed the police or testified in criminal proceedings, making it very difficult to bring to court "the perpetrators of violations of the fundamental rights of trafficked persons[278]".

The Israeli government had taken no steps to investigate and prosecute such violence. Moreover, the women were generally treated as criminals rather than victims. Indeed, according to Israeli law, almost all of the girls were irregular immigrants, residing in Israel without a work contract or with false documents. Many of them were arrested after police raids on brothels or massage parlours. Some were imprisoned for a short period of time before being expelled from the territory, but others were imprisoned for much longer, in some cases on the basis of a Justice Ministry order preventing them from leaving the country before testifying in court. Many imprisoned women had suffered significant physical and psychological trauma, and there was no counselling service to address their needs.

During their visit to Israel in April-May 1999, Amnesty International delegates had visited the Neve Tirza women's prison in

---

[278] The term "fundamental rights" is constantly repeated in the report.

order to meet young women imprisoned for prostitution-related activities and awaiting repatriation.

This was the testimony of Anna, 31, originally from St Petersburg. She was a physics teacher in Russia, and had been lured to Israel with a promise of a job paying $1,000 per month, twenty times the salary she was earning in Russia at the time. The Israeli citizen who had offered her the job had warned her that he was involved in the sex industry, but what he had offered her was clearly not the real thing. Ana arrived in Israel in 1998 on a tourist visa. On arrival at the airport, she was taken and locked in a flat with six other women from the former Soviet Union and her passport was immediately confiscated. Ana was then successively sold at two auctions. The second time, she was bought for $10,000 and taken to Haifa where she was held hostage with two other women. The windows of the flat were barred and the rare times they were allowed to leave they were always accompanied. Much of the money they earned was extorted by the pimps in the form of fines.

Ana had been arrested in March 1999 for prostitution following a police raid on the flat where she was being held. She had signed statements presented by the police in which she acknowledged engaging in prostitution, although all the documents were in Hebrew, a language she could neither read nor write. Only later, at the court hearing, did she learn that she was accused of running a brothel. She was never allowed to meet the Russian consul, and remained in jail for another month until her expulsion from the territory.

This is what Ana said: "I don't know how the trial ended. I only know that Abraham [the pimp] is free. I spoke to him on the phone. When the policemen arrested us, they did not let us pick up our belongings, which were left there. Abraham[279] knows my address in St. Petersburg and my phone number as well as my passport. I left my eight-year-old daughter there. He has threatened me that he would find me in Russia if I didn't do what he wanted."

Tatiana, originally from Belarus, had arrived in Israel in April 1998 on a tourist visa. She had been promised a job as a cleaning lady at a hotel in the Eilat resort, being told that her salary would allow her to provide for her mother and six-year-old son. Tatiana was taken in Eilat by a man allegedly sent by the hotel where she was to work. She was taken to another place where she was forced into prostitution. She was told that she had to reimburse her "selling price" and the cost of her journey.

Tatiana had devised several escape plans, but was finally released

---

[279] The drafters of the Amnesty International report had chosen the name "Arturo".

after a police raid: one of her friends had contacted the Belarusian consulate, which had alerted the police. Tatiana was placed in detention as an illegal immigrant in Neve Tirza prison pending her repatriation. A few days after her detention, she found an anonymous letter on her bed threatening her and her family with death if she told what had happened to her. Tatiana wanted to testify but feared reprisals from the traffickers who knew all the details in her passport as well as her family's address in Belarus. An injunction was therefore submitted to the police director to explain that it would be too dangerous for Tatiana to testify in court if she was not protected. He replied that the Israeli police could not guarantee the safety of any individual outside Israel. Tatiana finally testified in June 1999 and was repatriated at the end of the month. Although she had requested to be sent to Poland or Lithuania to return to Belarus by road from there, the Israeli authorities had sent her directly to Belarus, where one of her relatives had allegedly taken her to an unknown destination.

The following is the case of Valentina, a 27-year-old Ukrainian psychologist. She had come to Israel in August 1998 to work as a representative. The Israeli citizen who had offered her the job had arranged the visa and made the travel arrangements. Valentina was met at the airport and taken to a hotel. The next day, her money, passport and return ticket were confiscated. She was then sent to a flat where she was held for two months. Valentina recounted her ordeal in Israel: "The living conditions were terrible. One girl worked in the cellar for eight months, she caught tuberculosis because of the damp. Most of the girls suffered from various venereal infections. I wouldn't wish my enemies to suffer what they inflicted on us... I had a nervous breakdown, Valentina explained. I wanted to run away, but there were bars on the windows and the guards were always present, day and night. One day, I asked a client for help, but it turned out that I was part of their group and the owners beat me. I had nowhere to go..."

Valentina, however, managed to escape with another woman by jumping from the first floor of the building. When they returned to the house of prostitution to try to help another of their friends escape, they were arrested by the police operating at the time. Valentina was arrested in March 1999 for illegal residence. Happy with the police intervention, Valentina was afraid to testify because the pimps knew her family's address in Ukraine. Valentina did not know how long the Israeli authorities would keep her in detention.

Nina was a nineteen-year-old girl from Minsk in Belarus. She too had arrived in Israel at the end of 1998 on a tourist visa, unaware of what awaited her. She was kidnapped for three months in a Haifa brothel and then abducted under the threat of a gun, sold for $10,000, beaten and raped. After managing to escape, Nina returned to the first brothel in the hope of earning enough money to pay for her ticket back to Belarus. Nina was then arrested during a police raid on a Tel-Aviv massage parlour in March 1999 and imprisoned in Neve Tirza prison before being deported. The Haifa district attorney had forbidden her to leave Israel to testify against the three men who had abducted her." I want to go home," Nina said, "but the trial of Moses [the man accused of raping her] may not take place for another six months. I want to be sure that Moses[280] goes to prison."

She is a criminal," explained Haifa police spokesman Moshe Nissan. She has been living in Israel without a residence permit. It is obvious that she would not testify if she were not in detention." Nina was finally repatriated in June 1999 after being imprisoned for more than two months.

Amnesty International was unable to obtain from the Israeli authorities any statistics on the number of legal proceedings instituted, or data on complaints or convictions handed down in such cases against pimps. According to 2001 research by the *National Council of Jewish Women*, of the 392 prostitutes arrested and expelled from Israel in 2000, 46% were Ukrainian, 28% were Russian and 17% were Moldovan. The remaining 9% were from other republics of the former Soviet Union.

Similar testimony appeared in an article in the *Jerusalem Post* of 13 July 2000, which recounted the trial of 18-year-old Boris Yasser. He was accused of kidnapping, threats, forgery of documents, physical assault, pimping and rape. Boris Yasser was accused of helping his father smuggle in four young Ukrainian women and forcing them into prostitution. The four young women aged 19 to 22, who were also arrested for having entered the country illegally, explained that they had been offered a job as saleswomen. Once they had accepted the job, they were taken to Israel via Cyprus. In Haifa, their passports were taken from them and they were given false Israeli identity documents. Two of the girls were then sold to a brothel in Tel Aviv for 3,000 dollars each. The other two were kidnapped from a flat in Rishon Lezion and forced into prostitution. Boris Yasser drove the young women to the clients, between 15 and 20 per day. The girls were not paid a penny. One of them had been violently beaten after she had tried to run away. They later managed to telephone their parents in Ukraine for help. They contacted the Ukrainian embassy.

---

[280]The report simply said "X".

In 1998, the Hungarian Consul in Tel-Aviv, Andrea Horvath, also complained that four young Hungarian women, who had met their employer in a discotheque in Budapest, were being held against their will in houses in Tel-Aviv and forced into prostitution.

According to the CEDAW report of April 1997, there was a strong correlation between prostitution and drug use. Of the 200 young women incarcerated in Neve Tirza prison, 70% were addicted to heroin, the most common drug in Israel. The young women were effectively drugged to make them even more dependent on the pimps. In the end, they became totally addicted and prostituted themselves simply to pay for their heroin doses. The girls were not allowed to see a doctor; any medical assistance was denied. If they became pregnant, the pimps would not pay for the abortion. They were forced to work for five more months and thrown out on the street.

In the *New York Times* of 11 January 1998, Irina, who had experienced the same experiences in Israel, confided to the reporter with tears in her eyes: "I don't believe that the man who ruined my life will one day be punished, she said softly. I'm stupid... I'm a stupid girl from a small town... Sometimes, I sit here and wonder how all that could have happened, even if it really did happen." Like many others, Irina had been beaten and raped after refusing to prostitute herself.

The CEDAW report further noted that advertisements for the sex industry had multiplied in the daily press to such an extent that a committee had been set up to ban advertisements that explicitly mentioned the age of girls under 18 and to moderate the pictures accompanying such advertisements. There was a booming child pornography market in Israel[281]. The number of Eastern European girls under 18 prostituted in Israel was probably large, but unknown.

The American magazine *Moment*—"the magazine of Jewish culture"—had published an article in April 1998 in which one could read that Russian girls were highly valued by Israeli clients. There were all kinds of men; lawmen, policemen, but above all a significant proportion of these clients were ultra-orthodox Jews who came because they could not have relations with their wives due to religious proscriptions[282]. On Thursday afternoon, fleets of buses took them from Jerusalem to Tel Aviv.

The prostitutes also included Arab women, virtually reduced to a

---

[281]On this topic, see the chapters on the subject in *Psychoanalysis of Judaism* (2006) and *Jewish Fanaticism* (2007).
[282]On religious proscriptions, see also *Psychoanalysis of Judaism* (2006) and *Jewish Fanaticism* (2007).

state of slavery. Some of the Jewish clients came after a Palestinian attack to take revenge on the Palestinian prostitutes.

But the pimps also took advantage of the Arabs' anger, as one could read in a book by an Israeli writer entitled *The Promised Land, Not Yet*, published in 2002. This is what the author wrote about those "Russian" gangsters in Israel: "The Russians are white Africans. They pounce on everything that glitters. They are willing to do anything to succeed, the worst rackets, the worst misdeeds. I read in the paper that a Russian was prostituting girls dressed as soldiers in the Territories. It's not nonsense. By dint of being beaten up by the military, the Arabs must be in the mood[283]! "

International Affairs magazine in 2000 spoke of the "Natasha trade". The white slave trade generated between seven and twelve million dollars a year and carried few risks compared to drug or arms trafficking. Yitzhal Tyler of the Haifa police explained to Michael Specter of the *New York Times* in 1998: "With about ten girls, each taking 15 to 20 clients a day, multiply by 200 sequels, that's 30,000 sequels a day and at least 750,000 a month, that's 215,000 dollars. A pimp who owns five brothels, as is often the case, earns a million dollars per month."

In fact, there were "no laws in Israel against human trafficking or prostitution", reported the *New York Times* of 11 January 1998. Indeed, there was no law prohibiting the importation of young foreign women into Israel for prostitution, confirmed the CEDAW report of 8 April 1997. Linda Menuhim further explained (Reuters, 23 August 1998), "The problem is not finding the good article in the penal code, but finding a woman who dares to go to court."

The report published by the Haifa Feminist Centre was another important source of information. It was mainly based on interviews with 106 women victims of trafficking who were interrogated between 2001 and 2002 in Israeli prisons and various shelters. The authors pointed to the inability of the authorities to deal with the mafias and also blamed some of the police officers involved as clients of the brothels, but also as collaborators of the pimps.

The women questioned had been sold for between 5,000 and 10,000 dollars. They had worked without interruption, without holidays, even during their rules. A third of them were victims of daily aggression. The clients and the pimps considered them as objects and

---

[283] Michaël Sebban, *La terre promise, pas encore*, Ramsay, 2002, p. 99. Jews from Russia—more than a million since the fall of communism—were called "Russians" by Israelis.

beat them continuously. About 10% of them were poorly fed, half of them confessed that many policemen regularly frequented these brothels and that they were not only friends with the pimps, but were often in business with them.

This industry was still booming in 2005, if one is to believe the report of an Israeli parliamentary commission of enquiry revealed on 23 March 2005 and reported by Agence France Presse. White slavery in Israel was an activity that generated a turnover of nearly one billion dollars per year. The report stated that between 3,000 and 5,000 women were smuggled into Israel each year to work as prostitutes. These women were abducted from 300 to 400 brothels in different regions of the country. They were sold for between 8,000 and 10,000 dollars and then served as sex slaves every day of the week for between 14 and 18 hours a day[284]. They received only 20 sekels ($4) of the 120 paid on average for each client. The rest of the sum was pocketed by the pimp; but some received nothing at all. The study carried out at the request of the commission had also shown that the Israeli public did not consider the trafficking of whites as a violation of human rights.

The commission pointed out the weaknesses of the Israeli justice system in these cases. In fact, the investigation of complaint cases took a long time, which allowed and encouraged threats and even the murder of the complainants. The report noted that judges were often bribed by pimps. Prosecutors demanded minimal sentences and did not even demand damages for victims. Magistrates also benefited pimps with immunity by posing as suspected crime informants for the police.

However, some orthodox Jews reacted to what they saw as an invasion of Israeli cities by pimps and prostitutes. On 15 August 2000, the Associated Press reported that four women had died in a criminal fire in Tel-Aviv; four Russian women who had been unable to escape because the armoured door was locked and the windows sealed with bars. The four women had been held hostage in a flat behind a bar that served as a brothel. The investigation revealed that a religious Jew had thrown an incendiary bomb. Yariv Baruchim, 34, explained to the police that he wanted to purify Tel-Aviv of all its brothels. He had set fire to eight brothels and *sex shops*. That time there were four victims: Ina Takorsky, Lila Zachs and Yelena Pomina died. The fourth girl could never be identified.

Some Israeli filmmakers—and it is to their credit—took an interest in the ordeal of these young European women. Eyal Halfon's

---

[284] European women of childbearing age today represent less than 2% of humanity. They are a scarce and valuable "commodity" highly prized by pimps.

film *Welcome to Israel* (2005) showed women who came from Ukraine in the hope of earning some money in Israel. But contrary to the promises they were given, they ended up enslaved, raped by their pimps and forced into prostitution. The film also showed Thai labourers working as convicts on a farm in Israel.

Also on the same theme is Amos Gitai's film, *Promised Land* (2005), which recounted the ordeal of young Eastern European women trapped in prostitution rings. They are sold like cattle at auction, in the middle of the night, in the desert and end up in brothels on the edge of the Dead Sea. *Promised Land* begins with a scene of a night auction of these women in the Sinai desert. When I became interested in the criminal networks that operate across the borders of the Middle East," explains Amos Gitai, "I realised that trafficking in women was a new form of slavery on the rise. For these international networks that organise the White slave trade, women are simply commodities. They are transported from their country of origin, mostly Eastern Europe, via the Sinai in Egypt. They easily cross the Israeli border and are then distributed in different Israeli cities or in the territories... Before filming the *Promised Land*, I spent a lot of time documenting myself thanks to reports from NGOs working in Israel and other parts of the world to defend human rights. Hundreds of pages of testimonies from victims of white slavery show in detail how these international networks operate... Some women believe that they will be able to escape from misery thanks to such deals. They try to persuade themselves that it is only for a while and then they will have some money. They are abused on all levels, physically and emotionally, to an unimaginable extent... Auctions of women are known to take place in many places. I decided to film the sale at an auction at night, in the desert. The women are surrounded by a group of vehicles, like an arena, to create a sense of claustrophobia... The common thread of *Promised Land* is the fate of these women. We have followed them along this road on which they are transported from one place to another. There is a constant change of location in the *Promised Land*. From Tallinn to Haifa, from Cairo to Ramallah via Eilat, the women pass from hand to hand, from the desert to the car parks, from an immense aquarium built underwater in the Dead Sea to the various vehicles, lorries, motorways, etc.....".

Of course, Israel is not the only destination for these girls from the East. The Jewish mafia in Russia had contacts with the Jewish mafia all over the world. According to the Ukrainian Ministry of the Interior, 400,000 young Ukrainian women under the age of thirty had left the country during the 1990s. They may not all have fallen into prostitution rings, but the International Organisation for Migration estimated the number of young women from the former Eastern bloc trapped in rings around the world at 500,000. The *New York Times* article of 11 January 1998 indicated that Slavic women were sent to Turkey, and as far away as Japan and Thailand.

Many girls from the East had come to the former Yugoslavia. An article by Oksana Havrylenko, a Ukrainian, told us about her own ordeal. We have translated it from English: pimps recruited mainly through small advertisements in newspapers, offering a well-paid job abroad as a waitress, dancer or cleaning lady in Italy, except that it was not possible to get a direct visa for Italy, so they had to pass through the territory of the former Yugoslavia to cross the Adriatic Sea by ferry. In Bosnia-Herzegovina, where there was no Ukrainian consulate, the girls then understood the fate that awaited them. One girl who had categorically refused to prostitute herself had been beaten, tortured and killed in front of the other girls in a camp. Finally, the pimps had slit her throat. Girls who were too difficult were resold in the Muslim area. The pimps said that none of them had ever managed to escape.

The Italian authorities put the number of young women illegally employed in the country at 30,000. The *New York Times article* on the "Naïve Slav women" provided the testimony of another young Ukrainian woman. In Milan, Italy, a week before Christmas, a police operation had interrupted an auction. The girls were presented on boxes, half-naked and sold like cattle for an average of $1,000. Michael Platzer of the United Nations explained that prostitution did not present many risks as it was almost legal in many countries. In fact, in Israel, there was no law against the sale of human beings. It seems pertinent to point out here that, according to the Talmud, non-Jews are often considered as animals[285].

---

[285] The Talmud frequently discusses and denies that gentiles are human persons. As for example in *Keritot, 6b*: "The Mishnah includes in its list of persons liable to *Karet* [punishment]: One who applies anointing oil to his skin. The Sages taught in a *Baraita* [tradition, teaching, but outside of the Mishnah]: He who applies the anointing oil to animals or vessels is exempt, and he who applies it to gentiles or corpses is also exempt. The Gemara objects: It is true that one is exempt in the case of animals and vessels, since it is written: "On the flesh of a person it shall not be applied" (*Exodus 30:32*), and animals and vessels are not the flesh of a person. It is also clear why one is exempt if one applies it to a corpse, since once someone has died, the body is called a corpse and not a person. But if one applies anointing oil to the gentiles, why is he exempt—are they not included in the meaning of the term person [Adam]?
The Gemara explains: Indeed, they are not. As it is written, "And you, my sheep, the sheep of my pasture, are people [Adam]" (*Ezekiel 34:31*), from which it follows that

The American website Jew Watch, a kind of observatory of Judaism, revealed this information about a network of pimping of young Russian women in Florida: in 1996, a certain Sergey Skobeltsyn had bought two nightclubs, the *Pure Platinium* and the *Solid Gold* for eight million dollars. Ludwig Fainberg, for his part, had bought the *Porkys* and was involved in a prostitution ring that 'imported' Russian women.

In the *Jerusalem Post* of 31 January 2000, we were informed that the spiritual leader of the Jewish community in Chicago, Joel Gordon, 51, former "cantor" of Congregation Shirat Emet, had been arrested with his wife, Alison Ginsberg, 23, both accused of having opened several brothels.

On 15 September 1997, the *New York Post* reported that one Roman Israilov, from Brooklyn, had kidnapped and raped a 20-year-old Russian immigrant girl whom he had tried to sell. The police had been tipped off by a neighbour.

Such tragedies do not usually make the headlines in the Western media, and we never hear politicians or show business celebrities protesting against such infamous trafficking. Imagine now what the reaction would have been if Europeans had enslaved and subjected thousands of young Jewish women to all sorts of humiliations. But the media's silence on these issues is understandable when we see the links between the gangsters and those in charge of the small "international media community".

Certainly, young European women, especially blondes, are highly appreciated by Jews, judging by what we can read in literature. Listen for example to the famous American novelist Philip Roth: "How do they manage to be so beautiful, so healthy, so blonde? I despise their beliefs, but that is more than compensated for by my adoration of their physique, the way they move and laugh and talk[286]."

We find the same image of the Jew and the beautiful blonde in the Yiddishwriter Isaac Bashevis Singer, winner of the Nobel Prize for Literature in 1978, in his novel *The Slave*, published in 1962. The story follows the life of Jacob, a poor Jew in 17th century Poland, who has been sold into slavery to a peasant in the mountains after a pogrom destroyed his community. Isaac Bashevis Singer described the Polish peasants in the most insulting and contemptuous terms. Among those

---

you, the Jewish people, are called Adam, but the Gentiles are not called Adam." https://www.sefaria.org. (NdT).

[286] Philip Roth, *Portnoy's Evil*, Penguin Random House Debols! llo, Barcelona, 2008. p. 158, 159.

human-like animals lived, however, a beautiful young woman, Wanda, the daughter of her Polish master." At twenty-five, she was taller than most women. Blonde and blue-eyed, she had a fair complexion and harmonious features." Isaac Singer then plucked that pretty flower from the dung on which it grew, for one must take what is most beautiful from the filthy goyim. The only creature worthy of respect among these Poles was betrothed to the Jew[287].

In Stefan Zweig's novel *The Dangerous Piety* (1939), a respectable and very wealthy Hungarian castle owner named Von Kekesfalva turns out to be a Jew who has gone to great lengths to conceal his true identity, Lämmel Kanitz. The family doctor, Dr. Condor, reveals the secret and Stefan Zweig, through his character, described the individual in no uncertain terms: "What impressed me about Kanitz from the beginning was his truly demonic will to increase his knowledge as well as his fortune... He studied all the law books, commercial law as well as industrial law, to become his own lawyer ... and he was versed in all investments and transactions like a banker." This Jew, who had built up a colossal fortune in a somewhat dubious way, "had the possibility of making more money in twenty-four hours than he had hitherto made in twenty-four years of small and deplorable rackets at the expense of a Hungarian peasant". He had also married a young woman, a very kind person, a beautiful Aryan, a *"shiksa"*: "how could he, an almost old man, a Jew, a dingy, ugly, money-grubbing, money-grubbing, itinerant broker, propose in marriage to a girl of such a distinguished soul, such a delicate soul[288]."

In Robert Bober's novel *Novels of War*, the matchmaker, "Madame Sarah", was returning from a tour of the Parisian dressmaking workshops with her little tokens. This is what the narrator wrote, revealing the obvious envy of this people so strongly marked by genetic defects: "In our family we have always liked rosy cheeks. They are a sign of good health, my mother used to say. In Poland, when she saw Polish girls on the pavement in front of her, she always envied their rosy cheeks under their blonde braids. She could only console herself with a curse[289]."

---

[287] Isaac Bashevis Singer, *The Slave*, 1962, Epublibre, digital publisher German25 (2014), p. 48; Hervé Ryssen, *Psychoanalysis of Judaism*.
[288] Stefan Zweig, *La Piedad peligrosa*, Acantilado, Barcelona, 2006, p. 70, 82, 90 quoted in Jacques Le Rider, *in Europe*, 1995, p. 40, 41. Shiksa: gentle woman, derogatory.
[289] Robert Bober, *Quoi de neuf sur la guerre?* Folio, 1993, p. 19. On matchmaking and genetic defects, see *Psychoanalysis of Judaism*.

Cyprus and migrant smuggling

In Cyprus, the situation was manifestly identical to that in Israel, at least in the Turkish-dominated north of the island. The area conquered by the Turks in 1974 had become, in the words of a European diplomat, a "rogue state". A state recognised only by Turkey and which served as a refuge for all international criminals. The real lord of this "Turkish Republic of Northern Cyprus" was the chief of staff of the Turkish military contingent. He ruled over 35,000 men in countless garrisons. The 100,000 Turkish Cypriots already present in 1974 were joined by soldiers from Ankara and their families, as well as 30,000 illegal workers from Anatolia. The Ankara government, which subsidised everything from roads to civil servants, had ordered the construction of 320 mosques in the region and banned the restoration of the 200 Orthodox churches that had fallen into ruin.

On paper, the Turkish side was known to be poorer than the Greek side, but tourists could watch the non-stop parade of luxury cars. The state was covered with hundreds of brothels and 37 casinos where drug money was laundered.

Mansions as big as castles grew like mushrooms at the same pace as the multicoloured brothels around the Turkish military bases. That part of the island was indeed a reference point for the mafia. *Le Figaro* of 28 December 2005 quoted the words of a European policeman: "A dozen British and Israeli ringleaders are refugees there and cannot leave the territory. They prosper because the drug route from Afghanistan passes through Turkey and the money is laundered there[290]."

Girls from Eastern Europe were "placed" in the island's military brothels, before continuing on to Albania and ending up on the pavements of European cities. Elena Potoran was on the verge of this misfortune. Elena, 20 years old, was born in Chisinau (Kichinev) in Moldova and would remember her stay in Cyprus all her life. The young woman's nightmare began a year earlier after she accepted a contract as a waitress and was immediately sold to a brothel owner upon her arrival in Nicosia. The *Crazy Night* was located next to the *Sexy Lady,* the *Harem Night Club* and the *Lipstick* and in the evening they were filled with Turkish soldiers. Elena's "owner", a pimp named Ailan, first had her raped by clients before having her undergo surgery in sordid conditions to widen her vagina. During her convalescence, Elena managed to warn her father in Ukraine. The latter was able to inform a

---

[290] The "Brits" were also Israeli nationals. The US Center for Strategic and International Studies estimated the amounts at $1 billion per month at the time.

non-governmental organisation specialised in defending victims of human trafficking, Strada International. In Cyprus, a Russian Orthodox priest, Father Savas, acted as a liaison and contacted the Russian authorities. He said: "The officials in the north replied that they could do nothing, that the owner of the cabaret was an influential man." A European diplomat confirmed his words: "The people with power in Cyprus are all in cahoots with the mafias who have money."

The priest was not discouraged and contacted Matthew Palmer, Washington's chargé d'affaires in Cyprus. He managed to free Elena. The fact is that Ankara could not deny the Americans anything, as they were the most fervent supporters of Turkey's accession to the European Union at the time[291]." Today, Elena has been able to return home, but she is completely traumatised, explained Father Savas."

More than 10,000 Pakistani, Syrian and Bangladeshi Muslims arrived on the island every year. Indeed, Turkey issued visas to citizens of OIC countries, visas that were valid for the "Turkish Republic of Northern Cyprus". In exchange for 4,000 dollars, these fake tourists were taken to the demarcation line between the north and the south, which was poorly guarded by the UN Blue Helmets, and then shipped as fake seamen or in containers to mainland Europe. Turkey had thus become an accomplice in one of the most effective illegal immigration networks to the EU. Some of these migrants stayed on the Greek side of the island. There, without work permits, they were treated like slaves. Melopi, a young Sri Lankan woman, had signed a 15-year work contract stipulating that she would "work 78 hours a week, and 18 hours a day every Friday, Saturday and Sunday".

It is not difficult to understand that open borders and mass immigration are a blessing for all mafias and other multinational companies: immigrants—legal or illegal—lower wages and contribute to the destruction of the national identity of the countries where they settle. The big international financiers obviously have a vested interest in dissolving the boundaries and references of traditional society, in order to eradicate any form of national resistance to their hegemony and to the transformation of individuals into docile and acculturated consumers. It is in such environments that mafias thrive. Large Jewish-owned companies are notable for the fact that their subordinate employees are always from the third world. Indeed, Jewish businessmen hire immigrants as a matter of priority and quite legally,

---

[291] The close ties between Israel and Turkey can be explained by the influence of the Dönmehs on successive Turkish governments. The Dönmehs are Muslims, but only in appearance (see *Psychoanalysis of Judaism*).

whereas a French industrialist would be condemned—in his own country—for hiring his compatriots as a matter of priority. For their part, Jewish intellectuals, journalists and politicians, whether Marxist or liberal, atheist or religious, Zionist or "perfectly integrated", have always encouraged immigration and the building of a multicultural society. This is because it is in their best interests[292].

Since the 1980s, the Israeli state had also had to rely increasingly on foreign workers to replace Palestinians. After the second Palestinian Intifada that began in September 2000, restrictions were tightened even further, and there were only a few thousand Palestinian workers left in the country. They had been replaced by more submissive workers, who accepted to work under more difficult conditions and even lower wages. Half of the immigrants in Israel were now of Asian origin (China, Thailand, Philippines) and 45% came from Eastern Europe, mainly Romania and Moldova.

These workers initially worked legally but then lost their jobs or changed employers. As the work permit only allowed them to work for a specific employer, they therefore became illegal. Of the 300,000 workers, 60 per cent were in an illegal situation. Most of the time, Israeli employers had confiscated their passports.

The Golden Age of the White Slave Trade

The white slave trade did not begin with the fall of the Soviet empire. Already at the end of the 19th century, Western populations were alarmed by the phenomenon.

In Central Europe, where most of Europe's Jews resided, pimps travelled the impoverished countryside to convince peasants that their daughters could earn money in the United States as cleaning women. They explained to the parents that after some time, their daughters could repay the cost of the journey and start a better life in the land of freedom. This is how tens of thousands of young women ended up in the brothels of New York, Rio de Janeiro or Buenos Aires. The daughters of the peasants were not the only victims. The whole mass of domestic servants, workers and immigrants were potential victims of trafficking.

In the Austro-Hungarian Empire, the Jewish population was the largest. By 1900, the Habsburg capital counted more than 150,000 Jews, and as in Poland and the Ukraine, the brothels and traffickers of women to America and the Orient were members of this small community. The

---

[292]On multicultural society: Hervé Ryssen, *Planetary Hopes* (2005), (2022).

Austrian capital served as a transit point between Galicia and Poland on the one hand and Serbia, Turkey and Romania on the other. These suppliers and merchants of women invaded public places with their presence.

Galicia and Bukovina, in the south of present-day Poland, were major centres of trafficking. Between 1904 and 1908, the authorities identified more than a hundred of these Galitzian Jewish traffickers, forty of whom were women. These criminal networks of girl recruiters took the form of family businesses. Some of them even had links with Argentina and India. About fifty pimps from Chernivtsi (which had 30,000 Jews) were connected to Bombay. At the head of these family clans of gangsters, hereditary specialists in the white slave trade, we often found energetic matrons, organisers of international prostitution, from Constantinople to Buenos Aires. Rosa Langer, for example, ran an organisation that supplied all the Balkan countries with meat for pleasure[293]. In 1896, she was arrested and imprisoned in Vienna.

It should be noted that Jewish pimps not only raided Christian "merchandise", but also thrived on the exploitation of women from their own tribe: "There were undoubtedly Jewish traffickers engaged in the exploitation of women from their own nation", wrote Professor Jacques Solé in his book entitled *The Golden Age of Prostitution, 1870 to the present day*[294].

The French journalist Albert Londres[295] had written a book on the subject in 1927, entitled *La Trata de Blancas, El camino de Buenos Aires*. His research would lead him to Poland, in an entirely Jewish town, forty kilometres from Warsaw. This is what Albert London wrote: "It was last May. I was going through the Polish countryside, in search of the Pilsudski revolution. And here is what I found: a Jewish camp. A camp many times a hundred years old. No tents, but houses and streets, even a square, but a camp nonetheless. Tired of wandering, the tribe stopped there one fine day, one day in the course of a century far

---

[293] Raphaël Viau et F. Bournand, p. 91, 93, 97; in Georges Valensin, *La Vie sexuelle juive*, Les Éditions philosophiques, 1981, p. 65, 66

[294] Jacques Solé, *L'Age d'or de la prostitution, de 1870 à nos jours*, Plon, 1993, p. 80. Jacques Solé has based his research mainly on the book by the American Jewish historian Edward J. Bristow: *Prostitution and Prejudice. The Jewish Fight against White Slavery, 1870–1939*, Clarendon Press, 1982. Jacques Solé's 650-page book contains only one chapter on the subject, but what is described there is sufficiently eloquent to give an idea of the importance of the trade.

[295] Albert Londres (1884–1932) was a French writer and journalist. He was one of the founders of investigative journalism, critical of the abuses of colonialism and forced labour prisons.

removed from ours. And the grandchildren settled permanently in the temporary dwellings with hundreds of years of use."

Apparently, the Jews in the area were not very hospitable: "Perhaps they had never seen people of my kind before, so there was no other kind of people? I passed by: the shutters and windows were closed. Some groups of Jews, who filled the streets, dispersed... When they saw me, they took refuge in mysterious corridors, never ceasing to turn their heads to spy on me. If I looked up, the windows on the first floor were empty. They would have greeted me with water, in buckets, but would have refused me a glass, had I had it. I had never seen anything like it, except in wild country. The camp lay on an immense tapestry of dung, and the vague silhouettes of those Jews seemed to rise from that haystack, like emanations of vapour which had assumed vaguely human forms."

Nor were they prone to cleanliness, and Albert Londres's testimony confirmed other points: "Those black frock coats, the dirt on which gave them whitish highlights, that never-washed hair, in a ringlet on the left cheek, those flat, round caps, ending in a sort of cover for those virgin beards[296]...".

Albert London narrated how the poor girls of the Polish "shtetls" were sent by their families to prostitute themselves in South America to build up a dowry and then return to the country to marry[297]. The journalist showed us the game of the pimps: "And as traders they disembark in Warsaw. Not all of them are Jewish, but the travellers, the dealers who go from fair to fair, are. It is indispensable to get into the families. Because they don't do their work in the streets, like in France, but there they operate at home. First they deal with the parents, and then, and only then, they talk to the girl. They don't steal her, they buy her... In Warsaw, in Krakow, in Lvoff, in villages like "my" village, there are old women, whom they pay all year round, who have no other occupation than to point out good merchandise to them. That house is worthless: the daughters are not in good health. Be wary of that family: the parents intend to ask a lot. But there, and there, and there, and there, you will find what suits you, O little brother. Show yourself very religious in that place... Take the youngest, the eldest is lazy... They buy them from the poor by "contract". An acrimoniously discussed contract, duly signed, beautifully substantiated... The family asks for

---

[296]On dirt, read also General Patton's testimony in Germany in 1945.
[297] Encyclopedia Judaica, volume XIII, p. 415. Georges Valensin, *La Vie sexuelle juive*, Les Éditions philosophiques, 1981, p. 65, 66. Shtetl: small town or village populated by Jews in Eastern Europe.

one hundred and fifty zlotis per month for at least three years. The buyer offers only a hundred. The father's beard trembles under the indignation. He brings his daughter closer, shows her once more. Is she a virgin? He swears by the sacred Torah... A family saved from misery! To another[298]! "This is how thousands of young Jewish girls emigrated from Poland to the new world.

As early as 1869, in his book entitled *The Jew, Judaism and the Judaisation of Christian peoples*, Roger Gougenot des Mousseaux gave this testimony: "For a quarter of a century, and we could not go further, moralists have been asking, and rightly so, what happens that in all the great cities of Europe it is observed that among women of bad life, Jews are more numerous than Christians? This question is unfortunately well-founded; for, in Paris, London, Berlin, Hamburg, Vienna, Warsaw and Cracow, in what has been agreed to be called the middle world, in public places and even in lupanars, one finds more Jewesses than Christians, considering the proportion which exists between the two populations[299]."

Promises of work or marriage thus managed to convince families to let the fourteen-year-old girls go. Roger Gougenot also quoted an article in the St. Petersburg newspaper *Golos*, dated 3 October 1869, which noted how some Jews from Galicia and Romania "marry several times, in different places, beautiful young Jewish girls, to sell them immediately in the East and in Africa", and leave them in toleration houses (Court of Neusande). Then, a poor young Jewish girl, in order to escape the ill-treatment of her unnatural parents, seeks refuge in a Catholic convent, and the people, inflamed by the Jews, will break down this asylum in order to snatch the young girl from there[300]! "

In 1872, according to Jewish historian Edward Bristow, 17% of prostitutes in Warsaw were Jewish; they were 27% in Krakow and 47% in Vilna. In 1889, in Poland and the Ukraine, 22% of the women held in houses of prostitution (1122 out of 5127) were Jewish. Most of the

---

[298] Albert Londres, *Camino de Buenos Aires*, Editorial Prensa Ibérica; Clásicos de la Prensa, Barcelona, 1998, p. 131-136.
[299] Archives israélites, XV, p. 711; 1867, in Roger Gougenot des Mousseaux, *The Jew, Judaism and the Judaisation of Christian peoples*, pdf version. Translated into English by Professor Noemí Coronel and the invaluable collaboration of the Catholic Nationalism team. Argentina, 2013, p. 127
[300] Hermann Kuhn, *Monde*, 1 November 1869 and *Correspondance allemande*, in Roger Gougenot des Mousseaux, *The Jew, Judaism and the Judaisation of Christian peoples*, pdf version. Translated into English by Professor Noemí Coronel and the invaluable collaboration of the Catholic Nationalism team. Argentina, 2013, p. XIX, XX (introduction). Jewish women were to become the most prominent leaders of the feminist movement a few decades later.

prostitutes were therefore Christians, held in Jewish houses. In fact, the American consul noted in 1908 that the prostitution "business" was almost exclusively Jewish[301].

In Warsaw, 16 of the 19 known brothels had Jewish managers. The prostitutes received 40–50 clients per day, and up to 60–70 on busy days. In 1905, part of the Jewish community in Warsaw had revolted against the presence of these brothels, which degenerated into an intra-communal pogrom that resulted in 40 brothels being destroyed and eight people killed, including one prostitute.

The pimps saw no contradiction between their activities and their religious faith. Shilem Letzski had organised a small synagogue in Warsaw for prostitutes, madams, pimps and thieves. This criminal community also had its rabbinical court to judge disputes between pimps[302]. Many Jews considered this profession "perfectly honourable".

Jewish pimps exported their wares. In St. Petersburg, the city was off-limits to Jews. However, one of them, Aaron Simanovitch, resided there and became a supplier of female prey to Rasputin, to whom he was close[303]. Between Russia and Germany, border residents helped their fellow pimps to cross the border with the women they were going to prostitute. A small town in Austrian Galicia served as their headquarters before crossing the border: Oswiecim, today better known as Auschwitz[304]. But in the late 1870s, the more daring entrepreneurs transferred their hut from Poland to Argentina.[305]

The great Austrian Jewish writer Stefan Zweig, who had gone into exile in Brazil after Hitler came to power, left a testimony about the prostitutes of Rio de Janeiro. In August 1936, he wrote: "Pitch-black women like ebony carvings—with matted hair and open breasts—who look at you with apparent indifference; French make-up girls, who wear gaudy blouses or provocative shorts and sing in a provocative way;

---

[301] Edward J. Bristow: *Prostitution and Prejudice. The Jewish Fight against White Slavery, 1870–1939*, Clarendon Press, 1982, p. 23, 63, 56.

[302] Edward J. Bristow: *Prostitution and Prejudice. The Jewish Fight against White Slavery, 1870–1939*, Clarendon Press, 1982, p. 60, 61.

[303] G. Dupé, *Plaidoyer pour les maudits, Raspoutine*, Éd. Lefeuvre, Nice, 1978, in Georges Valensin, *La Vie sexuelle juive*, Les Éditions philosophiques, 1981, p. 65, 66.

[304] Edward J. Bristow: *Prostitution and Prejudice. The Jewish Fight against White Slavery, 1870–1939*, Clarendon Press, 1982, p. 124, in Jacques Solé, *L'Age d'or de la prostitution, de 1870 à nos jours*, Plon, 1993, p. 121, 122.

[305] Jacques Solé, *L'Age d'or de la prostitution, de 1870 à nos jours*, Plon, 1993, p. 117-119.

Eastern Jews who promise the craziest perversities; mulattoes who give reality to all gradations of café au lait. There are the very young and the mature, the delicate and the crude[306]…"

Brothels were a well-known feature of Brazilian society. In 1879, thirty-nine Jewish pimps were expelled from the country, although despite numerous and repeated expulsions, pimps remained in the country until the First World War.

The girls arrived first via Buenos Aires, via Hamburg. The famous German shipping company owned by Albert Ballin, a Jewish businessman and owner of the Hamburg-America Line, served as a carrier thanks to some complicity and thus supplied the brothels of Buenos Aires with beautiful girls. Edward Bristow rightly pointed out here one of those traits so characteristic of a certain very particular mentality: "For those who still harboured some illusions, the sea crossing was the moment of truth. The change of tone of their protectors, charged with demoralising them, was enough to announce their tragic fate[307]."

The Brazilian historian Marc Raizman put it this way: "Some of them would go around central Europe looking for a beautiful young Jewish girl to marry. After the marriage, the pimp would use his business as a pretext to go away, offering a ticket to Buenos Aires and promising to meet her there. When he arrived in Argentina or Brazil, the husband was not there and instead a woman appeared who introduced herself as his aunt. The young women, who were usually no older than 18, fell prey to pimping. Many committed suicide."

In the 1920s, the journalist Albert Londres recounted what he had seen in the same place: "Franchutas! Polacas! The Franchutas form the aristocracy: five pesos. The Polish women form the lower class: two pesos." The pimps were Jews from Poland: "The white slave trade, the real one, the one that the term evokes in the popular imagination, is the one practised by the Poles. They work with misery… There is not a single Pole in Buenos Aires who does not have five or six women. Or seven or eight. However, they are not nice. For two days, they refused to serve me a drink in their café on Talcahuano Street. I didn't drink: that's all they earned. And as they didn't bust my eyes, I looked at them, I took a good look… Officially, they call themselves fur traders. Fur,

---

[306] Stefan Zweig, *Diarios (1931–1940)*, Ediciones 98, Madrid, 2021, p. 78.
[307] Edward J. Bristow: *Prostitution and Prejudice. The Jewish Fight against White Slavery, 1870–1939*, Clarendon Press, 1982, p. 124, in Jacques Solé, *L'Age d'or de la prostitution, de 1870 à nos jours*, Plon, 1993, p. 121–123.

it's true, is also a skin, and skins, human skins, are their business[308]." In reality, they were mostly pimps.

The import trips to Europe for supplies never ceased during this period: three to six times a year. This vice industry had organised itself towards the end of the 1890s, forming a kind of trade union called the Zwi Migdal. Later, in 1906, the gangsters were legally constituted as an association. Thanks to the support of the police and corrupt politicians, their network of brothels and girls really came into its own in the 1920s[309]. The syndicate was dominated by a certain Dickenfaden, "the true Napoleon of the Jewish pimps of Buenos Aires", wrote Jacques Solé. He had arrived from Warsaw in 1885 and died immensely rich and highly regarded.

The Zwi Migdal bosses organised real sales of women. Once landed in Buenos Aires or Montevideo, the girls were taken to Argentinean brothels where they were sometimes offered for sale at auctions after being completely undressed[310]. The traffickers strutted ostentatiously in theatres or at the opera, wearing elegant dresses and big diamonds on their fingers. They had their clubs, their organisations and their secret codes.

Of the 199 houses of prostitution in Buenos Aires in 1909, 102 were run by Jews, with Jewish names (although we know that many Jews often change their names); and some of the prostitutes were Jewish. To these must be added a large number of pimps. These were often driven out of the country to Brazil and then expelled to Poland, but they always returned to Argentina, maintaining their relations with Warsaw. In 1930, 400 individuals were officially profiting from prostitution in Buenos Aires, while in Warsaw around 600 were suspected of feeding the trade.

Women and pimps were shunned from the Jewish community. They were not allowed, for example, to be buried in Jewish cemeteries. The members of Zwi Migdal, excluded by their more orthodox moral brethren, had organised a second Argentine Jewish world in parallel to the official organisations. They thus had a separate cemetery, their mutual aid and assistance societies and their own synagogues. The Jewish pimps, in search of respectability, had not abandoned Jewish

---

[308] Albert Londres, *Camino de Buenos Aires*, Editorial Prensa Ibérica; Clásicos de la Prensa, Barcelona, 1998, p. 133-134.
[309] Jacques Solé, *L'Age d'or de la prostitution, de 1870 à nos jours*, Plon, 1993, p. 122, 123.
[310] Edward J. Bristow: *Prostitution and Prejudice. The Jewish Fight against White Slavery, 1870–1939*, Clarendon Press, 1982, p. 309, in Jacques Solé, *L'Age d'or de la prostitution, de 1870 à nos jours*, Plon, 1993, p. 135.

traditions.

The Zwi Migdal was still very powerful in the 1920s, with its hundreds of brothels and thousands of prostitutes. The gangsters who ran it had also invested in other criminal activities: cocaine and heroin trafficking, extortion of funds, racketeering, burglary and, in the United States at that time of prohibition, the clandestine alcohol trade.

In 1929, however, the complaint of a Jewish woman against her husband who wanted to force her into prostitution in a brothel had led to a major general investigation. The following year, 112 suspects were arrested. Most were released in 1931, but Jewish prostitution in Argentina never recovered, and its promoters left the country[311].

Marc Raizman noted that the Portuguese word for "pimp" was "cafetão[312]". He explained that it was a word derived from "caftan", the name given to those long black coats worn by Eastern European Orthodox Jews. This is also what Edward Bristow wrote: "In Rio de Janeiro, Jewish immigrants from Russia, Poland, Hungary and Romania were so identified with pimping in the late 1880s that the "caftan", the traditional Jewish long coat, was synonymous with pimping." (page 13).

The Jewish population of Brazil at the end of the 19th century was 150,000, of whom 70,000 lived in Sao Paolo, the commercial heart of the country, and 30,000 in Rio. Marc Raizman was very proud to be able to give us the surnames of all those Jewish personalities in Brazil who had succeeded in business, show business and the cultural industry. In the late 1990s, the president of Brazil was called Fernando Henrique Silva Cardozo, and his daughter had married a Jew." He has a grandson whose surname is Zylberstein," wrote Raizman. And the historian pointed out that Cardozo was a "converso" surname, i.e. Catholic, but only in appearance. Multicultural societies are, as we well know, conducive to the rise of the children of Israel[313].

Before the First World War, London was also an important centre for Jewish pimping. Numerous young women ended up in houses of depravity behind the facades of supposedly family homes[314]. In London's East End, Isaac Bogard, called *"Darky the Coon"* because of

---

[311] Edward J. Bristow: *Prostitution and Prejudice. The Jewish Fight against White Slavery, 1870–1939*, Clarendon Press, 1982, p. 309, in Jacques Solé, *L'Age d'or de la prostitution, de 1870 à nos jours*, Plon, 1993, p. 135.

[312] Cafiolo, cafishio, cafiche in Argentina, Uruguay and other parts of Latin America.

[313] In 2008, the France of Nicolas Sarkozy, Jacques Attali and Bernard Kouchner, among others, was a good example of this.

[314] L. Gartner, p. 183, in Georges Valensin, *La Vie sexuelle juive*, Les Éditions philosophiques, 1981, p. 264.

his very black hair, was the ringleader who ran the local prostitutes and clubs at the beginning of the 20th century. Then there was Harry *"Little Hubby"* Distleman. A Jewish author like Chaïm Bermant wrote in the *Jewish Chronicle* of 15 January 1993 that at that time (1903–1909), 151 foreigners ran such establishments in England and that most of them were Jews[315].

From London, girls could be quickly shipped to the United States. Since the 1870s, some pimps had set up brothels in New York, but it was the 1890s that represented the heyday of the Jewish kings of New York prostitution. The lust for riches was undoubtedly the main motivation of the 6000 pimps present in the United States in 1914 who exploited no less than 30,000 prostitutes. According to the testimonies of contemporary Jews, being a pimp was a normal activity in this community when one was young and poor. The pimp was a model of social success. There were also competing French and Italian pimps, but, as in Buenos Aires, the Jews were far superior in their organisational skills[316]. Later on, some of them were clever enough to break into the Democratic electoral machine and were thus able to count on the support of the police.

Young French women were numerous in these New York brothels. In 1907, the two most represented nationalities were French and Jewish, wrote Edward Bristow (p. 165). Americans called these houses *"French houses"*, although the owners were Jewish. Motche Greenberg controlled in 1912 the business of eight brothels and their 114 girls. He was one of the kings of vice[317].

A 1908 investigation carried out by the Commission on Immigration in the United States gave the following figures: of the 2093 cases tried, 1512, that is to say three quarters, concerned girls born in the territory, with a predominance of Jewish girls. Of the 581 foreign nationals, 290 were Irish, 225 Jewish, 154 French, 64 German, 31 Italian and 10 Polish.

An association maintained order within prostitution, including through the murder of disobedient girls. At the time, a whole literature on the subject flourished. In the United States, between 1911 and 1916, the newspapers were full of stories of virgins sacrificed on the altar of

---

[315]Jacques Solé, *L'Age d'or de la prostitution, de 1870 à nos jours*, Plon, 1993, p. 79.
[316]Jacques Solé, *L'Age d'or de la prostitution, de 1870 à nos jours*, Plon, 1993, p. 125, 126.
[317]Albert Fried, *The Rise and fall of jewish Gangster in America*, 1980, Columbia University Press, 1993, p. 8, 18.

vice, women seduced, sold and subjugated[318]: in 1910, the whole of New York was gripped by the story of a virgin sold by a German Jew. There was a real collective panic at the time, obviously justified.

Yiddish-speaking brothel hookers and ruffians recruited mainly in nightclubs or through small advertisements, promising jobs as trainers. The naive victims were mainly destined for export, especially to South Africa[319].

But by 1910 the campaigns against the White slave trade began to have their greatest successes. More than a thousand pimps were arrested between 1910 and 1915. The testimonies of the victims and of the police, together with the investigations of the press, confirmed the totally organised nature of the traffic.

Sergio Leone's beautiful film, *Once Upon a Time in America* (1984), told the story of New York gangsters from their native Poland at the turn of the century. In it, they are seen to be engaged in bootlegging and all kinds of trafficking and racketeering. They rob a jewellery shop, knock off their competitors, own a discotheque, and don't hesitate to prostitute the women of their tribe. In the end, the gang leader (James Wood) changes his identity and becomes a senator.

In New York, of all the Jewish "madams", brothel managers, Polly Adler, who was of Polish origin, was the best known in the 1920s–1930s. A few years earlier, Rosie Hertz had been the most prominent "madame" in the city. Together with her husband Jacob, she had opened several brothels in the 1880s. During her trial, the judge called her the "godmother of prostitutes". A century later, in the 1970s, the famous Xaviera Hollander would occupy such a position, as she herself recounted in her book sold more than 17 million copies[320].

The most famous New York *sex club* of 1979 and 1980 was *Plato's Retreat*, owned by one Larry Levenson. In November 1999, Steve Kaplan, owner of the *Gold Club*, an Atlanta strip club that was also a local luxury prostitution emporium, was put on trial. Steve Kaplan was closely linked to the New York Mafia. He was charged with pimping, credit card fraud, money laundering and corruption of officials. In addition, Kaplan had ordered the beatings of more than twenty people who had been unable to repay the interest on usurious loans he had

---

[318] Judith Walkowitz, Ruth Rosen, *Prostitution and Victorian Society Women*, Cambridge University Press, 1980. Ruth Rosen, *The Lost Sisterhood Prostitution in America, 1900–1918*, The John Hopkins University Press, 1982.
[319] I. Howe, p. 96, in Georges Valensin, *La Vie sexuelle juive*, Les Éditions philosophiques, 1981, p. 65, 66
[320] On Xaviera Hollander read *Jewish Fanaticism* (2007).

made to them[321].

From 1895 onwards, New York pimps and prostitutes came under increasing police repression and some left for Buenos Aires and Johannesburg, where they came to dominate the world of prostitution. In Johannesburg, observers did indeed note the presence of large numbers of New York Jews from the Russian Empire among the prostitutes. Alongside the "Russian Americans", there were also black and mixed race, French and German prostitutes. Pimps of Jewish origin were numerous and most of them also came from New York.

Joe Silver dominated the "Polish-American" world. He was born in Poland in 1869 and had worked in London as a recruiter of prostitutes. In 1898, he boarded a ship in Southampton for South Africa. A rabbi, who had seen him embark in June, noted that he was accompanied by his wife—herself a prostitute—, fourteen henchmen and twenty-five girls. Thanks to his talents as an organiser, he quickly established himself as the king of vice in Johannesburg. He created the famous "American Club", a local association of Jewish pimps of which he was president. From this position, Joe Silver managed the problems arising from the supply of this traffic, especially the renewal of "stocks". Polish Jews were not the only ones doing this work, but they were by far the biggest traffickers and maintained, here as elsewhere, close links with the criminal world[322].

Joe Silver was finally arrested in Pretoria in April 1899 and sentenced to two years' banishment, a sentence that hardly interfered with the cosmopolitan traveller's habits. He moved to Cape Town with other pimps and their prostitutes. As in Johannesburg ten years earlier, the city's business world supported him, while the Christian religious authorities protested. Europeans were especially outraged that Jewish pimps linked Blacks with Whites[323]. In 1902, repressive measures forced them back into exile. They left for Bloemfontein, but quickly had to leave the city once again. They then settled in Durban, but again had

---

[321] Jean-François Gayraud, *Le Monde des mafias*, Odile Jacob, 2005, p. 116.

[322] Charles von Onselen, *Studies in the Social and Economic History of the Witwatersrand, 1886–1914*, T.1, The New Babylon, 1982, p. 106, in Jacques Solé, *L'Age d'or de la prostitution, de 1870 à nos jours*, Plon, 1993, p. 110.

[323] They promote by all means immigration and miscegenation among other peoples, but defend their own blood against any foreign contamination. In cinema and television, this obsession with miscegenation is recurrent. It is one of their trademarks, but there are others: drugs, transvestites, incest, homosexuality, "gore" films, attacks on the Catholic Church, the apology for market democracy and the war against the "bad guys", and so on. See the chapters on cinema in Hervé Ryssen, *Planetary Hopes*, *Psychoanalysis of Judaism* and *Jewish Fanaticism*.

to flee in 1903. Finally, Joe Silver left for the Transvaal, thus personifying the wanderings of the "wandering Jew", always innocent, always persecuted for no reason.

After New York and Buenos Aires, Constantinople was the third largest centre of prostitution. In the brothels of the Ottoman capital, Greek and Armenian prostitutes mingled with prostitutes from neighbouring European countries in Turkey, as well as many women from Central Europe. There, too, Jewish pimps were in the limelight. They transported their 'merchandise' via routes from Budapest through Romania, although the Black Sea port of Odessa was also an important point of this traffic.

From Constantinople, international pimps then organised the export to Egypt, East Asia or South Africa[324]. The Constantinople authorities were for a long time tolerant of this traffic until they started to dismantle it at the beginning of the First World War.

In 1903 in Alexandria, the traffickers came mainly from Galicia and Romania. As early as 1850 in Tunis, the French historian and traveller A. Vilhau spoke of the "brokers in debauchery, almost all of them Jews[325]." A century later, the pro-Nazi (National Socialist) newspaper *Je suis partout* made the same observation: "The Tunisian Jew is a pimp, the provider of innumerable clandestine brothels and the organiser of the trafficking of Aryan women[326]."

In North Africa, confirmed Georges Valensin, "by exception, Jewish prostitution has been very active up to the present day. Before independence, we read in various sources that Jewish pimps were "always ready to draw a knife for their protégés, which provoked the scorn of pious men"[327]. According to André Chouraqui, in his book *The Jews of North Africa*, since their emigration to France, pimping had become increasingly important[328]."

Beyond the Suez Canal, Asia and East Africa would have seen

---

[324] Edward J. Bristow: *Prostitution and Prejudice. The Jewish Fight against White Slavery, 1870–1939*, Clarendon Press, 1982, p. 181, in Jacques Solé, *L'Age d'or de la prostitution, de 1870 à nos jours*, Plon, 1993, p. 127.

[325] A. Vilhau, in Georges Valensin, *La Vie sexuelle juive*, Les Éditions philosophiques, 1981. Georges Valensin was a Jewish doctor from Algeria who published numerous books on sexuality.

[326] *Je suis partout*, 11 December 1942. [*Je suis partout* was a weekly newspaper published in France between 1930 and 1944. Described as "openly profascist and anti-Semitic", it adopted a collaborationist position during the German occupation. Prominent French authors contributed to its pages].

[327] *Les Nouveaux cahiers*, No. 42.

[328] Georges Valensin, *La Vie sexuelle juive*, Les Éditions philosophiques, 1981, p. 62, 65, 66

prostitution of European origin from 1870 onwards. Christian women were even more numerous in Asia; in Ceylon, Calcutta, Bombay, Singapore and Manila. In Manchuria too, Jewish women mixed with French or Japanese women in brothels, and even in Port Arthur and Shanghai. The poet Guillaume d'Apollinaire evoked the theme. In his anthology of poems *Alcohols* (1898–1912), at the end of his poem entitled *Marizibill*, he spoke of a prostitute from Cologne, in Germany: "In the buff she was being left/ By a rosy and red-haired pimp/ Who was Jewish and smelled of garlic/ And coming from Formosa had/ Taken her out of a brothel in Shanghai[329]."

Such was the expansion of that activity that, in the common parlance of the world in the 1900s, a Jew was commonly regarded in all latitudes as a dealer in human flesh and a potential pimp.

The Lemberg trial

The white slave trade began to scandalise European public opinion from the 1880s onwards. Especially in 1892, with the highly publicised Lemberg (now Lvov) trial in Galicia. Twenty-eight Jews were accused of pimping. The network was made up of recruiters, transporters and local agents in Turkey. The girls were sent to Constantinople, Egypt, South Africa, India and America.

In 1899, François Trocase, a French journalist who had lived in Austria-Hungary for 22 years, published an interesting book on the situation in the country entitled *Contemporary Austria as it is*. Here is a passage from that book: "In Austria, the Jews have instilled in the female youth a dissolute morality, pitiful habits, an unheard-of demoralisation. The inherent baseness of their feelings, money and absolute lack of conscience predispose them singularly to the role of seducers. Thus, prostitution lurks behind every door for young women, who in the big cities become in large numbers the servants of the Jews. We can safely say that most of the unfortunate girls who are corrupted and prostituted in the large Austrian cities owe their first fall to the Jews... Of course, of all the crimes under the sun, Christians have their share; but never until now in Austria have they been reproached for practising the trade of exporting Christian virgins. This shameful speciality which disgraces our century belongs exclusively to the Jews. This infamy must be left to them. For a long time the details have been

---

[329]Guillaume Apollinaire, *Alcoholes/El Poeta asesinado*, Ediciones Cátedra (Anaya), Madrid, 2001, p. 221.

ignored. We saw many young women disappear mysteriously, without any further news of them. It was a trial held in 1892 in the capital of Austrian Poland, in Lemberg, that finally revealed everything. Twenty-eight Jews were accused of kidnapping and trafficking young girls. These wretches had cleverly lured into a trap many Christian girls, most of whom were still at school. They had promised them advantageous working conditions to persuade them to go abroad. As soon as they crossed the border, they were treated as slaves and all attempts to escape were severely punished. Once in Turkey, they were sold to prostitution houses for an average price of 1,000 marks. Now, who are the owners of such houses in Turkey? Only the Jews. Those of these poor victims who wanted to resist were locked up in underground dungeons and subjected to ill-treatment. When the police finally decided to intervene, sixty of those girls were released. They managed to free them from the clutches of the barbarians, but unfortunately they were lost in body and soul. The trial lasted ten days, revealing and clarifying all the monstrous details. It was clearly established that hundreds of young women had been driven by that Lemberg gang to disgrace, despair, disease and death. Due to loopholes in the legislation, the culprits were sentenced to no more than insignificant penalties. The leader of the gang, Isaac Schafenstein, was sentenced to one year in prison. The others spent a few months behind bars and returned to the sinister trade, applying themselves with more cunning and mystery. The most outrageous aspect of this sad case was that, at the beginning of the trial, the signatory of the sale and delivery contracts had the cheek to proclaim his innocence: "You have no business to meddle in my affairs," he told the judges; "whether I sell clothes, fruit, calves or women, it matters little. I am in business and nobody has anything to say about it". As we well know, by speaking in such a manner, the accused was placing himself on the ground of Jewish morality which permits any business with human beings that is not forbidden by the Talmud towards animals[330]."

The Lembergtrial was naturally exploited by anti-Semites. In 1918, there were riots against Jews in the city, proof that the traffic had not been interrupted. At that time, the Austrian parliament was debating

---

[330] François Trocase, *L'Autriche juive*, 1899, in Léon de Poncins, *Israël destructeur d'empires*, Mercure de France, 1942, p. 88-92. [For example in the Talmud *(Yevamot 98a)*, we read: "Learn from this, that the Merciful One strips the male gentile of his offspring, as it is written concerning the Egyptians: 'Whose flesh is the flesh of asses, and whose semen is the semen of horses' (*Ezekiel 11:20 p.m.*), i.e. the offspring of a male gentile is considered no more related to him than the offspring of asses and horses." [NdT].

the disappearance of Christian maids who were taken to brothels abroad.

According to François Trocase, "two million Jews living in the country had as many maids as the 28 million Austro-Hungarians; nine-tenths of them were Christians; they often had the task of looking after the child of the house, "so that he would not be ill before marriage"." François Trocase evoked the role of the Israelite employers. One of them, an obese industrialist in the Silesian textile industry, boasted of having possessed more than a thousand of his female workers. And Trocase concluded: "The abuses committed by Jews against women have strongly contributed to the explosion of anger and anti-Semitism in Austria... Just talking about it, the hatred became indescribable[331]."

Dr Georges Valensin, an Israelite originally from Algeria, confirmed the role of Jewish pimps during the First World War. He wrote in 1981, in his book entitled *Jewish Sex Life*: "After 1918, in the profiteering and profiteering world that swarmed in Berlin, Jews were seen hanging around in the discotheques where young women of the aristocracy and the bourgeoisie in distress, after having sold their last jewels, came to prostitute themselves[332]. In 1920, on the façades of the Reichstag, a huge poster warned honest German women that behind the face of a pure and beautiful German woman, a disturbing man with Semitic features lurked in the shadows, lying in wait for her: "Hebraic lubricity was embodied in the features of the famous Jew Joseph Süss Oppenheimer, who was hanged in 1738 in Stuttgart. After that damning description, Georges Valensin wrote, as if wishing to take his distance: " After Hitlerism, its fanatics have persisted in believing in Jewish sexual perversities[333]."

Adolf Hitler had mentioned the subject in *My Struggle*: "In Vienna, as probably in no other city in Western Europe, with the exception perhaps of a port in the south of France, the relations of Judaism with prostitution, and even more so with the white slave trade, could best be studied.

Walking through the Leopold quarter at night, one was, wittingly or unwittingly, a witness at every step to facts which remained hidden from the great majority of the German people..." And Hitler added: "I

---

[331] François Trocase, *L'Autriche contemporaine telle qu'elle est*, Éd. Pierret, Paris, 1899, p. 148-157, in Georges Valensin, *La Vie sexuelle juive*, Les Éditions philosophiques, 1981, p. 142-144.
[332] H. Andics, p. 215
[333] Georges Valensin, *La Vie sexuelle juive*, Les Éditions philosophiques, 1981, p. 142-144.

shuddered when for the first time I thus discovered in the Jew the heartless, calculating, venal and shameless merchant of that irritating traffic in vice, in the dregs of the big city. I could take it no more, and from then on I never shirked the Jewish question[334]."

In France, in 1936, Léon Blum had become the head of the Popular Front government. In 1907, he had published a book entitled *On Marriage*, which was republished shortly before his accession to power. Léon Blum explicitly advocated sexual vagrancy for young Christian women: "Let them give themselves up whenever they please", he wrote (page 279)." Virginity, cheerfully rejected at an early age" was for him the solution (page 265)." Let a woman, before marriage, unburden all that is ardent in her instinct, all that is labile in her caprice; let her exhaust herself by innumerable adventures." (page 25). Léon Blum insisted: "It is barbarous that, in the full vigour of her youth, the virgin, on pain of degradation and dishonour, should have to restrain in herself the instinct which is the very movement of nature." (page 296). Blum was addressing the young women of France directly: "The feeling of honour which protected you was artificial and stupid..." (page 265)." (page 265).

The old prejudices handed down by reactionary Catholicism therefore had to be done away with: "I believe that in the future there should be nothing left of these customs." (page 280)." Your prejudices are reduced to nothing, as soon as we isolate them from the savage customs or religious asceticism that once prevailed. They are, as it is often said, a relic of the bygone days of civilisation." (page 292).

On the other side of the RhineRiver, in National Socialist Germany, Julius Striecher, the editor of the anti-Semitic newspaper *Der Stürmer*, wrote an article about Léon Blum's book. His conclusion was perhaps a little brutal: "It pretends to deal with the sexual problem. In reality, that book is an appeal inviting all Jews to systematically and methodically defile non-Jewish women and girls."

Eros centre in defeated Germany

After the Second World War, the Allied armies stationed in Germany had provided a fruitful market for all kinds of trafficking: food, alcohol, cigarettes and prostitutes. Yossef Buchman, a "survivor

---

[334] Edward J. Bristow: *Prostitution and Prejudice. The Jewish Fight against White Slavery, 1870–1939*, Clarendon Press, 1982, p. 84; Adolf Hitler, *My Struggle (Mein Kampf)*, Jusego Chile electronic edition, 2003, p. 40.

of the crematoria" as Jacques Derogy described him in his book *Israel Connection*, knew how to profit from the post-war period. With his accomplices, he had set up a small organisation to eliminate the competition. They disguised themselves as US military police officers, drove around in jeeps and set traps for the other traffickers. They would stop them, seize their goods and then pretend to be careless and let them escape." A few months later," Derogy wrote, "the young Polish Jewish refugee was driving a Kaiser, wearing a suit and only going out accompanied by bodyguards and *Gretschens* as attractive as they were docile."

Yossef Buchman then threw himself into trafficking in dollars, real or fake. He had created such a profitable network that his treasurer was tempted one day to flee with hundreds of thousands of marks in his suitcases, but an unexpected stabbing got in the way of his plans.

Yossef Buchman thrived near the US bases. Kaiserlautern had become a notorious centre for prostitution, drugs and smuggling. A US army newspaper, the *US Overseas Weekly*, had denounced Yossef Buchman as "the king of the crime town", but Buchman denounced the paper and its editor was brought up on libel charges. One cannot insult a Holocaust survivor in vain.

In the community magazine *L'Arche* in November 1977, an article confirmed that in the 'ruins of Berlin' in 1945, one did indeed meet 'groups of Jewish survivors who were engaged in unorthodox, let alone *"Kasher"*, profit-making activities'. The journalist Arnold Mandel specified that these "no longer believed that they had moral obligations."

The famous Moselstrasse in Frankfurt was the work of Buchman. He had moved there in 1956 to open a house of prostitution next to the train station. Forty prostitutes and *strippers* made up the staff. In the early 1960s, Frankfurt am Main, the Rothschilds' historic city, had become the European centre of the underworld.

With his friend and business partner Israelovitch, Yossef Buchman undertook the construction of fourteen to twenty-storey towers to house the girls. These towers were the first Eros Centers. Buchman generated so much money that he became a prominent personality within a few years. He was received in German high society, he hung around the ministries and the headquarters of political parties, not forgetting, of course, the Israeli embassy. For "Yossele" Buchman remained a good Jew and Zionist, and always used his free time between business trips to Israel. In fact, he was a major donor to the Israeli army, especially during the Six Day War and the Yom Kippur War[335].

Meir Cohen was another emblematic figure of the mafia world in Germany. A former soldier in the Israeli army, he had left Israel to settle in Frankfurt in the 1970s. Within two years he owned three discotheques and employed German prostitutes. Frankfurt, the city of the famous Rothschild bankers, was at that time the centre of drug trafficking and pimping in Germany.

The pimps also recruited Jewish women. The Jewish monthly *L'Arche* in February 1976 had published an article on organised crime in Frankfurt. This is what we read in its pages: "In Frankfurt in 1975, many street girls had come from Israel with their pimps; one out of three wore the Star of David. They spoke Hebrew and kept in touch with their families. They left the big German city when their protectors were convicted and imprisoned for heroin trafficking[336]." Indeed, prostitution almost always goes hand in hand with discotheques, drug trafficking, extortion of funds, murder and money laundering.

In 1980, Jacques Derogy, himself of Jewish origin, was struck by the evidence with this observation: "Curious phenomenon, in fact, this settlement of hundreds of Israeli criminals in Frankfurt, Hamburg and Munich, in this Germany that has barely emerged from Nazism... Curious phenomenon the irresistible rise of these Israelis to the Germanic heights of the international Mafia where prostitution, drugs, swindling and armed robbery can be seen everywhere[337]."

In 1994, *US News and World Report* published the testimony of a Frankfurt policeman: "It all came from the Jews", declared Bernd Gayk in the vicinity of the "hot" district. There was only one cabaret run by a German. In 1998, Marvin Wolf, a Jewish captain in the US army serving in Germany, explained: "After the war, in 1945-46, Jews who were already receiving a monthly pension recruited lonely, desperate and hungry women in Frankfurt to open the first brothels. They took their revenge and became enormously rich."

At the beginning of September 1999, the death of Ignaz Bubis, the president of the Jewish Community of Germany, had been in the news because of an incident in Jerusalem during his funeral. A Jew had protested by defacing the coffin of the deceased, accusing him of property speculation. The weekly *Rivarol reported that* Ignaz Bubis had indeed diverted funds received from the German government to

---

[335] Jacques Derogy, *Israël Connection*, Plon, 1980, p. 170, 171.
[336] *L'Arche*, in Georges Valensin, *La Vie sexuelle juive*, Les Éditions philosophiques, 1981, p. 264.
[337] Jacques Derogy, *Israël Connection*, Plon, 1980, p. 169.

compensate the victims of the "holocaust" to buy blocks of houses in Frankfurt. He had converted them into brothels along with other Eros Centers that he had had built. These facilities had made him an immense fortune.

For some Jews, this business seemed to be a normal activity, judging by the tendency to engage in it as a matter of course. Thus Samuel Pisar, a Jewish survivor of the gas chambers and later a multimillionaire, recounted in one of his books his experiences after liberation in 1945, after four years in the Nazi camps. He was 16 years old at the time. Fortunately, he and his comrades were always in good health and started their businesses as soon as they were liberated by the American soldiers: "The occupation of Germany," he wrote, "offered everyone attractive and fruitful possibilities. The left hand acquired in the camps, stimulated by our new and ambitious energies, was looking for a field in which to put it into practice. We quickly found it. Most of the Germans lived in abject poverty as opposed to the good-natured Americans, immersed in a solitary abundance, accompanied by enormous waste... I could not believe my eyes. We could act as intermediaries between these two worlds. For a carton of Lucky Strike cigarettes we could bring a drunken black GI and a complacent German Frau into contact."

By selling needy and frightened German women to black American men, Samuel Pisar and his friends were indulging in pimping and probably also satisfying an unspeakable desire for revenge against the German people.

Samuel Pisar explained his traffic in the German town of Landsberg: "In exchange for a pound of second-hand coffee, we got a bottle of first-class *schnaps*. For five bottles of this liquor, plus a docile blonde, the American drivers who drove the huge tanker trucks agreed to transfer part of their petrol load. The new activity was thriving so spectacularly that we were on the verge of rendering the entire American division stationed in the region almost non-operational... Nico had become an easy-going man who collected women and suits of the finest cut. Draped in a blue overcoat and wearing a carelessly knotted white scarf around his neck, he strolled through the city, his silhouette indolent... Years spent in the death camps had convinced me that he was immortal."

But little Samuel and his friends were again confronted with anti-Semitism and barbarism: "One morning, Nico went out on his rounds and found himself in prison. He was arrested at the home of the daughter of a former Wehrmacht general by two American policemen in white helmets who took him away in a Military Police jeep. I was shocked. A victim of Nazi persecution was once again deprived of his freedom... I thought it was monstrous. I thought it was monstrous. What had we done, except to respond effectively to the law of supply and demand? [338]"Here are some thoughts that speak volumes about the underlying tendencies of Judaism.

Before the war, patriots in all European countries were alarmed by the spread of pornography and the white slave trade. Especially in Berlin, the capital of a country defeated in 1918, the Jews seemed the absolute masters. In the weekly *Je Suis partout* of 15 April 1938, Lucien Rebatet wrote: "The whole night-time industry of obscene variety shows, dens of inverts, dens of rogues and cops, dens and narcotics which had made the Berlin of 1930 the strangest and most dubious, the most vicious capital in the world, was in the hands of Israel."

This was exactly what Nobel laureate Elie Wiesel described Berlin in 1928 in his book *Testament of a Murdered Jewish Poet*: "The defeated Germany gave the impression that everything was permitted on its territory except taking itself seriously," wrote Wiesel. Idols were broken, statues were dismantled, the habits of the religious were hung up, the sacred was mocked, and to make matters worse, laughter was sacralised for the sake of laughter[339]... The capital, in permanent effervescence, was reminiscent of the sinful cities of the Bible. The Talmudist in me blushed and looked away. Prostitution, pornography, depravation of the senses and the spirit, sexual perversion and so on; the city undressed, made itself up, humiliated itself without qualms, brandishing its degeneration as an ideology. Around the corner from *Chez Blum*, in a private club, men and women, or women with each other, danced naked. Elsewhere, people were taking drugs, whipping each other, crawling in the mud, transgressing all limits; it reminded me of the habits and customs of the Sabateans[340]. Values were inverted, taboos were lifted, did people feel the storm approaching? "And two pages later, Elie Wiesel wrote naively: "Berlin seemed to be dominated by Jews... Newspapers and publishing houses, theatres and banks, department stores and literary salons. The French anti-Semites who saw the Jew everywhere were right ... at least in the German case. The

---

[338] Samuel Pisar, *La Sangre de la esperanza*, Editorial Planeta, 1990, Barcelona, p. 98-102. Read in *Psychoanalysis of Judaism*.
[339] Elie Wiesel, *Le Testament d'un poète juif assasiné*, 1980, Points Seuil, 1995, p. 100.
[340] On Sabbateanism and Sabbateans read Hervé Ryssen, *Psychoanalysis of Judaism* (NdT).

sciences, medicine, the arts: the Jew set the standard, imposed it341."

A long tradition

According to Jacques Solé, the white slave trade would have reached its peak at the end of the 19th century. But the phenomenon was much older. In fact, Solé wrote: "Since its appearance in the West in the 1830s, the term white slave trade has been associated with trafficking of a Jewish nature[342]."

The Jewish historian Edward Bristow, whose work is the source of this information, nevertheless tried to make us admit that this traffic had died out in the 1930s, under the blows of repression: "The great traffic in women, inaugurated between Eastern Europe and South America in the 1870s by Jewish immigrants, died out after sixty years." Bristow, while admitting that this traffic had been "obscured by official historiography", also wanted us to believe that it was "no earlier legacy". The development of the trade in the 1860s would have been for the Jewish people a kind of "historical aberration[343]". According to him, an explanation had to be sought "in the economic, social and cultural problems specific to Eastern European Judaism at the end of the 19th century." As for Jacques Solé, who merely reproduced Bristow's observations, he made no further mention of the role of the Jews in the White slave trade in his voluminous 650-page book. He would even be very careful not to mention anything in his chapter on post-Soviet Russia.

In reality, the preponderant—and even exclusive—role of Jewish traffickers in international pimping goes back much further. In the *Persian Letters*, Montesquieu wrote in 1721: "You ask me if there are Jews in France. You should know that where there is money, there are Jews." And later, in another of the letters: "What would not be my despair to see that my sister was not at home. A few days before my arrival the Tartars had raided the town. Seeing that my sister was very beautiful, they seized her and sold her to some Jews who were on their way to Turkey, leaving at home only a child she had given birth to a few months earlier. I followed those Jews and caught up with them about

---

[341] Elie Wiesel, *Le Testament d'un poète juif assasiné*, 1980, Points Seuil, 1995, p. 124, 126.
[342] Jacques Solé, *L'Age d'or de la prostitution, de 1870 à nos jours*, Plon, 1993, p. 110.
[343] Jacques Solé, *L'Age d'or de la prostitution, de 1870 à nos jours*, Plon, 1993, p. 116, 117. As we also saw in the first part, Jacques Attali used the same fallacy with regard to Jewish gangsterism in the 1920s and 1930s: "historical aberration". [See note 85.

three leagues from there. My entreaties and my tears were in vain, and they asked me for her thirty tomans without lowering me a single one[344]."

"In the 17th century, wrote Dr Valensin, the Jews of the Ottoman Empire were specialists in the sale of slaves, skilled in all kinds of depravity, and the trade in women belonged entirely to them, as did the brothels... There were also in Constantinople Jews who had no other function than to verify the virginity of the girls sold as pleasure meat[345]." But one can go even further back in time: "In 1387 in Barcelona, a Jewish pimp was already punished with a fine[346]."

Already in the Middle Ages, testimonies testify to the feverish activity of the merchants of this community in the slave trade: Christian slaves in the early Middle Ages, then African slaves sent to the Americas. Women and children, as is well known, were not spared either, insofar as they could generate profits for the traffickers.

Let us recall the papal bull of Clement VIII in 1593, *Cum hebreorum malitia*: Jews are forbidden to encourage prostitution, gambling, receiving and pederasty.

The archbishop of Lyon, Agobard, in the ninth century, shortly after the time of Charlemagne, denounced the "cohabitation" of some Christian women with Jews. In a letter to the bishop of Nibridiius, he wrote: "Many of the women of pleasure are officially servants, others are hired domestics, some are corrupt; in reality they are all prostitutes, either under the yoke and dominion of the latter or else surrendered to the pleasure and deceit of the latter; the children of the devil indulge in this very thing with malicious hatred and false flattery..."

But perhaps we should simply go back to the sources. The Old Testament, the Torah, presents this eloquent passage that probably legitimised the prostitution of Jewish women by their own kinsmen: "If someone sells his daughter as a slave, the girl may not go away like male slaves. If the master does not take the girl as a wife because she is not to his liking, he must allow her to be ransomed. Since he rejected her, he may not sell her to any foreigner. If the master gives the girl to his son, he must treat her with all the rights of a daughter[347]."

The American nationalist author David Duke provided further

---

[344] Montesquieu, *Cartas Persanas*, Consejo Nacional para la Cultura y las Artes, Mexico, 1992, p. 112, 129–130.
[345] M. Yarden, in *Les chrétiens devant le fait juif*, Éd. Beauchesne, Paris, 1929, p. 131, in Georges Valensin, *La Vie sexuelle juive*, Les Éditions philosophiques, 1981, 65, 66.
[346] M. Kriegel, *Les Juifs à la fin du moyen âge*, p. 249, in Georges Valensin.
[347] *Exodus, 21, 7–9*, (New International Version Bible 1999).

explanatory elements for understanding the trafficking of Jewish women by their own kind. Duke cited in particular Evelyn Kaye's book, *A Hole in the Sheet*, published in 1987 in the United States. Evelyne Kaye, who had grown up in an ultra-orthodox Jewish home, exposed the inferior position of women in Jewish tradition: "Menstruation taboos are responsible for serious psychological damage to Jewish women: I have often encountered women who knew nothing of the Torah except that they could not touch the holy book during the period of its rules[348]." We know that in one of their prayers, pious Jews thank God every day that they are not women[349]. We believe that this is the origin of the feminist movement[350].

But all this did not prevent the great French philosopher Bernard-Henri Lévy from declaring: "Judaism in its entirety is an incomparable school of true respect, without deceit or feigned devotion, for the uniqueness of women[351]."

Philip Roth, the ultra-mediatic American novelist, also distinguished Jewish women from the human livestock of the rest of humanity. This is how he put it through the mouth of one of his characters: "Don't mess with Jewish girls. Save it for the gentiles, don't bother the Jewish girls[352]."

As for the rape of Christian maidservants or Russian girls by Israeli pimps, they could find legitimacy in the Talmud. Indeed, the Mishnah (Oral Law of the Talmud) states that anyone who forces another out of wedlock must be punished, but the Gemara (the commentaries of the law) teaches that there are exceptions, especially for female slaves: while she sleeps, the young servant girl is considered innocent. If she is conscious, the Pharisee is guilty. However, if he penetrates her by unnatural means (anally), or if she withdraws before orgasm, the act is considered as a "simple sexual contact" without moral consequences. In that case, the Pharisee is "undefiled, as if she had been asleep." This is probably one of the reasons for the large number of cases of psychiatrists or psychologists who raped their patients after

---

[348] Evelyn Kaye, *A Hole in the Sheet: a Modern Woman looks at Orthodox and Hasidic Judaism*, Secaucus, New Jersey: L. Stuart, 1987, p. 236–241, in David Duke, *Jewish Supremacism*.
[349] Talmud *Menachot*, 43b.
[350] See *Psychoanalysis of Judaism* (2006) and *Jewish Fanaticism* (2007).
[351] Bernard-Henri Lévy, *Questions de principes*, Grasset, 1986, Livre de Poche, p. 278.
[352] Philip Roth, *The Sabbath Theatre*, Epublibre, Titivillus, 2016, p. 158. The French translation differs: "Don't go out with Jewish girls. Save that for the shiksa, hé. Don't be mean to the Jewesses, never." *Shiksa:* pejorative Hebrew term for a goy woman.

giving them drugs or sleeping pills[353].

The dialectic of Jewish intellectuals

In May 1969, in the peaceful city of Orléans, a rumour began to spread: young girls who had entered clothing shops run by Jewish merchants had mysteriously disappeared. They had been lulled to sleep with chloroform and then kidnapped to be handed over to prostitution rings on the other side of the Mediterranean. The rumour, which had grown out of control, had rekindled a 'nauseating' anti-Semitism that recalled 'the darkest hours of our history'.[354]

The eminent Jewish historian Léon Poliakov explained: "What happened in the quiet city of Orléans in May 1969? Nothing much, after all. Some high school students spread a rumour that the fitting rooms of some clothing shops in their town, run by Jewish shopkeepers, were the starting point for a network of white slave traders. Before fading away, this small delirium nevertheless managed to drive part of the population of Orléans crazy, while the local Jews, for their part, thought they suddenly saw the spectre of the pogrom resurface for an instant[355]."

However, Poliakov had to admit it on pain of losing all credibility, albeit discreetly. Indeed, some forty pages after having ridiculed the Orleans rumour, he wrote simply: "Several Jewish personalities were engaged in this abject traffic at the beginning of the 20th century[356]."

The following year, similar, if less spectacular, phenomena occurred in other French cities, notably in Amiens, but also in Chalon-sur-Saône, Dinan, Grenoble and Strasbourg, fuelling the wildest fantasies and the most "delirious" accusations.

Manifestly, this crazy rumour persisted for several years: "As late as 1977, in a high school on the outskirts of Dijon, there was a rumour that abductions were taking place: pupils were disappearing in the shop of a Jew, mysteriously[357]."

A Sephardic writer like Albert Memmi denounced these absurd rumours, this "astonishing accusation of serial rapes, supposedly

---

[353] See *Jewish Fanaticism* (Chapter: Violations in Psychiatry).
[354] The darkest hours (*Les heures les plus sombres*): is an expression coined and used by the French cultural and media sphere that refers to the 1930s and the Second World War. It is a sort of reminder invocation on the memory of the public whenever it is uttered (NdT).
[355] Léon Poliakov, *Histoire de l'antisémitisme, 1945-1993*, Seuil, 1994, p. 141.
[356] Léon Poliakov, *Histoire de l'antisémitisme, 1945-1993*, Seuil, 1994, p. 181.
[357] *Le Matin*, 12 January 1978. Georges Valensin, *La Vie sexuelle juive*, Les Éditions philosophiques, 1981, p. 146.

organised by Jewish shopkeepers on their chloroformed clients[358]."

Faced with the danger of a resurgence of anti-Semitism, the much-mediated sociologist Edgar Morin (a Sephardite himself, born Nahoum) felt it was his duty to write a 250-page book to explain to the French that this was a grotesque rumour. In his book, Morin gave a lenificent overview of all the explanatory factors: urbanisation, fashion, female psychology, teenage girls, the bourgeoisie and social classes, etc.; everything except the essentials[359].

Thus, the reader had to understand that these accusations were totally delusional. It was an "immense superciliousness" (page 35)." The fantasy has become a myth, a delusion" (page 37, 39). The rumour was "an echo of the great medieval fears", resurrecting "the same anti-Jewish fantasy". The Jew, once again, was the "scapegoat", the "congenital culprit rooted in two millennia of the Christian West" on whom Christians dumped all their problems (page 52).

In reality, as you have understood, it was the Christians who were guilty. The Jewish merchant was assigned "the mission to fix and purge the guilt of a real libidinous fantasy and of a pseudo-traffic of white slave trade." (page 52). Thus, the Jew would act as "the fixer of anguish and guilt in the Western world." (page 56). We must therefore believe that the Europeans have had their spirits altered by two thousand years of Christianity.

The White slave trade was in the end nothing more than a "myth": "It is delusional to attribute the White slave trade to the Jews", insisted Edgar Morin (p. 73). And to those in Orléans or Amiens who dared to say that "if the river sounds, it is because there is water in it", Edgar Morin replied: "It is a scandalous amalgam" (page 239)." The Jew is completely absent from the news, reports and mass media fictions concerning the White slave trade, and his appearance in provincial rumours is both surprising and absurd[360]."

These fantasies were thus of the same order as the accusations of ritual crimes practised by Jews on Christian children in the Middle Ages. It is equally ridiculous to accuse Jews of controlling the financial system, the press, television and cinema in the Western world. It makes no sense at all. In the same way, Jews play no role in the pornography industry, nor in the global trafficking of heroin, cocaine and ecstasy, nor do they have anything to do with the West's wars against Muslim countries in recent years. Jews are innocent, fundamentally innocent of

---

[358] Albert Memmi, *Le Racisme*, Gallimard, 1982, réédition de poche 1994, p. 41.
[359] Edgar Morin, *La Rumeur d'Orléans*, 1969, Points Seuil, 1982.
[360] Edgar Morin, *La Rumeur d'Orléans*, 1969, Points Seuil, p. 48.

anything that can be blamed on them.

In cinema, some cosmopolitan directors have typically projected the guilt of their fellow human beings onto others. In Roger Hanin's (Lévy) film, *The Protector (*1974), Natalia, an eighteen-year-old girl, disappeared in Paris. To find her, her father, Samuel Malakian—a poor Jew—had to deal with a network of white slave traders run by an aristocrat, Baron Metzger. In Jean Tulard's *Film Guide*, Claude Bouniq-Mercier, who systematically praised the films of his peers, made his usual comments: after basing himself on "meticulous research", Roger Hanin aims to "denounce a social scourge without demagogy". See also the erotic film by "Jean Rougeron", *Police des mœurs (*1987): Séverine, 18 years old, falls into the trap of a pimp. Worried about her disappearance, her relatives alert the police. The investigation leads the police to the "Horsh" network, a network of white women traffickers. These bastards kidnap girls to sell them to rich foreigners. They are all Nazis, big blond Germans with light eyes[361].

The white slave trade of Jewish traffickers was apparently a fashionable topic at the end of the 1960s, judging by what one could read in the novel by Patrick Modiano, a well-known "French" writer. In *The Place of the Star*, published in 1968, Patrick Modiano imagined a completely delirious, buffoonish and sympathetic character. The action takes place in June 1942 in Paris; the narrator, Schlemilovitch, is a delusional, quixotic hero who imagines himself to be a great writer. Under a grotesque guise, Patrick Modiano puts into his mouth such astonishing and caricatured words about the Jews that no sane reader could read them without noticing their ridiculousness. Anti-Semitism is a hallucination. What the Jews are accused of is so enormous to the average reader that the accusations come across as a psychiatric disorder of the person making them. That is why Patrick Modiano could afford to write them. But let's hear Schlemilovitch speak:

"For the rest, my deeds and my sayings contradicted those virtues cultivated by the French: discretion, thrift and work. From my oriental ancestors I got black eyes, a taste for exhibitionism and lavish luxury, and incurable laziness. I am not a son of this country... I led the world Jewish conspiracy by orgies and millions... Yes, the war of 1939 was declared because of me. Yes, I'm something like a Bluebeard, an anthropophagus who eats young arias after raping them. Yes, I dream of ruining all the French peasants and turning the whole Cantal region Jewish...".

---

[361] In Luc Besson's popular film series *Taken (2008, 2012)*, the bastards are Albanians (NdT).

Lévy-Vendôme replied: "You, Schlemilovitch, you have time ahead of you. Make the most of it! Use your personal trump cards and pervert the young Aryan girls. Later on, you will write your memoirs. They could be called "The Uprooted": the story of seven French girls who could not resist the charms of the Jew Schlemilovitch and found themselves one day interned in Oriental or South American brothels. Moral of the story: they should not have listened to that seductive Jew, but stayed in the lush alpine meadows and green groves[362]." Anti-Semitism will definitely never be credible to the average Goy citizen.

The celebrated historian William Shirer, author of a monumental history of the Third Reich, did not elaborate much on the question of anti-Semitism. Of the 1500 pages of his two volumes, only one page was devoted to explaining Nazi anti-Semitism, which is perhaps a little insubstantial. Hitler, wrote William Shirer, "discovered the moral taint of this 'chosen people'... Was there any form of filth or licentiousness, particularly in cultural life, without at least one Jew mixed up in it? "Shirer simply quoted a few brief excerpts from *Mein Kampf* on prostitution and the White slave trade: "*Mein Kampf* is strewn with lurid allusions to strange Jews seducing innocent Christian girls and thus adulterating their blood. There is a great deal of morbid sexuality in Hitler's ranting about the Jews." Thus, for William Shirer, there was nothing to explain "this terrible hatred, which would contaminate so many Germans[363]". The bottom line is that it was the Germans who were sick, not the Jews, by any stretch of the imagination. This is an analysis that leaves no doubt as to the origin of its author[364].

A minor writer like Michel Herszlikowicz had written some interesting pages in his *Philosophy of Anti-Semitism*. He quoted for example a German author who wrote in 1890: "The mass of Jews who have taken over the field of brothels pursue systematically and on a large scale the transformation of the female part of the Aryan peoples into prostitutes. All cases of prostitution and trafficking in Blancas are almost exclusively in the hands of Jews[365]."

And Michel Herszlikowicz commented, in the most Talmudic style possible: "Jewish domination is realised through the lower

---

[362] Patrick Modiano, *The Place of the Star*, Pdf, http://Lelibros.org/, p. 14, 15, 26, 42–43

[363] William L. Shirer, *Auge y caída del Tercer Reich*, volume I, Planeta, Barcelona, 2013, p. 54, 55.

[364] See the chapters on accusatory inversion in *Psychoanalysis of Judaism, Jewish Fanaticism and The Mirror of Judaism*.

[365] A. Berg, *Juden Bordelle*, Berlin, 1890, p. 10, in Michel Herszlikowicz, *Philosophie de l'antisémitisme*, Presses Universitaires de France, 1985, p. 108.

passions, through the lowest sexuality. Nazism has made this argument one of the fundamental elements of its system, not because Jews were numerous in the profession, but because anti-Semitism was supposed to be the antithesis of the Germanic superman. Prostitution, as an inferior necessity, prevents the realisation of the mission of the German people, and the cause of that failure can only be Jewish."

We see very well here how ignominious the Nazi ideologues had become, always ready to hurl accusations against the poor Jews for the sole purpose of satisfying their will to dominate the rest of humanity.

4. The Black slave trade

Jewish traders clearly had no moral barriers to limiting themselves solely to trafficking in women for prostitution. The African slave trade was also a source of prosperity for some large traders.

The Atlantic Trade I: The Portuguese

On 2 January 1492, the Catholic kings Ferdinand and Isabella solemnly entered Granada, the last Muslim stronghold on the Iberian Peninsula. After centuries of struggle against the Muslim invaders, the Reconquista was over. But the case of the Jewish community, which had done so much for the Muslims from the beginning of the invasion, remained to be settled[366]. On 31 March 1492, Isabella signed the decree expelling the Jews, who were to leave the country by 31 July. The historian Leon Poliakov wrote: "In vain did they offer the treasury immense sums of money", and later added: "It seems that the great majority of the Christian population was not moved by the departure of the Jews[367]". On 2 August of the same year, Christopher Columbus' three caravels set sail westwards to discover the new continent. The three most important events in Spanish history had taken place in the space of a few months.

However, some Jews had converted to Catholicism in order to stay in Spain. They were now good Catholics who went to mass on Sunday, took communion and respected Christian traditions ... but only in appearance. For in reality, most of them continued to curse Christ and Christians. Those falsely converted Jews were called "marranos" by the Spaniards, and that is the word still used today to designate a Jew who hides and acts behind a religious mask, which is very frequent[368].

---

[366] On the role of the Jews in Spain during the Muslim conquest, see Hervé Ryssen, *Planetary Hopes*.
[367] Léon Poliakov, *Histoire de l'antisémitisme, tome I*, Point Seuil, 1981, p. 171.
[368] On the Marranos, the Dönmehs and the Frankists (false Catholics and false Muslims), read *Psychoanalysis of Judaism*." (…) They were still, in their inner selves, as Jewish as they had been before. Apparently, they lived as Christians. They had their children baptised in church, although they hastened to wash away the traces of the ceremony as soon as they returned home. They went to the priest to get married, but they were not satisfied with that ceremony, and privately performed another, which

In Spain, the Jewish community had controlled much of the trade and was immensely wealthy. The Marranos who had stayed behind still had powerful financial means, enough money to arm the ships of Christopher Columbus's expedition. In his *History of the Marranos*, a landmark work published in 1932, Cecil Roth wrote that wealthy Marranos had financed part of the venture. Chief among them was Luis de Santangel, to whom a royal decree had granted the right to export grain and horses to America[369]. Cabrero, the royal treasurer, and Santangel, invested 17,000 ducats. Alfonso de la Caballería and Diego de Deza also contributed funds; Abraham Ben Samuel Zacuto had provided the astronomical and navigational equipment.

Leon Poliakov confirmed this: "Support and financial contributions came from New Christians, which allows us to admit that beyond the spirit of adventure or profit, they were interested in the discovery of new lands in which, if necessary, they could take refuge. The fact is that the New Christians, whether sincere or not, played a major role in the colonisation of America[370]."

Christopher Columbus was accompanied on his expedition by seven baptised Jews. On the caravel Santa María were Mastre Bernard, the doctor; Luis de Torres, the interpreter; Marco Bernal, the surgeon; Alonso de la Calle, the navigator; and Gabriel Sánchez, an inspector. There were also Juan de Cabrera on the Pinta, and Rodrigo de Triana on the Niña. So some Jewish scholars naturally claim Christopher Columbus as one of their own. But an important point contradicted this hypothesis. In 1498, Gabriel Sanchez and the other Marranos had convinced Colomb to capture 500 Amerindians to sell them as slaves in Seville. However, Colomb did not receive a single cent from the sale. Be that as it may, that operation was the beginning of slavery in the New

---

completed it. Sometimes they went to the confessional; but their confessions were so unreal, that a priest, it is said, asked one of them for a piece of his garment, as a relic of a soul so immaculate. Behind this purely external fiction, they remained what they had always been. Their lack of faith in the dogmas of the Church was notorious. They furtively frequented the synagogues, for the illumination of which they regularly sent oil lamps. They also formed religious associations, ostensibly for Catholic purposes, under the patronage of some Christian saint, and used them as a screen, enabling them to observe their ancestral rites. By their race and faith, they remained the same as they had been before their conversion. They were Jews in all but name; Christians in nothing but form." In Cecil Roth, *History of the Marranos*, Editorial Israel, Buenos Aires, 1946, Ch. I, p. 26, 27.

[369] Cecil Roth, *History of the Marranos*, Editorial Israel, Buenos Aires, 1946. *History of the Marranos*, Jewish Publication Society of America, 1932, p. 272-273.

[370] Léon Poliakov, *The Samaritans*, Grupo Anaya & Mario Muchnik, Madrid, 1992 p. 77. 77

World.

Another very lucrative phenomenon also saw the light of day at that time: the tobacco trade. It was Luis de Torres who introduced tobacco to Spain. He set up his plantations in Cuba and then exported his profitable production all over Europe.

Many of the Jews expelled from Spain had settled in Portugal. But in 1497, they were also expelled from that kingdom. They left for Calvinist Holland or the Ottoman Empire. Some preferred to remain subjects of the Portuguese crown, but in their colonies in order to escape the Inquisition, which tracked down Christians suspected of being Jews in disguise. This is why so many Jews settled on the island of Madeira, and later in Brazil, where they quickly established trading emporiums.

On the island of Madeira, some Jews were involved in the sugar industry. At the beginning of the 16th century, according to the Jewish historian Morechaï Arbell, there were about 150 sugar cane mills. In 1516, the Portuguese King Manuel I had decreed that people who wanted to emigrate to Brazil to start sugar production would receive all the necessary material from the crown and would benefit from the assistance of experts. The "New Christians" (also called "marranos" or "conversos"), specialised in sugar production, began to emigrate to Brazil." Sugar cane was imported into Brazil from the island of Madeira in 1548 by Jews expelled from Portugal", wrote historian Don Antonio de Campany de Montpalan in 1779[371]. The New Christians were not always identified as Jews, but documents attest to their involvement in three stages: sugar cane cultivation, sugar production and marketing.

In his studies on Brazil, historian Herbert Bloom wrote in 1932: "The Jews owned huge sugar plantations... The Jews controlled the sugar trade in Brazil[372]." Another researcher, Gilberto Freyre agreed: "The Jews were the most active agents in the conquest of the sugar market in Brazil during the first hundred years of colonisation. The Jews were also the most efficient in the technique of sugar cane mills[373]."

When the activities and investigations of the Inquisition expanded, many of the New Christians were growers, traders and owners of the sugar industry. The arrests led to a drop in sugar exports, so much so that, to avoid shortages, the King of Portugal ordered at the

---

[371] Leon Huhner quotes him in the article *"Brazil"*, in *Jewish Encyclopedia* (New York, 1902), vol. III, p. 359.
[372] Dr. Herbert J. Bloom, *Study of Brazilian Jewish History*, in *Publications of the American Jewish Historical Society*, 33 (1934), p. 52 and 55. Quoted by Mordechaï Arbell, *Les Juifs séfarades des Antilles et le sucre*.
[373] Gilberto Freyre, *The Masters and the Slaves: Study in the Development of Brazilian Civilization*, New York, 1946, p. 12.

beginning of the 18th century that sugar cane mills should no longer be confiscated[374]. But Dutch Brazil had already become the main sugar centre.

In Calvinist Holland, religious tolerance and commercial prospects had attracted many Jews expelled from Spain and Portugal. Some officially returned to Judaism, but others still kept the mask on for some time. Some quickly invested their funds in diamond cutting, sugar, silk, textiles, tobacco and foodstuffs. The United Provinces became the centre of Jewish power and wealth in Europe. Marcus Arkin estimated that in the 18th century, 25% of the shares in Dutch international companies were owned by Jews[375]. Ships then carried out the triangular trade between Europe, Africa and the Americas. They traded manufactured goods from Africa against slaves to Brazil, the Caribbean and the United States, and returned to Europe with sugar and other commodities.

The Dutch occupation of Brazil between 1624 and 1654 was to be of considerable benefit to their business. Dutch soldiers, led by the Prince of Nassau, defeated the Portuguese and secured the Dutch presence in Pernambuco, in the north-east of Brazil. Two hundred Jews who were part of the expedition, attracted by the gold trade, immediately started their fruitful business. The Jews had invested massively, first in the famous Dutch West India Company, founded in 1621, which engaged in all kinds of trade, including the slave trade. With their centuries of mercantile experience and their networks of friends and family scattered all over the world, they played a very important role in the merchant capitalism of the time.

In Pernambuco, in 1630, the population was 12,703 people, of whom 2,890 were Whites. But in reality, half of these "Whites" were Jews. In fact, they built the first synagogue in Recife in the same year. The Brazilian Jewish historian Marc Raizman based himself on the important work *Historia dos Israelitas no Brasil* that his father had published in 1937. As they found the Indians not very hardy enough to cut sugar cane, they decided to import black slaves. The West India Company owned the ships, but once they were landed, "the Jews were responsible for the buying and selling of these black slaves," wrote Marc Raizman." They resold them often four or five times more expensive than what they had paid to the Company."

The preponderance of Spanish and Portuguese Jews in the

---

[374] Testamento Político da Carta Escrita pelo Conde D. Luis da Cunha, p. 54, in Arnold Wiznitzer, *Jews in Colonial Brazil,* New York, 1960, p. 151.
[375] Jewish Publication Society of America, 1975, p. 44, 45.

cultivation of sugar cane on the other side of the Atlantic was confirmed by another Jewish historian, Arnold Wiznitzer, who also mentioned the slave trade: "In addition to their dominant position in the sugar industry, they also dominate the slave trade. From 1636 to 1645, a total of 23,163 Blacks had arrived from Africa, being sold for 6,714,423 guilders. The buyers at the auctions were all Jews, and due to this lack of competition in the slave business, slaves were bought at low prices. Also, because of this same lack of competition in the slave trade, slaves were paid on credit until the following sugar selling season. If the auctions coincided with a Jewish holiday, they were automatically postponed[376]."

In Ouidah and Porto Novo, the two fortified Portuguese towns on the Dahomey coast, Jewish slave traders had made deals with the kings of the coast to buy the captives. The captives were rounded up and crammed into Aného, the border town, with a view to shipment. Soon, the raids of the local populations were insufficient and the coastal tribes penetrated north to hunt slaves on the mainland. The enslavement of the Blacks was indeed an African affair, for Africans had always practised the subjugation of opposing tribes. The traditional legends of the Mali empire, as well as those of Behanzin in Dahomey (present-day Benin), echo this. It was a scourge that no colonial administrator had been able to remedy before the independence of African countries in the 1960s. Often, indebted parents borrowed money and left a child as collateral until their debts were paid off. Today's colonial and African court records are replete with such cases.

Jewish slave traders thus supplied hundreds of thousands of black slaves to the plantations of South America and the Caribbean, and contributed extensively to making Portugal the first Western slave nation.

Moshe Kahan wrote that in 1653–1658, "Jewish Marrano merchants had control of the Spanish and Portuguese trade." Daniel Swetschinski estimated that Jews dominated 75% of Jamaica's trade, with Jews making up 10% of the white population.

The American historian Marc Lee Raphael, himself a Jew, confirmed that the Jews had in turn taken control of "a very important part of the Dutch slave business". In Recife and Mauritius, a tax ("*imposta*") of five "*soldos*" had been established for each black slave

---

[376] In David Duke, *Jewish Supremacism* (2003). Arnold Aaron Wiznitzer, *Jews in Colonial Brazil*, 1960, p. 72, 73. Arnold Aaron Wiznitzer was a professor at the University of Vienna in the 1920s, doctor in Hebrew literature, professor emeritus at the University of Judaism in Los Angeles, former president of the Brazilian-Jewish Institute of Historical Research.

bought by a Brazilian Jew in the colonies." In Curaçao in the 17th century, but also in the British colonies of Barbados and Jamaica in the 18th century, Jewish merchants played a very important role in the slave trade." Jewish merchants therefore played "a fundamental role" in the slave trade." In fact, in all the American colonies, whether French (Martinique), English or Dutch, Jewish merchants played a preponderant role[377]."

In an important book of Jewish historiography, *New World Jewry, 1493–1825*, Seymour B. Liebman provided additional details: "The trade was then a royal monopoly, and Jews were often appointed agents of the crown. They were the principal suppliers for arming the ships of the entire Caribbean region, where the trade was primarily a Jewish enterprise. The ships were not only owned by Jews, but were under the command of captains and crews composed of Jews[378]."

After the defeat of the Dutch in 1654, most of the Jews were expelled from Brazil by the Portuguese and left the Pernambuco region. About 150 Jewish families (600 people) then decided to return to Amsterdam with the Dutch. Others went to other Dutch possessions, such as Curaçao—an island north of present-day Venezuela—Bermuda and other Caribbean islands. Twenty-three Jewish merchants marched to New Amsterdam, which would become New York after the English conquest in 1664. The Dutch did all they could to promote these settlements and issued a series of decrees in favour of the Jews.

The West India Company wanted from the beginning to make Curaçao, with its large natural harbour, the centre of its slave trade network in the Caribbean. The economic life of the Jewish community revolved mainly around the sugar cane plantations and thus the slave trade. Jewish merchants created a slave market there that grew considerably from 1643–1648. The Jewish merchants of Curaçao had an outstanding network of contacts and relations that covered the entire Caribbean and Europe, with Amsterdam as its centre. A decade after their arrival, Jews owned 80% of the plantations.

Other Jewish refugees settled in London. The English had also encouraged Jewish entrepreneurs to settle in their colonies, especially on the island of Barbados where they had been allowed to settle since

---

[377] Marc Lee Raphael, *Jews and Judaism in the United States, a Documentary History*, New York, Behrman House, Inc., 1983, p. 14, 23–25. http://www.blacksandjews.com. Rabbi Raphael was for 10 years editor-in-chief of *American Jewish History*, the journal of the Jewish Historical Society of Brandeis University in Massachusetts.

[378] Liebman S. B., *New World Jewry 1493–1825: Requiem for Forgotten*. KTAV, New York, 1982, p. 170, 183. Quoted by David Duke in *Jewish Supremacism*.

1654. Jewish merchants thus spread throughout the Caribbean.

In 1655, before the Dutch occupation, the English had encouraged Jews to settle in Suriname, where they were considered full English citizens. The "Jewish Savannah" was a region almost exclusively populated by Jews and a major sugar centre. After the occupation of the Dutch in 1667—Suriname was renamed "Dutch Guiana"—the English considered bringing the Jews to Jamaica to develop sugar production, but the Dutch objected. In 1694, the Savannah was populated by about 100 Jewish families (570 Jews in all) who worked some 10,000 black slaves on some 40 sugar cane plantations. By 1730, they owned 115 plantations and had a near monopoly on sugar exports to Europe and the New World.

In his book *A History of the Jews*, another Jewish historian named Solomon Grayzel confirmed the same: "The Jews were the most important slave traders in European society[379]." The Jewish historian Henry Feingold wrote: "The Jews who were often at the centre of the trade could not fail to contribute, directly or indirectly, in a similar proportion to the slave trade. In 1460, when Jews had become experts in nautical science in Portugal, Portugal was already importing between 700 and 800 slaves every year[380]."

Today, Sephardic Jews still play a considerable role in the food trade. The international trade in sugar, cocoa, cereals, oilseeds and almost all the raw materials from these regions are in the hands of companies, generally family-owned, almost all of them belonging to Sephardic Jews, whether declared or not.

The famous historian Leon Poliakov also recognised the importance of the role of the Jews in the sugar industry and the Atlantic trade, but he apparently preferred to be more discreet about the role of his fellow Jews in the slave trade: "What is certain is that the Marranos were the great artisans of the colonial economy in South America: and first of all in Brazil, where, being more numerous than the Old Christians, they founded great commercial dynasties which today, aware of their origins, prefer to conceal them[381]."

---

[379] Salomon Grayzel, *A History of the Jews: From Babylonian Exile to the End of World War II*, Philadelphia, Jewish Publication Society of America, p. 312.
[380] Henry Feingold, *Le Sionisme en Amérique: L'expérience juive du temps des colonies jusqu'à ce jour— Zion in America: The Jewish Experience from Colonial Times to the Present*, New York, Twayne Publishing Inc., 1974, p. 42, 43.
[381] Leon Poliakov, *The Samaritans*, Grupo Anaya & Mario Muchnik, Madrid, 1992, p. 79.

The Atlantic slave trade II: in the United States

The slave trade brought several hundred thousand black slaves to the North American continent. Between Aného (Dahomey, on the border with Togo) and Newport (Virginia), and later Charleston (South Carolina), nearly half a million black slaves were bought, transported and sold in two hundred and fifty years (1600–1860) to supply the tobacco and cotton plantations.

Here, too, Jews were among the largest traders until the abolition of slavery was proclaimed in 1865, at the end of the Civil War. In the 17th century, slavery was forbidden in the northern American colonies. Four wealthy Philadelphia Israelite merchants, Sandiford Lay, Woolman, Solomon and Benazet, influenced the legislature to change the law and obtain its legalisation. Newport thus became a major centre of the slave trade and was home to the largest Jewish community in America at the time. In fact, the oldest existing synagogue in the country is located in Newport.

At the beginning of the 18th century, during the height of the trade, the slave trade operated through a fleet of 128 slave ships, almost all owned by Jewish shipowners from Newport and Charleston, the two great centres of the slave trade. The American Jewish historian Marc Lee Raphael admitted that Jewish merchants had been the protagonists of the slave trade. In all the American colonies, whether English, French or Dutch, Jewish merchants dominated the triangular trade: 'This was also true in the North American territories during the 18th century, when Jews participated in the triangular trade that brought slaves from West Africa in exchange for sugar cane molasses, which was exchanged for rum in New England. Isaac Da Costa of Charleston in the 1750s, David Franks of Philadelphia in the 1760s and Aaron Lopez of Newport in the late 1760s and early 1770s dominated the slavery business on the North American continent[382]."

The French historian Jacques Heers agreed: "At the height of the slave trade in the early 18th century, there were more than 120 slave ships, the vast majority owned by Jewish merchants and shipowners from Charleston in South Carolina and Newport on the Chesapeake Bay in Virginia (Moses Levy, Isaac Levy, Abraham All, Aaron Lopez, San Levey), or Portuguese, also Jewish, established in North America (David Gomez, Felix de Souza), who had relatives in Brazil."

These ebony traffickers (African slaves), some of "Portuguese"

---

[382] Marc Lee Raphael, *Jews and Judaism in the United States, a Documentary History*, New York, Behrman House, Inc., 1983. Vol. 14.

origin, were strongly implanted on the African coast, even in the land, directly managing important trafficking emporiums, warehouses and wharfs, something that neither the English nor the French had done[383].

This was the list of slave traders in Newport in the 18th century, compiled by African-American researcher Louis Farrakhan in his book entitled *The Secret Relationship between Blacks and Jews*[384], in italics in brackets the names of their slave ships: Joseph and Samuel Frazon (the *Joseph and Rachel*), Abraham de Lucena (the *Mary and Abigail*), Modecaï Gomez (the *Young Catherine*), Rachel Marks (the *Lydia*, the *Barbadoes factor*, the *Charming Sally*, the *Hannah*, the *Polly*, the *Dolphin*, the *Prince Orange*), Nathan Levy and David Franks (the *Drake*, the *Sea Flower*, the *Myrtilla*, etc.), Isaac and Abraham Hart (the *General Well*, the *Defiance*, the *Perfect Union*, etc.), Samuel Levy (the *Deborah*), Moses and David Franks (the *Gloucester*, the *Delaware*, the *Belle*, the *Mars*).

In the 19th century, the owners of the ships were David G. Seixas (the *Jane*, the *Nancy*), John Bueno (the *Rebecca*), James de Wolf (the *Ann*), Isaac Levy (the *Crown Gally*, the *Postillion*), Jacob Franks (the *Duke of York*), Samuel Jacobs (the *Betsey*), Emmanuel Alvares Correa and Moses Cardozo (the *Pearl*), Moses Levy (the *Mary and Ann*), Moses Lopez (the *Rebecca*), Naphtali Hart (the *King George*).

Aaron Lopez, a Portuguese marrano, was the most powerful of these slave traders. He owned dozens of ships and imported thousands of black slaves to American shores. Accounts from one of his ships, the *Cleopatra*, show that 250 slaves had perished during two voyages[385]. By 1774, Aaron Lopez alone controlled 50% of the trade to the American colonies.

Jacques Heers also gave other interesting information that highlighted the deep-rooted activities of these traffickers: "In Charleston," he wrote, "about twenty establishments, in no way clandestine, distilled a poor quality alcohol destined for Africa for the Black slave trade."

Jews were also the largest slave owners. One of Ira Rosenwaike's numerous studies, published by the American Jewish Historical Society, showed that in 1830, 75% of the two hundred thousand slave owners in

---

[383] Jacques Heers, *Les Négriers en terre d'Islam*, Perrin, 2003, Poche, 2007, p. 260.
[384] *The Secret Relationship between Blacks and Jews* (1991). Prepared by the Historical Research Department of the Nation of Islam. Chicago, Illinois: Latimer Associates.
[385] Platt, Virginia B. (1975). *And Don't Forget the Guinea Voyage: The Slave Trade of Aaron Lopez of Newport*. William and Mary Quartely, in David Duke, *Jewish Supremacism* (2003).

the Confederacy were Israelites.

Historian Jacob Marcus wrote that in the South, less than 10% of settlers owned slaves, but Jews were far more likely to own slaves than Gentiles. In 1820, more than 75% of Jewish families in Charleston and Richmond owned slaves and employed servants[386]. Naturally, some black women could also be exploited in prostitution rings.

In Martinique and Guadeloupe

In the French colonies, in Martinique and Guadeloupe, occupied in 1635 by the French, the slave trade also developed with the arrival of Jewish merchants who invested in the sugar industry. In 1654, seven or eight Jewish families accompanied by their black slaves had arrived in Martinique, expelled from Brazil by the Portuguese. These traders brought with them the techniques for manufacturing and refining white gold and set up a sugar factory[387]. The sugar craze took hold of the colonists and they all dreamed of becoming rich. In 1661, there were 71 cane mills in Guadeloupe, and slightly fewer in Martinique. Ten years later, 111 mills were operating in Martinique, and 172 in 1675.

In 1683, there were 23 such "Dutch" families in Martinique, representing some 90 people. This presence of slave-owners involved in the triangular trade with Dutch ships raised hackles. The Jesuits informed the King of France, and the expulsion of the Jews was ordered by a decree of 2 May 1684 registered with the sovereign council. This was the origin of the first article of Colbert's Code Noir of March 1685:

"Art. 1: ... it being so, we urge all our officers to expel from our said islands all the Jews who established their residence there, whom, as declared enemies of the Christian faith, we order to leave within three months from the day of the publication of the present, under penalty of confiscation of goods and property."

Some left for Curuzao, but the colonial government apparently ignored Article 1, as many Jews continued to prosper on the islands. The French Revolution, which declared the principle of equal rights, ensured their hegemony in the slave trade as agents (intermediaries) of European slave trading companies. From 1786 to 1792, 50% of the French slave ships were assembled in Bordeaux. The main shipowners were called Nairac, Cabarrus, Balguerie, Baour, Gradis.

---

[386] Marcus, J. (1989, *United States Jewry*). 1776–1985. Detroit: Wayne State University Press, p. 586, quoted by David Duke, in *Jewish Supremacism*.
[387] Armand Nicolas, *Histoire de la Martinique*, Tome I, Éditions L'Harmattan, p. 73, 74.

The Gradis dynasty illustrated the history of the Jews in the French colonies quite well. The house had been founded in 1685 by Diego Gradis, the scion of an old "Portuguese" family settled in Bordeaux. He had passed it on to his son David Gradis (1665–1751), who launched the commercial enterprise in Saint-Pierre de Martinique and opened a branch in French Saint-Domingue in 1724. His trade typically consisted of a triangular exchange between Europe, the Caribbean and North America. In Bordeaux, the "King David" armed twenty-six ships in those years. He had become so powerful that the colonial government was unable to banish him from Martinique. When David died in 1751, his son Abraham successfully continued his father's work and further increased the wealth and power of the family. His influence was so great that in 1779 he was granted "the rights of the French", a distinction never before granted to a Jew. When he died in 1780, his fortune was valued at 8 million pounds, i.e. half the value of Martinique's exports to France. Abraham Gradis was remembered long after his death by the inhabitants of Bordeaux, who called him the famous Jew Gradis, "the king of Bordeaux". In 1789, the Gradis house was hard hit by the Revolution and the abolition of slavery. However, it managed to rebuild itself with the transport and sugar business in Martinique.

Isaac Mendès was another great Caribbean slave trader. A Sephardite from Bordeaux, where some Portuguese Jews had settled, he called himself Mendès France, to distinguish himself from the Portuguese branch of his family. Isaac Mendès France was at the centre of a controversial trial in 1776, under the reign of Louis XVI. He had returned to France with two Congolese slaves: "Black Gabriel Pampy, 24 years old, and Black Amynte Julienne, 18 years old". But they had left their master in Paris, so Mendès France had them brought to justice. Leon Poliakov wrote that, during the trial, the slaves accused Mendès "of cruelty, listing several examples[388]". But Poliakov gave no further details.

The court finally ruled in favour of Pampy and Julianne. The Code no longer applied in the metropolis, and any slave who entered the kingdom was immediately freed. It is true that another royal edict forbade "Negroes" from entering the kingdom, as well as intermarriage.

Mendès France nevertheless continued its trade, as demonstrated by a document of the time dating from 1785: "Account of the sale of 524 heads of blacks from the coast of Angola landed in the port of Léogane by the ship *Agamemnon* on 19 December 1785. They were sold to Mendès France 105 black tails, including 9 sick and one of the

---

[388] Léon Poliakov, *Histoire de l'antisémitisme, tome I*, Seuil, 1981, p. 448, 449.

pian: 16 blacks, one black, 62 little blacks, 26 little blacks for a total sum of 192,000 pounds. The total load of blacks from the *Agamemnon* amounted to 1,215,960 pounds." The politician Pierre Mendès France, Prime Minister of France in 1954–1955, was a descendant of this slave-owning family.

The Debate

All this evidence did not prevent the mainstream press from claiming that Jews had never been involved in the slave trade. This is what we could read for example in the weekly *Le Point* of 4 May 2006: To the question: "Were the Jews the architects of the Atlantic slave trade? "Answer: "False: This is the thesis of the American populist Farakhan, defended in France by Dieudonné [a mulatto humorist at odds with the French Jewish community, cf *The Planetary Hopes*]. It is in contradiction with the Black Code. Dixit: "We urge all our officers to expel from our said islands all the Jews who have established their residence there, whom, as declared enemies of the Christian faith, we order to leave within three months...". Although some Jewish financiers had participated in the conquest of the New World, the journalist noted, it seems that it was rather Christians, especially Protestants, who had organised the Treaty from Liverpool, Nantes, Bordeaux, La Rochelle, Le Havre or Amsterdam." Evidently, this was without counting the Marranos, who were good Catholics, at least in appearance.

A year earlier, on 3 March 2005, another large-circulation, left-wing weekly— *Le Nouvel Observateur* —published a major dossier on the subject, entitled: "The truth about the slave trade". We read these lines: "Did the Jews take part in the Atlantic slave trade? —False, replied Olivier Pétré-Grenouilleau. And the best proof that this is a lucubration without historical basis is to be found in the Code Noir, promulgated in 1685 by Louis XIV. The first article of this text, which regulated slavery in the West Indies, French Guiana and Louisiana, formally excluded Jews from these territories: "We urge all our officials to expel all Jews from our said islands...". On the other hand, in La Rochelle, Nantes and Bordeaux, large Protestant families prospered thanks to the triangular trade."

Thus, we see that while diversity of opinion still exists in the democratic system, it is only apparent when it comes to debating substantive issues.

In 2004, historian Olivier Pétré-Grenouilleau published a

"reference book" in France entitled *The Slave Trade*. He wrote: "The myths about the role that Jews are said to have played in the slave trade must be corrected immediately." He added: "Seymour Drescher has provided a brilliant synthesis on the subject. In it, he underlined the fact that two thousand Jewish children were deported by the Portuguese to São Tomé after 1492 and that their descendants were the first traders on the island." Indeed, in his book Pétré-Grenouilleau referred mainly to Jewish historians...

Regarding the role of the Marran community, Grenouilleau again quoted Seymour Drescher: "Its overall impact was modest in Europe, Africa and the Atlantic, even at the times of greatest Jewish influence (1640–1700). Drescher concluded that "its presence in the trade was simply too ephemeral, localised and limited to stand out in any appreciable way[389]." So if Seymour Drescher said it, it must be true. That was the only reference to the role of Jewish traders to be found in Olivier Pétré-Grenouilleau's 700-page book.

As we know, Jewish intellectuals have a strong tendency to transfer onto others what they probably feel a little guilty about. Naturally, newspaper articles in *Time* or *Newsweek*, *Nouvel Observateur* or *Le Point* have denied the role of Jews in slavery. In the same way that Steven Spielberg's film about the slave trade, *Amistad* (USA, 1997), does not show the irrefutable role of Jewish traders in that tragedy and rejects the full weight of the infamy on Christians.

In 2006, in *The Modern World and the Jewish Question*, the Sephardic sociologist Edgar Morin (born Nahoum) admitted the involvement of Jewish slavers, although he settled the question with a single sentence: "The flight of the Marranos from Spain and Portugal provided the Netherlands and England with the ferments of their economic boom, and more generally of all the economic growth of modern times, for better (intellectual openness and cosmopolitanism) and for worse (contribution to the subjugation of the Indians of America and the practice of the slave trade)[390]."

But this was an exceptional intellectual honesty, for Jewish intellectuals usually prefer to blame others. Edgar Morin himself had been willingly on the attack in his 2005 book, kindly entitled *European Culture and Barbarism*. Europe is "potentially criminal[391] ", said the

---

[389] Olivier Pétré-Grenouilleau, *Les traites négrières*, Gallimard, 2004, Folio, 2006, p. 65, 66.
[390] Edgar Morin, *Le Monde moderne et la question juive*, Seuil, 2006, p. 55.
[391] On blaming, see *Planetary Hopes, Psychoanalysis of Judaism* and *Jewish Fanaticism*.

indispensable Bernard-Henri Lévy.

Let us now highlight the words of another "French" intellectual, Stéphane Zagdanski, who in 2006 wrote a short dialogue about the French-Cameroonian mulatto humorist Dieudonné ["*Diosdado*" in Spanish, ndt] who had discovered and understood the role of Jewish traders in the slave trade:

"Since he cannot choose between his father and his mother, or rather, since the racism of others has done it for him, he retaliates by attacking the "fraud-less" root of his surname.

—Result: He explicitly calls Judaism a "scam"!

—And the Jews become largely responsible for their own existential malaise?

—Precisely! You can't even imagine what fantasies this pale cretin has given credence to: the Jews would have massively enslaved the Africans!

—This is a most original inversion of the truth, due to a commonplace anti-Semitic hatred. The Jews are precisely the only people in the world who bear absolutely no responsibility for the continuing tragedies and misfortunes of Africa[392]."

This is a very good example of what Jewish intellectuals are capable of doing, driven by their usual "*chutzpah*", i.e. the height of impudence that allows them to defend the exact opposite of the truth. Jewish intellectuals always tend to project their own faults onto others, including the one that consists in projecting their faults onto others. We also know that they have a regrettable tendency to insult their opponents.

Another constitutive element of the Jewish spirit is that they are prone to treat their opponents as mentally ill. For example, this is what Zagdanskiwrote about Louis Farrakhan: "The black American leader with a growing following, whose anti-Semitism is simply sickening. This is evidently another manifestation of the "projection syndrome" [393]"

Moreover, Zagdanski confirmed that Jews encouraged immigration and the establishment of multiracial societies in the West. They had always supported the integration of Blacks into European and American societies, he wrote. Farrakhan, according to him, disavowed and nullified "what the emancipation of Blacks owed to the active assistance on the part of the Jewish community in America."

---

[392] Stéphane Zagdanski, *De l'Antisémitisme*, Climats, 1995, 2006, p. 346.
[393] On the accusatory inversion and the tendency to insults, read the chapters on *Psychoanalysis of Judaism* and *Jewish Fanaticism*.

Jewish intellectuals obviously have much more sympathy for docile blacks: "The anti-Farrakhan is the smiling Nelson Mandela," wrote Zagdanski. As soon as he was elected president, he went to the great synagogue in Johannesburg to thank the South African Jewish community for its participation in the struggle against apartheid[394]."

However, it should not be forgotten that the Jews and the state of Israel had long been the Apartheid regime's strongest international supporters, allowing them to benefit from the exploitation of South Africa's gold and diamond mines. Equal rights for the black population did not change anything. In all multi-ethnic societies—with or without Apartheid—Blacks are always at the bottom of the social ladder, while Jews are at the top. In South Africa as elsewhere, Jews had favoured equal rights not because it represented a moral duty, but because the aim was to undermine white society, to dissolve ethnically homogenous identities and communities in order to avoid a possible nationalist backlash against their domination.

The help that Jews had given to immigrants in the West had not really been a disinterested or unfounded vocation, it did not correspond to humanitarian sentiments. The depth of the Jewish soul was quite different. Here for example is an extract from the *Mishneh Torah* of Maimonides, the eminent 12th century Talmudist, who died in Cordoba in 1204 and whom the Jews also call "the medieval Moses": " The Turks of the far North and the blacks in the far South and their fellows in our climes are to be regarded as irrational animals below men and above apes."

Let us also listen to the famous American novelist Philip Roth, in 1967, talking about his parents' cleaning lady: "The cleaning lady is obviously a shiksa[395], but she doesn't count, because she is black[396]".

Mordecai Richler was another well-known Jewish novelist born in Montreal, Quebec. The author of a dozen novels and several screenplays, he was naturally described, like all Jewish novelists, as a "genius" by the press. He had received numerous awards, an obvious manifestation of this famous community solidarity. His novel *Joshua Then and Now* was "considered by critics to be one of his best books". If the critics said so, it had to be true. We do not doubt it: Mordecai Richler was a marvellous literary genius.

Here is an excerpt from his work: "Look at the blacks, for

---

[394] Stéphane Zagdanski, *De l'Antisémitisme*, Climats, 1995, 2006, p. 256, 257
[395] Shiksa: non-Jewish woman (pejorative).
[396] Philip Roth, *Portnoy's Evil*, Penguin Random House Debols! llo, Barcelona, 2008. p. 92.

example. They come in all shades, from coal black to brownish brown, like Sugar Ray, to a light tan[397]." The depths of a people's soul are always best glimpsed in his novels.

On the back cover of the book, you could read the following review: "Joshua Shapiro, son of a boxer turned smuggler and small-time hustler, has had a pretty good life. Writer, journalist, television star, he falls in love with the dazzling Pauline, daughter of a senator who moves in the distinguished society of Montreal... We follow the turbulent journey of this insolent and irresistible hero. Mordacious, ferocious, Richler's humour never ceases to amaze us."

A pity, however, that the word "shit" appeared every other page. Over the course of 615 pages it is perhaps too much.

---

[397] Mordecaï Richler, *Joshua*, Buchet/Chastel, 2004, p. 280, 443

5. Christian slaves

The black slave trade to America became really important at the end of the 17th century and stopped in the middle of the 19th century. But since ancient times, and until the height of the slave trade in the 18th century, most of the slaves bought and sold by Jewish traders were white.

Towards America

The truth is that even at the time of the slave trade it was easier to procure white slaves than African slaves. Coastal tribal chiefs had to be paid to go and capture slaves within African lands and the hunts could last for weeks at a time. By contrast, white slaves were within easy reach of English traders.

In 1615, the English parliament with the support of King Charles I had granted the power to the magistrates to allow the deportation of the poorest subjects in order to encourage the development of the English colonies and further the expansion of the British Empire. In 1618, a petition had been brought before the Council of London by representatives of the aristocracy to request the deportation of wandering children to Virginia. For their part, plantation owners called for the legalisation and expansion of *kidnapping,* and in February 1652 beggars from England left for America in chains.

The 1796 edition of the *Dictionary of Vulgar Tongue* defined a *kidnapper* as follows: "A person who steals children to send them to the colonies, in the plantations of the Caribbean". In 1670, according to the historian Edward Channing, in his *History of the United States,* ten thousand children were kidnapped in this way and deported to the United States.

Ireland was also to suffer hard times with its English neighbour. The country, which was invaded by Cromwell's troops after the fall of the English monarchy, paid heavily for its attachment to the Catholic faith. More than 100,000 men, women and children were deported and only a fraction survived the difficult conditions of the 9–12 week Atlantic Ocean crossing. In September 1655, Cromwell demanded that an additional 1,500 Irish boys aged 12 to 14 be sent to Jamaica and the

English Caribbean to alleviate the high mortality rate. In *The Curse of Cromwell: A History of the Ironside Conquest of Ireland*, Rose Esson claimed that Irish priests were systematically put in internment camps and deported to America along with old men over 80.

In February 1656, Cromwell gave the order to capture and deport 1200 English women, another 2000 followed the next month. In the same year, Cromwell had all homeless Scots deported, and later all political prisoners and also English beggars. By contrast, the very puritanical Cromwell, so steeped in Old Testament values, had allowed the return of the Jews in England, expelled from the kingdom in 1290 by King Edward I.

In a book entitled *They Were White and They Were Slaves*, the American Michael A. Hoffman, citing the case of a captain whose ship was loaded with 200 to 300 white slaves bound for Carolina, explained that a white slave was less valuable than a black slave because the latter was more accustomed to the tropical climate of Virginia or Florida. The Virginia state treasurer, George Sandys, traded, for example, seven white slaves against 150 pounds of tobacco. In 1657, a white slave was traded for a pig. In *Sugar and Slaves: The Rise of the Planter Class in the English West Indies*, historian Richard Dunn showed that the sugar cane plantations in the English Caribbean were the tomb of the white slaves, as 80% died within the first year of their arrival.

Not far from Martinique, in the Barbados Islands, sugar cane plantations employed mainly white slaves in the 17th century. In 1640, 21,700 of the 25,000 slaves were white. French, Irish and Scottish soldiers of the Jacobite army were deported there after the defeat of Culloden in 1746.

Slavery in the Mediterranean

Slavery in the Mediterranean has been studied by the American historian Robert C. Davies in a book entitled *Christian Slaves, Muslim Maters,* published in 2004. That flourishing industry of human abduction by Barbary pirates lasted approximately three hundred years, from 1500 to 1800. For most of that period, European navies were too weak to effectively oppose it. Salé in Morocco, Tunis, Algiers and Tripoli were the great slave capitals[398].

---

[398] After several failures in the 18th century, the Spanish monarchy and its allies managed to stop Barbary piracy thanks to the Bombardment of Algiers in 1784, commanded by Admiral Antonio Barceló. The French conquest of Algeria in 1830 put a definitive end to their activity.

Until recently, except for a few specialists, the captivity of Christians in the hands of the Berbers was thought to be nothing more than an anecdote. Novelised accounts of captivity, such as that of Miguel de Cervantes, contributed to this legend. Moreover, it was very difficult to grasp the significance of the phenomenon." Davis's study provides for the first time a quantitative analysis," wrote Olivier Pétré-Grenouilleau, commenting on the book." We realise that this was a fairly large-scale slavery and that it remained ignored for a long time. By the 16th century, the number of Christian slaves kidnapped was greater than the number of Africans deported to America. Although it is true that the slave trade did not really develop until the end of the 17th century, with the sugar revolution in the Caribbean."

If this traffic was ignored for so long, it is because it did not leave many traces. The white slaves were mainly men, 90% of them, and unlike the Africans in America, they did not take root and leave no trace in the land of Islam.

At first, the Berbers engaged in piracy and raiding operations along the Mediterranean coasts. Later, the Christians mobilised to rescue their relatives from slavery into which they had fallen. It became very profitable. This financial motivation intensified the Muslim raids from the 16th century onwards. Because they were saleable, prisoners were seen as more affordable prey than ships or cargoes. The Berbers multiplied their raids along the Mediterranean coasts, especially in southern Italy. After a few years, the Christian slaves were bought and returned to their country. The others were employed as servants, farm labourers, but many rotted in the presidios, where they quickly disappeared, as the mortality rate was quite high: around 15%, according to Davis. The less fortunate died of exhaustion in the galleys. Slaves in the Turkish Sultan's fleet were kept at sea for months, chained to their oars, even in harbours. Their galleys were prisons for life.

Pirates kidnapped most of their slaves by intercepting ships, but land attacks could also be very fruitful even if they were more risky than on the high seas. Italy was the most prized target. Sicily was only 200 km from Tunisia and had no strong central government that could organise resistance to the invasion. For example, the Algerians kidnapped 7,000 people in the Bay of Naples in 1544. The raid caused the price of slaves to fall so low that it was said that you could "trade a Christian for an onion". In 1554, pirates sacked Vieste in southern Italy and took no fewer than 6,000 prisoners. Spain also suffered wide-scale attacks. After a raid on Granada that took 4,000 men, women and children prisoner, it was said that "Christians rained down on Algiers".

For each of these major raids, there were probably dozens of lesser ones.

Incidentally, Muslim pirates never failed to desecrate churches and shrines. They often stole the bells, as the metal was of great value, and thus also silenced Christianity.

Only from the 1700s onwards were the Italians able to begin repelling these spectacular land attacks, although piracy by sea remained unhindered. Throughout the 17th century, Arab pirates had operated freely, even in British waters. In three years, from 1606 to 1609, the British navy lost 466 English and Scottish merchant ships to attacks by Algerian privateers. The ships of the Arab privateers had a clear advantage over their adversaries because they had two means of propulsion: wind and oarsmen. The ships' crews and passengers were therefore the main source of white slaves, and if the pirates ran out of slaves for the galleys, they could immediately put some of their prisoners to work. But the prisoners were usually sent to the hold for the return voyage. They were crammed together, barely able to move, amid filth, pestilence and vermin. Many died before they reached port.

On arrival in North Africa, the tradition was to parade Christians through the streets so that people could mock them and children could throw rubbish at them. In the slave market, men were forced to jump up and down to prove they were not lame. Customers wanted to see them naked to see if they were in good health. Buyers, hoping to make a good profit from the possible ransom, would examine the earlobes for earring marks, a sign of wealth. It was also customary to check the prisoner's teeth to see if he could survive a harsh slave regime. White women were naturally of great value. All these slave capitals in turn had a thriving homosexual network.

Professor Davis noted that while much research had been carried out to establish as accurately as possible the number of Blacks taken across the Atlantic Ocean, there was no similar study of the extent of slavery in the Mediterranean. In fact, it was far from easy to get a reliable account—the Arabs themselves generally did not keep records—but after ten years of research Professor Davis had developed a method of estimation.

The data collected suggested that from 1580 to 1680, there had been an average of 35,000 slaves in the Barbary countries. The researcher's conclusion was therefore that between 1530 and 1780 there were more than one million white European Christians enslaved by Muslims in the Mediterranean.

The European powers had been unable to put an end to this traffic, which, although it had slowed down considerably at the end of the 18th century, had increased again during the chaos of the Napoleonic wars. This issue was still being discussed at the Congress of Vienna in 1815. The Barbary slave adventure finally came to an end in 1830, with the final seizure of Algiers by the French, ordered by the French King Charles X. General Bourmont's soldiers then discovered that 120 white slaves were still held captive in the port's prison.

One might wonder about the role of Jewish traders in the slave trade, but neither Robeert Davis nor Olivier Pétré-Grenouilleau answered this question.

In the Middle Ages and in Antiquity

Indeed, Jews have always played a prominent role in international trade. In the Middle Ages, as in our own time, they had relations, members of their families in all the countries of the world, which fostered the trust necessary for commercial exchanges. Payments were then made by letters of credit, which avoided the transport of large amounts of gold over long distances. Jews could easily use their family ties to guarantee these exchanges and payment by means of these letters of credit. Blood ties ensured the smooth conduct of business. On the other hand, Jews did not have the scruples that restrained Christians—especially Catholics—in their commercial ventures.

The great Russian writer Aleksandr Solzhenitsyn gave an example of the role of Jewish merchants in this traffic. In the 13th century, the Jews, who had been invited to settle in Kiev by the Tatars, had earned the hatred of the other inhabitants of the capital. Solzhenitsyn quoted a certain Karamzine: "These people bought the right to collect tribute from the Tatars and practised exorbitant usury towards the poor, and, in case of non-payment, declared them slaves and took them captive. The inhabitants of Vladimir, of Suzdal, of Rostov, lost patience and rose up unanimously, ringing their bells, against these wicked usurers: some were killed, the rest expelled."

Jewish merchants enjoyed immense fortunes. Solzhenitsyn cited another source: *The Little Jewish Encyclopedia*, published in Jerusalem in 1976: "15th century archives mention Jews from Kiev, tax collectors, who enjoyed substantial fortunes[399]."

A few centuries earlier, in the time of Charlemagne, Jewish merchants already seemed to have a monopoly on international trade,

---

[399] Aleksandr Solzhenitsyn, *Deux Siècles ensemble*, Tome I, Fayard, 2002, p. 21.

so that the words *"judaeus"* and *"mercator"* appeared as interchangeable terms in Carolingian documents[400]. And since business is business, there was no reason why the slave trade should escape the rule.

Trade to Asia was in their hands: "Here too," wrote Jacques Heers, "the Jews ensured a surely important part of the exchange of products with distant Asia, through the steppes and the deserts of the high plateaus. The historian and geographer Ibn Khordadhbeh devoted a long passage of his description of the world to those Radhanite Jews[401]."

Very few sources exist for the Radhanites, those Jewish merchantmen of the early Middle Ages who dominated trade between the Christian and Muslim worlds. From the Rhone valley, they travelled down to North Africa, via Spain or Italy, progressed to the Middle East, and then to India and China, crossing the Asian continent. Ibn Khordadhbeh, director of the postal service and police in the province of Jibal, wrote around 870 in his *Book of Routes and Kingdoms*: "These traders speak Arabic, Persian, Greek, Frankish, Spanish and Slavic. They travel from east to west, by land and by sea. They transport from the west eunuchs, slave women, children, silk, swords, beavers, sables and other furs."

Traders could also take another route—from the Rhone valley—through Germany and the Baltic countries, or north through Russia. During the early Middle Ages, they were the only ones to trade with the Middle East and Asia. Cecil Roth and Claude Cahen placed the Radhanite centre of operations in the Rhone valley, whose Latin name is Rhodanus. But other experts claim that the name comes from Persian, from *rah* ("way") and *dan* ("he who knows").

The Radhanites played an essential role in the Slavic slave trade that spread widely in the 10th century. Verdun was then an important trading centre and one of the first slave markets. In his book *France in the Middle Ages* (1965), André Cheville wrote that slaves were captured from the Slavic and pagan tribes in the eastern markets of the Carolingian Empire and resold throughout the Muslim world. The trade was controlled by Jewish merchants: "The trade must have been important because the word *servus* disappeared in favour of the word

---

[400] Marcus Arkin, *Aspects of Jewish Economic History*, Jewish Publication Society of America, 1975, p. 44–45. And in Encyclopedia Britannica, 1973, article "Jews", in Arthur Koestler, *La treizième Tribu*, Calmann-Levy, 1976, Poche, p. 198, Koestler quoting Cecil Roth. (Translation from the PDF Arthur Koestler, *Jews Khazars, The Tribe number 13*, p. 185)

[401] Jacques Heers, *Les Négriers en terre d'Islam*, Perrin, 2003, Poche, 2007, p. 20.

slavus from which "slave" was formed. We know however that the Jewish community of Verdun, known to be at the head of this trade, had only a few dozen members[402]."

Verdun was also an important place for the castration of slaves. Eunuchs were sent to Andalusia to be sold to Muslims. Roberta Strauss-Feuerlicht, a Jewish historian, confirmed this: "The golden age of Jewry in Spain owed much of its fortune to the existence of an international network of Jewish merchants." In Central Europe, "Jews from Bohemia bought Slavs and resold them to Spanish Jews, who in turn resold them to the Moors[403]."

The medieval historian Jacques Heers did not elaborate too much on the role of Jews in the slave trade, but he also admitted that, in Muslim Spain, the main traffickers were Jews: "The authors, Muslim and Christian, insist particularly on the role of the Jews, who, in Muslim Spain, constituted the majority of the population of the great cities, especially in Granada, commonly called in the 8th century the "city of the Jews". Traders in luxury goods, metals, jewellery, silk and moneylenders used to group together in small societies of relatives and friends (…) and probably underwrote a large part of the transactions of the two worlds on their own. It was also said that since the Muslims refused to do so, these Israelite traffickers ensured the smooth running of the slave castration centres."

In the 10th century, Jacques Heers claimed, slave traders from the countries of Islam were reluctant to travel to Gaul, "where they found only hostile populations. They were not seen to frequent the slave markets, whereas the Jews were commonly designated as the masters of that wretched trade[404]." As we can see, the poor Jews, who had been cruelly deprived of being able to work the land, were forced to sell human livestock or practice usury in order to survive.

The Jewish author Julius Brutzkus wrote in his turn: "Already in the 10th century, Jews owned salt mines in Nuremberg. They deal in weapons and exploit the treasures of the churches. But their great speciality is slavery."

Israel Abrahams noted in the *Jewish Encyclopedia* (Volume II, page 402) that, in the 12th century, the situation had hardly changed: "The Spanish Jews owed their fortune to the slave trade." The Jewish

---

[402]André Cheville, *La France au Moyen Âge*, Presses Universitaires de France, 1965, p. 28.
[403] Roberta Strauss-Feuerlicht, *The Fate of the Jews*, New York, Time Books, 1983, p. 39.
[404] Jacques Heers, *Les Négriers en terre d'Islam*, Perrin, 2003, Poche, 2007, p. 17.

Encyclopedia further noted that "the first Jews whom the Poles encountered must surely have been merchants, probably slave traders called in the 12th century Holejei Rusyah (Travellers to Russia)."

Human trafficking is apparently an underlying trend rather than an anomaly in Jewish history, and some Jewish historians have acknowledged the role of their fellow Jews. David Duke's well-documented book mentioned the American Jewish historian Jacob Marcus, author of an article on the subject in the *Encyclopedia britannica*, who noted that in the Middle Ages the trade, especially the very lucrative slave trade, was "largely" dominated by Jews[405].

The chronicles of Antiquity and the Middle Ages underline their preference for European women and children. Christians were horrified when they realised that children could be sexually abused. The archbishop of Lyon, Agobard, author of *De Insolentia judaeorum*, who lived in the 9th century during the reign of Charlemagne's successor, also reproached the Jews for practising the slave trade. Agobard cited a number of reliable facts, such as the arrival in his diocese of a Spaniard from Cordoba, who, twenty-four years earlier, had been stolen by Jews from Lyon and sold into slavery when he was still a child. The Cordovan had managed to escape with another victim, originally from Arles, who had been in the same situation for six years. Agobardo had requested an investigation into this shameful traffic, which had revealed that the theft and sale of Christian children by Jews was not exceptional[406].

Different popes had warned Christian rulers against such abuses. Thus, in 1205, a bull by Pope Innocent III, *Etsi non displaceat*, made a list of accusations against the Jews: usury, blasphemy, arrogance, trade in Christian slaves, etc. The bull had been sent to the French king Philip Augustus to take action against the Jews.

Further back in time, we find more interesting testimonies. The *Jewish Encyclopedia* (volume II, page 402), for example, stated that in the 6th century, in the time of Pope Gregory the Great (590–604), Jews were already "the principal traders" of slaves[407].

Under the Roman Empire, Jews already followed the victorious legions to procure defeated soldiers and civilians. The *Jewish Encyclopedia* stated: "The slave trade constituted the main source of

---

[405] Marcus, J. (1952). *Jews. Encyclopedia Britannica*, vol. 13. p. 57, in David Duke, *Jewish Supremacism*, 2003.
[406] Let us remember that 800 children disappear every year in France. See Hervé Ryssen, *Psychoanalysis of Judaism*.
[407] Lady Magnus, *Esquisses d'Histoire juive, Outlines of Jewish History*, Philadelphia, Jewish Publication Society of America, 1890, p. 107; Jewish Encyclopedia, New York & London, 1905–1916, vol II, p. 402.

income for the Jews of the Roman Empire and many decrees were issued against this traffic in 335, 336, 339, 384, etc[408].

Perhaps we should go to the sources and open the Old Testament to find the moral and theological support for such a practice. This can be read explicitly in Leviticus XXV (*The Sabbath Year of the Land and the Year of Jubilee,* 44–46):

"The slaves and bondwomen you may have shall be from the nations around you; from them you may acquire slaves and bondwomen.

You may also buy them from among the children of foreigners residing among you, or from among their families who are among you, from those who were begotten in your country. They will become your property:

You can keep them as property for your children after you, to inherit them as perpetual property. You may treat them as slaves. But as for your Israelite relatives, none shall rule harshly over the other." (Israelite Nazarene Bible Version 2011).

---

[408] *Jewish Encyclopedia,* in 12 volumes, Funk and Wagnall's, vol. 10, p. 460.

6. Organ trafficking

On 23 July 2009, a huge corruption scandal broke out in the United States. A shady businessman and unscrupulous real estate agent, Solomon Dwek, a resident of the small town of Deal in New Jersey, had paid tens of thousands of dollars to various public figures in order to obtain building permits. According to the *New York Times*, the son of a rabbi, a member of the Syrian Jewish community who owned more than two hundred properties in New Jersey and Brooklyn (New York), was forced to cooperate with the police and to wear a wire to reduce his sentence. This police operation revealed the existence of double trafficking with local and international ramifications. On the one hand, investigators had traced a system of corruption involving local politicians; on the other hand, they uncovered a money laundering network involving rabbis in Brooklyn and New Jersey.

After ten years of investigations, eavesdropping and infiltration, three Democratic mayors, a city councillor and two members of the New Jersey State Assembly had been arrested: these politicians, both Democrats and Republicans, were newly elected and had won the election on a single campaign issue: the fight against corruption! Among those arrested were also notables, public works inspectors and city planners. Several synagogues had been searched, as well as five rabbis.

The FBI had gone all out for this gigantic raid, as more than 300 agents had been mobilised to arrest 44 suspects. On 23 July 2009, the FBI had to prepare a few buses for Solomon Dwek's interlocutors, as he had shown a great talent for putting them in confidence. Money transfers, bribes, dollars hidden in cereal boxes, smuggling of luxury goods and ... organ trafficking were the ingredients of the scandal.

To launder hundreds of thousands of dollars, the corrupt politicians had enlisted the services of rabbis in Brooklyn (a borough of New York) and Deal, New Jersey, who charged a 10 per cent commission. The *Jerusalem Post* of 24 July 2009 reported that the rabbis were accused of having laundered $10 million through their charities in the United States and Israel. They were Saul Kassin, 79, spiritual leader of the Syrian Jewish community in Brooklyn, Eliahu Ben-Haim, 58, Mordechai Fish, 56, and Lavel Schwartz, 57. The rabbis sent a portion of the proceeds to yeshivas in Israel linked to the Shas religious party, led by extremist Rabbi Ovadia Yosef[409]. Rabbi Eliahu Ben-haim worked closely in Israel with Rabbi David Yosef, the son of the great "sage" Ovadia Yosef. The latter had repeatedly drawn attention to himself by comparing the Palestinians to cockroaches.

Solomon Dwek's secretary, who also worked for the FBI, had pretended that her uncle was seriously ill and needed a kidney transplant. The New Jersey rabbis then put her in touch with Levy-Izhak Rosenbaum, 58, another Brooklyn rabbi. He offered to buy an organ from a Palestinian in need for his uncle. According to investigators' documents, the man had been involved in this type of trafficking for several years. The police then discovered that part of the money laundered by the rabbis came from the trade in human organs. Levy-Izhak Rosenbaum was convicted along with the four other rabbis who were involved in money laundering.

Rosenbaum later confessed that he bought kidneys from modest people in Israel for $10,000. The buyers in turn paid $160,000 for the transplant, and Rosenbaum collected his commission in the process. In the United States in 2014, more than 37,000 people were on the waiting list for a transplant. The situation was similar in Israel, where the average wait was six years. But in that country, organ donors were rare due to religious prohibitions.

The bodies of the Palestinians

It was during the summer of 2009 that organ trafficking made headlines in the Western media. Rabbi Rosenbaum's case lit the fuse of the scandal that erupted in August after an article published on the 17th by the leading Swedish daily *Aftonbladet* revealed that the bodies of young Palestinians killed by the Israeli army were used to extract "spare parts". At the beginning of 2009, the Israeli army had launched a massive and bloody blitzkrieg on the population of the Gaza strip, maiming and killing thousands of innocent civilians, hundreds of whom were children. The bombardment of the villages had lasted more than

---

[409] Ovadia Yosef had declared at a public event: "The Goyim were born only to serve us. Other than that, they have no purpose in the world; only to serve the People of Israel." In *JTA, Jewish Telegraphic Agency*, October 18, 2010: *Sephardi Leader Yosef: Non-Jews exist to serve Jews*. In 2013, his funeral was the largest in Israel's history, gathering nearly 800,000 attendees during the last procession." Public figures sent their condolences, remembering a giant of Jewish thought", in *The Times of Israel*, October 7, 2013. (NdT).

twenty days, and many of the victims had been sent to the medico-legal institute in Abou Kabir for autopsy. After a long on-site investigation, the Swedish journalist Donald Boström accused Israeli doctors at the medico-legal institute in Abou Kabir of having removed organs (heart, kidneys, liver) from the bodies of young Palestinians killed by the Israeli army in Gaza and the West Bank. The bodies were sometimes returned to the families, stuffed with cotton wool and stitched from top to bottom, but most often buried in numbered graves. Donald Boström suggested that the International Criminal Court in The Hague open an investigation into the case.

The journalist gave as an example the case of Bilal Ahmad Ghanem, 19, who was shot by the Israeli army during the invasion of his village." According to villagers who witnessed the incident, Bilal was shot in each leg. Two soldiers ran out of the carpentry workshop and shot him again in the belly. They then grabbed him by the feet and dragged him down the stone stairs of the workshop (...) Badly wounded, Bilal was loaded into a jeep by Israeli soldiers towards the outskirts of the village where an army helicopter was waiting for them. The boy was transported to an unknown destination for the family. Five days later, Bilal returned dead, his body wrapped in a green hospital sheet." Boström recounted that during the burial his torso was uncovered as his body was lowered into the grave, and that witnesses saw that it was badly stitched from stomach to chin.

This was not the first time. Khaled from Nablus, Raed from Jenina, Mahmoud and Nafes from Gaza had all disappeared for a few days before their bodies were returned at night after an autopsy." Why did they keep the bodies for at least five days before letting us bury them? Why do they perform an autopsy against our will when the causes of death are obvious? Why do they return the bodies at night? Why with a military escort? Why do they close the area during the burial? Why do they cut off the electricity? "

"We know that the State of Israel needs a lot of organs," explained Donald Boström, "that there has been a large illegal trade in organs for several years, and that the authorities are aware of this and that doctors in major hospitals are involved in it, as are officials at all levels. We also know that young Palestinians have disappeared, returned dead after five days, at night, in total secrecy, stitched up after being cut open from abdomen to chin. It is high time to put the spotlight on this sinister trade, to shed light on what has happened and is happening in the territories occupied by the State of Israel since the beginning of the Intifada."

A few days after the publication of the article by Swedish

journalist Donald Boström, a Palestinian journalist, Kawthar Salam, published an accusatory article entitled *The Body Snatcher of Israel*[410]. It is summarised below:

"I want to present to my readers what I have seen, heard and observed during my 22 years of work as a journalist under Israeli military occupation in the West Bank and Gaza." The Israeli military had started capturing and storing the bodies of dead Palestinians in the early 1970s." Since the early 1970s, thousands of Palestinians were buried in secret graves. Since the early 1970s, thousands of Palestinian victims of the occupation have been "autopsied", and numerous bodies kept in anonymous numbered graves. Most of the murdered resistance members have been taken for "autopsy" and others who had only been wounded were taken from the hospital by Israelis... During the first Intifada[411] and during the so-called peace period, I have personally seen how the Israeli army took the bodies of Palestinians and seriously wounded from the emergency room of the Princess Alia Hospital in Hebron (Al Khalil in Arabic). A few years later, I have seen how the Israeli army took the bodies of dead Palestinians from the new El Ahli Hospital: the whole area had been declared a military zone, the hospital was surrounded and invaded by troops and no one was allowed to move inside the building. All the bodies of the dead Palestinians, and also the wounded, were taken to Abu Kabir for "autopsies[412]"."

This practice had ceased to be widespread by the time the Palestinian Authority came to power. In the areas it controlled, deceased persons were no longer "autopsied", although this was still the case for those killed or injured in Israeli-controlled areas." Why transfer the bodies of the victims to Abu Kabir, when the causes of death were known?" In fact, all the deceased Palestinians had been shot in the head or chest by elite Israeli marksmen.

The journalist quoted the names of the main Israeli army officers involved in this trafficking. They told the Palestinian families that they were doing their best to "convince the army headquarters to release the body", as if it were a favour." Military commanders Shammi, Goldstein, Nagar, demanded that the bodies be buried in the dark." The families of the victims were called after midnight (usually between one and three in the morning), and "no more than ten people" were allowed to attend the burial which had to be held immediately in the dark of night for

---

[410] Article dated 23 August 2009, published on the website *Kawthar.info* and translated into French by the *Tlaxcala* network.
[411] The First Intifada (1987–1993) ended with the Oslo Accords.
[412] A kidney taken from a living person is more viable than one taken from a corpse.

alleged "security reasons". In addition, women were not allowed to participate in the funeral, also for "security reasons". The Israeli authorities actually wanted to prevent the mourning cries of the victims' mothers, sisters and daughters from being heard throughout the neighbourhood. Officials followed the funeral procession in their grey armoured cars and waited for the end of the burial; other military vehicles also accompanied the procession.

All the families of the victims knew that the bodies were stuffed with cotton wool. Hundreds of victims were thus buried in the dark, and hundreds or thousands of other bodies were kept by Israel in numbered graves. After this, Palestinians began to evacuate the wounded and dead fallen in the demonstrations themselves, and many were buried under their homes or under a tree rather than being taken to a hospital.

"All Israeli officials and civilian staff in the West Bank, since the early 1970s, have been involved in the harvesting of organs taken from Palestinians, or were at least complicit in it," said Kawthar Salam. All Israeli doctors and staff who have worked in Abu Kabir since the early 1970s have been involved in the harvesting and sale of Palestinian organs. All of the IDF's elite marksmen and soldiers who have shot Palestinians during peaceful demonstrations and protests have been complicit in the mafia that harvests and sells organs of deceased Palestinians. The IDF command centre and most, if not all, of the officers in the chain of command down to the rank and file knew full well what was going on."

At the end of September 2009, Arab-Israeli MP Mohammad Barakech also accused the Israelis of organ theft. We have the right to know the reasons why the state of Israel abducts the bodies of martyrs and what secret it is trying to hide," he said." On 21 December, Fathi Abu Mughli, the Palestinian Authority's health minister, said that Israeli doctors had "removed parts of the corpses, such as corneas, bones and skin without the permission of the Palestinian families", and called for an investigation. Eissa Qarape, Minister of Prison Affairs, accused Israel of keeping Palestinian corpses in secret cemeteries "to hide the theft of organs from their bodies."

Two days earlier, on 19 December 2009, the second Israeli television channel, Channel 2 TV, had broadcast an interview with Yehuda Hiss, the former head of the National Forensic Institute, the famous medico-legal institute in Abu Kabir. The interview was ten years old, from July 2000, and was given to an American university student named Nancy Scheper-Hughes. An anthropology professor at Berkeley University in California, she had founded the Organs Watch

Project and had conducted research on all continents. She was the specialist on the issue, although she had not dared to make the interview public out of fear. This is what she explained in an article of 25 October 2010 in the US monthly *Counterpunch*.

Dr Yehuda Hiss acknowledged that organs had been removed from the bodies of Palestinians in the 1990s without the permission of the families of the deceased. His confessions actually dated back to November 1999, explained Nancy Scheper-Hughes. They had been published in the local Tel Aviv daily *Ha'ir*, which revealed that Yehuda Hiss students performed autopsies and that organs were transferred to other clinics without the families' permission. In 2000, the major Israeli daily *Yediot Aharonot* had even published a price list of organs that Hiss sold to universities and medical schools.

Chen Kugel, his assistant, had claimed that Hiss had "a real organ depot" in Abu Kabir. It took two years before the Israeli judiciary intervened, and another two years before it issued a sanction. In 2004, Hiss received a reprimand from his management and was relieved of his duties, although he retained his job at the institute as a doctor with seniority that guaranteed him a salary promotion. He was therefore able to continue his activities, which he presented as necessary for medicine and for the defence of the State of Israel.

In that July 2000 interview, Dr. Yehuda Hiss explained that the Israeli army provided human skin for burn victims, taking only skin from the back and thighs.

Here is how he and his subordinates proceeded to disguise the disappearance of the corneas: "We closed the eyelids with glue." His assistant, Dr. Chen Kugel, who had been dismissed after complaining to the Ministry of Health, had declared that organs were sold to anyone; all they had to do was pay. A femur cost $300, for example. And organs were harvested indiscriminately from Jews or Muslims, soldiers or stone throwers, terrorists or victims, immigrants or tourists[413]. Bodies were stuffed with toilet paper rolls, held in place with broom handles, and glass eyes were placed in the empty orbits... Clearly, Chen Kugel claimed, it was less risky to harvest organs from new immigrants, or better still: from Palestinians." When families complained, they were the enemies, and naturally they were said to be telling lies, and no one

---

[413] Rachel Corrie was a 23-year-old American woman. On 16 March 2003, she was crushed under the tracks of an Israeli army bulldozer while protesting with other militants against the destruction of a Palestinian house in Rafah (southern Gaza Strip). Dr. Hiss then performed her autopsy in his own way.

believed them[414]."

After the broadcast of this interview on *Channel 2 TV*, the army and the health minister had admitted to harvesting organs from Israelis and Palestinians in the 1990s, but claimed that such practices had stopped in 2000: "These activities stopped ten years ago, it doesn't happen anymore."

In an interview on *Al-Jazeera* television in 2002, the historic Palestinian leader Yasser Arafat had accused the Israeli regime of murdering Palestinian babies, children and young people in order to harvest their vital organs for transplants." They murder our children and use their organs as spare parts. Why does the whole world remain silent? The state of Israel is taking advantage of this silence to intensify its oppression and terror against our people," Arafat was outraged. During that interview, which took place on 14 January 2002, Arafat had shown photographs of mutilated children's bodies.

Since it is forbidden in Judaism to desecrate the human body, Judaism does not permit the chopping up of Jewish corpses. Since Jews do not donate their organs, they must be found in the goyim. The State of Israel was until 2008 the only country in the world where the medical profession did not condemn the organ trade and did not take any action against doctors involved in the trade.

Fresh meat from Moldova

Rabbi Levy-Izhak Rosenbaum, arrested in New York in July 2009, was also accused of having persuaded Moldovan donors." He was targeting people in precarious situations," said Mark McCarron, the deputy U.S. attorney. Rosenbaum then made all the arrangements for the donor's travel to New York where the operation took place. Donors were recruited from poor countries, where desperate people were willing to sacrifice a part of their body for a small price compared to the final price charged to the recipients. Evidently, donors were not informed of the medical risks.

Mike Levinski, an Israeli citizen, was the pioneer of the Moldovan network. The weekly *Le Point* of 15 February 2002 reported on this trafficking. The Moldovans were citizens of a small country between Romania and Ukraine, many of them destitute and reduced to having to sell a kidney to survive. Israeli scouts canvassed the country, offering

---

[414] Article by Nancy Scheper-Hughes, 25 October 2010, published by the left-wing US magazine *Counterpunch*.

donors $3,000. The commission charged by these scouts was around $30,000 per kidney, while the surgeon's fee ranged from $100,000 to $200,000 per operation. Donors and patients met in Turkey at Dr Sönmez's clinic. The traffic was clearly extremely profitable, judging by the number of advertisements in the Israeli press.

The "donors" were not always aware of what was going to happen to them. After benign operations, appendicitis or otherwise, young Moldovans like Serghei Thimus would wake up with scars out of place. They were then told that a malfunctioning kidney had had to be removed, or—as in Serghei's case—they would later learn on the radio that the surgeon had simply stolen a kidney.

In December 2001, the Israeli daily *Haaretz* reported that the Romanian ambassador to Israel had asked to be received by the minister of social affairs for talks on an issue that was becoming a scandal in his country. He had been asked to explain a list of children born in Romania, and "with all their organs inside their bodies", who had been taken to Israel for adoption. It thus appeared that the adoption of Romanian children in Israel was not just a charity. Nancy Scheper-Hughes, the organ trafficking specialist, had visited villages in Moldova where, she wrote, "20% of the men had been recruited to be kidney sellers."

In July 2009, we were informed this time that three individuals accused of egg trafficking were arrested. The two managers of the Sabycclinic, a father and a son, were Israelis. Two other Israelis who worked at the clinic were also imprisoned. The clinic paid donors between 800 and 1000 lei (approximately 190 to 238 euros) despite the fact that Romanian law strictly forbids remuneration for organ or cell donations. According to Romanian media, the beneficiaries were all Israelis. They paid between twelve and fifteen thousand euros for in vitro fertilisation. The eggs came from young Romanian women in social difficulty. These arrests did not stop the trafficking from continuing, for in February 2013, the *Jewish Telegraphic Agency* reported that Dr. Rapahel Ron-El, a specialist at the Assaf Harofeh hospital in Israel, and his assistant Daphna Komarovsky, had been arrested for egg trafficking.

In Israel, more than 1000 people were waiting on an organ donation list, half of them for a kidney. Some were therefore receptive to newspaper advertisements, and willing to spend more than $150,000. Indeed, there was no law in Israel prohibiting such trafficking in human organs, and a health ministry directive even allowed Israelis, until 2008, to go abroad for a transplant—legal or not—and be reimbursed up to

USD 80,000 by the Israeli health service. The rest could be reimbursed by a mutual insurance company[415]. Israeli health agencies considered a kidney transplant to be much less expensive than dialysis and long-term care for the sick.

In an interview in July 2009, Nancy Scheper-Hughes explained: "I had begun to follow the ramifications of the whole network, a criminal network with a mafia-like ring. The headquarters of this pyramid structure was in Israel, with intermediaries in Turkey, in New York, in Philadelphia, in Durban, in Johannesburg, in Recife in Brazil, in Moldova, and many other places. I used my ethnographic research skills to scour the terrain and try to put the pieces of the puzzle together. In the end, I came to identify Isaac Rosenbaum as Illan Peri's main intermediary in Israel, the mastermind of the operation, a very slippery guy[416]."

In early October 2009, we learned that Rabbi Rosenbaum's network was also operating in Morocco. Professor Mustapha Khiati, president of the National Foundation for the Promotion of Health and the Development of Medical Research, revealed that the operations were carried out in clinics in Oujda. Rabbi Rosenbaum was in charge of financing the equipment necessary for the surgical operations and the transport of organs to New York and Israel.

At the end of 2014, we read that Levy-Izhak Rosenbaum had been sentenced by the US justice system in 2012 to two and a half years in prison, but that he would not be deported from the United States after his release from prison. He was so far the only person to be convicted of organ trafficking in the US.

From Brazil to South Africa

Illan Peri's name had already been mentioned in a January 2004 Agence France Presse article informing us that a retired Israeli army officer named Gedalya Tauber had been arrested in Brazil in 2003 along with another Israeli named Eliezer Ramon and six other Brazilians. Tauber recruited donors in Recife, in northeastern Brazil, in the favelas where very poor people lived. At first, donors were paid $10,000 per kidney, the equivalent of about ten years' salary for them; then prices dropped to $3,000, given the number of donors. All had been operated on in South Africa at the Saint Augustine hospital in Durban by Israeli

---

[415] Article by Larry Rother in the *New York Times*, 23 May 2004.
[416] Nancy Scheper-Hughes had informed the FBI since 2002 about Rabbi Rosenbaum's activities.

surgeons and for Israeli recipients. Gedalya Tauber had later testified in court that the Israeli government financed the operation and that an official, identified as "Illan", had put him in contact with an intermediary in Brazil.

Nancy Scheper-Hughes had first heard of organ thieves in 1987, when she was working in northeastern Brazil. A rumour was rife in the shantytowns of Alto do Cruzeiro, above the town of Timbaúda in the Pernambuco region." It was said that foreigners drove along the dirt roads in yellow vans looking for unattended children who were kidnapped and killed to steal their organs. The children's bodies were later found in roadside ditches or hospital dumpsters."

The university student had good reason to be sceptical. During her study of poverty and childbearing in the slums, she had questioned the region's funeral parlours, as well as the officials responsible for the death registers. The infant mortality rate was tremendous, but there was no trace of surgically dismembered bodies." These are stories invented by the poor and the illiterate," the director of the municipal cemetery had replied[417].

However, even though she knew that these rumours were not entirely true, Nancy Scheper-Hughes had refused to ignore them outright. The inhabitants were well aware that wealthy people from Brazil and abroad had access to better care." The people of Alto do Cuzeiro easily imagined that their bodies were coveted as spare parts stock for the rich," she wrote in her 1992 book on violence in Brazil, *Death Without Weeping*. In 1995, she had been the only ethnologist invited to speak at a medical congress on organ trafficking in Bellagio, Italy. Although there was no hard evidence that people were being killed for their organs, the same rumours were circulating from South America to Sweden, Italy, Romania and Albania. The conference organisers had then asked him to explain the persistence of such macabre myths.

He had testified before the parliamentary commission of Pernambuco (Northeast Brazil) that the trafficking had started in the early 1990s, under the impulse of a certain Zaki Shapira, former director of the Tel-Aviv hospital. Zaki Shapira had performed more than 300 transplants, even taking his patients to other countries, such as Turkey. The donors were very poor people, not only from Brazil, but also from Eastern Europe, the Philippines, and other Third World countries.

A *New York Times* article of 23 May 2004, written by Larry Rother, told the story of Alberty José da Silva, 38, the son of a prostitute

---

[417] Article by Ethan Watters in the *Pacific Standard Magazine* of 7 July 2014, quoted on 20 August 2015 in *Sept-info*, a Swiss online newspaper.

who lived in a favela near the airport. He had sold his kidney to Gedalya Tauber for a recipient living in Brooklyn, "a 48-year-old Jewish woman who was very religious". He had been on dialysis for 15 years and had been on two transplant waiting lists for seven years, so he had finally accepted the idea of a transplant on the parallel market. She was one of 60,000 people in the United States waiting for a kidney. Her family in Israel had put her in touch with Illan Peri's network.

Alberty José da Silva and the woman from Brooklyn had met at the Saint Augustine Hospital in Durban, on the edge of the Indian Ocean. When I was asked to sign a document attesting that the recipient was my cousin, I realised that something didn't add up," José da Silva explained, but it was too late."

An interview with other donors showed that the Brazilians did not enjoy the same medical care as the Israeli recipients. The latter were housed on the beachfront in front of the sea before the operation and after the operation were kept under observation, even after returning home. Donors, on the other hand, were kept under surveillance for no more than three days before being driven to the airport. More than a hundred operations had been performed this way in St. Augustine in less than two years." *They treated me Ok untill they got what they wanted,*" one donor told Nancy Scheper-Hughes." *Then I was thrown away like garbage.*" They treated me OK until they got what they wanted. Then I was thrown away like rubbish." [418].

"In my case, the complications appeared almost immediately," said José Carlos da Conceiçao da Silva, an agricultural worker. Three days after the kidney ablation, he had felt the first effects." I am always tired and I can't carry heavy things. My blood pressure goes up and down all the time and my scar hurts a lot." On top of that, when he returned to Brazil, his 6000 dollars were stolen from him at Sao Paulo airport, despite his tearful pleading with the thieves and showing them his scar[419].

Seven people were arrested in Durban in May 2004. In court, Sushan Meir had testified that, in addition to the 100 transplants performed in Durban, he had organised some 35 in Johannesburg, but investigators estimated the total number at around 200. But investigators estimated the total number at around 200. The hospitals belonged to the private company Netcare, based in South Africa. Their website advertisements claimed that South Africa was then "the

---

[418] Attitude characteristic of the community mindset. Article by Ethan Watters in the *Pacific Standard Magazine* of 7 July 2014.

[419] It is estimated that around 5,000 people illegally sell an organ each year.

transplant capital of the world".

The case of the South African network came to a head in September 2010: Richard Friedland, the chairman of Netcare, South Africa's leading private healthcare company, and five surgeons were accused of having transplanted kidneys to wealthy Israelis from Brazilian donors in the Recife region and from Romanians who had received as little as $3,000 per kidney. The private Saint Augustine Hospital in Durban, run by Netcare, was also accused of performing 109 operations between 2001 and 2003 on behalf of Israeli nationals. But Richard Friedland was adamant in his defence. In a statement relayed by Agence France Presse, he strongly denied any wrongdoing: "For several years, we have cooperated fully with the South African police and provided numerous documents to the inspectors. We are very surprised and disappointed to see that the prosecutor has deemed it necessary to indict us."

In Brazil, Gedalya Tauber had been sentenced to eleven years in prison, but in 2009 he managed to escape from the Henrique Dias prison in Recife by taking advantage of an escape. At the age of 77, he was arrested again at the beginning of June 2013 in Italy, at Rome's Leonardo Da Vinci airport. On 8 November 2015, he was extradited to Belgium, arriving handcuffed at Antwerp airport.

Chinese suppliers

In Brazil and South Africa, Illan Peri's associates were in prison; he remained in Israel. But some media reported that Israeli intermediaries were operating in China.

Israelis took full advantage of the opportunities offered by the opening up of the country to international trade. According to Amos Kanaf, president of the Association of Kidney Patients, interviewed by *Le Monde* (24 April 2006), around twenty Israelis waiting for a transplant travelled to China every month. The patients paid in cash and were reimbursed by the Israeli social security system, which accepted this solution due to the severe shortage of donors in their country. The official version was that these organs were taken from the bodies of the 3,000 people who died in traffic accidents every week on Chinese roads. In reality, the organs were taken from the bodies of those condemned to death. Recently, the Chinese had started dismembering the bodies at the place of execution. A mobile surgical unit parked nearby would remove the kidneys, eyes and tissues (but not the heart, which is only kept for a few hours). The spare parts were then transported to hospitals where medical tourists awaited transplantation.

From Ukraine to Azerbaijan

Israeli prospectors were also active in Ukraine and Central Asia. In the *Jerusalem Post* of 20 August 2010, we read that "twelve people, including several Israelis" had been arrested in Ukraine for organ trafficking. Transplant operations were carried out in Kiev, as well as in Azerbaijan and Ecuador.

On 2 December 2010, Agence France Presse reported that three doctors had been arrested in Ukraine. The information had not been published in any French newspaper, but was published on the Swiss website *Romandie.com* where we found details of the case[420]. In an interview with the daily *Gazeta po-Kievski*, the Ukrainian Deputy Minister of the Interior had stated that three other people had been imprisoned. These were people who recruited and transported donors to Baku, the capital of Azerbaijan, where most of the donors had been operated on. Other surgeries took place in a well-known clinic in Kiev." As of today, we have discovered 25 people who have been induced to sell their kidneys. We are looking for more." The three arrested doctors had extracted kidneys from citizens of Ukraine, Moldova and Uzbekistan. As for the recipients of the transplants, they were "mostly Israelis" who paid between 100,000 and 200,000 dollars.

Traffic continues in Israel

In Israel, organ trafficking had been outlawed by the *knesset* (national assembly) in 2008, and since then transplants performed abroad were no longer reimbursed unless they were legal—and they all were, at least on the face of it. However, due to the needs, hunting down the traffickers did not seem to be a priority for the government.

In April 2010, Israeli police arrested half a dozen men in the north of Israel. The suspects arrested, according to the Israeli daily *Haaretz* on 7 April, included a brigadier general and two lawyers. The investigation was prompted by the complaint of a 50-year-old woman from Nazareth who had answered an Arabic-language advertisement offering $10,000 to donate a kidney. She had flown to an Eastern European country where the operation took place, but on her return to

---

[420] We published an article on the subject entitled "Organ trafficking: Israel at the centre of the network" in the weekly *Rivarol* on 10 December 2010.

Israel she reported that the agreed sum of money had not been paid. The investigation uncovered a network of organ traffickers." The network operates throughout the country and not only in the north." The organ traffickers managed to gain access to the information of patients on transplant waiting lists and offer them their services as an alternative. The network then recruited donors through advertisements in newspapers and on the internet, the police officer said.

On average, a kidney transplant was billed $120,000 (90,000 euros) to the recipient. The donors, who were people in precarious situations, never received more than $10,000; sometimes even less, or nothing at all. The donors were required to sign a contract with the traffickers, with false clauses and declarations, especially those attesting that they had a family relationship with the recipient, which was a legal requirement in the countries (Eastern Europe, Philippines, Ecuador) where the transplant was to take place. They were then sent back to Israel without any medical records, putting them at risk in case of post-surgical complications, which was frequent.

A 17 August 2014 article in the *New York Times* mentioned the names of other organ traffickers: Avigad Sandler, a former insurance agent suspected of trafficking since 2008 and a former Israeli army officer; Boris Volfman, a young Ukrainian émigré close to Sandler who had set up his own company Leshem Shamaim ("*Au nom du ciel*"); and Yaacov Dayan, a businessman known in the real estate world. These Israeli "organ brokers" billed transactions between $100,000 and $200,000, but the investigation had shown that in 2012, a wealthy Texan had paid $330,000 to Sandler for a transplant. The three men were arrested in June 2013.

Ophira Dorin had bought a kidney from a poor neighbourhood in Costa Rica in 2012, and the transplant was performed in a luxury hospital in Tel Aviv. Other clients had received organs from Sri Lanka, Turkey, Egypt, Pakistan, India, China, Kosovo and Eastern Europe.

Kosovo's yellow house

Kosovo is that historic province that was seized from Serbia in 1999. An overwhelming ethnic Albanian majority demanded autonomy for the region, leading to bloody clashes with the Serb population. US bombing raids against the Serbs enabled the Muslim Kosovars and Albanians to win the battle. From then on, the territory came under the control of the former KLA, the liberation army, whose former leaders became the country's leading political figures.

According to Victor Ivanov, head of the Russian Federal Drug Control Service, "Kosovo has become an enclave where drug traffickers feel completely free. Every year, up to 60 tonnes of heroin pass through its territory, bringing in around 3 billion euros for the criminals."

Carla del Ponte, the prosecutor of the Hague war crimes tribunal for the former Yugoslavia, had published a book in 2008, entitled *La Caccia (The Hunt, War Criminals and Me)*, about her eight-year experience in the Yugoslav case. Four months after leaving office, she revealed that hundreds of young Serb prisoners had been trucked to northern Albania where their organs had been harvested. Carla del Ponte had seen the house where the carnage had taken place and had met the people involved in the events.

In the weekly *L'Express* of 17 April 2008, we read: "The alleged trafficking in which, according to her, leaders of what is now independent Kosovo were involved at the end of the 1990s, includes the current Prime Minister Hashim Thaçi. The details it reveals are chilling. Around 300 prisoners were allegedly transported during the summer of 1999 from Kosovo to Albania where they were locked up in a kind of prison. The harvested organs were allegedly "sent to clinics abroad to be transplanted into paying patients", while the victims remained "locked up until they were executed to harvest other organs"." But according to Florence Hartmann, her former spokesperson at the International Criminal Tribunal for the former Yugoslavia, Carla del Ponte did not have "the slightest shred of evidence" to prove her accusations. In an opinion piece published in the Swiss daily *Le Temps*, Ms Hartmann called it "irresponsible" and "unworthy" of the judge to present "as proven facts what was in fact impossible to prove".

The Serbian judicial authorities, however, had taken these reports very seriously and had opened an investigation into the case. On 6 November 2008, the arrest of three people in Pristina (Kosovo), two of them doctors, on suspicion of illegal kidney transplants, was widely reported in Serbia. In an article published on 14 November 2008 in *Courier international, the* weekly of the very Zionist press director Alexandre Adler (article signed Alexandre Lévy), we were informed that the Belgrade press had closely followed the trip to Tirana (Albania) of Vladimir Vukcevic, the Serbian war crimes prosecutor. He had presented his Albanian counterpart with "new evidence" concerning the trafficking of organs harvested from Serbian prisoners during the 1999 war." International investigation into organ trafficking", headlined the daily *Politika*, which reported the arrest of doctors Lutvi Dervishi and

Tuna Pervorfraj of the private Medicus clinic in Pristina by Kosovar and international police. The police had in turn issued an international arrest warrant for a "Turkish" doctor, Yusuf Erçin Sönmez, suspected of organising the trafficking. According to the Sarajevo daily *Oslobodjenje*, "this urologist, banned by Turkey from practising medicine, was part of the international organ trafficking mafia. He was also targeted by the Bulgarian and Romanian authorities."

In January 2010, a Council of Europe correspondent, the Swiss Dick Marty, had travelled to Kosovo accompanied by two investigators and subsequently confirmed the trafficking of Serb prisoners[421]. Finally, in February, a senior UN official, Philip Alston, asked Albania for its full cooperation in the investigation. Information then emerged that the abducted individuals had been held and operated in a house with yellow facades, hence the name "Yellow House".

According to Carla del Ponte, Bernard Kouchner—former minister of the "socialist" president François Mitterrand—who was the UN High Representative in Kosovo between 1999 and 2001, was aware of this trafficking but had decided not to make the case public. In June 2009, Bernard Kouchner[422] was now foreign minister under right-wing liberal President Nicolas Sarkozy and was receiving in Paris the former head of the KLA, Hashim Thaçi, who had become prime minister of Kosovo. Bernard Kouchner declared himself "happy" to have received his "friend". However, Bernard Kouchner's "friend" was a man linked to the mafia, "identified by several intelligence services as a key figure in organised crime in the Balkans[423]."

During his visit to the Serbian enclave of Gracanica in March 2010, Bernard Kouchner was asked by a *Voice of America journalist*, Budimir Nicic, to comment on the case of the "yellow house" that had served as a clandestine clinic. Kouchner had replied: "What is that, the yellow houses? What yellow houses? Why yellow? You should look it up. There have been no yellow houses, there have been no organ sales. People who tell such things are bastards and murderers! "We all remember his indecent laugh: "You are crazy, you believe any nonsense[424]! "

---

[421] His report on organ trafficking was presented to the European Council in December 2010.

[422] Bernard Kouchner had distinguished himself by campaigning before international bodies in defence of the principle of humanitarian interference. In 2010, *The Jerusalem Post* ranked him 15th among the 50 most influential Jews in the world. (NdT).

[423] Article by Silvia Cattori on the *Mediapart* website of 13 June 2013.

[424] "*Mais vous êtes fous, vous croyez n'importe quelle connerie!*" The video of the scene is famous and is still circulating on the internet (NdT).

On the *Mediapart* website, dated 13 June 2013, an article by Silvia Cattori returned to this case. Journalist Budimir Nicic was "offended and insulted" by Bernard Kouchner's reaction: "Everyone was shocked by his behaviour. The most terrible crimes took place while he was in charge of Kosovo. He has not kept any of his promises to find the perpetrators of the crimes against the Serbs. They were empty words." Naim Miftari, former head of the KLA, now testifying in the open in several ultra-sensitive trials, went further than Budimir Nicic: "In 1999, no crime could have been committed in Kosovo without Kouchner being informed."

When the "Yellow House" in Albania was repainted in white after the war, organ harvests were carried out at the private Medicus clinic in Pristina, Kosovo's capital. The establishment had been closed in 2008, and Turkish doctor Yusuf Sönmez had been sentenced in absentia to eight years in prison at the end of 2008. An international arrest warrant had been issued for him by the Pristina regional court, and he was finally arrested two years later, on 12 January 2011, at his mansion on Istanbul's Asian shore. Yusuf Erçin Sönmez was nicknamed "Doctor Frankenstein", or "Doctor Vulture".

On 12 January 2011, *Le Figaro* published an excellent article written by Cyrille Louis. It reported that Yusuf Sönmez, who had just been arrested, had been released on bail with a ban on leaving the territory. According to the indictment drawn up by the Kosovo prosecutor's office, the investigation had begun on 4 November 2008, purely by chance, following a check at Pristina airport. Yilman Altun, a Turkish citizen, was preparing to fly to Istanbul when police officers noticed his obvious weakness. A doctor called to examine him then discovered a fresh scar still fresh on his back. Exhausted, Yilman Altun admitted that he had just come out of the operating theatre at the Medicus clinic where he had had a kidney removed. Earlier, on 4 August in Istanbul, a certain Ismaïl had offered him to earn a lot of money by donating one of his kidneys, after he had received a letter from the Medicus clinic along with his plane ticket. At the end of October, Yilman Altun took off for Pristina. He had been assured that he would receive 20,000 euros in cash on his return. In the meantime, his kidney had been transplanted into the body of Bezalel Shafran, an Israeli citizen suffering from a serious illness. Questioned in turn by investigators, Shafran had indicated that he had contacted the criminal network through a compatriot based in Turkey, Moshe Harel. In exchange for 90,000 euros, the latter had assured him that he could have a "new" kidney transplanted. On 30 October, the Israeli had landed in

Pristina, where he was introduced to Yilman Altun at the Medicus clinic. Before entering the operating theatre, the two men had been asked to sign a letter declaring the benevolent and "humanitarian" nature of the transplant. Fresh off the plane, Dr Yusuf Sönmez had been in charge of handling the scalpel.

The investigation had been overseen by Prosecutor Jonathan Ratel, an international magistrate attached to the European civilian mission Eulex that contributed to the establishment of the rule of law in Kosovo. Jonathan Ratel had succeeded in circumscribing responsibility for the entire case. Dr. Lufti Dervishi, head of the urological service at Pristina hospital, had met Sönmez during a urology congress in 2006. Moshe Harel, who was now under an international arrest warrant, had managed the matching of donors recruited in Turkey, Moldova, Kazakhstan and Russia with the recipients. His bank accounts had been used for all payments. In total, and on the basis of the anaesthesia records seized from the Medicus clinic, 27 operations were carried out in 2008.

The police were interested in the complicity of traffickers within the Kosovar administrative apparatus. For example, the former permanent secretary of the Ministry of Health, Ilir Rrecaj, was accused of having granted an authorisation of complacency to the Medicus clinic.

In March 2012, another story came out that a Canadian from Toronto, Raul Fain, a 66-year-old Jew, had paid $105,000 to an Israeli citizen in 2008 to arrange a kidney transplant at the clinic. He had decided to seek a foreign donor after his doctors told him that he might be waiting twelve years before receiving an organ in Canada. Raul Fain had met Israeli Moshe Harel in Istanbul. They had travelled together to Kosovo accompanied by a German man who was also due to receive a kidney and two Russian women who were going to donate one of their kidneys.

On the *bloomberg.org* website, dated 1 November 2011, we read an article entitled "Organ trafficking gangs force poor to sell their kidneys to desperate Israelis". In Belarus, Sasha, 29 years old and up to his neck in debt, had also agreed to sell one of his kidneys, travelling to Pristina after answering an internet advertisement promising $10,000. He had been met in Istanbul by Yuri Katzman, an Israeli of Belarusian origin. Katzman had introduced him to Moshe Harel before landing in Pristina on 26 October 2008. His kidney had been sold to an old Jew from New York. After that, Moshe Harel had fled.

Other surgeries took place in Turkey. Dorin Razlog, a 30-year-old shepherd from Ghincauti in Moldova, claimed to have been operated on in Istanbul in August 2002. He had been paid 7,000 dollars instead of the 10,000 offered, although 2,500 dollars were counterfeit notes." They said that if I reported to the police they would destroy my house and kill my family."

Moshe Harel, one of the nine people charged in the Kosovo organ transplant case, was arrested in May 2012 in Israel. Jonathan Ratel, the Eulex special prosecutor investigating organ trafficking, had confirmed that Moshe Harel and other suspects had been arrested.

On 26 April 2013, the five doctors of the Medicus clinic were finally sentenced in Pristina, Kosovo. A hundred witnesses had appeared in court. The harshest sentence, eight years in prison, was handed down to urologist Lutfi Dervishi, the clinic's owner. His son, also a doctor, Arban Dervishi, was sentenced to seven years and three months. Three other defendants in the case, also doctors, were sentenced to between one and three years in prison. The culprits were also ordered to pay 15,000 euros in compensation to seven of the victims. The daily *Le Monde* headlined: "A lucrative market for the mafia", but did not specify which mafia was involved. Twenty-four victims had been identified: Israelis (probably Palestinians), Turks, Kazakhs, Belarusians, Russians, Ukrainians and Moldovans. All were vulnerable and needy people who had undergone surgery between March and November 2008 at the Medicus clinic. All had first been contacted in Istanbul, where they had been promised substantial sums, "even if they were never paid" according to the newspaper *Le Monde* of 29 April 2013. Six donors had testified in court, either in person in the courtroom or by videoconference. For their part, the clients had paid between 80,000 and 100,000 euros." They came from Israel, Canada, Poland, the United States and Germany, and were generally wealthy people, eager to shorten waiting times in their own country. They were also all Jewish," the *Le Monde* journalist said. Yusuf Sönmez and Moshe Harel were absent during the trial, as their extradition requests to Turkey and Israel were not granted. Indeed, these countries do not hand over their citizens to foreign courts.

On 13 May 2015, seven Israelis were indicted in Tel Aviv for belonging to an international network of organ trafficking and illegal transplants in Kosovo, Azerbaijan, Sri Lanka and Turkey, according to the Israeli Ministry of Justice. One of the defendants, Avigad Sandler and Boris Wolfman, located Israeli patients in order to offer them the organs of people from Kosovo, Azerbaijan and Sri Lanka. The third defendant, Moshe Harel, also operated in Kosovo with the Turkish doctor Yusuf Erçin Sönmez.

Another defendant, Dr Zaki Shapiro, was considered an expert in organ transplantation. He had been the head of the organ transplant service at Beilinson hospital near Tel Aviv until he retired in 2003. At the beginning of 2007, this Israeli was arrested in Turkey with three other fellow citizens. The *Jerusalem Post* described him at the time as one of the most important organ transplant specialists. Organ harvests and transplants were carried out in private clinics in Istanbul, in one of which Dr. Shapiro had been arrested under extraordinary circumstances. Four armed men had broken into the medical centre to demand reimbursement of his money. According to the Turkish press, the four men had fired on the medical staff. The police were immediately alerted and a policeman was wounded in the shooting. The police investigation revealed that, after multiple warnings, the clinic had been ordered closed down by the judiciary months earlier because of the illegal transplants. In addition to Dr. Shapiro (or Shapira), sixteen other people had been arrested, including two Turkish doctors.

In 2002, university professor Nancy Scheper-Hughes had already mentioned the name of this Zaki Shapiro before the US House of Representatives: "Dr. Zaki Shapiro, head of the transplant service at Beilison Medical Center near Tel-Aviv, had gone outside the law in the early 1990s when he used Arab middlemen to find organ sellers among the working poor in Gaza and the West Bank." Zaki Shapiro and Yusuf Sönmez were also associates of the elusive Illan Peri.

On 9 December 2015, the Russian news agency *sputniknews* reported that, according to the German *Deutsche Welle*, the Ukrainian-born Israeli citizen Boris Walker (whose real surname was Wolfman) had been intercepted at the Atatürk airport on the outskirts of Istanbul. He had travelled to Turkey with the aim of retrieving the organs of Syrian refugees fleeing Islamic State. Forty days after his arrest, the Turkish judiciary ordered the extradition of the alleged trafficker to Israel, although the Turkish and Israeli authorities declined to comment. As of 2015, no organ trafficker had yet been convicted by the Hebrew state's judiciary.

The accusatory inversion

The typical accusatory inversion was once again verified in the cinema with the film *Dirty Pretty Things* (UK, 2002): Okwe is a poor black man of Nigerian origin living in England, in London. He is a clandestine, illegal immigrant, and his life is not easy. But he works hard to get by. He is a taxi driver by day and a receptionist at night in a palatial London hotel. But strange things manifestly go on in the hotel, and Okwe discovers that the palace hotel is home to an organ trafficking operation run by the man in charge who takes advantage of the plight of the immigrants. In exchange for one of their kidneys, the poor immigrants from the third world can thus obtain a passport or a visa: a kidney in exchange for a passport. The operations are performed in a hotel suite by inexperienced doctors. Pursued by the immigration services (two very bad white Englishmen), Okwe does not dare to denounce what he has just discovered. He will therefore proceed through alternative channels to try to dismantle this traffic, aided by a Turkish cleaning woman, a black prostitute and a Chinese man working in a morgue. The poor illegal immigrants (they were then called "sin-papeles") are victims of blackmail, pressure, rape and crime, while the Whites, once again, play the role of the bastards. The film is by director Stephen Frears, who is not a "White", you understand.

We also know that the blood of Christian children may have been trafficked in the past for religious reasons. In February 2007, a very unpleasant case broke out in Italy and caused a great scandal. Professor Ariel Toaff had just published a 400-page book entitled *Pasque di sangue (Passover of blood, the Jews of Europe and the blood libels)*. Professor Toaff, of Bar-Ilan University in Jerusalem and son of the former chief rabbi of Rome, caused a media stir by acknowledging that ritual murders were practised by some Ashkenazi Jews in northern Italy and that the blood of these Christian children was a commodity trafficked on both sides of the Alps. Accusations of ritual murder had erupted everywhere in Europe and the Middle East since the 11th century[425].

Naturally, here too, some Jewish filmmakers had to make films related to the theme. For example, *The Haunted* (USA 1987): In New York, young boys are kidnapped and victims of ritual murders. The psychologist Jamison discovers the existence of Santeria, a sect that practices a Cuban variant of voodoo. The film is by John Schlesinger, who is not a member of a voodoo sect.

In Peter Webber's film *Hannibal Lecter, the Origins of Evil* (2007), which reveals the childhood of the famous Hannibal Lecter, the cannibalistic psychopath from *Silence of the Lambs*, we see in one scene how a child murderer can also be a good Catholic who takes his children to church.

---

[425]On ritual murder, see *Jewish Fanaticism* (2007) and our *History of Antisemitism* (2010).

Against the unrelenting drumbeat of Hollywood propaganda, a Turkish production from 2006 stood out: *Valley of the Wolves,* a film depicting the crimes committed in Iraq by US troops, as well as the humiliations suffered by the resistance fighters in Abu Ghraib prison. The film also denounced the organ trafficking for which Israeli doctors were responsible in that Iraqi prison. We saw a Jewish American doctor delicately remove a kidney from a living Arab prisoner and carefully place it in a container labelled *"To Tel-Aviv".* As the film had been remade into a television series, episodes of which were repeated on Turkish television, the state of Israel had expressed its displeasure. In January 2010, Turkish ambassador Oguz Celikkol was summoned to the Israeli Ministry of Foreign Affairs, where the second in command of Israeli diplomacy, Danny Ayalon, after having kept him waiting for a long time in the corridor, received him without shaking his hand and invited him to sit in an armchair on a lower step than those occupied by Israeli diplomats. Afterwards, the Turkish ambassador declared that in 30 years of his career he had never been so humiliated.

In August 2009, following the publication of the article by Swedish journalist Donald Boström, the Israeli leadership decided to respond immediately with an attack, at the risk of provoking a diplomatic crisis. The Swedish government was to immediately condemn the anti-Semitic article." We are not asking for an apology from the Swedish government, we want a condemnation of the article from them," declared Prime Minister Benjamin Netanyahu during the council of ministers. Finance Minister Yuval Steinitz told reporters: "The crisis will last as long as the Swedish government has not changed its attitude towards this anti-Semitic article. He who does not condemn it is not welcome in Israel," adding: "The Swedish government can no longer remain silent. In the Middle Ages slander was spread accusing Jews of preparing unleavened bread for Passover with the blood of Christian children, and today Tsahal (Israeli army) soldiers are accused of killing Palestinians to harvest their organs."

The head of Israeli diplomacy, Avigdor Lieberman, reproached his counterpart in Stockholm for his silence: "It is shameful that the Swedish foreign minister refuses to intervene in a case of incitement to murder Jews. This attitude is reminiscent of Sweden's during the Second World War. At that time, it also refused to intervene against Nazi genocide." Sweden's ambassador to Tel-Aviv, a member of the wealthy and influential Bonnier family, who owned most of Sweden's newspapers, television stations and cinemas, expressed her deep "state of shock[426]".

A certain unease spread through the editorial offices of the major Western media. The mainstream press spoke of "tensions" between Israel and Sweden. The French weekly *Le Point*, for example, headlined: "Israel raises its voice against Sweden after an article judged to be anti-Semitic". This avoided discussing the basic issue of organ trafficking.

On 11 December 2009, an incredible article entitled *"Mengele stole my Kidney"* appeared in the English online newspaper *Dailymail*, the second largest English daily. We read that an 85-year-old Israeli, Yitzchak Ganon, had just been operated on by a cardiologist in Tel-Aviv. When he woke up in his hospital bed, the surgeon who had just saved his life was very surprised. He had indeed found that his patient was missing a kidney. I know," he had replied. The last time I saw it, it was throbbing in the hands of a man whose name was Josef Mengele." Yitzchak Ganon then began to tell his incredible story.

Josef Mengele was "the terrible Nazi doctor who worked in Auschwitz". Yitzchak Ganon, who was a survivor of Auschwitz, had been chosen by that "diabolical doctor, who appeared on the arrival platform of train convoys to choose human guinea pigs for his atrocious experiments."

The following is the full text from the English newspaper: "Once the number 182,558 had been tattooed on his left arm, Mengele—whom his victims called 'the angel of death'—tied Y. Ganon on an operating table: 'He thrust his knife into me without anaesthetic. The pain was indescribable. I felt every cut of the knife. And then I saw my kidney throbbing in his hand. I cried out like one possessed, I cried out this plea: "Hear, O Israel: the Lord is our God, the Lord is One". And I prayed for death to come, so that I would no longer have to endure such suffering." But Mengele, who wanted to discover how to clone the perfect SS supermen for his Führer, was not finished with him." After the operation they gave me no painkillers and put me to work. I had to clean the room behind the bloody operations performed by Mengele."

Six months later, Mengele tested him again. This time, he was immersed in a bath of ice-cold water, while Mengele watched him at intervals: he wanted to see how his lungs worked." Then I was selected for the gas chamber because my body was no longer worth anything." On the morning of the gassing, Y. Ganon was incredibly lucky (like Elie

---

[426] A German Jewish ancestor, Hirschel, had changed his surname to "Bonnier". The Bonnier family from Sweden also owned numerous media outlets in Finland.

Wiesel, like Samuel Pisar and other survivors[427].) I was "the 201st to be sent to the gas chamber—but after 200 people the room was full": "That saved my life. And they sent me back to the camp."

When Auschwitz was liberated, Ganon was able to return to Greece, where he was reunited with his brother and sister who had also survived, and subsequently emigrated to Israel in 1949.

We then understood why, after 64 years, this Israeli refused to see a doctor. For all that time, the man had kept this terrible secret that explained his distrust of the medical profession. His family members had always been surprised by his refusal to see a doctor." Whenever he had a cold, a cold, an infection, an ecchymosis, a cut or any other illness, he managed on his own," said his wife." When he was sick he said he wasn't sick, he said he was just tired." When Yitzchak Ganon had a heart attack, his secret was out. On the website of the newspaper that published this incredible story, the comments were fortunately open to readers, and the irony of some internet users showed us that we had to keep hope in humanity.

Cosmetic surgery

Cosmetic surgery developed considerably in the 1990s. This medical discipline had a large number of practitioners in the community. An article in the magazine *Le Point* of 27 July 2001, entitled *The hidden face of cosmetic surgery*, made us understand that the operations nevertheless entailed certain risks. A traumatised woman had had the courage to speak out publicly." It was my hairdresser who recommended this surgeon. He seemed very sure of himself, he told me he was the best, so I said yes. So I said yes." On 19 July 2000, Chantal L., 55 years old, had an operation in a cosmetic surgery clinic in the Yvelines. Chantal was a petite brunette, an accountant in the Paris region, who had saved 37,000 francs to offer herself more generous breasts and an eyelid lift.

"The next day, the surgeon came to see me to tell me that I had bruised my eyelids, but I was blindfolded and couldn't see anything. A few days later, after returning home, I realised the carnage: my right eye was ruined, my lower eyelid drooped, and a very visible scar up to my temple. My right breast is crumpled and dented, with one nipple still missing and also positioned much higher than the left one. I later

---

[427] Read the account of these "survivors" in Hervé Ryseen, *Le Miroir du Judaïsme (The Mirror of Judaism)*, Baskerville 2009.

discovered that the surgeon had placed the right breast prosthesis in front of the muscle and the left breast prosthesis behind..."

Chantal L. was one of the "unsuccessful" cosmetic surgery victims. How many were there? Nobody knows," admitted Dr François Perrogon, president of the Association for Medical Information in Aesthetics. The same conclusion was reached by the Association of the successes and failures of cosmetic surgery, which brings together 1,500 victims. When insurers are asked, they reply that there are 20% of litigation against 2% in other medical disciplines." In ten years, litigation has increased by 117%, of which a third is said to be related to breast surgery," explained Nicolas Gombault, legal director of Sou Médical, which insures 160 cosmetic surgeons. He acknowledged: "Sometimes we are forced to do without some of our partners who have too many accidents."

In reality, the number of disputes that reached the insurers was underestimated, as patients rarely dared to call their surgeon to account after a failure." Suffering a cosmetic operation failure is like a rape, you don't want to talk about it", explained Valeria F, who had been living for more than twenty years with mutilated breasts after a cosmetic operation. After a long psychotherapy, she could hardly begin to talk about her ordeal." I was 51 years old at the time and wanted to reduce the size of my breasts. I went to see a surgeon in Paris who had his own practice. After the operation, when I lifted the bandage, I saw that my left breast no longer existed. I started screaming. The nurses came and told me: "it will be all right". A week later, when I went back to see the surgeon for the post-operative visit, I thought he would explain what had happened. He just said, "It looks great on you, anyway, you already look like a man". I didn't protest, because I'm one of those women who aren't exactly pretty, but it left me shattered. I never wanted a man to touch me again, I withdrew into myself with depression after depression, and I even ended up selling my restaurant. There must be many victims like me who don't dare to speak out..."

Some surgeons offered to "fix" them at a cheap price, or, more rarely, to pay them back on condition that they signed a paper in which they undertook not to disclose the matter. This confidentiality clause had no legal value, but it made it possible to silence the victims of failure. A legal complaint was not feasible. Few took the step." It is a long and costly procedure, and the result is very random," explained Martina L., who had been fighting for seven years with the surgeon who had performed liposuction on her." I go from one expert opinion to another, and each time it's a pain. I am forced to show off my atrociously stitched and dented belly. On top of the fact that I have to pay for it, I have no right to have it repaired before the end of the procedure." And this woman added: "I have discovered that in this type of case, the surgeons appointed for the expertise rarely dare to criticise the work of their colleagues. It is a world in which everyone covers their backs, at the expense of the victims."

It was clear that some clinics were more careful to choose their lawyers than their surgeons, and easily hid behind the excuse of "therapeutic risks" or the absence of any obligation to achieve results. In reality," said Dr François Perrogon, "between 10 and 30% of cosmetic surgery operations require at least a few touch-ups. But the professionals do not shout it from the rooftops." During the consultation, the surgeon was supposed to inform about the risks of the operation and possible complications, but he or she did not say so from the lips. On the other hand, everything was done to "inebriate" the future client:

Lidia, 60, recalled her experience: "They invited me to a glass of champagne and canapés, showed me photos of 'successful' patients and even videotapes. I didn't ask any more questions, I was seduced. Besides, the atmosphere in the waiting room was electric, the surgeon had just been on TV. His appointment book was full." Lidia had paid 75,000 francs without batting an eyelid, half in cash, for a facelift and a steatomy. When the patient resisted the siren's call, the assistant who had just had an operation and whose impeccable silhouette was living proof of the surgeon's know-how would come in.

The managers of the Rond-Pointclinic on the Champs-Elysées, a luxurious 3000 square metre establishment employing more than 70 people and which had just been floated on the stock exchange, had profited greatly from their media relations. This is what we read in the weekly *L'Événement du jeudi* of 14 May 1998: "Thousands of women have entrusted their breasts, their faces, their love handles to the surgeons of this chic Parisian clinic with the endorsement and authorisation of the Ministry of Health. How could they have suspected? For years, the media gave a publicity platform to doctors Guy Haddad, Bernard Sillam and Martial Benhamou, owners of the establishment, together with doctor Michel Cohen. Articles in *France-Soir, Femme actuelle, Télé 7 Jours,* praising the merits of the practices of the Rond-Point clinic; participations in television programmes, publication of a book, *Jeunesse pour tous (Youth for all).* —At each of his interventions, a telephone number was communicated to the public: that of the French Society for aesthetic development which forwarded the call to the clinic."

Advertising was strictly forbidden by the code of ethics for doctors, but this prohibition did not apply to these clinics, which enjoyed the status of a commercial establishment. The Rond-Pointclinic on the Champs Elysées profited from this to a large extent, with an advertising budget of up to ten million francs per year. In May 2000, its manager was sentenced to a fine of 400,000 francs for misleading advertising. Indeed, the clinic stated in its advertisements that it was "authorised by the Ministry of Health", which was untrue, as no such agreement existed for this type of establishment. The judges had noticed other misleading formulas: the four doctors, supposedly "the best specialists" in "reconstructive and aesthetic plastic surgery" were in fact only general practitioners. Their advertising slogans had all the makings of success: "permanent hair removal"; "get rid of cellulite for good"; "remove fat from the hips"; "remove double chin"; "baldness vanquished".

As for the prestigious societies that provided a kind of professional endorsement for the establishment ("Société française de développement aesthétique", "Fédération internationale d'aesthétique médicale"), the researchers had discovered that these were phantom associations created by the clinic's directors for strictly commercial purposes and whose aim was to direct all those who called to enquire about cosmetic surgery to their practice[428].

The clinic had been severely criticised during an inspection by the Fraud Control and by the provincial directorate for health and social affairs. The investigators had noted several breaches of the most elementary rules of hygiene and, even more serious, anaesthesia performed by unqualified general practitioners." The operations were carried out in shivering conditions," wrote the journalist. A complaint had been submitted to the Order's council, and more than 70 testimonies from colleagues had been submitted to the national body to denounce dubious practices. However, only one patient had decided to go to court, which showed that the system was really tight. One of the clinic's surgeons, a medical advisor to the establishment, was also a legal expert at the French Court of Cassation.

---

[428] Before the French Revolution, the guilds of craftsmen and tradesmen forbade and banned advertising. It was only used by Jewish merchants, who later popularised it. On this subject, see the well-documented study by the German sociologist and economist Werner Sombart, *Les Juifs et la vie économique (1911)*, republished in French in 2012. (Also translated by the Complutense University in 2008, *Los Judíos y la vida económica.*)

Contacted by telephone, Dr. Benhamou denied the allegations against him. The four doctors had, however, been provisionally suspended for six months, an unusual and "particularly harsh" sanction. The clinic was officially closed "for works", but continued to operate as an outpatient clinic, mainly for liposuction, which represented the major part of its activity. For surgical operations (breasts, eyelids, nose), clients were taken by limousine from the Champs Elysées to the Hartmann clinic in Neuilly, which provided interim care." During the building work, business went on as usual," journalist Marie-Françoise Lantieri concluded ironically.

On 2 May 2001, the manager of the Rond-Pointclinic on the Champs Elysées was again sentenced to a fine of 20,000 francs by the Paris correctional court, this time for discrimination in employment. In a medical journal, he had published a job offer reserved for "foreign surgeons". The court had underlined that hiring foreign surgeons, whose qualifications were not valid on French territory, allowed this establishment to benefit from a highly qualified cheap workforce, incomparable to the salaries it would have had to pay to a French doctor or surgeon.

Some scalpel aces had not hesitated to commission general practitioners, beauticians or hairdressers." When I created the Association for medical information in aesthetics in 1991, several professional colleagues came to see me to offer me a commission of 10 to 15% on each patient I would refer to their clinics", revealed François Perrogon.

Another trick to inflate turnover was to "advise" the client on procedures that he did not require. Irene, 52, had asked for a facelift: "I saw Dr. S. on TV, he looked great." The appointment was arranged at a Parisian clinic, a sumptuous mansion named after a 14th century humanist poet. In May 1999, after three consultations, Irene was operated on. This was her testimony: "A few minutes before the operation, just after I had been given an anxiolytic, Dr. S. came to propose breast prostheses in addition to a facelift. I refused, but he insisted, talking to me about a three-month credit, then a six-month credit, and finally said: 'I'll give you 30,000'. I was out of my mind because of the medicine and I agreed. He then made me sign a document called "informed consent for surgery". I thought we were going to discuss the operation, the size of the prostheses, but the anaesthetist showed up to give me an injection and I fell asleep." The next day, after the visit of "doctor S." to her room to make her sign a promissory note, Irene discovered her new breasts: "They were too big, I had a 95 C, when before I had an 85B. From then on, everything went wrong. One of the prostheses deflated and the facelift was ruined. I have sagging in the lower part of my face."

The sanctions of the Council of Order, as well as the investigations of the health authorities, were rarely made public. Nor was it possible for candidates for cosmetic surgery to detect doctors who had been convicted by the courts, as civil convictions were not published and those on appeal or in cassation were only mentioned in specialised and confidential legal journals.

Organ trafficking and Jewish morality

In his famous play, *The Merchant of Venice*, William Shakespeare had imagined a horrible character, a Jew named Shylock who claimed his pound of flesh from an insolvent debtor. Four centuries later, thanks to advances in surgery and transplantation possibilities, Shakespeare's imagination seems to have been realised on a grand scale.

In any case, organ trafficking had a certain legitimacy in the discourse of religious leaders. Yitzhak Ginzburg, a celebrated kabbalist in charge of the Od Yosef Hai yeshiva in Israel, had thus declared in *Jewsih Week*, the most important Jewish publication in the United States: "A Jew is authorised to remove the liver of a goy if he needs it, because the life of a Jew is more valuable than the life of a goy, just as the life of a goy is more valuable than that of an animal... Jewish life is of infinite value. There is something infinitely more sacred and unique in a Jewish life than in a non-Jewish life[429]."

The goy was sometimes even equal to an animal, as we have been able to read in some works by Jewish intellectuals. In *The Last Righteous*, the novelist André Schwarz-Bart told the story of poor Mordecai, who, attacked by Polish peasants, managed to defend himself—an incredible thing for a poor Jew—and defeat his assailants: "Mordecai, stunned and almost drunk with blood, suddenly discovered the Christian world of violence... That same night, on his return home, he knew that from now on he would outstrip his fellows, how derisory and insignificant! of a body closely linked to the earth, to plants and trees, over all harmless or dangerous animals—including those bearing the name of men[430]."

Martin Gray, the famous author of the bestseller *In the Name of*

---

[429]Israel Adam Shamir, *Notre-Dames des douleurs*, BookSurge, 2006, p. 241. See also statements by Yitzhak Ginzburg in *Psychoanalysis of Judaism*.
[430]André Schwarz-Bart, *The Last Righteous*, 1959.

All My People, tended to feel the same contempt. He was seventeen in 1941 and lived in the Warsaw ghetto. When a German Gestapo policeman began to interrogate him about the merchandise trade he had set up, which enabled him to enrich himself considerably ("My profits are enormous..."), Martin kept silent. Martin Gray then wrote of this policeman: "He belonged to the world of the rabid beasts that must be killed because they are noxious... I and my people were the men with the faces of men. And the rabid beasts could not defeat us even if they killed us." In other passages, he spoke of "beasts with the faces of men[431]."

Readers of our previous books know the extent to which contempt for the goyim is glimpsed in certain Jewish literature. Thus, it is natural for them to think that the corpse of a Jew should not be touched, let alone desecrated by the goyim. We understand better why Jewish intellectuals, on the whole, are firmly opposed to the death penalty in the countries where they have settled432.

---

[431]Martin Gray, *Au nom de tous les miens*, Robert Laffont, 1971, Poche, 1984, p. 125, 220, 286.

[432]"Never, as far as I know, has any philosopher as such, in his own systematic philosophical discourse, never has any philosophy as such contested the legitimacy of the death penalty. From Plato to Hegel, from Rousseau to Kant (undoubtedly the most rigorous of them all), each one, in his own way, expressly took sides in favour of the death penalty." Jacques Derrida and Élisabeth Roudinesco, *Y mañana, qué...* Fondo de cultura económica, Buenos Aires, 2002, p. 159.

PART THREE

SWINDLERS AND TRAFFICKERS

Jewish criminals and gangsters were not all organised in mafia or criminal networks. Some acted alone on their own and specialised in scams of all kinds. In the June 1989 issue of the Jewish monthly magazine *Passages*, devoted to '*The truth about Jewish crooks*', a lawyer named Bernard Cahen stated the following: 'The magistrates who leave the courts specialising in financial crime, such as the 11th or 31st criminal courts in Paris, recognise that in the end they are close to harbouring anti-Semitic feelings. The number of Jews they had to judge far exceeds the percentage of Jews in the population. This is a fact."

At the end of his interview in the same magazine, Thierry Levy, a lawyer, unburdened himself: "I come from a very assimilated family from the East. In my family, many felt ashamed whenever a Jew was involved in a scandal. Today, I no longer feel that shame. And if there are reactions like those of these judges, that pleases me. Fuck them!"

1. The big scams

All Jews are not swindlers, and all swindlers are not Jews. But judging by the judicial chronicle, the big financial swindles are exclusively carried out by "highly assimilated" Jews.

Claude Lipsky, "the swindler of the century".

Claude Lipsky was one of those great swindlers that only the Jewish community seems capable of spawning. The man had become famous in the 1970s with the case of the *Patrimonio territorial* y de la *Garantía inmobiliaria*, a 43 million franc (6.56 million euros) swindle that had wiped out the savings of more than 8,000 small savers. Nicknamed in France the "swindler of the century" since that swindle, he had been sentenced to eight years in prison in 1976. But eleven years after his conviction, Lipsky decided to return to action.

Starting in 1987, and for a decade, Lipsky offered incredible investments to retired or active French soldiers on the African continent. Officers or non-commissioned officers, some of these soldiers had amassed comfortable savings thanks to their pay as soldiers on mission abroad. In Africa, a sergeant earned 25,000 francs a month, and a colonel 80,000 francs a month, even if he was not the father of a family. These savings had aroused Claude Lipsky's interest, from which he hoped to profit handsomely.

To make contact with his clients, Lipsky found two good chumps to prospect for him in military circles: Pierre Haubois, 66, a former general who had commanded the Djibouti base, and Claude Derusco, a former pilot and lieutenant-colonel of the same age, also retired. Their membership of the army removed all doubt and they were given a red carpet welcome on their visits to the garrisons. Lipsky's name was on the mailing list as director or administrator, but he never travelled to Africa, leaving it to his associates to approach the military.

During the period 1987–1999, Claude Lipsky had thus launched subscriptions for French military personnel stationed abroad, mainly in Dakar, Djibouti and Libreville, to whom he promised very attractive returns on real estate investments thanks to a computer programme capable, he claimed, of analysing long-term stock market flows. The trio assured their interlocutors that if they handed over their savings, their investments could generate an annual return of 10% net of tax with an initial capital of 50,000 francs. Under these conditions, hundreds of soldiers took advantage of this golden offer.

But in 1998, the military became disillusioned. Instead of receiving the agreed sums, they received emails with evasive explanations asking for patience. Sensing the swindle, they filed complaints with the courts and a judicial investigation was opened for "aggravated breach of trust and swindling" (*Le Figaro*, 23 September and 31 October 2000). Some did not receive interest. Others were unable to recover their initial capital.

The military quickly discovered to their astonishment that Claude Lipsky was a former fraudster. They also discovered that his company had moved between Geneva, Monaco, Cyprus and the British Virgin Islands under different names such as Neiman Trust, Neiman Corporation and Moneywise Investissement Limited. Some of the military men went to Cyprus to investigate the matter further: "It was really just a postal address with a single employee that Claude Lipsky had never seen," said one of them. Tens of millions of francs had passed through companies based in Geneva, Monaco or Cyprus before evaporating.

For many, this represented a loss of millions of dollars: "All my savings are gone at once," said Thierry Pineau, a former pilot officer in Dakar. The soldiers swindled by Claude Lipsky had formed an association, *Ardiplent*, in order to recover their money." We have 342 members in an association, but today there are nearly 500 victims registered," declared the president, Jean-Francis Comet, a former officer in Djibouti. He explained that the two retired soldiers working for Claude Lipsky had inspired confidence in them: "Their past commanded respect. They came to visit us twice a year, in October and March. That was enough. Military bases are like small towns: word of mouth works very well. And we passed on the word of these juicy investments to each other. In the beginning, the customers got their investments back. Everyone was satisfied... Everything changed dramatically in 1998, when some of them could not recover their start-up capital. In spite of the letters we received telling us about the temporary bad situation, suspicions grew. The letters contained too many contradictions. It was then that the addresses of the companies—Monaco, Geneva, Cyprus—began to worry us. We realised that we had been taken for fools... Many families had made important investments. They lost everything." This huge scam had wiped out the savings of nearly 500 military personnel. The overall loss in this case amounted to 175 million francs (26.7 million euros).

On 11 May 2000, the judicial machine was finally set in motion. The two prospecting officers were arrested in Djibouti and placed under judicial control. They claimed that they too had been victims of the same underwriting, denouncing their former boss for breach of trust and fraud. They received a 3% commission but swore they never knew anything about Claude Lipsky's scandalous past.

He was arrested at his home in September in Chesnay, in the Yvelines, imprisoned and charged with aggravated breach of trust and fraud. However, he assured investigators that he had never intended to defraud his clients, but that he had been the victim of bad economic times and bad investments. When heard by the examining magistrate, Claude Lipsky denied any embezzlement. As he had declared to several "clients" who had come to his home to ask him for accounts, his business had collapsed in the storm of the Asian stock market crisis.

Beyond these initial explanations, the duped soldiers had regained some hope after seeing Lipsky indicted.

The Ministry of Defence had gone to great lengths to keep the scandal out of the public eye. The DPSD (formerly Military Security) had taken matters into its own hands. At the general assembly of the defence association set up by the military, the DPSD representative, solemnly accompanied by the minister, had described the scam as a "defence-confidential" affair. The soldiers had had to sign a document in which they undertook not to divulge anything about the bad move. They were asked to suffer in silence.

Apart from this military aspect, we learned that other people had also fallen victim to the swindler. Claude Lipsky had also offered his "juicy" investments in the metropolis to businessmen and pensioners. In this case, the intermediary was the deputy director of a Crédit Agricole agency. Lipsky would then go personally to negotiate the contracts.

This was the testimony of Suzette, a 54-year-old restaurateur in the Loir-et-Cher: "He was introduced to us by our banker. So, even though I had some doubts, I gave him 750,000 francs. When I later realised that I had been tricked, I went to see Lipsky in the Var, where he has a sumptuous property. The interview was fruitless and I denounced him."

The case of Pierrette and Louis, aged 73 and 77, was identical: "We handed over 900,000 francs, the proceeds from the sale of our frozen food business when we retired. We have nothing left," they declared, devastated.

On 26 May 2001, the press informed the public that the "swindler of the century" had been "miraculously released". Due to a simple error in the lawyer's summons deadline because of a faulty fax, Claude Lipsky, 69 years old, had been released from Bois-d'Arcy prison. It was a blow to hundreds of civil parties in this case who were still hoping to get their money back.

In addition, some 100 military personnel had lodged a complaint in the Principality of Monaco. In fact, Lipsky had moved his activities from Geneva to Monaco in 1997. In April, the Principality's judiciary issued an arrest warrant for the fraudster, who was absent from the hearing "for medical reasons". Lipsky had appealed against the sentence and in September 2001, the Monaco Court of Appeal upheld the sentence of 5 years imprisonment and a fine of 20,000 euros handed down at first instance.

The court of appeal had in turn confirmed the sentence of two years in prison and a fine of 20,000 euros imposed on Lieutenant-Colonel Claude Derusco, considered to be an accomplice of Claude Lipsky. On the other hand, General Pierre Haubois was released on appeal despite having been sentenced to the same penalty as Derusco at first instance. The conviction had been pronounced by default. In fact, Claude Lipsky had once again been unable to appear "for health reasons".

The Monegasque part of the case had been tried, but on 21 May 2007, "the swindler of the century", now 75 years old, appeared before the court in Versailles." The French-Israeli businessman", based in the Chesnay in the Yvelines (*Le Parisien*, 21 May), still claimed his innocence. He had not siphoned off funds: "They were lost. As in all financial companies, sometimes it works very well, and sometimes there are problems," he told journalists before entering the courtroom.

Claude Lipsky further stated that he was "very, very, very bad" about the retrial "because it's not nice to be in the middle of all these people, because I'm going to be asked many, many questions that I'm going to have to answer."

On 15 June, however, the last day of his trial, Lipsky finally admitted to the gigantic swindle (*Le Parisien*, 16 June 2007). Absent from the hearing "for medical reasons", Claude Lipsky had finally confessed through his lawyer, Raphaël Pacouret, who declared in his plea: "My client realises belatedly, but he has understood the pain inflicted on the civil parties." In passing, the presiding judge read a short letter written by the accused: "With a different sense of values, given my advanced age, my state of health and my more human concerns, I can only say that I regret the consequences of my actions."

His lawyer explained that his client's mentality had really changed: "He is tired of this tumultuous existence. He only aspires to end his life in peace with his wife." The journalist added: "The septuagenarian would like to be perceived as 'someone human'. Hospitalised, he wanted to make a gesture to his victims by giving them 1.5 million euros from the sale of a property in the south of France."

Claude Lipsky's confessions had provoked the anger of the lawyers of his alleged accomplices, Claude Derusco and Pierre Haubois, who had called for the release of their clients. The sentence was pronounced on 26 July 2007: Claude Lipsky was sentenced to five years in prison and a fine of 375,000 euros for this case of false investments to the detriment of the military. Together with his co-defendants, he also had to pay 17 million euros in compensation to the military. Colonel Claude Derusco and General Pierre Haubois were sentenced respectively to three years and thirty months in prison. They were also ordered to pay a fine of 150,000 euros. The bank Sofipriv, which had opened an account in the name of Claude Lipsky, was sentenced to a fine of 700,000 euros for aggravated money laundering and complicity in fraud.

In England, Lipsky was a surname that had long remained in popular memory. A century earlier, in 1887, a certain Israel Lipski had been found guilty of poisoning a young English girl in London, and 'Lipski' had been a term used to insult Jews ever since.

Jacques Crozemarie and the ARC scandal

The ARC scandal was quite notorious in France in the late 1990s. Jacques Crozemarie, the president of the Association for Cancer Research (ARC), regularly appeared on television in commercials to convince viewers to send him their money. People were unaware, however, that hundreds of millions of francs were siphoned off by the swindler to finance his luxurious lifestyle.

The scandal had erupted in January 1996. The Court of Auditors' report had then revealed that only 26% of the donations received by the ARC actually reached the scientists. The rest was embezzled through front companies and a system of over-invoicing. Crozemarie had subcontracted its communication campaigns to the company International Developpement, run by two businessmen, Michel Simon and Pascal Sarda. The company overcharged for its services and immediately returned undue salaries to the fraudster. 327 million francs had thus been diverted between 1990 and 1995, as revealed by the trial that took place in May 1999, which was the equivalent of 8,000 euros per week in cash.

In his book *La Banda del cáncer*, the journalist Jean Montaldo provided some information on these two characters: "They are Crozemarie's two protégés," he wrote. Illiterate and uneducated, the two ruffians went about their business in the same way as they extorted the donations collected by the ARC for cancer patients." (p. 45). Michel Simon was "a true leader of men". He was the son of a wealthy family who had made a reputation in beauty products." His father had the good fortune to return alive from the Mauthausen deportation and extermination camp, where the arrival of American troops had saved him in extremis, on the verge of death." Pascal Sarda was "the evil genius of Michel Simon, the evil alchemist who taught him to turn lead into gold, and to turn his hitherto rudimentary rackets into great industries of theft, fraud and swindling. We are at the beginning of the Mitterrand years, the time of the *golden boys*, of easy money, of dirty money... Without this Simon-Sarda gang, the fervent contributors to the ARC, a charitable association recognised as a public utility, would never have been so systematically robbed and on such a large scale[433]."

The *Nouvel Observateur* of 14 August 1996 reported that the financial director of International Developpement was another Israeli called Ronald Lifschutz. At the beginning of June, the financial brigade had turned up in the morning at his building, a social housing unit of the Paris city council. Unfortunately, the cautious tenant had flown to Israel a couple of weeks earlier.

Since 1988, Jacques Crozemarie's power over the ARC was described as "almost theocratic" by the General Inspectorate of Social Affairs (Igas). Autocratic and proud, Jacques Crozemarie chased away criticism by persecuting the press and encouraging members to write to denounce attacks on the association. He had been forced to resign from the association's leadership, but he continued to claim his innocence, and, confident that he was right, he went before the correctional court in 1999, "giving the president a monumental dressing-down", accusing her of "doing nothing against cancer", and even questioning the competence of the Court of Auditors' magistrates: "Can't they count! "With phenomenal impudence, he then declared in front of the television cameras: "I would be a criminal if I had pocketed anything, but look at my representation fees, they are nil! They don't even reimburse me for the restaurant bills! "A report by Emmanuel Cohen, broadcast on the television programme *Secrets d'actualité* on 26 March 2006, showed him weakened, entering the courtroom with a cane to walk. But a few hours earlier, photos taken from behind him showed him walking normally at a petrol station without a cane. The programme also included the testimony of the association's accountant. She said that one day she had drawn his attention to invoices that had been paid in duplicate. Crozemarie became furious and threw her out of the office, wielding it so tightly that she was literally "lifted up", feeling as if her "feet were not touching the ground".

Jacques Crozemarie was sentenced in June 2000 to four years in prison, a fine of 380,000 euros and 30.5 million euros (200 million francs) in damages to be paid to the ARC. He was arrested at his villa in Bandol (Var), a few hours after his conviction, and imprisoned in the Santé prison. Michel Simon was sentenced to three years in prison, a fine of 380,000 euros and 15.2 million euros in damages. But of the

---

[433] Jean Montaldo, *Le Gang du cancer*, Albin Michel, 1997, p. 120-127.

300 million euros lost, only 12 million euros had been recovered.

In October 2002, after 33 months of detention in the Santé prison, Jacques Crozemarie was released, benefiting from remissions of sentence. He continued to claim his innocence and declared in an interview with the daily *Le Parisien*: "I am not a thief. I never understood why I was convicted, and I never will. I don't want to be condemned for the rest of my life. It makes me indignant. I have paid for nothing! I'm still waiting for the evidence against me".

His luxurious Bandol villa with heated swimming pool, his two Parisian flats, the furniture, the boat and the Swiss account had been seized and put up for sale by the ARC. Crozemarie had nothing left but his CNRS pension[434]. But neither the prison, nor the months of instruction, nor the taunts and spitting he had received during his arrest, had dampened his character. The taxi that had come to pick him up at the Santé on 11 October 2002 had taken Jacques Crozemarie to Audierne, a small fishing village in Brittany near Douarnenez, where Claude Legall, a former anaesthesiologist at the Villejuif hospital who had known him for a long time and who had agreed to help him find a place to live, was waiting for him. Thirteen days later, the Legalls said they had "had enough" (*Le Parisien*, 28 October 2002): "There was no question of giving him accommodation as I had found him a studio overlooking the sea. But as soon as he saw it, he told me that €182 (1200 F) per week was too expensive for him. He stayed in our house," said Claude Legall. It's horrifying, everything is owed to him, he treated my wife like his maid and had to be taken care of. Life with him quickly became hell... We lent him some money, housed him, fed him, washed his things, but he left without a word to us, without a thank you."

Contacted by telephone in a retirement home on the outskirts of Paris in February 2006 (*Secret d'actualité*), Crozemarie continued to deny everything: "You're joking!" It also emerged that his white coat was a disguise of circumstance: the head of the ARC had never been a doctor. With a degree in radio-electrical engineering, he had joined the CNRS in 1954 as "deputy chief of service" at the age of 29 thanks to a recommendation "from a friend of his mother's". He had never studied medicine, which had not prevented him, whenever the occasion arose, from posing in his white coat with other scientific authorities. Thanks to his impudence—the *chutzpah*[435]—he had gradually managed to control the wheels of the main association that solicited the generosity

---

[434] The Centre national de la recherche scientifique, better known by its French acronym CNRS, is France's largest public scientific research organisation.

[435] Yiddish Jewish word: shamelessness, impudence, extreme shamelessness.

of the French and to swindle 3.5 million from donors.

Some journalists recalled that he was a "former Indochina fighter", perhaps to make the Goyim believe that this despicable character was a militarist, even an extreme right-winger. But no journalist of the establishment press had pointed out that Jacques Crozemarie was also a doctor honoris causa of the University of Tel-Aviv and a member of the Masonic lodge of the Grand Orient of France, as revealed by the journalist Emmanuel Ratier. Jacques Crozemarie died on 24 December 2006 at the age of 81. The municipality of Bandol did not want to reveal the causes of his death.

Jacques Crozemarie's cries of innocence resembled those of another businessman named Marcel Frydman. Marcel Frydman was the founder and owner of Marionnaud perfumeries which had acquired most of the independent perfumeries in France. The group was in turn acquired in 2004 by a Chinese company, but Frydman's management had been called into question by an accounting report by the Autorité des marchés financiers (AMF), which accused him of having falsified the company's balance sheets. In December 2004, Marionnaud announced a loss of 93 million euros due to corrections of errors, whereas the previous year the company had declared a profit of 13 million euros. The AMF referred to "proven fraud". But Frydman gave his own explanations: "I messed up, but I didn't steal from anyone. I have not tried to enrich myself. I only have a house in which I live. It's my only asset." The report also mentioned "false documents to deceive the auditors" and "false account summaries drawn up by the accounting department" (*Libération*, 17 October 2005). Frydman responded to these unfounded accusations as follows: 'It is false. I did not ask the accounting department for anything. And as for the auditors, if they have been misled, it is worrying."

In *Psychoanalysis of Judaism*, we also recounted in detail the extraordinary scam of "Gilbert C". After the bloody attacks in London in July 2005, the man had posed as an agent of the French secret services. With his formidable brazenness, he had managed to manipulate a bank manager over the phone, convincing her to hand over millions of euros in banknotes in a suitcase. The damage amounted to some 23 million euros. In August, the police had foiled other such attempts by alerting the bankers in time. But in September, "Gilbert C" (his name was not disclosed in the press) had tried a variant that had brought him much more, obtaining international transfers from bankers to the accounts of alleged terrorists so that they could supposedly be traced. With his phenomenal gab, he persuaded them that they were serving the country in the fight against Al-Qaeda. The fraudster had thus managed to have millions transferred into accounts in front companies set up by his front men in Hong Kong and Estonia. Gilbert C, 40, and his brother Simon, 38, both born in Paris, had taken refuge in Israel, from where they continued to defy French justice. In January 2008, the press finally revealed their name: Gilbert Chikli. For the first time, Israel had agreed to extradite one of its own citizens.

The Sentier case

The Sentier, in the centre of Paris, was the clothing district. 5000 manufacturers and wholesalers worked every day with their employees. These were immigrants, often clandestine, exploited "the old-fashioned way", sometimes for more than fifteen hours a day. They worked with the sewing machines or on the streets, unloading the trucks and loading the rolls of fabric. These countless slaves from poor countries, who accepted a devastating job for a pittance, made the cosmopolitan employers happy. In 1997, the Sentier was in the news because of a gigantic *"cavalerie"* scam. This consisted of a system of issuing unfunded bills of exchange at maturity[436]: a bill of exchange allows a supplier to be paid immediately, instead of three months later. The bank, which pays in place of the customer, simply charges a commission, say 10%. The customer will pay the bank within three months. This is a win-win situation for all parties. However, if the customer immediately resells the goods at a profit, he can also be paid by another bank using the same system. Between what he pays the first bank in three months and what the second bank pays him immediately, he makes a profit by reselling the more expensive product. The second customer only has to do the same thing again with a third, and the third with a fourth, and so on. And since nobody is going to check whether the deliveries are real, it is not necessary that the goods are actually delivered. When the bill of exchange is due, the customer does not pay his debt to the bank, and the bank then turns to the supplier ... who has disappeared and gone bankrupt. The customer then claims that he cannot pay because the

---

[436] In this system, a fictitious window dressing is often used to simulate business transactions in the eyes of the bank or other lender in order to pass off the new loan amount as profit. Through this façade, the borrower feeds his appearance of respectability and solvency, and thereby the lender's trust, and thus his propensity to obtain new funds from the lender. The technique lends itself easily to snowballing: the fraudster can use the money to present himself as a solvent client of an accomplice, who in turn will obtain a larger loan, and so on. (NdT)

supplier has not delivered the goods, which in fact never existed. And that's it, this is the deception, the *"cavalerie"*.

Between April and June 1997, 2,700 bills of exchange were issued in the Sentier, a prelude to numerous bankruptcies. 93 companies left bankers and suppliers in the lurch to the tune of 540 million francs, "but if the investigation had covered the 768 companies potentially involved, the billion-franc mark would have been crossed" (Libération, February 2001)." (*Libération*, 20 February 2001). The companies were set up for this purpose, managed by unemployed individuals recruited for the scam.

In addition to the *"cavalerie"*, there was the *"carambouille"*. *Carambouille* is a slightly more primitive procedure consisting of buying goods without paying for them, selling them at a discount and disappearing at the right time. Insurance fraud had also occurred. Fires had destroyed warehouses in Aubervilliers. Warehouses of fictitious goods had supposedly burned down and the insurers had to pay out 16 million francs. All this made a policeman say: "I've never seen so many *Rmistas* [recipients of the RMI [minimum income] circulating in BMWs". When the banks decided to alert the public prosecutor's office in July 1997, it was too late.

In November 1997 and March 1998, two spectacular police raids resulted in 188 arrests. Investigators had uncovered nine interlinked *cavalerie* networks. They were led by Ekrem Sanioglu, Samy Bramy, Thierry Luksemberg, Jacky Benghozy, Gary Meghnagi, Philippe Gabay, Denis Gourgand and Gerard Atechian.

The mastermind of the operation, dubbed the "ditching of the bank", was Haïm Weizman, who used to wander around the neighbourhood dressed in Tsahal fatigues, as a reminder of his rank as a sergeant-chief in the Israeli army. His own network had mobilised 23 of the 54 "active" companies around which the scam was organised. 31 members of his team were indicted, but he had preferred to flee to Israel with other accomplices.

Samuel Brami, nicknamed *"petit Sam"*, or Samy the Weasel, was about to flee when investigators caught up with him in a Roissy hotel near the airport. He then declared that he had isolated himself to reflect and "take stock of the situation"." I have fled my home, but not my country," he told the police, assuring them that he had decided at the last minute not to take the plane and to return home. His right-hand man, Samson Simeoni, nicknamed *"grand Sam"*, had managed to flee to Israel. But one of Samy's lieutenants, Raphael Elalouf, had told everything in his first interrogations: "At the head was Samy, just to organise[437]..."

Another *cavalerie* network was run by a certain Thierry Luksemberg. A businessman named Gérard Cohen had had the misfortune to do business with him. The lawyer Hervé Témine, Gérard Cohen's lawyer, explained: "His responsibility is overwhelming, not only at the criminal level, but also because with his flight to the United States, after having tried to negotiate his appearance, he has deprived his co-defendants of a confrontation that would have exonerated my client[438]." Because Gérard Cohen was innocent, or so we had to believe.

Le Parisien of 23 April 1999 published on two pages "the confessions of the Sentier swindlers". Monsieur Albert and his lieutenants had agreed to talk: "Albert, Éric, Philippe, Denis. Average age, 34 years". Philippe, 27, had found a pearl: the director of a Crédit Mutuel agency on the outskirts of Metz." His biggest client before us was the local pastry chef, Philippe said. He would come to see him in a Porsche, invite him to great restaurants, show him the purchase orders from Carrefour or Monoprix, and leave him open-mouthed." Once he felt confident, the banker from Lorraine said yes to everything." He was not aware of anything, Philippe assured him. He never knew that the promissory notes were fictitious and that *cavalerie* was behind them." The naïve banker had been arrested and had been sleeping behind bars for eighteen months, while "Philippe, Albert, Eric and Denis", as the journalist wrote, were resting abroad with 150 million francs.

Almost all of the defendants had finally admitted their involvement in the gigantic scam after many verbal contortions. The investigators recalled some rather picturesque behaviour: the impromptu fainting of a woman "whenever the questions were annoying"; the consensual confessions after "great circumvolutions"; or the network leader who no longer recognised his cousin; or the confrontation that almost ended in a fight in the courthouse.

The Sentier case had taken eighteen months of judicial investigation. Fifteen people were still at large, and thirty-three banks had joined the case as civil parties. The trial took place in Paris from 20 February 2001 and had lasted about ten weeks, given the scale of the proceedings. 124 defendants had taken the stand, all accused of organised fraud.

Gilles-William Goldnadel[439], Samy Brami's lawyer, was scathing

---

[437] *Libération*, 20 February 2001, p. 17; 31 March 2001, p. 18; *Le Parisien*, 29 January 2002, p. 12.
[438] *Libération*, 19 May 2001." Témine" is part of the Hebrew onomastics.
[439] Gilles-William Goldnadel is a French-Israeli lawyer with a strong presence on the

about a show trial, which, according to him, was nothing more than the fruit of a "heterogeneous assembly of small and medium-sized swindles" that did not deserve so much scandal: "I find it hard to understand how the Sentier can be defeated in the realm of farce and provocation." The president of the court, Anny Dauvillaire, took things with phlegm. Only one thing irritated her: the incessant departures of the accused from the courtroom to make phone calls.

There was also a "serious incident", according to the journal *Actualité juive* of 24 May 2001: The lawyer Gilles William Goldnadel had decided not to let the verbal outburst of the public prosecutor, François Franchi, who, at the opening of the trial, had stigmatised the flight to Israel of some of the defendants' "congeners" present at the hearing, go unchallenged. He also considered that Israel was "placing itself on the fringes of the nations" by refusing to extradite them.

"It is regrettable that an ethnic connotation should be given to this case," thundered the lawyer Goldnadel, who then specified that he had consulted the definition of "congeneric", and added fulminatingly: "Israel on the fringes of the nations! How can one not be aware of the way in which this phrase, coming from the depths of time, can be felt? And not only by my fellow men? I ask Mr Franchi, representative of the Paris prosecutor's office, to be more humble". The lawyer had then urged the prosecutor to "publicly retract his words". Exceptionally, the prosecutor stood up and asked for twenty-four hours to be able to respond to the lawyer. The next day, in a tense atmosphere, the prosecutor's representative read out his response: "Your defiance of the prosecution is unacceptable and unworthy of a lawyer. I do not need your advice and moral lessons," he declared in substance." Mr Goldnadel, you are not, to my knowledge, the representative of the State of Israel. For my part, I stand by my words and the vocabulary I used. For I am of Latin culture... And I abide by the etymology[440]."

On 28 January 2002, the Paris correctional court had sentenced 88 of the 124 accused to prison terms. The harshest sentence - 7 years unconditional imprisonment—had been pronounced against Haïm Weizman. But he and twelve other defendants were still in Israel. Samy the Weasel was sentenced to five years in prison with thirty months suspended.

French political and media scene. He is also an essayist, associative and political activist. Right-wing and conservative, he is known for his pro-Israeli political commitment and fervent defence of the state of Israel. Gilles-William Goldnadel was the founder and president of Avocats sans frontières in 1993. (NdT)

[440]*Actualité juive*, 24 May 2001. Archives of Emmanuel Ratier.

In addition to the prison sentences, the charge of organised fraud, which had been retained, obliged the defendants to jointly and severally reimburse the banks and the suppliers. The sum they had to pay was 280 million francs: "They want us dead", lamented Samy Brami after the hearing." They want to kill us with the money[441]! "he finally shouted.

On 10 May 2004, the investigating chamber of the Paris court examined the Sentier II case, which focused on money laundering networks between France and Israel. 142 people were charged with money laundering: 138 individuals and four banks. Unlike Sentier I, traders (textile, leather, transport) and temporary employment agencies were not the only ones implicated. The banks were prosecuted as legal entities (such as Société Générale, Bred and American Express), and 33 bankers (such as Daniel Bouton, chairman of Société Générale) were prosecuted as natural persons[442]. The Sentier II trial began in February 2008 and was due to last until July.

Trafficking consisted in "endorsing" cheques, i.e. modifying the name of the beneficiary by a simple mention on the back with a bank stamp. Endorsement has been prohibited in France since the 1970s, as it is almost everywhere else in the world except in Israel. The cheque was given to a "moneychanger" in exchange for cash (minus commission). The moneychanger would then deposit the cheque in his Israeli bank and the latter would have the account credited by the French bank. The cash made it possible to defraud the French tax authorities or to pay salaries under the table. The Financial Investigation Brigade (Brif) had meticulously examined all the cheques of more than 20,000 francs that circulated between France and Israel, and it turned out that the traffic of cheques recycled into cash amounted to more than 1 billion francs.

The banks certainly could not verify everything, given the number of cheques in circulation—several tens of thousands per day. But investigators became suspicious when they realised that a bank would agree to transfer a cheque made out to the order of the Treasury or the Urssaf[443] to a third party with a simple mention in Hebrew on the back.

---

[441] In 1986, there had already been a case in the Sentier, in which 21 people had been charged. Three shell companies acted as intermediaries and provided false invoices and cash to pay illegal immigrants. The mastermind of the trafficking was one Seymon Blankenberg.

[442] *Libération* of 10 May 2004 and 19 June 2004, article by Renaud Lecadre. *Le Parisien*, 12 May 2004, p. 15." Bouton" is part of the Hebrew onomastics.

[443] In France, the Unions for the Collection of Social Security Contributions and Family Allowances (URSSAF) are private bodies with a public service mission that come under

With this system, it was effectively possible to recycle any stolen cheque, which explained the disappearance of numerous postal sacks in postal sorting centres. Sometimes, the beneficiaries of the stolen cheques were simply called "Mr. Urssaffi" or "Treasury advertisement". The two protagonists of this traffic, "Philippe B." and "George T." were on the run in Israel." George T." was Georges Tuil. He had set up the first network in 1997 from Mulhouse." Philippe B." was Philippe Besadoux. In November 2005, he was arrested in Prague under the identity of Harry Mervyn. In his pockets, Czech police officers found a plane ticket to Tel-Aviv.

The hundreds of Sentier cheques were collected and then sent to Israel instead of being cashed in French banks. Chabad-Lubavitch Hasidic Jews, in traditional dress and unlikely to be searched at the airport, were responsible for crossing the border, their suitcases full of cheques on the way to Roissy and cash on their return from Israel. Six rabbis from the Chabad-Lubavitch movement and more than twenty association leaders were involved. They supplied the merchants of the Sentier with suitcases of cash. In fact, a nebula of Jewish confessional associations was widely implicated. Rabbis and their teams of fundraisers offered donors a cash return of up to 50%. Between 1997 and 2001, 70 million euros transited in this way.

Two of the rabbis, Joseph Rotnemer and Jacques Schwarcz were among the main defendants. The Rotnemers were an important family in the Jewish community. They were at the head of one of the most important Jewish school networks in France. Rabbi Elie Rotnemer was the founder of the *Refuge*, a body collecting 1% for social housing. The *Refuge* and its 92 civil real estate companies controlled nearly 4000 social housing units. In the early 1990s, an investigation had revealed that *Refuge* funds were not going to social housing but to investments in commercial businesses.

When Elie Rotnemer died in 1994, his son Joseph Rotnemer became the new family patriarch. He had expanded and diversified his fund-raising methods in favour of a nebulous 150 associations (public schools, retirement homes...), all domiciled in Seine-et-Marne and in the 19th arrondissement of Paris—the two nerve centres of the Chabad-Lubavitch Hasidic Jews[444]: in five years (from 1997 to 2001), the

---

the "Collection" branch of the general social security system. (NdT).

[444] According to the Chabad-Lubavitch Hasidic doctrine, Jews must remain in exile in the midst of the material realm of Evil and Impurity—the *Qelipa* (*shell*) of the Gentiles—in order to raise the divine sparks held prisoner there, and thus precipitate their destruction and the advent of Redemption. On the Chabad-Lubavitch Hasidic Jews

Rotnemers had thus absorbed 450 million francs. Joseph Rotnemer and Rabbi Jacques Schwarcz were both on the run in Israel.

Rabbi Haïm Chalom Israel, 57, had founded private contract schools in France and raised funds in this way from members of his community. Donors' cheques were handed in against cash at 'Change Point', a bureau de change in the orthodox quarter of Jerusalem. As a Jabad-Lubavitch official acknowledged, a distinction had to be made between "kosher donations[445] ", which were real donations, and "non-kosher" donations, which were cheque transactions in exchange for cash. In November 2000, investigating judge Isabelle Prévost-Desprez had ordered the provisional arrest of Haïm Chalom Israel, considering that the amount of donations to Jewish charities was excessive and constituted an abuse of social goods. But five weeks later, in December, the indictment chamber ordered his release on payment of a bail of 300,000 francs." He's going to run away, that's for sure! "Isabell Prévost-Desprez exclaimed to herself on the phone. The examining magistrate then ordered the police to re-arrest the rabbi as he left the Fresnes prison so that he could be charged this time with aggravated money laundering and put back in prison. Three days later, the indictment chamber again ordered his release. It should be noted here that the indictment chamber was headed by one Gilbert Azibert[446].

Myriam Sitbon, one of the 142 people charged in the Sentier II case, was a trader who worked in the leather industry. She had to leave the neighbourhood after receiving threats, but had decided to testify: "In this world," she said, "they stick scissors in each other's back and the next day they slap each other. As soon as they see a weakness in someone, it is exploited: a flaw, whether in private life, a divorce for example, or in business. The prey is surrounded and the rapacious enter the square and the victim is stripped, even by his own friends... There is a mixture between private life and professional life... The terror is exercised even on wedding and party days... I came out of there

---

and their doctrines, see *Psychoanalysis of Judaism* and *Jewish Fanaticism*.

[445] See note 223.

[446] Religious Jews had also been indicted in the US. In late December 2007, Naftali Tzi Weisz, 59, spiritual leader of Spinka, an ultra-Orthodox Hasidic Jewish group in Los Angeles, appeared in court with five accomplices on charges of defrauding the tax authorities of some $33 million. Federal prosecutors accused the rabbi and his co-defendants of underhandedly reimbursing people who had donated money to Spinka's charitable activities. The money was laundered via a bank in Israel, but not before a tax exemption was applied in the United States. Rabbi Tzi Weisz was released after posting $2 million bail. On the other hand, a Tel-Aviv-based Israeli bank manager named Mizrahi had been arrested.

exhausted and ruined." In this article in *Le Parisien* (22 January 2003), the shopkeeper also revealed the existence of an organised mafia in the Sentier district: "The saleswoman in my clothes shop was raped and I myself was assaulted. I have been stripped of my goods, extorted, threatened. I have been terrorised so much that today I no longer want to be afraid, that's why I have decided to speak out. El Sentier is subject to the law of silence."

The article by Renaud Lecadre in the daily *Libération* of 20 February 2001 had pointed out the problem: on 10 July 1997, Emile Zuili had been kidnapped by four hooded men and subsequently released in exchange for his promise to pay 3 million francs. His friend, Denis Ouabah, explained to the police: "There are teams of extortionists in the Sentier who go to the perpetrators of fraudulent bankruptcies, either to collect unpaid debts or to extort a share of the profits." In this case, the Sentier knew that Zuili represented a major coup. But his kidnappers had not dared to attack his boss, Haïm Weizman, the mastermind of the Sentier scam. Wiretapping had made it possible to record some eloquent conversations: "The guy downstairs doesn't want to pay. Rafy is going to go there with Alex who has recovered his pipe in Alfortville." The day after his arrest, after his release, Emile Zuili left France for good with his wife and children.

Racehorses and mechanics

In 2004, another big scam had been uncovered. Sebastian Szwarc, alias M. Guerin, and his childhood friend Samy Souied, had set up a juicy business. The scam, which started in August 2003, consisted of selling advertisements in specialised publications published by police, gendarmerie, fire brigade and finance ministry associations. The idea was to seduce small traders into believing that an advertisement in a police magazine or a tax yearbook would help them to avoid a fine or a tax adjustment. The advertising spaces did not exist, but the cheques were cashed in Israel. In eighteen months, the fraudsters had amassed a haul of 55 million euros.

The Israeli bank Hapoalim was in charge of money laundering. Wiretaps had made it possible to trace the mastermind of the operation: Samy Souied, who had a business relationship with the head of the bank in Israel. In France, the Hapoalim bank had been searched in June 2004 and the head of the Parisian agency, her deputy and two employees were remanded in custody. In Israel, 180 bank accounts and 375 million dollars had been blocked. 200 clients were suspected, including Israel's ambassador to London, Zvi Hefetz, Vladimir Goussinski (owner of 27% of the Israeli daily *Maariv*), and Arcadi Gaydamak. A score of accomplices were being prosecuted by the French justice system for "aggravated money laundering" and "organised fraud".

Some of this dirty money had been invested in horse racing. Alain Szwarc was the owner of a dozen horses, including several champions, which, according to investigators, had been bought with dubious funds. Evidently, the purchase of these thoroughbreds led to under-the-table disbursements, as the purchase value was much higher than the declared price. In January 2005, just a few days before the Grand Prix of America, the arrest of Alain Szwarc and his son Sebastian by the police of the Financial Investigation Brigade (Brif) shook the equestrian world. The father and son had been indicted by a Parisian judge for money laundering and fraud.

Arrested on 16 January 2005 when he got off the plane, Sebastian Szwarc, 31, was remanded in custody. The young man, who drove around in a Porsche and a Ferrari, admitted that he had no income in France, but that his parents regularly gave him cash, a total sum amounting to 600,000 euros." I am a gambler, a spendthrift," he told police." My father supports me. He even finances me so I can play[447]."

Le Parisien of 4 September 2004 had also revealed the case of the mechanics, although on this occasion the television did not talk about it either." Huge French insurance swindle", we read in the pages of the press. It was "one of the biggest insurance scams ever uncovered in France." The basis of the scam was very simple: mechanics recruited victims of road accidents and established false files based on the declaration of damages. Then, with the complicity of experts, the damages were exaggeratedly overestimated. In the end, all that was needed was to fabricate false invoices in the name of real or not real garages. All of this—false damage declarations, false expert reports and false invoices—was sent to the insurers. The profits made by this highly organised group between 2000 and 2003 were estimated at 8 million euros, to the detriment of the main French insurers. All of the profits made by the group's leaders were transferred to Israel. In total, 1,200 fraud cases had been opened and some twenty people had been charged in Paris. Several international arrest warrants had been issued, including one for Bruce Chen-Lee, a 48-year-old "French-Israeli" on the run in Israel[448]. According to investigators, the alleged mastermind of the

---

[447] *Le Parisien*, 22 June 2004 and 28 January 2005.
[448] Surnames are sometimes misleading. Here, "Chen" is obviously missing a letter: perhaps an "O"?

gang, Chen-Lee owned a helicopter stationed in Greece, a twin-engine plane at an airport in the Paris region, as well as several villas in France and Israel. Before a hearing in Israel, he had denied being the instigator of the scam and presented himself as a hermit, a spiritual guide who devoted his life to writing religious books.

VAT fraud

In March 2008, a new scandal broke out. A gigantic VAT fraud network had been dismantled. Some fifteen individuals were accused of having stolen 100 million euros from the State. A record in France for this type of fraud. After two years of investigation, the mastermind, Avi Rebibo, a 38-year-old French-Israeli, and his gang were charged with organised fraud. Avi Rebibo had himself reimbursed in France for VAT he had never paid. The mastermind of the business managed Eurocanyon, a Luxembourg company specialised in mobile telephony. The scam consisted in buying phones before tax in England, a legal practice as they could be exported. The company then resold these phones without margin to some fifty front companies, this time including VAT, which was finally pocketed by the fraudsters. The shell companies then offered these batches of phones to the UK supplier. The money then left the system through a set of transfers between accounts opened abroad. Avi Rebibo was accused of being in control of the taxi company, nicknamed "VAT busting". Avi Rebibo's lawyer, Sylvain Maier, however, formally rejected these accusations. In his opinion, his client had been a victim of his clients who had not declared VAT. He had never broken the law, but "because he was in Israel, the managers of the accused companies had accused him", the lawyer declared. However, Avi Rebibo had appeared for his summons at the beginning of the year and had been remanded in custody since 21 January.

Defrauding the community

Jewish criminals do not hesitate to swindle their own co-religionists either. For example, there is the case of Israel Perry, a London-based Israeli lawyer who had siphoned off the pensions of concentration camp survivors agreed by the German state. In 1983, the Jewish state and the Federal Republic of Germany had effectively ratified an agreement according to which any former deportee with Israeli citizenship since 1953 could benefit from compensation of up to 100,000 marks, as well as a German pension and social benefits.

The little-known, but ambitious and clever lawyer had specialised in representing former deportees claiming their just deserts in Germany. The lawyer received his clients in a five-star hotel in Tel-Aviv, where he offered them his representation services by having them sign powers of attorney that the former deportees did not clearly understand the full extent of. In reality, by placing their trust in Israel Perry, the camp survivors were handing over part—or all—of their monthly allowances to an insurance company set up by the lawyer in a tax haven. In twenty years, the intermediary had thus processed thousands of files and siphoned off 320 million marks (nearly 150 million euros!), deposited in three banks in Zurich. The Israeli Ministry of Justice had, however, managed to enforce mutual assistance agreements with the Swiss justice system to block these deposits.

An article from September 2000, published on the website *www.sefarad.org*, informed us of this scam, as little publicised as the previous ones: "More than 1000 Holocaust survivors in Israel have denounced an Israeli lawyer." The information was confirmed by the Israeli Ministry of Justice. The case was mentioned in some newspapers, such as the German weekly *Der Spiegel*, the Swiss Sunday paper *Sonntags Zeitung*, as well as in *La Tribune de Genève*. When his clients complained that their claims were not progressing, Israel Perry invoked "German ill-will" and the slowness of international diplomacy. The "German pension scam" had been a huge scandal in Israel. In February 2008, Israel Perry finally appeared in court. His lawyer had denied any involvement on his part, but the swindler was sentenced to 12 years in prison. A radio presenter in Israel had addressed him in these terms: "You have a rat mentality and deserve to rot where you are[449]."

We have previously seen in these pages the case of Semion Mogilevitch who had enriched himself in the 1980s by proposing to Jews wishing to leave the USSR to buy their property, take care of the sale and then send them the money in Israel. We have also seen the case of Ignaz Bubis, the president of the German Jewish Community who had diverted funds received from the German government to invest in the Eros-Centers, as well as that of Mickey Cohen who organised charity galas in Los Angeles for the Israeli army and then lost the money

---

[449] In 1955, Salomon Margulies, originally from Romania, claimed to have had to go into exile and abandon all his possessions behind the Iron Curtain to escape racial persecution. The people he solicited did not resist his requests and donated large sums of money to him. On 16 December, he was arrested in a Paris discotheque after several complaints. The visas in his passport bore witness to his numerous journeys throughout Europe (*Le Soir*, 17 December 1955, archives of Emmanuel Ratier).

in poker games.

Two directors of the French Jewish French Television (TFJ), Ghislain Alloun and Michaëla Heine, were sentenced at the beginning of February 2008 to two years in prison, six months unconditional, for abuse of social assets. The two leaders were found guilty of having organised a fraudulent system based on fictitious agreements between the television channel, of which Mr. Alloun was president, and the production company Charisma Films, managed by Ms. Heine, his concubine. TFJ, which had been in receivership since 2005, had not been broadcasting since autumn 2006. The first complaints had been lodged by a lawyer, Elisabeth Belicha, a founding shareholder of TFJ, who had denounced the "methodical looting of TFJ" and accused the couple of having taken total control of the channel "without taking any cash", thanks to "a system of triangular invoicing and of offsetting debts in two stages".

Here is the case of another high-flying swindler called Didier Meimoun. This Tunisian Jew from Paris arrived in Brussels in the mid-1990s and invested his "clients'" money by guaranteeing them interest rates of 12 to 17.5%. Meimoun had invested in Radio Judaïca, and donated money to the good works of the community. At the age of 47, at 1.87 metres and 120 kilos, he was a respected man in the Brussels Jewish community. He had invested in numerous companies and owned villas in Knokke and Paris. He smoked cigars, was involved in show business, drove around town in his Jaguar XJ 8 coupé and kept his Ranger Rover for trips to the countryside, not to mention his wife's Rav 4. But by the beginning of 2001, doubt had crept into his environment. For example, he only used prepaid cards for his mobile phone, which he changed regularly. On 18 May 2001, those who had trusted him for years learned of his sudden disappearance. The evidence had to be accepted: the swindler had vanished with 50 million stolen from dozens, even hundreds of members of the community. With his false surnames—Meimoun Daida alias Meimoun Jerri alias Didier Lescure alias Didier Santerre, etc. —Didier Meimoun had multiplied the leads and was unaccounted for. He was sentenced in absentia: 3 years unconditional. Wherever he was, he probably didn't lose any sleep over it...

Looking further back in time, we find, for example, the unique case of Rabbi Menachem Porush of the ultra-orthodox Agudat Israel Party community. He had not hesitated to con a New York mobster, Joseph "Doc" Stacher, who had been arrested for aggravated violence, burglary, murder, etc. in 1965. Doc Stacher couldn't get over his astonishment. During the proceedings against the rabbi who had swindled him, Stacher was still stunned: "I can't believe it, a rabbi stole my money! A rabbi cleaned out all my dough[450]!".

Samuel Flatto-Sharon

Samuel Szyjewicz, nicknamed Flatto-Sharon, was born on 18 January 1930 in Lodz, Poland, to Josef Flatto and Esther Szyjevicz. Settling in France, he had adopted the name Flatto-Sharon to begin his career. He quickly got involved in all sorts of scams and after a few months in custody for swindling, he decided to flee first to Brazil and then to Dahomey, where he met the President, a former classmate from the Charlemagne Institute in Paris. He became the president's personal adviser and negotiated a $10 million loan with the World Bank. But the money received was immediately divided between the president and his ministers, with Flatto receiving half a million dollars "as expenses" in the process. Not to mention the forestry concessions with which he was rewarded by his presidential friend[451].

Five years later, he returned to Paris and entered the real estate sector with a partner of stature: Jacques Engelhard, a Strasbourg businessman with a special record at the police's Office of the Big Bandit: pimping, suspicions of contract killings." Jacky from Strasbourg" was his real estate negotiator and his henchman when it came to forcing recalcitrant tenants to vacate a building in the process of being demolished. Flatto gave the impression of ignoring everything about Engelhard: "My friend Jacques, he used to repeat, is the most slandered man in France!".

Flatto-Sharon had carried out twenty-nine real estate transactions, either on land to be built, buildings to be renovated or to be rebuilt after demolition. He resold them to shell companies set up by his accomplices. He had also benefited from the complicity of politicians who expedited building permits. The great financier of the Flatto group was Tibor Hajdu, a Jewish refugee from Hungary, a financial genius and the grey eminence of Flatto-Sharon. He was the organiser of the system of loans and front companies set up in the name of anyone he sent; chauffeurs, secretaries, and even errand boys. Once the loans had been secured and the land for the building paid for, the rest of the

---

[450] Robert Rockaway, *But he was good to his mother: The lives and the crimes of jewish gangsters*, Gefen publishing, 1993, p. 116–117.
[451] The family fortune of the famous media philosopher Bernard-Henri Lévy was also made in the African timber trade.

available funds would mysteriously make their way to Geneva, often in suitcases filled the same day at the counters of the lending banks.

Samuel Flatto-Sharon had thus pocketed 324 million francs (around 50 million euros). But that was not enough for him: he then invented fictitious renovation works and also took on debt to finance them. Thanks to straw men, the loans were withdrawn and immediately deposited in other financial institutions. His problems began when a tax investigation forced him to set sail for a country where there was no extradition convention with France, nor, in fact, with any country in the world: Israel. He applied for the country's nationality under the name Flatto-Sharon and got it without any problems after answering the usual question concerning a possible criminal past "against the Jewish people and the State of Israel". When the scam was finally uncovered in France in 1975, 550 million francs had evaporated. Arrested in Italy where he was to meet his lawyer Klarsfeld, he miraculously escaped before France could even request his extradition[452].

In 1974, Flatto-Sharon had bought a sumptuous 3,000 m² property in Savyon, on the chic outskirts of Tel Aviv. He soon met Betsalel Mizrahi, one of Israel's underworld bosses. An avowed patriot, he set up an arms export company and financed militias to protect synagogues in France, as well as a team of assassins to kill Chancellor Kurt Waldheim in Austria. He also funded a community centre for disadvantaged children. His generosity made him the idol of Israeli high society.

When his case was uncovered in France in the autumn of 1975, he volunteered to travel and stand trial. But on one condition: he demanded that Paris hand over the Palestinian Abu Daoud to Israel. Abu Daoud had been the head of the Palestinian commando responsible for the deaths of eleven Israeli athletes at the 1972 Munich Olympics.

In Israel, a committee was immediately set up to oppose Flatto-Sharon's extradition and tens of thousands of signatures of support were collected. Flatto was now a national hero. In order to avoid eventual extradition, he stood for election to the Israeli parliament in the ranks of Menahem Begin's Likoud party, financed by another great 'patriot', Begin's long-time friend, the Genevan Jewish billionaire Nessim Gaon[453]. Flatto was elected to parliament in May 1977 and made a triumphal entry into the Knesset. Interviewed on RTL, the French journalist asked him:

---

[452] For the rest of the case and Flatto-Sharon's obscure political relations with Jacques Chirac, see *Le Crapouillot* of March 1989.
[453] On Nessim Gaon, see note 139 above.

—So how many mandates have you achieved?
—Two, Flatto replied proudly.
—Bah, that's only thirty-four!

Allusion made to the thirty-two international arrest warrants issued by the French government after the scam[454].

Prosecuted for electoral corruption and fraud, Flatto was forced to resign his seat as a member of parliament in the 1984 elections. Imprisoned and convicted in Israel, he managed to raise bail to regain his freedom and was never extradited.

In 1990, Samuel Flatto-Sharon was once again implicated in a 20 million franc swindle to the detriment of an industrial butcher's shop in the Vichy region: Sobovidé. In October 1989, the ailing company had been sold to two wealthy buyers. The latter had guaranteed to keep the 196 employees and even to increase their salaries. The commercial court then gave its approval. Bernard Gliksberg had presented himself as the son of a large Belgian textile industrialist. Simon Abramowitz was a wealthy American financier in his fifties. He moved into the best hotel in Vichy, where he immediately had two telephone lines installed. From then on, Sobovidé knew no borders. Six million francs in false orders for tomatoes to a Parisian company; 3.5 million francs transferred to an account in Düsseldorf in the name of a false company to pay for calves from Poland that would never arrive; 1.4 million francs deposited in an Egyptian bank to guarantee a delivery of 4,000 tonnes of meat to a Lebanese company, and so on. After three months, the fraudsters fled, leaving 125 million francs in the company's debt. In addition, they had taken care to retain three cheques for 500,000 francs on behalf of Sobovidé before leaving, probably for travel expenses. Gliksberg had been arrested on 9 February 1990 under his real identity, his real name being Samy Prince. Abramowitz was arrested a few days later in Austria, in a palace in Vienna. Investigators had recorded 556 phone calls to Israel from the Vichy hotel, mainly to Flatto-Sharon. In April 1993, the court of Cusset, in the department of Allier, sentenced the two men to 5 years in prison. Flatto-Sharon chose not to appear[455].

---

[454] Jacques Derogy, Israël Connection, Plon, 1980, p. 130–136. Journalist's word play on *mandat d'arrêt* and *mandat de député* (arrest warrant and deputy's mandate).

[455] In 1980, three Tunisians, François Abitbol and his two sons, David and Mordecai, had managed in little more than a month to make off with a haul of four million francs by placing massive orders for meat from suppliers in the Creusot, Orléans and Rennes, for their butcher's shop in the 20th arrondissement of Paris. After selling everything, they settled in Israel, without paying the suppliers.

Another famous case of *"carambouille"*: in 1993, David Cherbit, a 28-year-old Rwandan owner of a *"Cash Menuiserie"* supermarket (windows, doors, stairs, cladding,

In April 2003, *Israel Magazine* published an interview with Samy Flatto-Sharon. In his Tel-Aviv residence, the walls were "covered with paintings by masters from Marc Chagall to Modigliani." Flatto-Sharon claimed to be an uncompromising Israeli patriot. Regarding the Jews who stole weapons to resell them to the Palestinians, he declared: "These people should be sentenced to heavy prison terms. We don't need these Jews. They are criminals, traitors who must be eliminated."

In England and the United States

Robert "Maxwell" was the son of Hasidic Jews from Slovakia who had taken the surname Maxwell, but whose real name was Abraham Hoch. He had become a British citizen in 1945. A Red Army liaison officer in Berlin, he had been in charge of interrogating various National Socialist dignitaries. Subsequently, he made his fortune in the press and publishing, controlling several newspapers. He had become a multimillionaire through various swindles, for example by siphoning off the equivalent of 4.3 billion francs from the pension funds managed by one of his investment companies. A large part of his money had been invested in Israel. In 1992, Robert Maxwell died in unclear circumstances. He was said to have fallen off his yacht off the coast of the Canary Islands, where his body was found in the sea.

His death was nevertheless suspicious. Loic Le Ribault, an international expert in criminology, was surprised that no examination of the yacht had ever been carried out. For him, Robert Maxwell's death was criminal in origin. Before falling into the water or being thrown overboard, the businessman had been brutally beaten. The fact is that Robert Maxwell left behind him a mountain of debts: no less than 34 billion francs, essentially unrecoverable[456].

---

etc.) decided to radically resolve his financial difficulties. At the head of S. A. Davidson, with a capital of 250,000 francs, David Cherbit did not hesitate to travel by helicopter to Paris to look after his business. He was a man who could be trusted. Even though he knew that his company was about to go into receivership—the hearing was set for 24 April 1993—he decided to place order after order with his suppliers. Semi-trailers full to the brim queued up in front of *Cash Menuiserie*. The goods were to be sold to unscrupulous salers against cash payment. The suppliers would never be paid. Within a few days, David Cherbit had issued more than two hundred bad cheques. A small company specialising in alarm systems had seen its cheque for 200,000 francs return from the bank marked "unprovided for", and had to declare bankruptcy. David Cherbit had left with his wife and sister for Israel. His brand new furniture was shipped to him in containers via Morocco.

[456] Robert Maxwell was the father of Ghislaine Maxwell, who was related to the famous Jewish American financial magnate Jeffrey Epstein, both involved in child trafficking

Another scandal, this time in the UK, had put the spotlight on Lady Shirley Porter. She was the daughter of businessman Jack Cohen, owner of a supermarket chain and mayor for a few years of Westminster. He had siphoned off $50 million and flooded Tel-Aviv University (built on the ruins of the Palestinian village of Cheikh Munis) with his generous donations. The Supreme Court had found him guilty and ordered him to pay a fine of £27 million. But as all his assets had been transferred to Israel, the fine was never paid[457].

The weekly *Le Point* of 20 July 2006 published an article about Michael Levy, a friend of Prime Minister Tony Blair whom he had met in 1994 at a dinner hosted by an Israeli diplomat. Levy had started fundraising among the big money for the Labour Party, until then mainly financed by the trade unions. That work had earned him the title of Lord Lord after Tony Blair's victory in 1997. In the summer of 2006, Levy had been accused of taking millions of pounds in loans from wealthy industrialists in exchange for honorary titles and seats in the House of Lords. The English have since dubbed him "Lord Cashpoint".

In the United States, cases of fraud were evidently rife. In February 2006, for example, seven members of the US occupation forces in Iraq were arrested for fraudulently misappropriating more than ten million dollars in reconstruction funds. Their leader, Robert Stein, 50, a former US officer, worked in the coalition interim government in Iraq and managed a budget of $82 million earmarked for the creation of a police academy and reconstruction projects in a region south of Baghdad. Stein was accused of stealing at least two million dollars from the Iraqi government and hundreds of thousands of dollars from the interim authority, as reported by the *New York Times* on 2 February 2006. Stein had used much of the money to purchase weapons for a private security company he had set up to protect the interests of a US reservist officer who had gone into business in Baghdad, one Philip Bloom. In return, he transferred money to the bank accounts of Stein's wife. Robert Stein and his wife, who lived lavishly at the expense of the US taxpayer, had bought a large property and several luxury cars. Stein was also rewarded for his services with airline tickets and enjoyed the villa Bloom owned in Baghdad. In 1996, Robert Stein was sentenced to eight months in prison in the United States for defrauding a financial institution.

In January 2006, the Abramoff scandal rocked the US political world. In *Le Point* of 12 January, we read that Jack Abramoff was a 46-

---

and prostitution for the US political and economic elite. (NdT).

[457] Israel Shamir, *L'autre visage d'Israël*, Éditions Al Qalam, 2004, p. 171.

year-old "brilliant lobbyist" close to the Republicans. He had just pleaded guilty to fraud, tax fraud and active corruption. He had bribed parliamentarians in exchange for favours for his clients. There was talk of 12 to 60 compromised congressmen, "one of the biggest scandals in the history of Congress." Abramoff and his clients had contributed some $4.4 million to the election campaigns of more than 250 congressmen since 1999[458].

A few years earlier, the American judiciary had exposed the brazenness of a major fraudster: Rabbi Sholam Weiss. Sholam Weiss, a Hasidic Jew born in 1954, had almost bankrupted an American life insurance giant, the National Heritage Life Insurance Company. In October 1999, Weiss was summoned to appear in court. His lawyer later recounted in the press Weiss's rantings, "berating" his accomplices by mobile phone in the courthouse hall and even inside the courtroom, behaving obnoxiously towards the court. In fact, he recalled that he "had to continually remind the court that his client was not being tried for his arrogance and rudeness, but for his swindling". Contrary to the opinion of all court observers, Weiss had obtained the right to remain at liberty by paying a ridiculous bail of five hundred thousand dollars, i.e. one thousandth of the enormous 450 million dollar haul. Predictably, Weiss disappeared, mocking the sentence inflicted in contumacy on 15 February 2000: life imprisonment, more than 845 years in prison. But in Israel, Weiss was free to enjoy the savings of 25,000 Americans, mostly retirees who had invested their pensions in that insurance company.

Americans will probably not remember the case of Martin Frankel, who had extorted more than 200 million dollars from insurance companies in more than five states and fled the United States in 1999; nor the case of the "New Square Four", those four Orthodox Jews from New Square City, outside New York, who had founded a fictitious yeshiva (Jewish university) in order to collect more than 40 million dollars in state loans. A few hours before leaving office, President Bill Clinton had commuted the sentences of the four criminals, Chaim Berger, Kalmen Stern, David Goldstein and Jacob Elbaum. The court simply sentenced them to repay the $40 million ... which was reason enough to put their feet up...

And that is because we must understand the very particular morality of the Jewish people. In the Israeli newspaper *Haaretz* of 24 March 1995, Rabbi Avner enlightened us with his interesting teachings: "A crime against a Jew is always more serious than the same crime

---

[458] On Abramoff, read *Psychoanalysis of Judaism*.

committed against a non-Jew according to the teachings of the Torah." On the other hand, it was also necessary to know that "one who robs a thief does not commit a sin[459]." It is therefore enough to consider other peoples as thieves and murderers, responsible for the misfortunes of the Jewish people.

Under the Third French Republic (1870–1940)

At the time of the Third Republic, financial scandals involving politicians provoked popular anger. In 1892, Edward Drumont, the famous author of *The Jewish France* and editor of the newspaper *La Libre Parole*, accused important politicians of having used their influence and votes to fraudulently grant the Panama Canal Company the right to issue a public loan of 700 million gold francs. In 1892, Edward Drumont's *La Libre Parole* denounced the corruption of parliamentarians, sparking the Panama scandal. Baron and banker Jacques de Reinach was directly accused. He was the distributor of funds that the Suez Company lavished on journalists, MPs and ministers. Cheques confiscated by the courts revealed that the baron had distributed four million gold francs. Most of the major republican newspapers had been bribed. When he learned that he was going to be indicted, the baron took his own life. But the financier's death did not put an end to the case.

The intermediaries in charge of contacting the political men whose cooperation the Company wished to secure were two other Israelis, Emile Arton and Cornelius Herz. Aaron, called Arton, had been particularly in charge of the Bourbon Palace (the seat of the Chamber). As soon as he was discovered, he fled to England, taking his list of "*panamists*" with him. His co-religionist, Cornelius Herz, was of a higher level. From a Jewish family in Besançon and of Bavarian origin, he was a Grand Officer of the Legion of Honour, close to Presidents Grévy and Sadi Carnot, a friend of Freycinet and Clemenceau, whose newspaper he financed. When the scandal came to light, he also fled to England. Arton was arrested in London in 1897 and extradited. He appeared before the judges, but was acquitted. Cornelius Herz was convicted in absentia, as his extradition was never authorised by England.

This is what the Jewish historian Leon Poliakov wrote about the

---

[459] Isaac Bashevis Singer, *The Slave*, 1962, Epublibre, digital publisher German25 (2014), p. 496.

affair: "At the centre of the scandal was a stubborn and megalomaniac old man, the "hero of Suez" Ferdinand de Lesseps, assisted by his son; then in concentric circles appeared a handful of corrupters, dozens of corrupted parliamentarians and hundreds of corrupted journalists, and finally tens of thousands, if not more, of ruined small savers. Now, the main corrupters were Jews (Lévy-Crémieux, Jacques de Reinach, Cornelius Herz, Emile Arton), so that, for once, one was tempted to say that the anti-Semitic propaganda was not gratuitous." But Poliakov could not leave this observation at that and sought to lead the reader to relativise the supposed importance of the influence of the Jews in France at the time, without realising that, in doing so, he was merely comforting the idea of the great harmfulness of the Jewish community: "Their total number was no more than eighty thousand (0.02 per 100 of the French population) of which half were settled in Paris[460]."

In May 1925, a report appeared in the French newspapers announcing that the Eiffel Tower, built for the Universal Exhibition of 1889, was in need of serious restoration, so much so that there were even plans to dismantle it. When this news was announced, "Count" Lustig, a Jewish man of Czechoslovakian origin who had recently landed in France, set to work. He had documents drawn up on the letterheads of the Ministry of Posts and Telegraphs, which was responsible for the tower, and set out to find the most important ferrous metal recycling companies. With his henchman Dan Collins ("Dapper Dan"), whom he had met in New York, he took up residence in the luxurious Hotel Crillon on Place de la Concorde and summoned the five main representatives of these companies to a "confidential meeting", taking great care to point out that only the President of the Republic, the Minister, the Deputy Minister (Lustig himself) and his chief of staff were aware of the project and that under no circumstances was this information to be made public.

The "Vice-Minister" announced the news in the most solemn tone: "Gentlemen, the government will have to demolish the Eiffel Tower! And you are here to bid for it! "A few days later, the "Vice-Minister" went to Mr Poisson's house to announce that he had been chosen. The latter had to present himself within two days with a certified cheque for half of the sum. Lustig had had the audacity to demand a bribe: "Nothing more normal," said the goy, who gave the swindler a substantial tip in addition to the cheque. The two swindlers immediately deposited the cheque and took the train to Austria where they stayed for a while before leaving for New York.

---

[460] Léon Poliakov, *Histoire de l'antisémitisme, tome II,* Point Seuil, 1981, p. 296.

Marthe Hanau came from a Jewish merchant family in Alsace. After the First World War, she opened a perfumery factory, and then, in 1925, she entered the world of finance. He published a newspaper called *La Gazette du Franc*, which became such a reputable selection of stock market tips that some stocks changed according to his buy and sell recommendations. Thanks to the reputation achieved by the newspaper, Marthe Hanau was going to offer all savers to invest their money at interest rates never seen before. But in December 1928, she was arrested for fraud and breach of trust, but was quickly released in 1930. She founded a new newspaper, *Forces*. Martha Hanau was arrested again in April 1932 and committed suicide in her Fresnes prison cell on 14 July 1935, after having been sentenced to three years' unconditional imprisonment.

The Burgundian genre writer Henri Vincenot expressed very well the old resentment of some small French savers in his wonderful book of childhood memories, *La Billebaude (*1978). This is how Henri Vincenot narrated it:

"The Hanau-Stavisky case, which all my contemporaries remember, ended in a huge scandal and an unsolved criminal case. What had happened was not well understood at the time, because, in our region, those schemes seemed very shady and perfectly ridiculous, although I certainly knew that that couple had swindled a lot of good people, such as farmers and craftsmen in our cantons, but also captains of industry who deserved it, and even financiers. It was one of the biggest crooks of all time. Mr Tremblot finally had the revelation of his recklessness and was furious. I was there precisely because it was August. I saw him take all the copies of the *Forces* newspaper that had been his bible and make a big fire on the compost in the vegetable garden.

—It will be used for manure," he cried out, shouting at all the gods of Olympus, furious at having lost his two best fields to buy a bundle of fictitious shares which he threw on the bonfire.

In the afternoon, I picked up the dictionary composed by my compatriot Pierre Larousse and, I don't know why, I looked up the word Forces, which was, as I said, the title of Marta Hanau's diary, and read: "Forces: from the Latin *forces*, large scissors used to shear sheep." Shearing sheep!

I thought it was so funny that I made old Tremblot read it to him, and when he put on his steel vaults, he laughed too, but with a laugh he couldn't wince any more. *Forces*! Hahaha! And we, the bream, we've let ourselves be shorn!

He had risen and, with his good-natured laugh, entered the cellar, saying:

—Shorn they left us my little Blaise, shorn and horned. Hahaha!

He came back with two bottles of the stuff, which he opened screaming:

—It's well deserved, caguën diola! It's well deserved! That's how the Gauls will learn their lesson!

Two customers then arrived to garrison a cavalry yoke; he brought out four large glasses. When they were filled, the bottle was emptied:

—Drink up, caguén diola! Don't miss such a good opportunity to mock the labourers! They've just tanned me till I bleed!

But it turned out that those two clients had also been swindled by the Ethiopian. Then the old man exploded:

—Come on guys, let's wake up the Ethiopian! Come with me! He's going to have a hard time!

The other two said quietly:

—But he didn't wait for you, Tremblot! He left the country a long time ago. He had already sold his house last January, and nobody knew about it!

And so we drank a second bottle, and a third, and with them a head cheese. I gallantly drank my half-litre of that *1909 échézeau* that cousin Petit gave us, one of the best years of the *Côtes-de-nuits*. The Old Man gave me no respite.

—Get yourself a good fuck, rapacious! So that you'll always remember the dirty trick Marta Hanau played on us, so that, as long as you live, you'll be wary of people who have a beautiful cartridge case and shit in the china...

As you can see, that story was for him nothing more than a good burst of sarcastic humour, but it reinforced tremendously the anti-Semitism that was already endemic in our regions, it must be said, the truth[461]."

Among the biggest scandals of the time, one cannot fail to mention the Oustriccase of 1930, whose fraudulent enterprises had cost French savings the trifling sum of two billion Poincaré francs. Albert Oustric was a highly sought-after banker who took a special interest in

---

[461] Henri Vincenot, *La Billebaude*, Denoël, 1978, Folio 1982, p. 319-321. The life of Marthe Hanau was brought to the big screen by the filmmaker Francis Girod, in the film *La Banquière* (1980). The character, played by Romy Schneider, and the script have erased any trace of Judaism in that story. The banker is presented as a victim of political and financial machinations.

companies in difficulty, lending them large sums in exchange for shares. He thus took control of these companies and placed men he trusted on their boards of directors. He increased capital by issuing shares and creating more or less fictitious companies that financed each other. His omnipotence was radiant until the collapse of his bank. The bank had gone bankrupt and other satellite banks followed in a chain. Albert Oustric had corrupted the Minister of Justice, Raoul Perret, who obstructed justice. It was the revelation of the relations between Albert Oustric and Raoul Perret that led to the fall of the Tardieu government on 4 December 1930. On 5 January 1932, Oustric was sentenced to 18 months in prison and fined 3,000 francs for irregularities in transactions involving the securities of shoe companies. He left behind him a 1.5 billion franc hole. Thirty years later, Oustric was a respectable pensioner decorated for deeds of resistance.

A swindler with a formidable charisma, Serge Alexandre Stavisky, nicknamed "Monsieur Alexandre", was at the origin of several scandals, never fully elucidated, which marked the history of the Third Republic. Serge Alexandre Stavisky was born in 1886 in Slobodka, Ukraine. He had come to France at the age of twelve with his father, a dentist, and had been naturalised French in 1910. The young Sacha quickly strayed from the right path, as he was already known for several swindles in 1909. At the beginning of the 1920s, he signed more and more bad cheques. He was indicted several times, but each time the evidence disappeared in a timely manner. The swindler evidently had connections even in the ranks of the police. The Stavinsky mystery had begun.

On 22 July 1926, Stavisky was arrested for the first time. Commissaire Pachot had managed to corner him in the village of Marly-le-Roi, where the swindler, who had been tipped off, was preparing to escape. However, on 28 December 1927, he was granted a medical dispensation and was provisionally released. On his release from prison, Stavisky was a different man, calling himself Serge Alexandre from then on. He then founded the company Alex: jewellery and goldsmiths. Emeralds pawned at the Credit Municipal d'Orléans earned him forty million francs. The emeralds were fakes, but "Monsieur Alexandre" had duly obtained a certificate of authenticity. He also created several companies, whose boards of directors included an inspector of finance, a general, an ambassador or a former prefect of police.

Monsieur Alexandre, always accused but never tried, had become the star of the Parisian elite. He had married a Channel model, Arlette Simon, and lived with her in a palatial mansion. He managed millions, received ministers at his table and got his lawyer elected deputy for Paris. Stavisky had many friends in politics, the press and finance and led a princely life between Paris, Deauville and Chamonix.

However, before the great scandal, he had to repay the Orléans pity fund. He then had the idea of founding his own institution. So, in 1931, he founded a Crédit Municipal in Bayonne, whose director, Tissier, was one of his friends. He did not officially appear on the organisation chart. Moreover, he enjoyed the complicity of the city's radical republican mayor.

Municipal credits were authorised to borrow by placing interest-bearing bonds with the public or with financial institutions within the limits set by law. When a borrower applied for a loan, the Municipal Credit, if it did not have sufficient funds to advance the requested money, had the legal possibility to issue bonds called "cash bonds". These bonds, taken from a cheque book, consisted of three parts. The counterfoil, which remained in the hands of the director of the cash office as a voucher or supporting document, the voucher, the debt security given to the contributor of the funds to the Municipal Credit, and the cheque, which remained in the hands of the controller of the Municipal Credit. In both Orléans and Bayonne, Stavisky, through two directors of Crédit Municipal, had induced the issuance of false bonds. The controller, confident in his hierarchy, agreed to sign blank bonds in advance to the cash manager. On the counterfoil and the voucher, the director would write, say 100 francs, which were entered as income in the accounts. But on the flyers, he would write down a larger sum, depending on the possibilities of the lender, who suspected nothing. Stavisky, who deducted the vouchers from the Municipal Credit, kept the whole sum while only returning to the Municipal Credit the sum corresponding to the amount that had been entered on the counterfoil and the voucher.

For three years the scam ran smoothly, until December 1933, when a routine check by a financial controller uncovered the fraud. On 24 December, Tissier was arrested, and on the 28th, the examining magistrate issued a warrant for Stavisky's arrest.

By the time this scandal broke, which shook the republican regime, 80 files had already been compiled on the case. At the time, before the war, the nationalist press was strong and relentlessly denounced the corruption of the parliamentary regime. The newspapers thus revealed that Dalimier, the Minister of Labour who had signed a circular recommending all banks to buy these safe securities—the Bayonne bonds—was a friend of Stavisky. France was stunned to discover the extent of the fraud: 250 million francs of counterfeit bonds had been put into circulation.

But other accomplices had intervened to obtain successive extensions of the trial. The Public Prosecutor's Office was headed by Pressard, who was the brother-in-law of the President of the Council, Camille Chautemps. In addition, Stavisky had secured control of the mainstream republican press by greasing the hands of journalists and newspaper editors.

Stavisky had fled to hide in a chalet in Chamonix in the Alps, rented under a false name. When police tracked him down and surrounded the house, a gunshot was heard inside: the conman had shot himself in the head and was lying at the foot of the bed. It took two hours to transport him to the nearest hospital where he died in the evening. That was the official version, but Charles Maurras' Action Française[462] accused Camille Chautemps of having him killed to cover up for her brother-in-law, the prosecutor Pressard. Chautemps, who had opposed a commission of enquiry called for by Parliament, set off the powder keg. On 9 January, the day after Stavisky's "suicide", thousands of demonstrators marched on the Boulevard Saint-Germain, shouting "Down with the thieves! In the days that followed, the rightists, the *Camelots du Roi* (King's Militants) and the patriotic leagues occupied the streets. Bars were torn off trees, benches and paving stones to make barricades. There were numerous injuries, hundreds of arrests. On the 27th, Chautemps resigned and was replaced by Daladier. On the morning of 6 February 1934, Action Française and the patriotic leagues gathered in front of the Assembly where the "thieves" had been "locked up". The communists also turned up. At about 4 p.m., the demonstration began its march in front of the Pont de la Concorde. Police cordons blocked the way to the Bourbon Palace. At 6 p.m., as night fell, nothing could be seen, the street lamps had been blown to pieces. The crowd was emboldened but was repelled by a charge of mounted guards. The horses skidded on the marbles that the demonstrators had brought in by the hundreds of kilos. At 7:30 p.m., a shot was fired and the mobile guards fired on the demonstrators. It was a massacre: 15 dead among the demonstrators and 655 wounded. The forces of order deplored one dead and 1660 wounded, but the Republic was safe. Preparations for war against Germany could begin.

Jacob-Leib Talmon, a philosopher and historian of the community,

---

[462] Charles Maurras (1868–1952): Important intellectual of the 20th century. He was the ideologue of the nationalist, monarchist, anti-parliamentary and anti-Semitic *L'Action Française* (NdT).

expressed quite well in his works the rise to power of the Jewish arrivals from Central Europe and Russia during the 19th century: "The social mobility of the Jews surpassed that of all other groups, he wrote. A father could have been a sacristan in a synagogue lost in a village and his son could have ruled an entire empire of capitalist enterprises. While nothing kept the Jew rooted in his town or village, everything appealed to him in the city. All anti-Semitic writers insisted on the alarming influx of Jews into the big cities and capitals. The Jews flocked to those agglomerations which are the centres of any country, where they shine the dazzling lights of publicity and attract the eyes of the whole world."

Already in 1870, it seemed that Jewish financiers held the fate of European nations in their hands: "Europe could not ignore the fact that a Jewish banker—Bleichröder—represented Germany in negotiations on compensation for war damages, while a Rothschild represented France. Emancipation had released volcanic forces that had lain dormant for centuries[463]."

And Jacob-Leib Talmon added: "The influence exerted on the press by Jews became public knowledge, and not only among anti-Semites... The Jewish surnames involved in the public scandals that rocked some countries, from the Panama case to Goldfine (Sherman Adams) or Gruenwald, attracted special attention because they sounded more shocking to the ear than surnames like Dupont, Smith or Schmidt, and because the Western world still regarded the Jew as the heir of Judas Iscariot. In France, when the Panama scandal splashed names like those of Baron de Reinach (born in Frankfurt), Dr. Cornelius Herz (American citizen) and Arton (Italian Jew), cries of "death to the Jews" mingled with those calling for a strong and pure man to cleanse the parliamentary stables and expel the corrupt deputies, just as Jesus had expelled the merchants from the Temple[464]."

On 20 April 1892, Edward Drumont had launched his newspaper, *La Libre Parole*. He wrote in the first issue: "I can perfectly accept, and so can most of the workers with me, that there are millionaires. But things change when we come across people like the Camondos, the Cahens of Antwerp, the Bambergers, the Ephrusis, the Heines, the Mallets, the Bichoffsheims, who have 200, 300, 600 million earned through speculation, who only use these millions to make millions more, who engage in endless gouging, who perpetually destabilise the country with their stock exchange strikes." And Drumont vehemently asserted: "The liquidation of the Jewish millions may be just as easy,

---

[463] See *Psychoanalysis of Judaism* and *Jewish Fanaticism*.
[464] J.— L. Talmon, *Destin d'Israël*, 1965, Calmann-Lévy, 1967, p. 51, 52.

and in any case infinitely less iniquitous, than the confiscation, a hundred years ago, of the dead hand property of the Church and the patrimony of the émigrés[465]."

In 1931, George Bernanos, in *The Great Fear of the Biemensants*, evoked the situation at the end of the 19th century and the 'Jewish conquest', something that Drumont had made 'evident to all'. Bernanos wrote: "A small number of foreigners, convulsively active, kept for centuries apart from national life, suddenly thrown into a society without references, impoverished by war, suddenly seize the very sources of money, immediately organise their conquest, patiently, silently, with a marvellous understanding of modern man, his prejudices, his prejudices, his faults, his immense and stupid hopes. Having become masters of gold, they soon ensure that, in a full egalitarian democracy, they can at the same time be the masters of opinion, that is to say, of morals and morality. They give the liberal bourgeoisie [...] their bosses, they impose themselves by means of the same vices that ruined them so often in the past, the frenzy of appearances, impudence, the cruelty of the satrap. Since the middle of the 19th century, in the first places of the Administration, the Banks, the Judiciary, the Railways or the Mines, everywhere, at last, the heir of the great bourgeois, the polytechnic[466] with glasses, has become accustomed to encountering these strange types who speak with their hands like apes [...] as if they had come from another planet, with their black fur, their features chiselled by millenary anguish[467]." Bernanos also denounced "the invasion by the Jews of the best places, of the best squares." And he added a little further on: "The peaceful invaders" had "first firmly installed themselves in the editorial rooms" where they pressed "as best they could against each other". One would have to be blind not to see "this dazzling success whose mere reading of the yearbooks would suffice today to convince the less well-informed[468]."

On 12 May 1921, Charles Maurras, the editor of the newspaper *L'Action française*, solemnly launched "an appeal to all the anti-Jewish forces of the Universe" for "a universal anti-Jewish policy." The trickery of some of the sons of Israel had clearly aroused the anger of

---

[465] Georges Bernanos, *La Grande Peur des bien-pensants*, 1931, Grasset, Poche, 1969, p. 186, 187. [The émigrés were the opponents of the French Revolution who left the country between 1789 and 1800. That is to say, the aristocrats].

[466] Graduates of l'*École Polytechnique*, the great French engineering school.

[467] Georges Bernanos, *La Grande Peur des bien-pensants*, 1931, Grasset, Poche, 1969, p. 380, 381.

[468] Georges Bernanos, *La Grande Peur des bien-pensants*, 1931, Grasset, Poche, 1969, p. 182.

many Frenchmen.

In Thouars, in September 1920, the retired Major Lécureuil had not hesitated to shoot down with a revolver a merchant who had swindled him, a certain Lévy. Major Lécureuil then took his own life to avoid justice, but his honour was safe.

A few years earlier, on 11 April 1907, the banker M. Benoist-Lévy had seen one of his clients, a certain M. Caroit, enter his offices at 132 rue Rivoli. The latter had asked for a few minutes' meeting with the banker, who received him in his office. Caroit then took two revolvers out of his pockets and, with both hands, opened fire on the banker, who fell, his chest riddled with bullets. The employees rushed to the aid of their boss and heard the man say: "He has ruined me, I have taken revenge." During his trial, his lawyer, Henri Robert, had declared: "If you believe that honest Frenchmen must be protected, then let them be exculpated without a doubt! Their wealth is made of our misery; their hopes, of our sorrows! The verdict you are about to render will have a great social impact. If well-earned wealth is respectable, the house of Benoist-Lévy is a factory of misery, and the jury must consider that the revenge of the victims is the professional risk of the unconscionable banker." His plea received great applause, and Caroit was acquitted. The Court awarded twenty duros in damages to Benoist-Lévy's widow[469].

---

[469] *Gazette des Tribunaux*, 10 and 11 March 1908; Archives of Emmanuel Ratier.

2. The Traffickers

Monsieur Michel and Monsieur Joseph

Two traffickers had amassed immense fortunes during the German occupation: Mandel Szkolnikoff, nicknamed Monsieur Michel, and Joseph Joanovici, nicknamed Monsieur Joseph. Monsieur Michel was of Russian origin and had specialised in textiles and foodstuffs. He had not hesitated to denounce to his SS friends, through his German wife (an Aryan), other Jewish competitors and to take over their business premises and warehouses. It was Monsieur Michel who led the German police to the Sentier warehouses. The occupied area was his hunting ground. His profits were so fabulous that he had acquired the largest hotels on the Côte d'Azur. He had bought hotel chains, real estate and trading companies, restaurants, cafés and breweries in Paris. This real estate fortune had been valued in 1945 at two billion 1985 francs.

Monsieur Joseph was a Bessarabian Jew. He was born in 1905 in Chisinau. He was a plump, seemingly harmless little man. In his early twenties, he had saved enough money to travel to Paris where he founded a scrap metal salvage company. He soon set up branches in Belgium and Holland. He travelled endlessly. By 1939, Joseph Joanovici had become one of the biggest scrap metal dealers in Paris and was proud to help Paul Reynaud's government forge the steel of victory. After the debacle of June 1940, the prudent dealer had converted to the orthodox religion and gone to work for Germany. He was engaged in discovering stocks of old metals useful to the German war machine, buying them at legal tender and reselling them to the Germans at bootleg prices. In the first six months, he had already made a profit of two billion dollars[470].

Joanovici had also taken over the leather market, a crucial and highly sought-after commodity for the Germans who had just invaded the Soviet Union. At the time, Monsieur Joseph's monthly turnover was around 200 million francs in 1989. He made other fabulous profits in

---

[470] In Canada, millionaire Morris Lax had been convicted in February 1977 for the theft of several tons of copper. Morris Lax frequented Israeli political circles and was a friend of Menahem Begin, the former Prime Minister of Israel. He was found murdered on his property in 1993.

the occupied zone in textiles and foodstuffs.

He rubbed shoulders with the crème de la crème of German Paris, SS, Wehrmacht officers, collaborators[471], and had made contact with the head of the French Gestapo in Lauriston Street ("*La Carlingue*[472] "), Henri Lafont. The notorious Dr. Petiot was part of the gang. Monsieur Joseph turned to him to make the corpses of his competitors, often Jews, rag-pickers and scrap merchants, disappear. The Romanian Jewess Eryan Kahane, a spy in the service of the Gestapo, served as a liaison agent between the Lafont-Joanovici gang and Dr. Petiot. She would send her co-religionists seeking to flee the country to the doctor. Petiot killed them and recovered for the gang the money and jewellery they wanted to take with them. On 9 March 1944, the fire brigade was alerted by neighbours who had been disturbed for several days by the smell coming from a chimney of Dr. Petiot's mansion at 21 rue La Sueur. After knocking on the door of the house and waiting in vain for the doctor to arrive, the firemen decided to enter by breaking a window. The hum of a boiler and the smell drew them directly into the cellar. There they discovered mangled human bodies ready to be incinerated. The fugitive Petiot managed to escape and enlisted in the French Forces of the Interior (FFI), rising to the rank of captain under the name "Valéry". Arrested in October 1944, he claimed responsibility for 63 murders during his trial, proclaiming that they were the corpses of collaborators and Germans. He was sentenced to death and guillotined in the Santé prison in May 1946.

When the Nazis decided to ruin the British economy by disposing of millions of counterfeit pounds sterling in neutral countries, Monsieur Michel and Monsieur Joseph, who had proved their worth, were recruited to put their skills at the service of this clandestine operation. Armed with Aryan passports, they travelled around Switzerland, Spain and Portugal, opening bank accounts for the future, collecting lion's fees in the process.

---

[471] Maurice Rajsfus published a study on the collaboration of French Jews with the Vichy regime and the German authorities: *Des Juifs dans la collaboration, L'UGIF (1941-1944)*, Éditions Études et Documentation Internationales, 1980. It deals with the institutional role of the UGIF (General Union of Israelites in France), the predecessor of today's CRIF, and how this organisation collaborated with the authorities to deport Jews fleeing from Eastern Europe (i.e. non-French Eastern Jews). This is a little-known, highly problematic and explosive taboo subject that has torn the Jewish community in France apart. (NdT).

[472] *The Carlingue* was formed on the basis of the collusion between the French underworld and the German authorities during the Occupation, both for the repression and torture of communist resisters, and for the plundering of the wealth, persecution and plunder of Jews.

But at the end of 1943, fortunes changed, and Monsieur Michel fled to Spain with his German muse and his French and Jewish agents. But in his wife's luggage, French police discovered jewellery and precious stones worth 1.4 billion 1989 francs. Monsieur Michel was eventually extorted in Spain by former Gestapo agents who had fled the execution squads. His body was found on 17 June 1945 in a field between Burgos and Madrid.

Monsieur Joseph was more far-sighted, for he had shared with a resistance group a portion of the fabulous profits he made from the Germans. He had bought from Lafont the weapons parachuted by the Allies and requisitioned by the French Gestapo, and then supplied a network of resistance fighters within the police prefecture. At the same time, he equipped and clothed the Free Guard of the Militia and the North African Brigade fighting the communist maquis. Monsieur Joseph had managed to get away with playing on both sides since 1943. Before the landings, he delivered to the Resistance stocks of arms and ammunition stolen from the Germans." Joano is a good guy, he's one of us! "he was said in the FFI. Indeed, hadn't he given the best proof of this by tipping off the whereabouts of his old friends Bony and Laffont, who were hiding at Baslin's farm in Seine-et-Marne." It was Bony who gave me the address. He wanted me to go with them to Spain. The poor guy, he hadn't heard anything about it! The next day, they raided Baslin's farm.

During the Liberation, Joseph Joanovici's power exceeded that of the prefect. In terms of business, a new market was opening up to him: that of American surpluses. He had a monopoly on French territory thanks to his relations with the government. Moreover, he had made the witnesses of his past disappear. In Paris and elsewhere in France, his former collaborators were mysteriously murdered. As for Petiot, he had been guillotined.

Monsieur Joseph knew above all how to be generous: "There is no secret," he would later reveal. When he earned ten, he distributed five and everyone was happy! "Only that the distribution involved huge sums, over two million per day (*Passages*, 18 June 1989). In September 1944, a magistrate who demanded an account from him was immediately called to order and sent back. Since he insisted, Joano preferred not to cause any more commotion and advised his friends not to do anything. He spent only a month in prison and was cleared of all suspicion. He resumed his activities, dealing in everything, metals, foreign currency, etc. It was a rather ugly case that led to his downfall two years later. Before the liberation, he had denounced to the Nazis some monks who were hiding weapons for the maquis, and a young resistance fighter, a witness to that crime, had been murdered by his men. An upright examining magistrate managed to convict him, but the sentence was incredibly light, reflecting the influence of the trafficker: five years' imprisonment, a paltry fine and national degradation and indignity, which this stateless man did not care about. On his release from prison, he was placed under house arrest in Mende, although this did not prevent him from regularly going on excursions to Switzerland. At the end of his life, Monsieur Joseph tried to settle in Israel, but death overtook him. He died in 1965 in a clinic in Clichy, taking his heavy and compromising secrets to his grave.

Shenanigans and company

The image of Jews has always been rather negative among the common people, both in Europe and in the Muslim world. Jews have always been collectively regarded as people who got the best jobs using dubious procedures. The Jewish philosopher Jacob-Leib Talmon wrote: "In the dictionaries of all European languages, the term "Jew" is defined as a synonym for thief, liar and usurer[473]."

Philip Roth, a rather mediocre but very famous American novelist translated into all languages, had one of his novel characters say the following: "Every industry with Jews in it is full of bribery and corruption and networking ... the guys end up sticking their noses in every business, and they fuck it up[474]."

We saw how they were the biggest international traffickers of alcohol and drugs. But from time immemorial, they trafficked in all kinds of goods. Here is another testimony, falsely naïve, from another famous Jewish writer, Joseph Roth, who was of German culture and writing in the early 20th century at the time of Sigmund Freud and Stefan Zweig. Listening to him, it seems that the condition of Jews in the Austro-Hungarian Empire was miserable: "They were smugglers. They brought flour, meat and eggs from Hungary. In Hungary they were put in jail because they hoarded foodstuffs. And in Austria they were locked up because they smuggled non-rationed foodstuffs into the country. They made life easier for the Viennese and put them in prison."

In his *memoirs*, Elie Wiesel, a native of the small town of Sighetu

---

[473] J.— L. Talmon, *Destin d'Israël*, 1965, Calmann-Lévy, 1967, p. 44 [Read the RAE definition of "judiada"].
[474] Philip Roth, *Operation Shylock*, Debolsillo Penguin Random House, Barcelona, 2005, p. 298.

Marmatiei in northern Romania, gave a convergent account of his childhood memories: "I was unaware that respected members of the community were engaged in smuggling and trafficking in foreign currency; I was also unaware that there was in our neighbourhood ... a brothel[475]."

Joseph Roth wrote about German Jews: "There are also East-Jewish criminals in Berlin. Pickpockets, bride swindlers, swindlers, counterfeiters of bank notes, inflation-mongers." But beware: "There is hardly a single mugger. And not a single murderer or robber who murders[476]."

The June 1869 issue of the *Revue des Deux-Mondes* published an article entitled *Le clan du vol à Paris (The Clan of Thievery in Paris)*, which described every imaginable category of thieves. Of these thirty-five pages, seventeen lines, i.e. a little more than a third of a page, or about one hundredth of the article, was devoted to the Jews:

"The thief who gathers and hoards is an anomaly found only in very few avaricious Jews." (...) There are families who seem destined to theft from generation to generation; "it is the Jews, chiefly, who, devoting themselves to humble but incessant mischief, fulfil these kinds of hereditary functions. They are to be feared, not for their daring, for they seldom murder, but for their persistence in evil, for the inviolable secrecy kept among them, for the patience they display, and the facilities they have for hiding themselves in the houses of their co-religionists. The Jewish robbers seldom go on the warpath against society; but they are always in a state of dull struggle; it would seem that they take revenge, that they are within their rights, and that after all they do nothing more than recover, when the occasion arises, a good which was violently taken from their ancestors by others. Sometimes they get together in gangs and steal in a big way, as when doing business; they have their correspondents, their intermediaries, their buyers, their account books... Everything is good for them: from lead in the pipes to a handkerchief in a pocket. The boss usually takes the title of merchandise commissioner, and makes expeditions to South America, Germany and Russia. The Hebrew-German slang they speak among themselves is incomprehensible and serves to mislead investigations[477]. They are the first receivers in the world and disguise their actions behind an ostentatiously practised trade[478]." "

---

[475] Elie Wiesel, *Mémoires, tome I*, Le Seuil, 1994, p. 47.
[476] Joseph Roth, *Judíos errantes*, Acantilado 164, Barcelona, 2008, p. 81, 83.
[477] See footnote 84.
[478] Roger Gougenot des Mousseaux, *Los Judíos y la judeización de los pueblos*

In a book published in Paris in 1847, Cerfberr de Medelsheim acknowledged that the number of convicted Jews was easily double that of other citizens: "These crimes are swindling, plagiarism, usury, trafficking, fraudulent bankruptcy, smuggling, counterfeiting of coins, cheating in collections, stellionate, bribery, fraud, fraud in all its forms and with all aggravating factors".

The publicist Roger Gougenot des Mousseaux, who reported these lines in 1869, also wrote: "Almost every week some monstrous trial of criminals of the worst kind takes place in the civil courts of Vienna. Jews mostly, the scandalous thefts, shameful swindles, amount to enormous sums. The illicit booty has long since been in safe keeping when the criminals are arrested; and after having spent a few years in the shadows, it is left to them to enjoy themselves at their leisure[479]." And Gougenot added: "To the disgrace and moral and material ruin of Austria, the press is almost entirely managed by Jews."

Also in 1847, in his *Letter on Kiev (Lettre sur Kiev)*, published by the Balzacian Notebooks in 1927, the great French novelist Honoré de Balzac recounted what he had seen in Central and Eastern Europe: "I have seen them in small towns, swarming about like flies, going to their synagogues in pontifical costumes whose strangeness made me smile." And he continued: "The Jews are extremely thievish, they are first cousins of the Chinese in that respect. You can't imagine how many horses are stolen, especially on the frontiers. A Jew does not shrink from murder as soon as a large sum is involved. This race has unique customs and superstitions, it has preserved wild traditions. Thus, when in a family appears a Jew lacking the spirit of rapine, incapable of washing ducats in acid, cutting up roubles, cheating Christians, and who lives in idleness, the family feeds him, gives him money, he is considered a genius; it is the opposite of civilised countries, where the man of genius passes for an imbecile in the eyes of the bourgeois; but then the saint of the Jewish family must continually read the Bible, fast and pray, like a fakir."

The famous Jewish historian Leon Poliakov also taught us in his monumental *History of Anti-Semitism* that Jewish criminality was an old story. This is what he observed in Germany: "A curious

---

cristianos, pdf version. Translated into English by Professor Noemí Coronel and the invaluable collaboration of the Catholic Nationalism team. Argentina, 2013, Introduction, p. XLV-XLVI.

[479] A. Cerfberr de Medelsheim, *Les Juifs, leur histoire, leurs mœurs, etc.* p. 2, 3, 29, Paris 1847. In Roger Gougenot des Mousseaux, *Les Juifs et la judeisation des peuples chrétiennes*, pdf version. Translated into English by Professor Noemí Coronel and the invaluable collaboration of the Catholic Nationalism team. Argentina, 2013, p. 145, 146

phenomenon, and how characteristic is that Jewish banditry of which the first traces can be detected at the beginning of the 16th century, and of which no equivalent can be found in the millennia-long history of the dispersion." According to Poliakov, this was probably a "great historical novelty".

In the following centuries," continued Poliakov, "there is evidence of the existence of organised gangs, some purely Jewish, others mixed, Judeo-Christian, about which the police officers make noteworthy observations. The Jewish bandits, we are informed, are good husbands and fathers of families, and lead an orderly family life; and, what is more, they are of exemplary piety and never steal on holidays and Saturdays... Although within the German underworld they constitute but a small minority, they set the standard[480]."

Let us recall here the words of Jacques Attali, in the weekly *L'Express* of 10 January 2002, when he presented his book *The Jews, the World and Money. Referring to* the Jewish gangsters of the 1930s in the United States, Attali declared without laughing: "A great historical novelty. Until then, Jews had a phobia of delinquency and criminality."

The gold rush

It is undeniable that the Jews had for centuries had the aptitude for amassing great fortunes. We have seen some examples in our previous books of how these cosmopolitan billionaires who work tirelessly for the establishment of a world without borders use their influence over the governments of still independent nations to open them up to more "democracy", to more "tolerance". In 2007, a study published by a major American newspaper, the American magazine *Vanity Fair*, showed that out of the 100 richest personalities, more than half belonged to the Jewish community. There were certainly poor Jews, but the fact was that Jews were vastly over-represented among the world's billionaires. A 26 February 2008 article in the *Jerusalem Post* also reported that Jews were the *wealthiest religious group in the United States*, with 46% having "six-figure incomes" per year, i.e. at least $100,000. Hindus reached 43%, but no other group reached 30% and the US average was 18%. All this evidence did not prevent Jewish intellectuals from regularly railing against these "hateful prejudices of another age".

The novelist Irene Némirovsky was born in Kiev in 1903. The

---

[480] Léon Poliakov, *Histoire de l'antisémitisme, Tome II*, Point Seuil, 1981, p. 379.

daughter of wealthy Jewish bankers, her family left Ukraine at the time of the Bolshevik revolution to settle in Paris. Her novel, *The Dogs and the Wolves*, tells the story of a family of Jewish bankers who settled in France after the First World War. Harry Sinner, the banker's son, marries a Frenchwoman named Laurence Delarcher, of the old Delarcher bank. Harry's uncles, who ran the bank, had in a few years acquired enough power to influence the French government: "We have taken over enormously important entities. The governments we have supported have provided us with solid, appreciable wealth in return..." (p. 169)." (p. 169)

Irene Némirovsky explained why Jews were so eager to amass money: "Money was good for anyone, but for the Jew it was like the water he drank and the air he breathed. How to live without money? How to pay bribes? How to get one's children into school when one had filled the quota? How to get one's children into school when the quota had been filled? How to get permission to go here or there, to sell this or that? How to get out of military service? Oh, my God! How to live without money? [...] for a Jew there was no salvation but wealth[481]."

But the Sinner bank went bankrupt after a financial scandal. The whole family gathered for the occasion, before the expulsion that had been ordered: "In the evening, one after the other, all Aunt Rhaissa's friends arrived, all the émigrés whom she had met in Paris. It was an extraordinary gathering of withered faces, thick hair, dull looks ... there were Jewish women from Odessa and Kiev; [...] wives or widows of financiers under suspicion, dead, on the run or in prison ... for all these women, the announcement of the expulsion of one of them had a precise and ominous meaning. It meant that, sooner or later, they could also be victims of the same measure[482]."

In another novel by Irene Némirovsky entitled *The Wine of Solitude*, we see again "the image of "the Jewish race" [...] always consumed by a kind of fever, by the gold fever." And about David Golder, the character in her eponymous first novel, we also read: "It is above all the "pride, the immense pride of his race" that characterises David Golder in Irène's eyes[483]." A journalist from *L'Univers israélite*, Nina Gourfinkel, had interviewed Irene Némirovsky before the war. Irene then tried to defend herself against certain accusations: "That's

---

[481] Irène Némirovsky, *Los perros y los lobos*, Ediciones Salamandra, 2016, Barcelona, p. 24, 25, 75

[482] Irène Némirovsky, *Los perros y los lobos*, Ediciones Salamandra, 2016, Barcelona, p. 210, 211.

[483] Jonathan Weiss, *Irène Némirovsky*, Éditions de Félin. 2005, p. 105, 106

how I saw them", she repeated several times without seeming to convince the journalist." They were Russian Jews, she replied again. Evidently, Jews love money."

After the triumph of the Popular Front, the resurgence of anti-Semitism in France had led him to rethink his way of seeing things. In *Les Nouvelles littéraires* of 4 June 1939, he expressed his regret: "How could I have written such a thing? If I were to write *David Golder* now, I would do it very differently... The atmosphere has changed so much[484]!". After the Second World War, both in film and literature, only poor and persecuted Jews were depicted.

In Prussia, before the French Revolution, Jews had taken control of great wealth, and the Berlin aristocracy, artists and philosophers seemed to have surrendered at their feet. In the salons of Berlin, wrote historian Léon Poliakov, "they surpassed the Christian businessmen in both initiative and wealth: in the words of Mirabeau, the only millionaires in Berlin were Jews." The richest of them "had lavish mansions built for them, and they were intimate with high society: high officials and members of the Prussian nobility hastened to their receptions." But dealing with the upper echelons caused these upstart Jews to disregard the law of Moses, and "some of them disregarded it altogether[485] ", claimed Poliakov, who continued: "In Berlin, this domination of the unjudaised Jews was that of the worldly cliques: to make a name for oneself, nothing was worth the patronage of a Jewish salon. Even the uncompromising Fichte sought such protection." His first Berlinese lecture actually took place in 1800, in the salon of Mme Samuel-Salomon Lévy. He had been introduced to Jewish circles by Dorothea Mendelssohn, the eldest daughter of the Jewish Enlightenment philosopher who embodied the Jewish *Aufklärung* (The Haskalah).

Leon Poliakov explained how Jewish merchants supplanted Christian ones: "Among the commercial stratagems used by the Jews to the fury and despair of their Christian competitors, some have long since become customary, while others are still reprehensible; but they all earned them the favour of their clientele, as well as an unflattering reputation; although on the latter side, they had little to lose. Here are some of them: Advertising and solicitation of clientele, i.e." sales promotion", practices strictly forbidden by corporate regulations, but favourite economic weapons of the Jews in the form of attracting customers in the public squares, in the halls of taverns and inns, and in

---

[484] Jonathan Weiss, *Irène Némirovsky*, Éditions de Félin. 2005, p. 59, 71
[485] Léon Poliakov, *Histoire de l'antisémitisme, Tome II*, Point Seuil, 1981, p. 89, 93.

the streets of the ghettos. And the exit of goods of dubious origin, whether they were spoils of war, contraband, plunder of soldiers, or robberies." And Poliakov wrote a little further on: "The ability of the Jews to cover up with their Jewishness all sorts of operations disloyal or contrary to the code of honour has certainly facilitated numerous spectacular ascensions[486]."

In Tsarist Russia, the situation was the same if one is to believe Kalinine, a Soviet economist and statesman who also recognised the superiority of the Jews in this field: "The Jews showed special abilities to enrich themselves by taking advantage of the conditions of the environment, whether honestly or dishonestly. It is evident that these Jews were a head above the Russian merchants[487]."

Money was a means to corrupt princes or deputies. In return, they covered the Jews with honours. Roger Gougenot des Mousseaux, who observed the situation in France at the end of the Second Empire, wrote for example: "The Jews, who form a compact body, a national association, a family whose members support each other... The Jews who possess gold, press, talent, character ... possess for this the highest degree of the gift of being noticed, of being feared, of being flattered and flattered by the powerful of the earth, and we see them always abusing this gift. Positions, public functions, privileges, honours, fall on Israel's head from all sides[488]."

In 17th century Poland, a scholar like Simon Starowolski rebelled against foreign domination: "In the domains of numerous powerful lords, the Jews become a beloved and protected nation [...] having perverted the hearts of their masters. Who leases Polish property? — The Jew! Who is the esteemed physician? — The Jew! Who is the famous merchant? — The Jew! Who collects the customs duties? — The Jew! Who is the most faithful servant? the Jew! — The Jew! Who enjoys the greatest protection from the civil authorities and from the autonomous noble institutions? — The Jew! Who has the easiest access to the master? — The Jew! Who has the greatest grace and confidence at court? — The Jew! Who most often wins trials unjustly and illegitimately? — The Jew! Who is most likely to get away without suffering the consequences of the greatest imposture, subterfuge,

---

[486] Léon Poliakov, *Histoire de l'antisémitisme, Tome I,* Point Seuil, 1981, p. 430, 442. [Werner Sombart in his seminal work, *The Jews and Economic Life (1911)* analysed these questions and others].

[487] Léon Poliakov, *Histoire de l'antisémitisme, Tome II,* Point Seuil, 1981, p. 220.

[488] Roger Gougenot des Mousseaux, *Los Judíos y la judeización de los pueblos cristianos,* pdf version. Translated into Spanish by Professor Noemí Coronel and the invaluable collaboration of the Catholic Nationalism team. Argentina, 2013, p. 327

treachery, plunder, robbery and other unpublished crimes? — The Jew[489]!"

Here is now the testimony of Isaac Bashevis Singer, a famous novelist from the Jewish community who won the Nobel Prize for literature in 1978. In his novel *The Slave*, he narrated the tribulations of Jacob, a poor Jew in 17th century Poland:

"The trade of Poland was still in the hands of the Jews, who even trafficked in ecclesiastical ornaments, although they were forbidden by law to do so. Jewish merchants went to Prussia, Bohemia, Austria and Italy; they imported silks, velvets, wine, coffee, spices, jewellery and arms, and exported salt, oil, linen, butter, eggs, rye, corn, barley, honey and furs. Neither the aristocracy nor the peasants understood business[490]."

Naturally, some Jews prospered from usury, an activity that had nevertheless caused them many problems for centuries: "The moneylenders choked their clients with their demands—circumventing the law against usury [...] Envy and avarice were hidden under a cloak of piety. The Jews had drawn no lessons from their misfortune; on the contrary, suffering had debased them[491]."

Jacob then met Mr Pilitzki in a Polish village. And he made no secret of his feelings about his fellow man: "We know, we know. Your damned Talmud teaches you to deceive Christians. You have been driven out everywhere, but King Casimir opened our doors wide to you. And how do you repay us? You have established a new Palestine here. You ridicule and curse us in Hebrew, spit on our relics and blaspheme our God ten times a day. Jmelnitski[492] taught you a lesson, but you did not have enough. And the Polish gentleman pointed out here a problem that is still topical through the centuries: "You love all enemies of Poland, be they Swedes, Muscovites or Prussians[493]."

The master then offered him a glass of wine, which Jacob politely refused: "Forgive me, your excellency, but my religion forbids it.

---

[489] Simon Starowolski, *La Vermine de la mauvaise conscience*, in Daniel Tollet, *Les Textes judéophobes et judéophiles dans l'Europe chrétienne à l'époque moderne*, Presses Universitaires de France, 2000, p. 208.

[490] Isaac Bashevis Singer, *The Slave*, 1962, Epublibre, digital publisher German25 (2014), p. 352.

[491] Isaac Bashevis Singer, *The Slave*, 1962, Epublibre, digital publisher German25 (2014), p. 328, 330.

[492] Khmelnitsky had raised the Ukrainian peasants in 1648 against the Polish overlords and the Jews.

[493] Isaac Bashevis Singer, *The Slave*, 1962, Epublibre, digital publisher German25 (2014), p. 462, 463. Jews do not stop encouraging immigration wherever they settle.

Pilitzki stiffened. —Oh, well, so your religion forbids it. So you can swindle Christians, but you can't drink with them[494]. And who forbids it? The Talmud, of course, which also teaches you to cheat Christians.

—Christians are not mentioned once in the Talmud; only idolaters are mentioned.

—The Talmud considers Christians idolaters... Sit down, Jew. I'm not going to hurt you. Sit here. Very well! The Countess and I believe that faith should not be imposed on anyone. Here we have no Inquisition, as in Spain. Poland is a free country, too free for its misfortune. That is why it is on the road to ruin. Let me ask you a question. You've been waiting for the Messiah for a thousand years. I say a thousand! More than fifteen hundred, and the Messiah does not come. The reason is clear. He has already come and revealed the truth of God. But you are a stubborn people and you stand apart. You consider our flesh unclean and our wine an abomination. You are not allowed to marry our daughters. You think you are God's chosen people. Well, what has He chosen for you? That you should live in dark Jewish quarters and wear emblems of yellow cloth. I have travelled and seen how Jews live abroad. They are rich and think only of money. Everywhere they are treated like spiders. Why don't you think it over and give up the Talmud?

—I can convince no one, your excellency," said Jacob, who was beginning to stammer. I have inherited the faith of my fathers, and I follow it as best I know how[495]."

Pillage of the defeated countries

Martin Gray was one of the hundreds of thousands of survivors of what were called, paradoxically, still at the beginning of the 21st century, the "death camps". In *In the Name of All Mine*, an international *best-seller* published in 1971, he recounted his ordeal in Treblinka. Miraculously, he managed to survive and make it through by joining a Polish partisan group immediately after liberation, where he was able

---

[494] Talmud, *Avodah Zarah* (72a and b): "[...] When you serve wine, do not let a gentile come near to help you, lest you let your guard down and rest the vessel in the hands of the gentile, and the wine will come out because of its strength and be forbidden..." *Yoreh De'ah* (120:1): "Whoever acquires from an idol worshipper a metal or glass vessel of food or vessels or vessels or covered with lead inside—even if they are new—must immerse them in a *mikveh* [purification bath] or in a stream that has forty *se'ot*." (www.sefaria.org).
[495] Isaac Bashevis Singer, *The Slave*, 1962, Epublibre, digital publisher German25 (2014), p. 500–505.

to unleash his "revenge"—a term that recurs in his text and in Jewish literature in general. After the war, he left for the United States, New York, where he would find his family, which, again miraculously, had not been exterminated[496]." I multiplied my activities, gambling, sales, services, shows. I accumulated dollars. At night, I would lie in bed, exhausted." (page 365).

Later, he would go into the antiques trade, especially porcelain, feverishly buying everything he could find. He travelled to Europe, which had just emerged from the war: "My principle was to buy and sell quickly. A small profit multiplied produces a big profit. The goods arrived. Berlin became for me a distant suburb of New York. For months I wandered like that, from one continent to another... I soon added London to my itinerary. I shopped, I phoned, I jumped from taxi to plane. A woman said to him one day: "Enjoy life, Martin," she said..." Learn to be happy, Martin, you're always running away." And Martin explained: "I preferred work to the peace she offered me. Maybe one day a woman would manage to curb my career, maybe one day I would take a liking to rest." (page 381)

"In Berlin the market was becoming difficult... All the antique dealers from the United States had descended on Berlin, emptying the city and the whole of Germany of its porcelain... —Buy, buy everything, Tolek," he said to his partner." I could see the inkwells piling up in piles, the cymbals untidy... Tolek said: 'You're crazy, Martin." They'd really been sweeping everything up." There's nothing left, Tolek repeated."

But Martin-Mendle-Miétek knew what he was doing: "After two days of searching, we found an old craftsman painter who was willing to repair our porcelain. But I hadn't reached my goal ... not yet," he says, "and I didn't want to give up. And I didn't want to give up. Never. I heard that there were factories in Bavaria. I rented a car and drove south. I stopped in Moshendorf. There I was at the spring. I visited a factory, saw the workers in their white blouses leaning over the porcelain, watching the kilns. I found the KPM, the Royal Porcelain Manufactory, a gold mine." Tolek laughed: "You're crazy, Miétek, crazy, the KPM is official, only for kings and presidents." But Miétek was a prince: "I was well worth its founder, the King of Saxony, we were well worth it, all of us, my people, those emperors, those kings,

---

[496] Martin Gray's book was written in collaboration with Max Gallo. He wrote in *Le Monde* on 28 November 1983, at the time of the premiere of Robert Enrico's film: "I wrote *Au Nom de tous les miens* with him, using both my profession as a historian and my vocation as a novelist."

those German princes for whom the KPM had worked exclusively since the 18th century. I, Miétek, a little Jew from the ghetto, decided that the KPM would work for me. It was long and difficult. I asked to see the director, and he received me. —You have a great tradition," I said. You will certainly be able to do this. —I put the models and photographs I had brought with me on the office table. He defended himself inch by inch, but I interrupted him, "I have money, and I buy everything. Finally, we closed the deal, and now I was not only an importer of authentic antiques, but also an imitator! The big cylindrical kilns of the KPM were set to heat up for my porcelain, for me, a survivor of Treblinka. This was also a revenge! And a stroke of genius." As you can see, Miétek was making authentic 18th century antiques in the middle of the 20th century: "The antiques made by the KPM were authentic. And the dollars I accumulated by the thousands built up the walls of my fortress[497]."

But it didn't end there: "My work became even more accelerated: New York, London, Paris, Frankfurt, Berlin, New York, the streets of those cities, the faces of those cities. The antique dealers who spoke Russian or Polish at the flea markets, the Germans in Berlin, the decorators who paraded in the shop on 3rd Avenue..." Boxes piled up in the shop." It started up again: New York, London, Paris, Frankfurt, Berlin, New York[498]." (page 382)." I accumulated dollars, invested, sold... I was now rich, a citizen of the United States, an importer, a manufacturer, I had opened a branch in Canada and another in Havana. I owned houses; I put my money in the stock market. I went from capital to capital, for me Paris and Berlin were suburbs in the suburbs... I went from one woman to another: none managed to silence in me the voices, the faces, the places that obsessed me." (page 387)

His friend Tolek said to him one day: "Whether you're hunting Nazis or inkwells, you're always the same, Martin. You'll never change. You get the fever. —I'm always late," he replied. I was late for a childhood, for happiness, I was running after them. I couldn't stop." (page 378).

"In Moshendorf, the factory worked for me; in Paris, London and Berlin my purchases continued. I added other imports to my boxes of objets d'art; I bought and resold European cars by the hundreds; I had

---

[497] Martin Gray, *Au nom de tous les miens*, Robert Laffont, 1971, Poche, 1984, p. 383, 384 and *In the Name of All My Own*, digital edition at https://es.scribd.com.
[498] The characteristic frenzy is recognisable here; see also Marek Halter, in *Planetary Hopes*; Samuel Pisar, in *Psychoanalysis of Judaism*; "Hannah" and "the flies", in *Jewish Fanaticism*.

antique chandeliers made in Paris, and from the West Coast, the South and the Midwest, antique dealers begged me to reserve them for them. I was rich and I was forced to work harder and harder to try to fill the abyss, to repress the nightmares. My journeys were even faster. Tolek kept saying: "You're a runaway horse, Miétek. One day, you will foam at the mouth." I was going in a straight line, and so I would go on till the end." (page 388). And again: "My business was never better: I cashed, I invested, I bought, I cashed again." (page 393). And all this, of course, "In the name of all my people". Thus Germany, the defeated country, was plundered from top to bottom.

After the fall of the Soviet Union, Russia, as we have seen in these pages, had also been the prey of major international predators. *L'Express* of 16 July 1998 mentioned the case of Andrei Kozlenok. This Muscovite had been arrested in Athens in January 1998 and extradited to Russia on 17 June. The scam in which he had been involved, with the approval of the highest authorities in his country, involved some 187 million dollars. Thanks to his contacts and support—he was close to Viktor Chernomyrdine, the former Russian Prime Minister—he had managed to illegally circumvent the monopoly of De Beers, which held the exclusive rights to market 95% of Russian rough diamonds on the international market. A friend of Boris Yeltsin's, Yevgeny Bytchkov, head of the former Russian Gemstones Committee, had commissioned him in 1994 to sell directly abroad. As part of this dubious trade, he was also authorised to take 5 tonnes of gold, jewellery, goldsmiths' wares, etc. from the Tsarist era out of the Gokhran (Federal Reserve). These treasures were supposed to serve as collateral for loans from the Bank of America.

In October 1917, after the fall of the Tsar and the victory of the Bolsheviks, Russia had already been subjected to the same treatment. The sons of Israel, so numerous in all echelons of power, took full advantage of the situation. The great Russian writer Aleksandr Solzhenitsyn had addressed the issue in his book on Russian-Jewish relations, *Two Hundred Years Together*, published in 2003, mentioning the case of the American businessman Armand Hammer, Lenin's favourite. Armand Hammer "unashamedly exported to the United States the treasures of the imperial collections. He returned frequently to Moscow, under Stalin and Khrushchev, to continue importing freighters full of Fabergé icons, paintings, porcelains and goldsmiths' wares."

These words were confirmed by Jacques Attali in *The Jews, the World and Money*: Armand Hammer (...) became one of the leaders of

East-West trade, reconciling his friendship with Lenin and his full adherence to the capitalist system. He exploits asbestos mines in the USSR, imports cars, tractors, and buys Russian works of art from the State in exchange for industrial products[499]."

Honoré de Balzac had portrayed a number of Jewish characters in his *Comédie humaine*. In *Cousin Pons* (1847), he depicted a Jew called Elie Magnus, who travelled around Europe in search of works of art to sell: "Élie Magus, by dint of buying diamonds and reselling them, of knocking about with paintings and lace, with valuable antiques and enamels, with precious sculptures and ancient goldsmith's work, had amassed an immense fortune without anyone knowing about it…" Balzac had previously specified, "In the Middle Ages, persecutions obliged Jews to wear rags to ward off suspicion, to always complain, to whine, to appear the most miserable."

---

[499] Jacques Attali, *Les Juifs, le monde et l'argent*.

3. Anti-Semitism

In every age since antiquity, in both the Christian and Muslim worlds, many illustrious men have been alarmed by the subversive ideas conveyed by the Jews, as well as by the manoeuvres of some of them. For Judaism, in its very essence, was fatally in conflict with the rest of humanity.

Jews have always been obsessed with "peace" on the face of the earth (*shalom*). They dreamed of a world in which conflicts would have disappeared, and this world of peace would, they believed, be the prelude to the coming of their long-awaited Messiah. To finally put an end to conflict on earth, there was no choice but to make all differences between men disappear, to abolish nations, frontiers and all particularisms, and to encourage by all means universal intermarriage and the dissolution of old traditions. Social classes were also to disappear. It was "ineluctable". Nothing was to remain of the old world. Thus, when all has been destroyed, when nothing remains of the old civilisations, when men are reduced to the role of mere consumers, the Jewish people will still be there, intact and triumphant. And at last they will be recognised by all as the "chosen people of God".

Anti-Semitism through the ages

In these conditions, we can understand why the Jews had been able to arouse fierce opposition to their politico-religious project, especially since many of them had acquired great wealth by methods that were not always considered honest by the natives. Anti-Semitism was therefore as old as Judaism itself. At the end of the 6th century AD, the Christian Gregory of Tours spoke of a "wicked and perfidious nation", although five hundred years before him, the Roman Tacitus already wrote about them: "No people has ever so hated others as the Jewish people, none in turn so repulsed them, and none have deservedly earned such implacable hatreds[500]." (*Beatus Rhenanus*). And even four hundred years before Tacitus, Hecataeus of Abdera, a Greek historian living in Egypt, had noticed the irreducible opposition between the Jews

---

[500] Léon Poliakov, *Histoire de l'antisémitisme, Tome I*, Point Seuil, 1981, p. 232, 361.

and the rest of mankind. This he said of Moses: "The sacrifices and customs he established were completely different from those of the other nations; in memory of the exile of his people, he instituted a way of life contrary to humanity and hospitality[501]"." But we shall not recapitulate here all the opinions expressed by illustrious men against the Jews, for it would be impossible.

Recriminations against Jewish "deceit" and "perfidy" have been recorded in countless writings throughout history. Jewish merchants were accused of hoarding wealth by unfair and sometimes more or less fraudulent methods. The actual afflictions of Christian merchants driven to misery were repeated from year to year, from province to province. Thus, for example, in 1734, the merchants' guilds of the city of Stendal in Prussia complained to the authorities: "The Jew is a pike in a tent-hole... He penetrates everything, takes the bread out of the merchant's mouth, sucks the blood of the poor, and, sordidly, does not pay the taxes[502]."

The deputies of the Chamber of Commerce of Toulouse had in their turn denounced in 1744: "This Jewish nation seems to be dragging itself along in order to better elevate itself and enrich itself..."." In the same year, the corporations of Montpellier declared: "We implore you to stop the progress of this nation." But the royal administration already seemed to have surrendered to the ideas in vogue in the "Age of Enlightenment".

We can also quote the famous 1765 injunction of the merchants and traders of Paris against the admission of Jews: "The Jews can be compared to hornets that enter beehives to kill the bees, open their bellies and extract the honey from their guts..."."

On the eve of the French Revolution, Malesherbes, Louis XVI's Minister of State, spoke in these terms: "There still exists in the hearts of most Christians a very strong hatred against the Jewish nation, a hatred based on the memory of the crime of their ancestors and corroborated by the habit of the Jews of all countries to engage in business which Christians see as the cause of their ruin[503]."

In 1753, the very liberal England had also experienced an anti-Jewish explosion after the government submitted a bill for the naturalisation of Jews to the Houses for approval. The popular agitation was "of a violence rarely equalled in the annals of English history",

---

[501] Georges Nataf, *Les Sources païennes de l'antisémitisme*, Berg Int., 2001.
[502] Léon Poliakov, *Histoire de l'antisémitisme, Tome I,* Point Seuil, 1981, p. 433.
[503] Léon Poliakov, *Histoire de l'antisémitisme, Tome I,* Point Seuil, 1981, p. 444, 446, 447.

wrote Léon Poliakov two centuries later. Naturally, Poliakov gave the phenomenon a very personal explanation. The historian denounced "dark ancestral fears which had risen to the surface at the mere thought that members of the deicide sect would be allowed to exercise full human and Christian rights[504]."

Léon Poliakov quoted the German Enlightenment philosopher par excellence, Immanuel Kant, who, in his *Anthropology*, advocated "euthanasia" for Judaism. Kant wrote: "The Palestinians who live among us have incurred by their usurious spirit since their exile, also as far as the great masses are concerned, the not unfounded reputation of defrauding others. It seems, it is true, extravagant to imagine a nation of defrauders; but it is not less extravagant to imagine a nation of mere merchants, of whom, by far the greater part, united by an old superstition, recognised by the list in which they live, do not seek civil honours, but wish to make up for this loss by the profits obtained by defrauding the people under whose protection they find themselves, and even by defrauding each other. Now this cannot be otherwise in a whole nation of mere merchants or non-producing members of society (e.g., the Jews of Poland); therefore, their constitution, sanctioned by ancient laws, even recognised by us, among whom they live (and who have in common with them certain holy books), though they make the saying "buyer, open your eyes," the supreme principle of their morality in dealing with us, cannot be abolished without inconsistency. Instead of drawing useless plans for moralising this people on this point of fraud and honesty, I prefer to state my presumption as to the origin of this singular constitution (i.e., that of a people of mere merchants[505])." Kant was, however, an optimist and believed that once freed from their "Jewish spirit", the Jews would know how to mend their ways." His conception was therefore more Christian than racist," wrote Poliakov.

At the same time, in Germany, the humanist thinker Herder used the same language while advocating assimilation: "For thousands of years, since its very beginning, the people of God, having its homeland established by Heaven, has been vegetating like a parasitic plant on the trunk of foreign nations; a cunning and sordid race..." For Fichte, on the other hand, the problem of the Jews could only be solved by their expulsion from German lands." To protect ourselves against them, I see only one way: to conquer for them their promised land and send them all away," he wrote in his first major work on the French Revolution in 1793.

---

[504] Léon Poliakov, *Histoire de l'antisémitisme, Tome I*, Point Seuil, 1981, p. 452.
[505] Emmanuel Kant, *Antropología*, Alianza Editorial, 1991, Madrid, note 1 p. 123.

In a competition organised by the Metz academy in 1785 on the theme: *Are there ways to make the Jews happier and more useful in France*, Abbot Gregory, a priest of the diocese of Metz, was awarded a prize for his essay entitled *Essay on the physical, moral and political regeneration of the Jews.* Abbot Gregory, who wanted to bring them by means of gentleness to the Christian religion, had no choice, he too, but to note: "They are parasitic plants that eat away at the substance of the tree they attack."

Lorraine and especially Alsace, regions where many Jews lived, had expressed their discontent. The book of complaints of the clergy of Colmar, in 1789, contained some explicit passages: "The Jews, by their vexations, their plundering, the greedy duplicity of which they daily offer such pernicious examples, [are] the principal and first cause of the misery of the people, of the loss of energy and moral depravity of a class of people once famous for that Germanic faith so highly praised." The popular reaction was such that, in 1789, thousands of Jews had to take refuge in Switzerland.

The conventional[506] Baudot, commissar of the armies of the Rhine and Moselle, proposed a new kind of regeneration for the Jews: "Everywhere they put greed before love of country, and their ridiculous superstitions before reason. I know that some of them serve in our armies, but—excluding them from the discussion we must have about their conduct—would it not be expedient to consider a *guillotine* regeneration with regard to them? " The II thermidor, the Jews were reproached for their continual agiotage, whereupon the district municipalities were ordered "not to take their eyes off these dangerous beings, who are citizen-devouring leeches[507]."

Under these conditions, the emancipation of the Jews proposed by the Revolution and the status of equal rights was tantamount to letting the fox into the henhouse. For Gougenot des Mousseaux, it was therefore necessary to protect Christians against the aggressiveness of the Hebrews. In 1869, he wrote in this connection: "A large Viennese newspaper (*La Presse*) edited and run by Jews has as its motto: Equal rights for all. But to accord the same right to people who know neither morality nor Christian duty, is to make vampires of those who are bound by Christian principles and who cannot imitate the wandering abuses of unbridled competition." " (page 146).

Napoleon had also sought to regenerate the Jews by de-Judaising

---

[506] Conventionnaires: Assembly members of the National Convention of the First French Republic (1792–1795). It was the constituent assembly.
[507] Léon Poliakov, *Histoire de l'antisémitisme, Tome II*, Point Seuil, 1981, p. 106, 111.

them: "The Jews," he wrote, "are a vile, cowardly and cruel people. They are caterpillars, locusts that plague the countryside... The evil comes above all from that indigestible compilation called the Talmud, where is exposed, alongside their true biblical traditions, the most corrupt morals when it comes to their relations with Christians." And about this "race", he said: "I would like to prevent it from spreading evil[508]." He proposed to the Jews to enlist in his armies to reconquer the Promised Land, but they turned a deaf ear to his appeal and the project was put aside along with other oriental mirages. At that time there was no organised authority, no central government of the Jews in France. Napoleon then decided to create a 71-member Grand Sanhedrin, which, after eighteen centuries, would re-establish the tradition of a government of Israel. The Grand Sanhedrin met for the first time in February 1807. Napoleon was then seen by all European princes as the Antichrist himself. A month after its solemn inauguration, the Sanhedrin was dissolved.

Recriminations against the Jews were recurrent, everywhere and at all times. We have seen what Tsar Ivan the Terrible thought in 1550, when he reproached his Polish ally for wanting to make him admit Jews into Russia: "They bring poisoned drugs into our state and cause much harm to our people." Ivan the Terrible's successors were equally suspicious. A century and a half later, Peter the Great, who, although he had invited valuable foreigners to come to Russia, had nevertheless expressed great reservations about the Jews in his *Manifesto*: "I would rather see Mohammedans and pagans in my dominions than Jews. They are thieves and deceivers. I extirpate evil, I do not propagate it; there will be for them in Russia neither lodging nor trade, in spite of all their efforts and attempts to bribe my environment[509]."

In the territories conquered by Peter the Great in the Ukraine, Catherine I, who succeeded him, had issued the following edict: "The male and female Jews in the Ukraine, and in other Russian cities, are all to be expelled immediately from the frontiers of Russia. From now on, they are not to be admitted to Russia under any pretext whatsoever, and it is to be strictly enforced everywhere." Such were the origins of the famous "zone of residence", which confined the Empire's Jews to the western periphery until the February 1917 revolution[510].

In the Holy Empire, the Jews had been expelled from Vienna in

---

[508] Léon Poliakov, *Histoire de l'antisémitisme, Tome II*, Point Seuil, 1981, p.
[509] Aleksandr Solzhenitsyn, *Deux siècles ensemble, Tome I*, Fayard, 2002, p. 29.
[510] Léon Poliakov, *Histoire de l'antisémitisme, Tome I*, Point Seuil, 1981, p. 420. On the "zone of residence" read the introduction to *Jewish Fanaticism*.

1670 by Leopold I, but they had managed to "persuade" the king, and fifteen years later they were back in the square. In Prussia, the Grand Elector Frederick William, the "sergeant king", had taken them in after their expulsion from Vienna. Only the nobility could have some sympathy for the Jews, because of certain services the Jews could render them (money lending, speculation). Among the advice on good government that the king gave to his son, the future Frederick the Great, were these lines: "As for the Jews, there are too many in our country who have not received letters of protection from me. You must expel them, for the Jews are the locusts of a country and the ruin of the Christians. I beg you not to grant them new letters of protection, even if they offer you money ... for the most honest Jew is a swindler and a scoundrel. You may be sure of it[511]."

In England, William Prynne, a very popular publicist in the mid-17th century, had rebelled against Cromwell's admission of the Jews into the country. They were "a race of evil-doers, a generation of vipers, greedily doing evil with both hands according to all the nations around them, as bad or worse than Sodom and Gomorrah[512]."

In the following century, his compatriot Alexander Pope, raised a prayer in one of his satires: "We beseech Thee Lord, remove from us the hands of the barbarous and cruel Jews who, though they have a horror of the blood of swine's pâtés, are no less vehemently bloodthirsty[513]."

Pierre de Lancre was born in Bordeaux in 1553, in a city that had welcomed some Spanish Marranos. He had studied law and theology in France and Turin, before becoming an alderman in the Bordeaux Parliament in 1582, before marrying Montaigne's grand-niece in 1588. He described the Jews as follows: "More perfidious and unfaithful than demons ... the Jews are worthy of all execration, and as true criminals of all divine and human majesty, they deserve to be punished with the greatest tortures: the brazier, molten lead, boiling oil, pitch, wax and sulphur all incorporated together would not generate torments sufficiently exact, sensitive and cruel for the punishment of such great and horrible crimes that those people ordinarily commit[514]..."

In Germany, Martin Luther had published his famous pamphlet *On the Jews and Their Lies* in 1542: "They possess our money and our

---

[511]Léon Poliakov, *Histoire de l'antisémitisme, Tome I*, Point Seuil, 1981, p. 435.
[512]Daniel Tollet, *Les Textes judéophobes et judéophiles dans l'Europe chrétienne à l'époque moderne*, Presses Universitaires de France, 2000, p. 172.
[513]Léon Poliakov, *Histoire de l'antisémitisme, Tome I*, Point Seuil, 1981, p. 451.
[514]Léon Poliakov, *Histoire de l'antisémitisme, Tome I*, Point Seuil, 1981, p. 318.

goods and are our masters in our own country and in their exile. A thief is condemned to hang for stealing ten guilders; if he steals on the way, he loses his head. But when a Jew steals and steals ten tons of gold through usury, he is esteemed even more than God Himself. As proof of this we cite the insolent boasting with which they strengthen their faith and give vent to their venomous hatred of us, thus saying among themselves: "Be patient and observe how God is with us, and does not forsake His people even in exile. We do not work, and yet we enjoy prosperity and leisure. The cursed goyim have to work for us, but we take their money." A few months later, he published another pamphlet entitled *Vom Schem Hamephoras*: "They are much stronger in scorn than I am, and they have a God who has become a master in the art of scorn, he is called the Devil and the spirit of Evil[515]."

Luther, who had observed how the vocabulary of the criminals was full of slang words from the Hebrew[516], wrote: "Besides, we do not know to this day which devil brought them to our country. It was certainly not us who brought them from Jerusalem. Besides, no one is holding them here now. The country and the roads are open for them to return to their land whenever they wish. If they did, we would gladly give them presents for the occasion, it would be a feast, because for our country they are a heavy burden, a plague, a pestilence and a real misfortune."

Jews were often depicted in the guise of a sow. The sow "who suckled them and fornicated with them on innumerable stone monuments", wrote Poliakov." One of these high reliefs (most of which have disappeared) is described by Martin Luther in his famous pamphlet *Vom Schem Hamephoras*, in the following terms: "Here in Wittenberg, in our church, a sow was hewn out of the stone: piglets and Jews suckle her, while behind her stands a rabbi lifting her right leg and with his left hand pulling her tail, bending down and diligently contemplating behind the tail the Talmud, as if he wanted to learn something very subtle and very special[517]"." Luther had written many letters to have them expelled or their privileges taken away. He had succeeded in Saxony, Brandenburg and Silesia. At the end of the 14th century, in Italy, artists assimilated them to scorpions. In paintings and frescoes, this perfidious animal par excellence was often present on the banners of the Jews, on their shields and on their robes.

In the Middle Ages, in the middle of the 12th century, we discover

---

[515]Léon Poliakov, *Histoire de l'antisémitisme, Tome I*, Point Seuil, 1981, p. 365, 367.
[516]See note 85.
[517]Léon Poliakov, *Histoire de l'antisémitisme, Tome I*, Point Seuil, 1981, p. 311.

the great figure of Peter the Venerable, the famous abbot of Cluny. At the time of the Crusades, he had revolted against the domination of the usurers and had sent an injunction to King Louis VII in which he strongly denounced the Jews and "vigorously rose up against the unimaginable invasions of this race which concentrates in its hands all the treasures of France." He judged that "it was urgent to repress the audacity". He asked the king why he was going to the other side of the world to fight the Saracens, when he left among his subjects "infidels infinitely more guilty towards Christ than the Mohammedans"." It is time that justice should be done, and far be it from me, however, to think "that they should be put to death; but what I ask is that they should be punished in proportion to their perfidy. And what kind of punishment more fitting than that which is at once a condemnation of iniquity and a satisfaction given to charity? What more just than to divest them of what they have accumulated by fraud? They have cheated and plundered like thieves; and, what is worse, like thieves secured to this day with impunity! What I say is widely and publicly notorious." "It is neither by the simple labours of agriculture, nor by regular service in armies, nor by the exercise of honest and useful functions, that they fill their shops with grain, their taverns with wine, their coffers with gold and silver. What have they not amassed with all that cunning enabled them to wrest from Christians, and to buy stealthily and at a vile price from robbers! "

In 1180, as soon as Philip Augustus was seated on the throne, recriminations against the Jews were again rife. They were accused, wrote Gougenot des Mousseaux, "of having ruined the people by their usury, of having made themselves masters, by this unjust means, of an infinity of lands and of almost half the houses of Paris; of having received as payment the sacred ciboria, the treasures of the churches and of having profaned them. It is further added that they reduced many poor Christians to slavery and that they crucify them every year on Good Friday". Philip Augustus, "at last persuaded of the malignity of the Jews, expelled them from his States in the year 1182; confiscated their property with the exception of their furniture; ... restored his subjects to the possession of the inheritances they had usurped and relieved them of all the debts they owed by paying him only one-fifth[518]."

In reality, the expulsions of the Jews were continuous throughout

---

[518] Roger Gougenot des Mousseaux, *Los Judíos y la judeización de los pueblos cristianos*, pdf version. Translated into Spanish by Professor Noemí Coronel and the invaluable collaboration of the Catholic Nationalism team. Argentina, 2013, p. 168, 170

history. Jews were expelled, sooner or later, from all European countries, from all European principalities, from Mainz in 1012 to Moscow in 1891, from Naples in 1496, from Hungary in 1360 and 1582, from Prague in 1557, and so on. But the Jewish financiers, using their power of corruption with the princes, always found a way to reintroduce their congeners into the square. The centralised states such as England, France and Spain were better able to defend themselves than the Holy Germanic Empire, which was fragmented into quasi-independent states.

In Paris, at the end of a great controversy between Jewish and Christian doctors, the Talmud had been condemned. King Saint-Louis had ordered the seizure of all copies found in the country, and on 6 June 1242, whole carts of books were solemnly burned in the Place de Grève. But neither Philip Augustus nor Saint Louis had used radical methods. It was Philip the Fair who expelled the Jews in 1306. The Jews were reintroduced soon after, under the reign of his son, and were again expelled before returning again under certain conditions. On 17 September 1394, on Yom Kippur, King Charles VI expelled them radically, for several centuries.

King Edward I of England had already expelled them in 1290, but the Jews had returned 350 years later, after a civil war and the establishment of a short-lived republic by Cromwell in the mid-17th century. Spain had been rid of them in 1492. In Germany, then divided into hundreds of principalities, expulsions were frequent. In 1388, the last general expulsion from Strasbourg had been declared; in 1394, they were expelled from the Palatinate; in 1420, they were expelled from Austria; in 1424, Freiburg and Zurich followed suit; in 1426, they had to leave through the gate of Cologne; in 1432, Saxony wanted no more to do with them; the city of Augsburg rejected them in 1439; Würzburg expelled them in 1453; Breslau in 1454, etc, etc, etc, etc. By the end of the century, the list of expulsions snowballed[519]. These expulsions could be followed by readmissions, so that the Jews of Mainz, for example, had been expelled four times in the course of history.

Rome was finally the only major city in Europe where Jews were never expelled[520]. In the 14th century, Italy was the main host country for Jews expelled from France and German countries. One day, however, there was a reaction. In 1555, after his election to the throne of St. Peter, Pope Paul VI proclaimed in his bull *Cum nimis absurdum*

---

[519]Léon Poliakov, *Histoire de l'antisémitisme, Tome I,* Point Seuil, 1981, p. 300.
[520]However, on 18 January 2008, we learned that eleven Jewish *souvenir* sellers had demonstrated against their expulsion from St. Peter's Square in the Vatican.

that it was absurd to allow Jews to live in the better quarters of the city, to hire Christian servants and to let them generally abuse Christian kindness. Paul VI took ruthless measures, first ordering the concentration of the Jews behind the walls of a ghetto on the edge of Tibre and forbidding them to trade except in second-hand clothes. Basically, these provisions were a summary of the canon law of past centuries, but contrary to all his predecessors, the uncompromising Paul VI had applied it to the letter.

The end of the Middle Ages was the time when the old Jewish quarters were transformed into ghettos. Jews were only allowed to frequent the Christian quarters during the day, and in the evening they had to enter the ghetto, the gates of which were locked. Behind the gates of the ghetto, the Jewish community was closed in on itself, which corresponded to the wishes of the rabbis who feared above all else the assimilation of the Jews into Christian society. In reality, however, the Jews had long since isolated themselves from the rest of humanity.

Nahum Goldmann, the founder of the World Jewish Congress wrote in 1976, in *The Jewish Paradox*: "The Jews are the most separatist people in the world. Their faith in the notion of a chosen people is the basis of their whole religion. Over the centuries, the Jews have intensified their separation from the non-Jewish world; they have rejected, and continue to reject, intermarriage; they have erected one wall after another to protect their existence 'apart', and they have built their own ghetto: their *shtetl* [Jewish villages] in Eastern Europe, the *mellah* in Morocco." And Nahum Goldmann insisted later in his text: "The ghetto is historically a Jewish invention. It is false to say that the goyim forced the Jews to separate themselves from other societies. When the Christians confirmed the ghettos, Jews were already living in them[521]."

The very famous Elie Wiesel said the same in his *Memoirs*: "In ancient times, Jewish quarters were created by the Jews themselves who feared foreign influences. This was the case with the communities of Rome, Antioch and Alexandria. It was only later that the ghetto was imposed on them under different names[522]."

In 2008, Théo Klein, former president of the Representative Council of Jewish Institutions in France (Crif)[523], stated unequivocally: "We were isolated before we were enclosed: the gates of the ghetto were

---

[521] Nahum Goldmann, *Le Paradoxe juif*, Stock, 1976, p. 16, 83, 84
[522] Elie Wiesel, *Mémoires, Tome I*, Éditions du Seuil, 1994, p. 83.
[523] French counterpart of the AIPAC (American Israel Public Affairs Committee) in the US.

installed around the places where we had previously regrouped[524]." Indeed, the first ghetto, that of Venice in 1516, was "originally a Jewish initiative[525]." According to Poliakov, an expression was apparently very common in the ghetto: "By God, I'll cut your throat and go and become a Christian". Baptism, in fact, was seen as a means of escape from criminal prosecution.

Jewish uniqueness

In his 1894 book *Anti-Semitism, its history and causes*, Bernard Lazare—an intellectual of the community—provided several explanations for the origin of Jewish uniqueness. The Jewish people, he explained, were too weak, numerically speaking, to be able to compete militarily with the Christians and Muslims: "They could not dream of attacking these two powers head-on. Therefore the Jew tried to triumph over them by cunning, and both developed in him the spirit of caution. He acquired a strange ingenuity and an uncommon subtlety." Money enabled him to triumph over his enemies: but it had a drawback: "The pursuit of gold, pursued unceasingly, degraded him. It weakened his conscience. It lowered him and gave him the habits of a liar." And Bernard Lazare added: "In the war which, in order to live, he had to wage against the world and its civil and religious law, he could not win except by intrigue and this wretch, destined to humiliations and insults and forced to cower under blows, grievances and invectives, could only by cunning avenge himself on his enemies, his torturers and his executioners. For him, robbery and bad faith became weapons: the only weapons he could use. He therefore contrived to sharpen, complicate and disguise them[526]."

Jewish historians were also in the habit of arguing that the Jews' practice of usury (lending at interest) was because all other trades were forbidden to them. In short, they had become rich because they had been oppressed. In fact, from time immemorial, and long before the Christian era, usury had been a very popular and lucrative activity among the Jews. Usury enabled Jews to devote themselves to the study of the Talmud, the most respected activity in the Jewish world. This was

---

[524]Théo Klein, *Sortir du ghetto*, Liana Levi, 2008, in *Philosophie Magazine*, March 2008.
[525]Michel Herszlikowicz, *Philosophie de l'antisémitisme*, Presses Universitaires de France, 1985, p. 76.
[526]Bernard Lazare, *Anti-Semitism, its history and causes*, Editions La Bastille, Digital edition, 2011, p. 156.

confirmed by Leon Poliakov: "Moreover, usury and study are not considered incompatible, quite the contrary: one text even specifies that usury has the advantage of leaving all the free time necessary for study[527]."

Gougenot des Mousseaux also recalled that of the six hundred and thirteen precepts (mitzvot) that Jews must observe, the one hundred and ninety-eighth commanded against usury with non-Jews[528].

Zalkind-Hourwitz gave us an insight into the Talmudic spirit. He was a Polish Talmudist who had been a clothier in Paris before becoming curator of the eastern department of the King's Library. Isolated in France, the man had become progressively detached from his community. In 1789, Hourwitz had published an *Apology of the Jews*, in response to the competition opened in 1785 by the Metz academy on the subject: *Are there ways to make the Jews happier and more useful in France?* In it, he fought the anti-Jewish polemicists: "They say that the Jews deserve to be oppressed because they are usurers and thieves; instead of saying that they are usurers and thieves because they are oppressed and because all legitimate professions are forbidden to them[529]." Two centuries after the emancipation of the Jews by the French Revolution, we can realise that the phrase in its first version was correct. Hourwitz, a "de-Judaised" Jew, as Poliakov defined him, had undoubtedly retained some very characteristic features of the Talmudic spirit.

The image of the poor Jew, oppressed and persecuted for no reason, was one that the Jews were happy to keep alive over the centuries. The very famous Elie Wiesel, for example, recounted in his *memoirs* the misfortunes that befell him and his family before the Second World War. Originally from a village in northern Romania, he had had to endure harassment by the authorities and manifestations of anti-Semitism." Special army and gendarmerie units burst into Jewish houses. Inspection, search, threats: you have to hand over jewellery, silver service, foreign currency, precious stones, valuables. My father tries to make us smile: "They will be disappointed... In most Jewish houses, they will only find misery... I hope they take that away too"." At that time, the Jews in Romania were poor, very poor, and persecuted for no reason.

However, a dozen pages later, Elie Wiesel incidentally wrote that,

---

[527] Léon Poliakov, *Histoire de l'antisémitisme, Tome I*, Point Seuil, 1981, p. 330.
[528] Roger Gougenot des Mousseaux, *The Jews and the Judeoization of Christian peoples*.
[529] Léon Poliakov, *Histoire de l'antisémitisme, Tome II*, Point Seuil, 1981, p. 65.

in the face of the danger, the family had hidden all their wealth, burying it carefully: "Last night, late into the night, we improvised buriers and dug a dozen holes under the trees to deposit what was left of our jewellery, valuables and money. For my part, I buried the gold watch I had received as a Bar-mitzvah gift[530]."

The Jewish drive for profit could also be explained by the teachings of the Torah. In the magazine *L'Express* of 10 January 2002, Jacques Attali presented his latest book, *The Jews, the World and Money*: "In the Bible, wealth is a means to serve God, to be worthy of him. One of the founding texts says: "You shall love God with all your strength" and one of the commentaries specifies: "That means with all your wealth". Therefore: "The richer you are, the more means you will have to serve God". Wealth is a means, not an end. Provided it is a created wealth, an increase of the wealth of the world and not a wealth taken from another. This is why fertile property (land, livestock) is especially prized. In fact, Abraham became rich from his flocks." Undoubtedly, that comment was very enlightening about the love of God.

Jacques Attali added another comment: "For the Jewish people, insofar as the fertility of goods is healthy, there is no reason to prohibit lending at interest to a non-Jew, since interest is only the mark of the fertility of money. Among Jews, on the other hand, one must lend without interest, in the name of charity. It is even prescribed to give loans at negative interest to the very poor."

In his book, Attali presented another example: "Isaac and Jacob confirm the need to enrich themselves in order to please God. Isaac accumulates animals." He got richer and richer until he became extremely wealthy. He had large flocks of sheep, large herds of cattle and many slaves" (*Genesis XXVI, 13–14*). Next, Jacob "became very rich, and had many flocks, and maidservants, and menservants, and camels, and asses" (*Genesis XXX, 43*). God blesses his fortune and allows him to buy his right of entailed estate from his brother Esau, proof that everything is monetised, even for a plate of lentils[531]…"

The Jews recognise themselves as the descendants of Jacob, who was depicted in Genesis as a gentle and delicate being, while the Gentiles were, according to them, the descendants of Esau, the elder

---

[530] Elie Wiesel, *Mémoires, tome I*, Le Seuil, 1994, p. 82, 94. Readers of our previous books know that Jewish intellectuals often say one thing and the opposite in their books, sometimes even on the same page. The word "paradox" is in fact recurrent under their pen.
[531] Jacques Attali, *Les Juifs, le monde et l'argent*.

brother, who was of a brutal, hunting and warlike nature. Jacob, as is well known, was also very cunning and unscrupulous: he had deceived his father and had managed to appropriate the inheritance that normally belonged to his elder brother.

Attali gave the example of the departure of the Jewish people from Egypt. According to tradition, in 1212 BC, the Jews left for the land of Canaan: "Egyptian texts of the time also mention the expulsion of a sick people, or of a people with a leprous king, and an uprising of foreign slaves." The Hebrews had left the country laden with wealth. Indeed, the day before, "the prediction made long ago to Abraham: "You shall go out of that land with great riches" (*Genesis 15, 13–14*) was fulfilled; then, the command given to Moses before the burning bush: "Every woman shall ask her neighbour and her host for vessels of gold and silver; garments with which you shall cover your children, and you shall despoil Egypt" (*Exodus 3:21-22*); then, the order conveyed by Moses to the heads of the tribes just before the departure: "Let every man ask for gold and silver" (*Exodus 11:1-2–3*); finally, the brutal summary of the situation, a little further on: "They asked and they despoiled" (*Exodus 12:35-36*)." "Tens of thousands of women, men and children set out, some rich in gold, silver and all kinds of goods, even with slaves" across the Sinai desert. The Hebrews were then going to make their golden calf. As for the Egyptian soldiers who pursued them and who ended up, it seems, submerged in the waters of the Red Sea, perhaps they were simply trying to recover what belonged to them?

In short, the Israelites had abused the trust of the Egyptians. And "to those who are surprised to see the slaves run away rich, commentators will reply, down the centuries, that these riches are due to them by way of compensation for the labour provided free of charge during the years of slavery, or as a parting gift, or even as tribute paid to the victors by a defeated army[532]."

Indeed, Jews felt the need to correct the injustice of which they believed themselves to be victims, through some kind of extra-legal self-compensatory action. In a way, as the Israeli publicist Israel Shamir (who became Israel Adam Shamir after his conversion to Christian orthodoxy) wrote, Holocaust museums represent "a not inconsiderable explanatory factor for the increase in Jewish criminality", as it reinforces in Jews the feeling of their victimisation.

In the June 1989 issue of the Jewish monthly *Passages*, entitled "*The truth about Jewish crooks*", lawyer Francis Terqem confirmed this idea: Jewish criminality, he said, "could be sustained by a somewhat

---

[532] Jacques Attali, *Les Juifs, le monde et l'argent*.

paranoid idea, by the feeling that, in the end, one acts against others because they have previously been hostile to Jews. We would thus have a kind of collective revenge."

The pursuit of profit and the love of riches surely represented one of the characteristic features of the Jewish community, and indeed they have most often been caricatured as such. It is clear that the Jews, who believed neither in hell, nor in an afterlife, nor in any reincarnation, were less subject to moral obligations than the other peoples of the earth and were more inclined to invest in their sojourn on earth.

Elie Wiesel, who had spent some time in India, had shared his reflections on the Hindureligion with his readers. That religion could not satisfy him: "I have no right to postpone my salvation to the next reincarnation, he wrote: what I do not do today, I will never have the chance to do again. Self-realisation is only possible in the moment it happens. I return from India more Jewish than before." Indeed, "in Judaism, it is in earthly life that man must fulfil himself[533]."

In the Old Testament, as Otto Weininger observed, there is no trace of a belief in immortality[534]. A French media philosopher like Michel Onfray—an atheist who nevertheless boasted of being a specialist on religions—did not seem to know that the Jews did not believe in an afterlife. During a television programme, *Culture et dépendance*, in 2005, journalist Elisabeth Lévy and essayist Jacques Attali had to confirm this for him to admit it.

"Most Jews I know do not believe in either heaven or hell," wrote Rich Cohen[535]. Another Jewish intellectual, Pierre Paraf, also wrote: "I do not believe in the future life as most religions teach us[536]." And we also know that all the Marxist intellectuals of all obediences, the great majority of whom were of Jewish origin, were complete atheists. It is therefore not impossible, after all, that fear of punishment in the hereafter was a major factor in forcing human beings into that minimum of morality and decency of which some Jews seem to be utterly devoid.

As we were able to study in our previous books, in reality the Jewish religion is above all the expression of a political project whose aim is to prepare for the coming of the long-awaited Messiah, working tirelessly for "peace" on the face of the earth, a peace that should be, according to them, "absolute and definitive". That is why Jewish intellectuals of all persuasions continually advocate cosmopolitanism,

---

[533] Elie Wiesel, *Mémoires, tome I*, Le Seuil, 1994, p. 288, 283.
[534] On Otto Weininger, read *Psychoanalysis of Judaism*.
[535] Rich Cohen, *Yiddish Connection*, 1998, Denoël, 2000, Folio, p. 242
[536] Pierre Paraf, *Quand Israël aima*, 1929, Les belles lettres, 2000, p. 9.

"tolerance", the disappearance of borders, immigration and universal miscegenation. When all civilisations, cultures and traditions and all peoples have disappeared, then only the small Jewish people will remain, who will finally be able to guide what is left of humanity. From this perspective, the disappearance of states and nations is indeed "ineluctable".

Incidentally, Bernard-Henri Lévy, a well-known philosopher, even outside France, had explained the problem very well in one of his books in 1994: "I believe that entire states will fall under the blows of the planetary mafias; and that if not under their blows, it will be at their hands. I think the world is on the way to becoming a ghetto and the planet a mafia... And I do not believe that we will get out of this by merely muttering, as some clever people are already doing, that the world has always been a conglomeration of ghettos, states a mafia in disguise, and civil societies a contractual association of evildoers, and that it is therefore better that things should be told as they are, that humanity should pass into confessions, and that we should not pretend surprise when the masks of the world fall. I believe in a future fragmentation of the world, in a pulverisation of states and a dissolution of the old, peaceful nations." And Lévy finally shared his opinion with us: "Isn't this better[537]?"

In short, Bernard-Henri Lévy declared to us the most simple thing in the world that justified the mafias, judged in the end to be less perverse than states and sedentary nations. In the end, perhaps that is the ideal of the *planetary* philosophers: the destruction of nations and, in their place, the control of the planet by transnational mafias.

Paris, June 2008
January 2016 for this second edition.

---

[537] Bernard-Henri Lévy, *La Pureté dangereuse*, Grasset, 1994, p. 184.

Epilogue

After the publication of *The Jewish Mafia* in June 2008, our research work on Judaism continued, as some of the information gathered concerned Jewish criminality.

Thus, our *Mirror of Judaism*, published in February 2009, contains a short three-page chapter on hustlers and traffickers before and after the Second World War.

In our *History of Antisemitism*, published in April 2010, we included a very instructive chapter of a dozen pages on Jewish criminality in Germany in the early 19th century. The information was taken from a German book published in Berlin in 1841, written by a high-ranking Prussian official named A. F. Thiele: *Die jüdischen Gauner in Deutschland, ihre Taktik, ihre Eigenthümlichkeit, ihre Sprache* (*The Jewish swindlers in Germany, their tactics, their idiosyncrasy, their language*). In the course of his work, Thiele had seen how the Jewish community produced the biggest criminals and the most dangerous criminals. Through police files and records, he described the "world", the mentality of the criminals, the nomadism of the Jews, their identity theft and the general scope of their criminal activities. His aim was to facilitate the work of German policemen, to show how organised gangs functioned and to provide investigators with a working tool. He denied being anti-Jewish: his work was simply that of a criminologist. The first edition of the book (*"auf Kosten des Verfassers"*, published at the author's own expense) sold out within two months.

It is also worth noting here the publication of a book that had escaped our attention. In 2004, an Israeli academic, Mordechai Zalkin, published a book on the criminals who plagued Eastern Europe before the Second World War. In an article in the *Haaretz* newspaper of 21 October 2004, available online, we read that the author had spent thirteen years examining the archives of Eastern Europe: "When I open the police archives, I find detailed reports on Jewish criminals. The archives contain enough material for a hundred historians to work for a hundred years, and even then they would not have finished."

Mordechai Zalkin concluded that before World War II, the criminal world in Warsaw, Vilnius, Odessa and other major cities in Eastern Europe was *largely controlled by Jewish syndicates*.

Zalkin presented the novel *In the Valley of Tears*, by a Yiddish writer named Mendel Mocher Sforim (pseudonym of Shalom Jacob

Abramovitsch, 1835–1917). He reportedly gave an 'exceptional description of an obscure Jewish criminal organisation'. In the book, Jewish gangsters used underhand tactics to kidnap young Jewish girls from the cities and force them to work as prostitutes.

The author also mentioned child kidnappers. A gang of Jewish criminals called the "Golden Flag" had kidnapped a child from a wealthy family for ransom. According to the police, the man who had organised this crime, Berl Kravitz, had belonged to Al Capone's gang a few years earlier. Zelig Levingson, the head of Bandera de oro, had given the green light for the operation despite the reluctance of some members. The kidnapped boy was a Jew named Yossele Leibovitch, a student at the Jewish school in Vilnius whose father was a moneylender. The operation was carried out by Abba Vitkin and Reuven Kantor outside the boy's school. The message sent to the family was short: "Money or death". The criminals demanded 15,000 roubles, as well as the family's gold, diamonds and pearls. The police had made a huge wave of arrests, so the gang had released the boy in his neighbourhood.

In Vilnius, Odessa, Warsaw, Bialystok or Lviv, Jewish criminals were the talk of the town. Their organisations, such as the "Golden Flag" or the "Brotherhood" were active in that part of Europe—the famous Yiddishland. The most famous of Odessa's gangsters was a certain Benya Krik—the very one who figures in the title of the book by Isaac Babel, a well-known Soviet author: *Benya Krik, The Gangster, and Other Stories*.

There were also bandits and highwaymen. In 19th century Russia, the best place to rob people was in the countryside or on the roads. There were not enough policemen to guard all the forests that covered the territory, so travellers and traders were easy prey. Saul Ginzburg, one of the leading historians of the Jewish world in Russia, described these gangs of Jewish robbers in his chapter "crooks and predators". A gang of fifteen robbers robbed a convoy and took refuge in the forest with their loot. One of the most famous robbers was Dan Barzilai, who led a gang of thirty men in the Warsaw region, half of whom were Jews. Armed with pistols and masked, they stole fur coats, jewellery and horses. Barzilai was captured in 1874.

We learnt in passing that some of the figures of the Warsaw ghetto resistance in 1943 came from the criminal underworld: "On 8 May, the Germans discovered the central bunker of the Jewish Fighting Organisation at 18 Mila Street. What is less well known is that this symbol of resistance, the headquarters of the fighters where the insurrection commander Mordechai Anielewicz fought to the death, belonged to the Jewish criminal Shmuel Isser."

Mordechai Zalkin further quoted Professor Israel Gutman, an eminent scholar at the Yad Vashem Institute for the Holocaust in Jerusalem, who had taken part in the Warsaw ghetto uprising at the age of 15: "In the ghetto, the criminals had rapidly enriched themselves, becoming the social elite thanks to smuggling." In his book on Warsaw's Jews during the war, Gutman quoted another testimony: "The smugglers made huge profits... Most of them had amassed millions. They were the richest class in the ghetto. They spent all their free time drinking and in discotheques."

According to Havi Ben Sasson, a 32-year-old doctoral student who had worked at the International Holocaust School at Yad Vashem, Jewish criminal organisations were part of the Warsaw landscape in those years." At 18 Mila Street, a symbol of ghetto resistance, there was clearly collaboration between members of the Jewish Fighting Organisation and the gangsters. In fact, the bunker belonged to the mafia. Huge quantities of food were stored in it, and only the gangsters could distribute them." Numerous testimonies recounted how the criminals were "welcomed like princes" by the fighters. All this was certainly confirmed by the testimony of Martin Gray, in *In the Name of All Mine*[538].

After the war, nothing had really changed in the behaviour of some members of this "elite people" in the Soviet Union. The famous Venezuelan-born anti-Zionist militant Ilich Ramirez Sanchez, better known as Carlos, left a testimony on this subject. On 13 January 1975, Carlos fired from the roof of Orly airport with a rocket launcher at a plane belonging to the Israeli company El Al; the shot had missed, but his exploits included the kidnapping of eleven OPEC (Organisation of Petroleum Producing Countries) ministers in Vienna in December of the same year. In 2016, Carlos was still a prisoner in a French jail. This is what he said about his stay at a Moscow university: "The KGB was not the only temptation I encountered in Moscow. At the end of his doctorate, just before returning to his country, a rather older student wanted to pass me the contact of the head of the Moscow gold mafia. He obviously didn't trust anyone, but he wanted me to keep the contact of an old Jew who was an eminent figure in the Moscow underworld. Gold bars in Moscow, on the black market, were at that time worth about twelve times in roubles the dollar price in Geneva and twice as much in Tashkent. My contacts with that world went no further and had,

---

[538]We are grateful to the historian and publisher Jean Plantin (Akribeia editions) for passing this article on to us.

of course, no political connotations, although I would discover somewhat by chance that most of the members of that network were Zionists[539]."

We can also note the publication in January 2010, in New York, of the book by the American Jewish historian Ron Arons, which tells the story of the Jewish gangsters who were incarcerated in the notorious Sing-Sing Prison, located some fifty kilometres north of New York City on the banks of the Hudson River. The 350-page book offers biographies of famous gangsters and lesser-known criminals, painting a vast panorama of New York's Jewish criminality. On Amazon's website, we read this brief review in English: "Sing-Sing Prison was built in 1828, and since then more than 7000 Jews have been incarcerated there... Alongside famous gangsters like Lepke Buchalter, thousands of Jews who committed all manner of crimes—from incest to arson to selling Manhattan's air rights—passed through."

Regarding scams and financial embezzlement, the cases that have accumulated since the publication of *The Jewish Mafia* in June 2008 have been so numerous and important that we had to write a 336-page book, published in September 2014: *Israel's Billions*, subtitled, *Jewish Swindlers and International Financiers*[540].

The first part is dedicated to VAT fraud, especially the large-scale VAT fraud on carbon emission allowances that was uncovered in spring 2009 and cost European countries' treasuries several billion euros[541]. The above scams almost seem ridiculous in comparison.

Let's move on from ad fraud, real estate scams, charity money, credit card fraud, market cameleers, counterfeiters and memory fraudsters, and focus on this new type of fraud: the "president's scams", which have been in the news for several years now. In February 2015, there were 700 known cases, 360 victim companies and at least 300 million euros in damages. The scam consists of impersonating the company's chairman over the phone and demanding an urgent "top secret" transfer to a bank account abroad. The fraudsters were exclusively from the French Sephardic refugee community in Israel. Only French companies suffered from these scams.

The second part of the book is devoted to financial sharks. The

---

[539] Jean-Michel Vernochet, *L'Islam révolutionnaire*, Ed. du Rocher, 2003, p. 21.
[540] "*Les Milliards d'Israël*. The cover of the book earned us three months of unconditional imprisonment (judgement of 26 May 2015 by the 17th court in Paris).
[541] Between 1.6 and 1.8 billion euros in France and between 5 and 10 billion euros in the EU according to Europol. Source wikipedia: https://fr.wikipedia.org/wiki/Fraude_%C3%A0_la_TVA_sur_les_quotas_de_carbone. (NdT).

Madoff case, which broke out in December 2008, was thought to be the biggest scam in the history of mankind. Bernard Madoff, who promised a reasonable interest rate to those who gave him their money, was in fact remunerating old clients with the money of new ones. Of the twenty billion dollars that had been handed over to him for twenty years, there was nothing left... Or so the press reported from the beginning of the case. Looking back a few years later, it is clear that the money was not lost for everyone.

But the Madoff case was ultimately small potatoes compared to the international financial crisis of 2008. On 15 September, the world's fourth largest investment bank, Lehman Brothers, with its 25,000 employees, filed for bankruptcy. At the root of this bankruptcy was the practice of "predatory lending", whereby banks lent money to more or less insolvent people for real estate projects, while reselling the loans to pension funds or foreign banks on the secondary markets, all with the approval of the rating agencies and the US Federal Reserve[542]. Here too, money was not lost for everyone.

Compared to these gigantic scams, Jordan Belfort, the 1990s financial swindler turned hero in Martin Scorsese's film *The Wolf of Wall Street* (released in November 2013), was nothing more than a small fry.

In fact, at the beginning of this millennium, the records for scams have been smashed. Not simply surpassed, but definitely "smashed", to such an extent that the cases described above seem to belong to another era.

For the rest (arms trafficking, drug trafficking, international pimping, diamond trafficking, etc.), as the information accumulates, it may be updated. But it will only be an "update"; the important thing is to understand the very particular mentality of these criminals.

Hervé Ryssen,
January 2016[543]

---

[542] From 1987 to 2018 the Chairmen of the Board of Governors of the US Federal Reserve System were Alan Greenspan, Ben Bernanke and Janet Yellen (NdT).

[543] On 18 September 2020, in execution of a series of sentences handed down between 2017 and 2020, Hervé Ryssen was imprisoned for seventeen months. (NdT).

Other titles

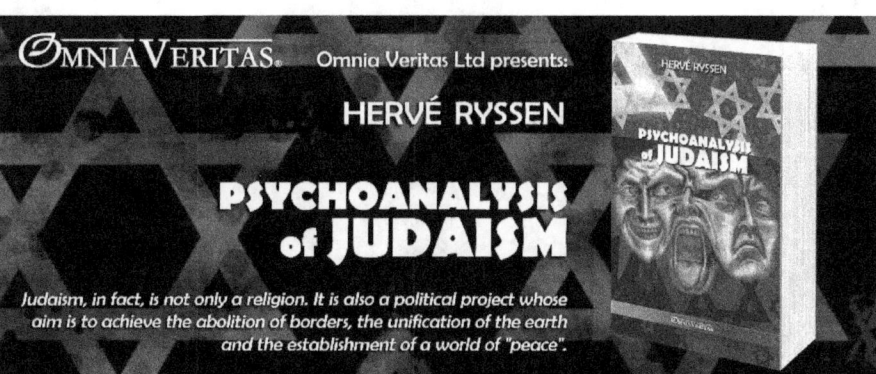

THE JEWISH MAFIA

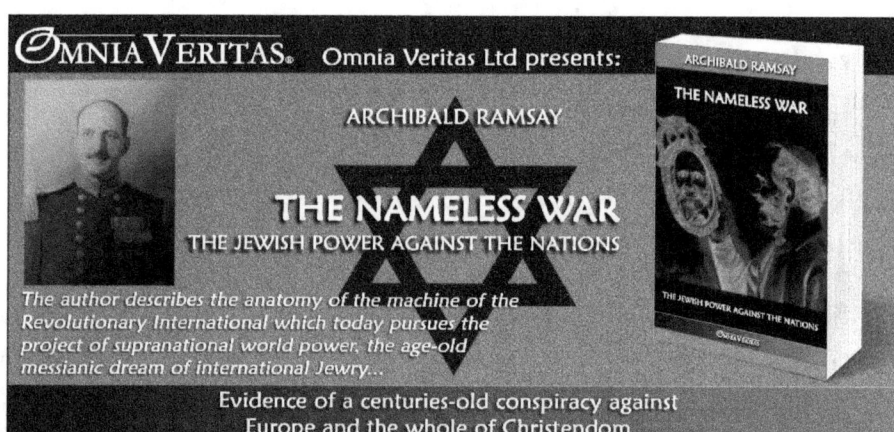

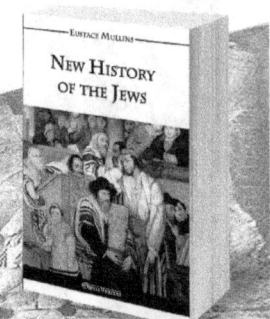

www.ingramcontent.com/pod-product-compliance
Lightning Source LLC
Chambersburg PA
CBHW071950220426
43662CB00009B/1073